CHRISTOPHER ARMSTRONG

AND H. V. NELLES

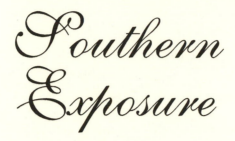

Southern
Exposure

CANADIAN PROMOTERS

IN LATIN AMERICA

AND THE CARIBBEAN

1896–1930

D0208492

UNIVERSITY OF TORONTO PRESS

Toronto Buffalo London

© University of Toronto Press 1988
Toronto Buffalo London
Printed in Canada

ISBN 0-8020-2660-5

∞

Printed on acid-free paper

Canadian Cataloguing in Publication Data

Armstrong, Christopher, 1942–
Southern exposure : Canadian promoters in
Latin America and the Caribbean 1896–1930

Includes bibliographical references and index.
ISBN 0-8020-2660-5

1. Investments, Canadian – Latin America.
2. Investments, Canadian – Caribbean Area.
3. Public utilities – Latin America – History.
4. Public utilities – Caribbean Area – History.
I. Nelles, H. V. (Henry Vivian), 1942–   .
II. Title.

HG5160.5.A3A75 1988   332.6′7371′08   C88-093854-4

This book has been published with the help of a grant
from the Social Science Federation of Canada, using
funds provided by the Social Sciences and Humanities
Research Council of Canada

For Emily, Jennifer, and Geoffrey

Contents

PART FIVE: CONCLUSION

TABLES

CHART

ILLUSTRATIONS

follow page 168

Preface

Winter alone did not make Canadians yearn for the south. Long before the airlift of vacationers to the Caribbean and Latin America, several generations of Canadian businessmen had already established advanced beach-heads of Canadian enterprise in the region, some of massive proportions. This book follows a group of ambitious late-Victorian and Edwardian Canadian entrepreneurs into the tropics of capitalism.

Beginning just before the turn of the century, Canadian businessmen channelled huge quantities of investments into the Caribbean, Mexico, Brazil, and later Spain, mainly into urban public utilities. Brazilian Traction, later Brascan, was only the best known of a flock of such enterprises promoted prior to the First World War. Before US capital penetrated this sector, Canadian businessmen developed an internationally recognized specialization in the finance and operation of utilities – tramway, telephone, light, power, gas, and hydroelectricity companies – in Latin America.

On the face of it, it was an unlikely North-South combination. Canadians had no extensive experience of either trading with or travelling in Latin America. The massive, rapidly growing, and aggressively imperialist United States lay between Canada and the tropics and presumably would have seized these opportunities before information about them reached Canada. And besides, what was Canada doing exporting capital when it did not have enough for its own needs? As Canadians looked to investments in Latin America, Canada itself was rapidly becoming one of the major fields for British investors.

How then did this happen? Who were the moving spirits behind these ventures? How were Canadians able to steal a march upon their US competitors from whom they had learned, after all, how to finance and build such companies in the first place? Where did the promoters find the money in a capital importing country? How did Canadian managers negotiate the unfamiliar shoals of diplomacy, war, revolution, economic nationalism, and exchange rate crises? And finally, what were the implications of these tropical enterprises for Canadian capitalism? These will be some of the questions we will pursue in the pages that follow.

To anticipate the narrative briefly at the outset, it must be emphasized that this outbreak of tropical capitalism in Canada occurred at a unique juncture in Canadian, Latin American, American, and European history. Great Britain and the countries of Europe had longstanding commercial and political connections with the Caribbean and Latin America. The door to Latin America had already been opened by generations of formal and informal empire, and in the major cities the process of industrialization and modernization had already begun. Latterly the United States had begun trading and investing more heavily in the continent where its Monroe Doctrine proclaimed hegemony.

Thus a tacit though somewhat fluid regime of multipartite suzerainty established fairly stable and well-understood rules of commercial conduct, financial links, lines of communication, and *in extremis* police forces. Exchange rates under the gold standard initially encouraged capital flows out from Europe to North and South America where an over-valued pound brought a good deal more than it did at home or on the continent and where interest rates were higher.[1]

Canada had nothing to do with either forging these connections or exercising quasi-imperial power, but citizens of Canada had access to and could take advantage of the prevailing system through their British imperial connections. Equally important, Canadian ties to the British capital market made it possible for Canadian entrepreneurs to tap the world's largest source of risk capital in support of their undertakings. The early twentieth-century Canadian financial community was strategically positioned: atop a small but extremely rapidly growing industrializing economy, poised alongside British capital during a peak expansionist phase, and not yet dominated by US finance.

It is not that the Americans were negligent in exploiting opportunities in Latin America at this time. Rather, in the sector in which the Canadians developed a specialty, the Americans were thoroughly occupied at the turn of the century in servicing their own exploding cities. And this must be emphasized; Canadian overseas investments were highly concentrated in the utility, insurance, and transportation fields. Canadian entrepreneurs rapidly exhausted the major public utilities sites at home, but still had access to ample capital for new ventures. So they looked abroad for opportunities of appropriate scale, just as Canadian real estate developers would do in the 1970s. And their leverage could be enhanced by tapping the vast financial resources of Great Britain if need be.

Such a political, economic, and technological moment would not recur later as the United States rose to hemispheric dominance in almost every field, and European capital, diminished by costly wars and driven out by US competitors, retreated from the Americas. But for one brief period, roughly from 1896 to 1913, there was a wonderful wave to be caught and ridden by the bold. It would subside and gradually disappear after the First World War, but the institutions created by this flow of foreign investment would live on, some until fairly recently.

This, then, was the broader context within which these business opportunities were perceived, a context that helps us understand why it was that Canadians were investing in Brazil and not vice versa. But the big picture does not explain why *these* particular people developed *this* sector – public utilities. Thus it is equally important to see these events from a lower level of abstraction, from the perspective of the human participants who took risks within this broader context and in so doing helped to shape it. For these actors, what seems inevitable and preordained to the economic historian seemed all too chancy and contingent at the time. In this book we hope to make a more intimate acquaintance with the actual participants, convey a sense of their style and ambition, and at that level show how chance, personality, and choice played their part in shaping the big picture. The great forces of history are composed, after all, of real people striving, contending against one another, succeeding, failing, coping, rationalizing.

Here the focus will be upon a group of individual 'Canadian' companies that contributed their mite to one of the major intercontinental capital flows. These pages catch Canadian capitalism at a particularly vital phase, as it deployed the electrochemical technologies and organizational forms of the second industrial revolution. Bursting with energy, capital, and confidence, Canada found itself strategically located between the technological dynamism of the United states on the one hand and the capital surplus of Great Britain on the other. Thriving and transforming, Canadian financiers and industrialists looked both inward to the opportunities of their own rapidly industrializing and expanding society and outward to the possibilities presented by the international economy.

'To overcome the inherent native advantage of being on the ground, the firm entering from abroad must have some other advantage not shared with its local competitor,' the standard textbook account of foreign direct investment begins. Surplus capital apart, what were the Canadian international comparative advantages in the public utilities sector that made Canadian investments more profitable abroad than at home, and more profitable than locally organized enterprises as well?[2]

In two words the answer was 'technology' and 'information.' A process of technology transfer from mature to marginal regions lay at the heart of this flow of capital. Canadian investors possessed world-class engineering capabilities, which allowed them to develop much larger hydroelectric energy sources in the urban hinterland than local entrepreneurs were capable of doing. Thus they could replace small-scale, high-cost thermal utilities with much more efficient hydroelectric facilities. Engineering knowledge was only half the story. For these entrepreneurs also possessed equally important managerial and financial knowledge, which made it possible for them to weld a whole complex of urban services into large-scale, integrated enterprises. Hardware and software together were exported with capital.

What induced Canadians to go abroad, apart from the salesmanship of promoters? First, the rate of return upon this imperfectly distributed knowledge promised to be higher in the foreign context than at home. Secondly, foreign promoters in possession of this knowledge held key advantages over local entrepreneurs operating without it. Had the engineering capability and information been more freely available, there would have been no need for foreign investment.[3] Market imperfections are what make economics interesting; they are also the seedbeds of great fortunes.

If international economic circumstances were propitious for this capital flow, Canadian domestic circumstances were too; about this more will be said by way of introduction below. For a brief moment Canadian businessmen ventured out into this greater arena carrying new technologies and management techniques and millions of investors' dollars. We will attempt to look at this process from the inside, focusing upon 'how' sorts of questions. Our interest will be with methods, personalities, conventions, and institutions of the nascent Canadian capital market and the linkage of

Canadian corporate finance to the web of an emerging global capitalist system. We are particularly keen to show how sophisticated international ventures of this sort arose within the emergent Canadian capital market, how they forced adaptation within that institutionally incomplete setting and, subsequently, how control migrated across the Atlantic to richer, more mature capital markets.

This book follows the fortunes of these Canadian enterprises from their inception until 1930, in effect from birth through mid-life crisis. This was the period for which reasonably full documentation was available. The period before the Depression was sufficiently cloaked in decent obscurity that private archival holdings were readily opened up to us without any restrictions. Obviously there is more to be said about these enterprises' subsequent death and transfiguration.

At the outset we must defend ourselves against predictable and probably justifiable criticism. We have not tried to write detailed company histories of all the Canadian utilities in Latin America and the Caribbean. For purposes of clarity we have focused only upon the largest and most important of the companies. Nor have we tried to examine all aspects of even those enterprises. Rather we have concentrated upon the problems of promotion, organization, and international finance – subjects that lie within our fields of competence.

If we are not company historians we are even less Latin American historians. We have never been to the cities we write about, lest anyone should suspect a monstrous Latin American travel grant disguised in these pages. We lack the languages and historiographical background necessary to say much about the social and political context in which these companies operated. For that we express our regrets, but plead by way of extenuation that by sticking close to home and keeping the focus upon the promotional and managerial matters we do know something about, we may enable historians of Latin America to be more fully informed about private corporate behaviour, a subject that seems to us to be something of a historiographical black hole – involving much theorizing about an intensely important matter that emits no light.

Theories concerning foreign direct investment, and its modern variant, the multinational enterprise, have proliferated in recent years and have become increasingly sophisticated. In particular, scholars have recently come to recognize the perplexing variety of this international economic phenomenon. Indeed, the complex history and diversity of foreign direct investment raises serious doubt about the possibility of developing any unified theory. Amidst all of this theorizing, what have been in rather short supply are archivally based histories of foreign investment decision making and international business behaviour.[4] By opening a window upon one particular and perhaps highly unusual capital flow, our book is intended as a contribution to that literature. Our location in Canada, a country that is itself a recipient of heavy foreign investment, gives us a slightly different vantage point and sensibility from metropolitan authors.

Because Canada was the birthplace and subsequently the legal domicile of these companies, a substantial quantity of documentation concerning Latin American economic and business history remains on deposit in public and private archives in Canada. On the basis of these unparalleled collections of papers, generously opened to us by their guardians, we have been able to write this history of Canadian enterprise in Latin America and the associated internationalization of Canadian capitalism after the turn of the century.

During the course of researching and writing this book we accumulated a host of social and intellectual debts and a wealth of stories. We are grateful to the House of Lords Record Office for permission to examine the Lord Beaverbrook Papers; to J. Trevor Eyton of Brascan Limited for access to the papers and records of Brazilian Traction; to the Compañía Mexicana de Luz y Fuerza Motriz, SA, for opening the records of Mexican Light and Power to us; and to Magnum Fund Limited, the successors of the Mexico Tramways Company, for permission to consult its minute books.

Blundering southward in pursuit of our subject we needed a great deal of assistance with the intricacies of Latin American and Caribbean historiography. John Wirth of Stanford University read early drafts of the Brazilian chapters and steered us towards material we might otherwise have overlooked. Our colleague Russell Chace gave the entire manuscript an extremely close reading, especially those parts pertaining to Mexico, providing us with twenty pages of detailed criticism. Duncan McDowall of Carleton University, whose history of Brazilian Traction, *The Light*, will appear about the same time as this book, selflessly shared his research material with us and guided us through the extremely rich Brazilian Traction collection. This book could not have been completed without the help of these scholars. We acknowledge our debt without in any way wishing to implicate our mentors in the results.

Research for this book has taken us to nearly a score of archives in Canada, Great Britain, and the United States. A grant from the Social Sciences and Humanities Research Council of Canada, as well as sabbatical leave fellowships for the authors, helped make that possible. The council also provided funds to the Social Science Federation of Canada to aid in the publication of this book. We gratefully acknowledge the support we have received from SSHRCC for this and earlier work. York University contributed release time to permit us to write and technical assistance in the production of the manuscript, which Gerry Hallowell and his colleagues at the University of Toronto Press have now turned into a well-designed book. For all that aid and comfort over many years we are grateful. From the wayward fetcher in the House of Lords Record Office to the more prosaic follies of the National Library and the Public Archives of Canada we found more than enough justification for laughter in our travels. And we ourselves, we gather, provided passing amusement to those who suffered our visits. All in all, pursuing the paper trail of our tropical entrepreneurs has been a pleasure nicely spiced by ironic amusements. We hope our enjoyment can be glimpsed in the pages that follow.

PART ONE

Context

1

The Paper Givers

The paper givers adorned their village with classical temples, exchanged elegantly inscribed papers within their clan groups, and were served by scurrying black-coated minions, some of whom habitually wore their hats indoors. Perched atop the commanding heights of the Canadian economy at the turn of the century they could see from coast to coast and as far as London and New York. In time an extraordinary group of junior associates would extend these horizons as far as Cuba, the Caribbean, Mexico, Brazil, and Spain.

Timing was all important. After 1896 the Canadian economy entered upon a phase of unprecedented growth, which lasted with only two minor pauses until 1913. Rarely has any country experienced such prodigious expansion as Canada during this period: virtually every indicator soared upward – population, homestead entries, exports, railroad mileage, construction. Between 1880 and 1900 Canadian gross national product doubled. It doubled again in the next decade. In the last two decades of the nineteenth century Canadian real incomes rose at a compound average annual rate of 3 per cent. During the first decade of the twentieth century annual real growth in GNP averaged 5.5 per cent. This burst of prosperity gave Canada one of the highest rates of aggregate economic growth ever recorded.[1]

Thus the new century dawned in a warm glow of prosperity and self-assurance that found even the country's bankers in an uncharacteristically expansive mood. Times had been so good for so long that the editor of Canada's leading financial journal fretted that younger businessmen had yet to learn the hard lessons of commercial adversity. Edmund Walker began his address to the annual meeting of the Bank of Commerce in 1900 in a tone of mock apology. Bankers were more accustomed to explaining why expectations had not been fulfilled, but in this instance, he said: 'Prosperity speaks readily for itself and needs little explanation.' E.S. Clouston, Walker's counterpart at the Bank of Montreal, welcomed the good fortune of the country and his bank more openly at his annual meeting with the exultant words: 'the year ends in a blaze of universal self-congratulation.'[2]

I

If London was 'The City' of western capitalism at the turn of the century, Canada was one of its outlying villages. During the previous decades a complicated network of interconnected financial institutions had matured, anchored by a highly concentrated branch banking system centred in Montreal and Toronto. Despite the growing volume of business, the Canadian financial world remained little more than a village in actual physical size, consisting of a few streets, fifty or so major banks and financial houses, and perhaps no more than forty key individuals. As the country got richer a large portion of this wealth flowed into the custody of these very men. A well-placed few, who controlled the major chartered banks, guarded the apex of this burgeoning pyramid of savings at the point where it met an incoming flow of foreign capital. There, at this golden nexus, in a mood of buoyant optimism, unorthodox ventures in unfamiliar places suddenly seemed possible.

Had the renowned cultural anthropologist Franz Boas taken as his subject this central Canadian financial community rather than Kwakiutl tribes on the west coast, he would have observed and mapped an equally elaborate and mystifying culture. Though this village society was function-ally related to the surrounding agricultural, mercantile, industrial, and political environment, it had its own clans, headmen, totems, taboos, myths and legends, language, and means of producing, holding, and redistributing wealth, which also set it distinctly apart.

The financial village was predominantly a market – in this case for capital – but it was very much a market embedded in an intricate web of social relations. Like other communities and traditional cultures, the financial village was not static, but rather a dynamic organism riven by tensions and anxieties as it struggled, often against its own inherited ways, to tame a capricious but essentially bountiful nature and draw the

TABLE 1
Canadian Financial Intermediaries, 1900

Type	Number	Assets ($ million)	%
Chartered banks	35	437.3	52.6
Mortgage and loan companies	86	134.7	16.2
Life insurance companies	52	108.7	13.1
Fire and casualty companies	49	27.6	3.3
Quebec savings banks	2	20.8	2.5
Trust companies	10	9.6	1.2
Fraternal orders	9	8.5	1.0
Investment dealers, brokers	25	—	—
Subtotal	278	747.2	89.9
Government notes and post office savings		84.5	10.1

SOURCE E.P. Neufeld, *The Financial System of Canada: Its Growth and Development* (Toronto: Macmillan, 1972)

maximum benefit from it. And to pursue the metaphor one step further, a company promotion, by its redistribution of wealth and social debts within the community, vaguely resembled a potlatch.

In this exchange economy, pieces of paper representing mutual obligations were inscribed, distributed, accumulated, and redeemed. Subtle and not easily described distinctions of social rank – sometimes even kinship – governed the process of exchange. Not all members of the community had equal opportunities to produce paper or participate in its distribution. And even as the economy grew and the volume and velocity of these cycles of distribution and redemption increased, paper tended to accumulate in relatively few hands. These social attributes were not incidental to the capital market; rather they were essential to it. Some measure of social control was necessary to reduce uncertainty, regulate behaviour, and temper some of the inherently destructive forces of a market.

The Canadian financial community at the turn of the century consisted of about 275 separate institutions controlling assets of $747,200,000. A decade later the number of financial institutions had contracted slightly (there were fewer banks [28] and mortgage companies, about the same number of life, fire, and casualty insurance companies), but they controlled assets of $1,628,900,000 – a 118 per cent increase. A smaller number of much larger firms were thus worth more than twice as much. Invisible in this classification were the equivalent of the great investment banking houses at the apex of metropolitan money markets, such as J.P. Morgan, Kidder Peabody, Brown Brothers, Kuhn Loeb, Seligman, and Lee Higginson in the United States and Rothschild, Baring, Glyn Mills, Sperling, and Hambro in Great Britain.[3] The institutions may have been absent, but the functions were performed by other means, as we shall see.

Most of the 275 formal members of the Canadian financial community were marginal, purely local undertakings, with only limited connections to the centralized capital flows coursing through the economy. They raised their capital locally, invested locally, and perhaps loaned surplus funds and borrowed short-term money from the larger metropolitan banks and insurance companies. To be sure they were important elements of the capital market, especially in financing merchants' inventories, housing, commercial real estate development, and municipal undertakings, but they were nonetheless peripheral and dependent, operating on the margins of the metropolitan financial community.

Banks and insurance companies came in all sizes, and only the largest of them could be thought of as full members of the financial village on King and St James streets in Toronto and Montreal. The savings banks, building societies, mortgage and loan companies, fire and casualty insurers were also absent because they operated in strictly local, geographically separated markets. Thus there may have been as few as twenty-five or thirty houses in this village in 1900, consisting of, roughly, the six largest banks, which accounted for 43.4 per cent of all bank assets, half a dozen insurance companies, which wrote 84 per cent of all life insurance, and perhaps a handful of the largest building societies and mortgage, savings, and loan companies centred in Toronto and Montreal. Three or four trust companies, about the same number of brokers and investment dealers, and two or three law firms, which wrote up the necessary paper, also figured prominently in this capital market, notwithstanding the relative insignificance of their assets. It was a very small world.

Moreover, kinship, group loyalties, and interlocking corporate directorates concentrated effective control of these financial institutions into even fewer hands. In this village society the individual members were neither independent nor equal. Most were affiliated with well-recognized groups or clans, each with its acknowledged leader. Thus while the formal elements of the Canadian capital market were connected by a process of functional interdependence, the individual members and their houses were held together by powerful social bonds and a keenly felt sense of hierarchy. In Montreal and Toronto there were distinct groups of companies and capitalists who did business with each other, sat on each other's boards, and often promoted new ventures together as a group. As in all such societies a delicate diplomacy linked the clans.

The 'ideal type' of such a group would be centred upon a large chartered bank whose directors were the nucleus of the clan. In loose orbit around the bank circled one or perhaps two life insurance companies, a mortgage, savings, and loan company, a trust company, and an investment house. Intersecting the paths of these institutions were the commercial houses, manufacturing companies, and railroad and shipping ventures that had produced the fortunes of the individual financiers in the first place and that continued to depend upon the financial intermediation provided. These companies were not formally linked as subsidiaries of a centralized organization. Nevertheless, a well-understood social hierarchy, signified by overlapping directorates, legitimized reciprocal commercial intercourse, controlled the conduct of individual capitalists, and helped guarantee exchanges among the separate houses.

The Cox group in Toronto came closest to approximating this 'ideal type.'[4] Senator George A. Cox was president both of the Bank of Commerce, Canada's second-largest bank with assets of $6 million, and the Canada Life Assurance Company, also the second-largest business of its type. Cox began as a local telegraph agent in Peterborough, promoted local railways in the 1870s, and in the 1880s gained control of the Central Canada Loan and Savings Company. This brought him into contact with the Bank of Commerce in the late 1880s. During the next decade he forced his way onto the board of Canada Life and, after seizing personal control in 1899, moved the company from Hamilton to Toronto, where he himself had relocated to be closer to the capital market. He also controlled the British American and the Western Fire insurance companies. Cox founded the Imperial Life to provide employment for his son, established his son-in-law as the president of his own brokerage firm, A.E. Ames and Company, and founded National Trust, headed by E.R. Wood, a young protégé, to handle the trustee functions of these numerous organizations. As Ian Drummond wryly observed: 'Cox had three great passions – his sons, railroads, and insurance. His wealth came largely from the last of these. He used his power massively to assist in the promotion of the second, and with the proceeds he was able to endow the first.'[5]

George Cox controlled companies with assets totalling more than $70 million in 1900 through his headship of a group that spanned the generations. Cox was not only father and father-in-law to the members of his group, he was among other things the landlord of the Toronto Stock Exchange. The Toronto market was very much a family affair.

Other members of the Cox group consisted of the directors of the Bank of Commerce and Canada Life; Edmund Walker, the highly respected general manager of the Bank of Commerce; J.W. Flavelle, an old Peterborough friend who had succeeded marvellously in pork packing and department stores; Robert Jaffray, a banker and publisher; and William Mackenzie, an aspiring utilities magnate and railroad contractor.

In Montreal, an institution rather than an individual formed the core of another group. There the directors of the Bank of Montreal, by far the largest bank in the country, with assets in excess of $12 million, integrated and co-ordinated most of the financial affairs of the metropolitan region. The Bank of Montreal, bound together in loose alliance the Canadian Pacific Railway, the Sun Life and the Royal Victoria insurance companies, the branches of us and British fire, life, and casualty companies, and the largest cotton manufacturers, shippers, and milling companies. This formidable constellation of capital lacked a single leader, perhaps because the headmen traditionally decamped to England with their titles, leaving operations in the hands of a trustworthy collective leadership, which in 1900 consisted of G.A. Drummond, William Macdonald, E.B. Greenshields, James Ross, R.B. Angus, A.F. Gault, W.W. Ogilvie, and E.S. Clouston, the general manager of the bank. Outside the boardroom, Sir William Van Horne, until lately the general manager of the Canadian Pacific Railway, Robert Mackay, C.R. Hosmer, Robertson Macaulay, president of Sun Life, the largest insurance company in the country, and his son, T.B. Macaulay, were also connected to this group.[6]

These two dominant groups communicated with one another through emissaries. In Toronto, E.B. Osler, a distinguished broker and banker, sat on the board of the CPR, and James Ross from Montreal was a business partner of William Mackenzie in Toronto. There were other aspiring groups in each city; most notably, the Howland group in Toronto and, to a certain extent, the Macaulays in Montreal stood somewhat aloof, partly as a result of old quarrels with some members of the élite, partly because so much of their business was conducted in the United States and abroad. In Halifax John Stairs, an astute merchant, shipper, banker, and trust company president, headed up a much smaller group of young men, the most prominent being the lawyer-promoter B.F. Pearson, who could draw upon the savings of a flourishing mercantile and industrial community. Centralization and amalgamation of certain sectors of Canadian industry–

especially textiles, coal and steel – brought this Halifax group into close contact with the Montreal group.[7]

Elevation to this élite bestowed enormous prestige and respect. This came not just as a result of successful private capital accumulation; it also recognized creditable conduct and business respectability over a long time. Not everyone could aspire to a directorship in the two core banks. When W.W. Ogilvie died in 1900 the obituaries dwelt upon the fact that he was the largest miller in the world and a director of the Bank of Montreal, the latter of which was 'another token of his character as a businessman.'[8] Thus distillers, sharp operators, and 'unclubbable' men need not apply.

These two main groups constituted the inner circle of Canadian capitalism at the turn of the century. Three or four smaller affinity groups and one or two outstanding individuals could also be said to have a claim upon membership. The core consisted of approximately forty individuals, known to each other and in a few instances related by marriage. All were bound by mutual obligations and a shared understanding of busines conventions. The cohesiveness of these groups can easily be overstated. George Cox offended a number of people by his rough takeover of Canada Life; his eccentricities, single-minded devotion to the careers of his family members, and somewhat abrasive behaviour at length lost him the unswerving loyalty of Flavelle and Walker. The Macaulays in Montreal trod upon a few toes in their seizure of Sun Life. Affinity could not completely eliminate family feuds. Nevertheless, a clear social hierarchy and compatible social origins helped both to bring this market into existence and to exert a measure of control over it.

In 1900 the elders of the financial village were in fact quite ancient; their average age was 61.5 years. Half of them were native born. More than half the members of the élite could claim Scottish origins; 25 per cent were immigrants from Scotland. All but two of the recognized chiefs were Presbyterians, Anglicans, or Methodists. About half the native-born members had moved from smaller towns to Montreal and Toronto as recently as the late 1880s; in the metropolitan centres business interests and affiliations opened channels of upward mobility into the emerging financial élite. Thus the principal financiers were even more likely to be immigrants and Scotsmen than the more broadly defined industrial élite of the same era.[9]

The elders were not, however, a self-sufficient group. They made the decisions whether to go ahead with a project or not and on what terms, but they depended upon a much larger cadre of younger technicians, specialists, and lawyers to manage their individual companies, generate ideas for new company promotions, execute decisions, and inscribe and distribute the resulting paper. And of course some elders had more leadership power and access to capital than others. The marginal members could raise only one or perhaps two million for a venture on their own. The Cox group and the Bank of Montreal could raise five million or more.

The technicians, managers, promoters, and lawyers upon whom the core group depended were, on average, a decade younger than the 'elders.' The general managers of the two key banks, E.S. Clouston of Montreal and Edmund Walker of Toronto, were representative of managers who had risen to the highest ranks by virtue of their large responsibilities and accumulated obligations over the years. Most men like them remained on the outside of the core group, though they commanded great respect and prestige. They did not, however, command capital, and that was the key difference.

Zebulon Lash, of the firm of Blake, Lash and Cassels, was the pre-eminent corporation lawyer of the Cox group. He was so highly regarded that he also did much of the Montreal work. His partner, S.H. Blake, who had once held this position, was getting on in years. Younger lawyers, such as Newton Rowell and Allan Aylesworth, also did a certain amount of corporate work. But Lash was most in demand. The Montrealers tended to come to Toronto for legal advice; Montreal lawyers were used primarily for property transactions and political liaison. In Halifax B.F. Pearson's law firm, which included Robert Harris and C.H. Cahan, handled the transactions of the Stairs group.

The promoters and investment dealers were all in their thirties and forties in 1900. The Cox group depended most heavily upon William Mackenzie, the hard-driving contractor and utilities magnate, for promising new propositions. Associated with him were men with some understanding of the new electrical technology, such as Frederic Nicholls, who had been a principal in the development of the Canadian General Electric Company. Henry Mill Pellatt, son of a stockbroker, was an electrical entrepreneur as well. In Montreal the stock broker L.J. Forget and the young utilities executive Herbert Holt seemed to perform this scouting role.

The distribution of the paper beyond the inner circle was the weakest link in this chain of capital. Outside the financial village the market for paper was not as well developed as the branch banking and insurance networks. Several young scions of the Toronto elders dedicated themselves to this task, among them A.E. Ames, Cox's son-in-law, and E.R. Wood, a Cox protégé from Peterborough who ran Dominion Securities. Ambitious newcomers, such as W.T. White at National Trust and J.H. Deacon, carved out niches for themselves by specializing in new types of securities. In Montreal the Hanson brothers, Charles, Edwin, and William, and E. Mackay Edgar worked at broadening the market along with the somewhat mercurial L.J. Forget and his associates. They were greatly aided in this task by banks and insurance companies, awash with liquidity, that made convenient call loans available to brokers and clients on the collateral of this very paper.

Forty or so men presided over the mounting piles of Canadian and later foreign savings. They relied upon their minions to develop appropriate investment vehicles into which the large streams of the capital flowing to their banks, insurance, savings and loan, and trust companies could be directed and in the process multiplied. Of course they never met as a formal council to discuss such matters – apart from the regular board meetings of the major financial institutions. But decisions taken by the leaders were quickly communicated to those on the margins, who positioned themselves as best they could.

At the top, then, the capital market, was a small tribal village. Hierarchy, strict social conventions, ethnic harmony, and an elaborate code of reciprocal benefits and obligations reigned. The market process was not autonomous or impersonal; rather it was embedded in a complex social matrix. Semi-organized groups of Scottish and native-born Canadian capitalists attempted to impose a certain order upon this rapidly growing market to maximize their institutional and personal fortunes. The market consisted of these men, who loaned each other the funds entrusted to their care. It helped that the circle consisted of friends, kith or, even better, kin.

These men reared the main temples of finance along the main streets of their village around the turn of the century. Usually these took the form of neoclassical Graeco-Roman temples, formidable masses of masonry on the outside and vast, vaulted, echoing halls on the inside. The façades and the interiors aimed to awe the visitor with their majesty. Plinth, pedestal, portico, and pediment, Greek and Roman orders, colonnades, domes, lintels, friezes and balustrades, grillwork, high arching windows, and filtered light playing upon polished marble, gold leaf, and mosaic spoke firmly in every possible way of Property, Law, Order, Stability, Security, Responsibility, Equity, Trust, and Authority. Across the Dominion in branches and regional offices these same sentiments were echoed in ever-diminishing grandeur.[10] These concrete statements reassured those involved in this somewhat mystical process. Architecture buttressed the faith both of those investing and those receiving someone else's hard-earned surplus on trust and committing it to others for mutual benefit.

Off in the distance, well beyond the ordered columns of the village, finance capital was transmogrified into real assets. In this modern alchemy, amidst much smoke and sweat, paper became property: metal was smelted and moulded, crops were planted, harvested, and shipped, towns built, bricks and rails laid, equipment ordered, lumber sawed, and merchants' shelves stocked with the latest goods. But in the village everything was made of paper. It was also a volatile, unpredictable, insubstantial world of mutual trust and hope. That was what the architectual illusion was meant to hide.

II

Between the banks and the financial houses in the village two new buildings appeared early in the twentieth century, lower and less massive than the monuments to capital around them but nevertheless affecting the same grandeur and evoking the same reassuring symbolism. The one built in Montreal in 1904 was said to be modelled after the Temple of Vesta in Tivoli.[11] Corinthian columns in Montreal, Greek Ionic in Toronto announced the emergence of that most mysterious paper-distributing institution, the stock exchange.

Size spoke of their relative importance; their columns and friezes spoke of their aspirations. These modern temples were intended for money changers; here the property rights to the capital being amassed in the largest financial institutions, railroads, industries, and utilities were divided up, bought, and sold. In this, the most callow and capricious financial intermediary, the architecture of reassurance achieved its purest and most sublime form.

Stock exchanges had been in continuous existence in Montreal and Toronto since 1874 and 1878 respectively. The first permanent home of the stock market in Montreal was the Italian Renaissance-style Merchants' Exchange Building on St Sacrement Street where it shared quarters with the city's more important produce and commodity markets. The same was true in Toronto where stockbrokers were very much the junior tenants of the stately Greek Revival Exchange Building. The rotunda, an impressive oval room fifty by thirty feet, surrounded by a gallery, and surmounted by a circular dome of glass and iron, housed the major market, the grain exchange.[12] Stocks were traded in a much smaller chamber off to one side.

At the turn of the century both exchanges moved to newer, larger quarters, as befitted their growing volume of business. In 1900 the Toronto Stock Exchange relocated in the National Trust building at 20 King Street East, the ground floor of which was occupied by A.E. Ames and Company. Thus George Cox quite literally housed and supported the Toronto market. Shortly afterwards in the summer of 1904 the Montreal Stock Exchange moved into its St James Street Temple of Vesta, designed by the New York architect George B. Post. The Toronto Stock Exchange did not acquire its own exclusive building, a more restrained, four-columned Ionic affair punctuated with deep-set windows, until 1913.

Stock exchanges were very much the struggling aspirants of the financial village. Though they had been in existence for some time, the exchanges had never handled very much business or played a particularly key role in the process of capital formation. Rather they performed the relatively minor and subordinate function of providing a market for the claims against physical assets. Typically the business of the exchanges consisted mainly of handling transactions in bank stock and to a limited extent municipal debt. As the number of credit instruments available for purchase and sale was extremely small in the late nineteenth century, the stock exchanges had little to offer investors, and thus volume remained slight.

In 1890 there were twenty-nine seats on the Toronto exchange, a figure that remained more or less steady until 1899 when thirty-seven firms and individuals held seats. As a reflection both of the limited business available in the early 1890s and the rising trade in the last few years of the century, seats could be purchased on the Toronto exchange for as little as $1,500 between 1890 and 1898. In the last year of the century, however, the price of a seat shot up to $4,000, and the next year $10,000 was the asking price. A similar phenomenon occurred in Montreal. During the last years of the century the price of a seat rose from $3,500 to $6,700, and reached an unbelievable $25,000 in 1903.[13]

Certainly there was not much money to be made from stockbroking in the 1890s. It has been estimated that total commission income from transactions on the Toronto exchange fell from $24,400 in 1891 to $16,300 in 1894. A Montreal broker publicly complained that, because bankers had restricted credit, business was so slow that his commission income had been reduced to five dollars a day out of which he still had to pay his office expenses. The *Journal of Commerce*, notably unmoved by his plight, heaped sarcasm upon this plea for what amounted to 'a free run of the bank larders.' Beginning in 1897 business began to pick up and with it commissions: Toronto's brokers divided $43,200 in 1897 and more than $100,000 in 1901.[14]

Trading on the Toronto Stock Exchange peaked at 340,200 shares in 1882, then sagged to less than 100,000 later in the decade. During the recession of the 1890s trading fell off to a mere 92,800 shares in 1894, then it bounded up to more than 200,000 the next year, at which level it remained until the turn of the century. January to March were the busiest months; the spring and summer were very quiet. The pace did not pick up appreciably until September and sometimes October. During the late 1890s, as the volume of trading increased once again, this seasonality of the market became less pronounced.

In Montreal the leading investment dealers at the turn of the century were L.J. Forget and Company on Notre Dame Street, Hanson Brothers, R. Wilson Smith, McCuaig and Rykert, Burnett and Company, and McDougall Brothers on St James Street. Toronto brokers, clustered close to the exchange on King Street, seem to have been slightly more numerous judging from notices in the financial press and city directories. On the other hand, they may simply have been more aggressive advertisers, which may explain in part Toronto's eventual eclipse of Montreal as the dominant exchange in Canada. The leading Toronto firms were A.E. Ames and Company, A.P. Burritt, Fergusson and Blaikie, Aemilius Jarvis and Company, H. O'Hara and Company, John Stark, Osler and Hammond, Pellatt and Pellatt, J.H. Deacon, and George Stimson and Company.

Both the Toronto and the Montreal markets were extremely narrow in the late nineteenth century and dominated by the securities of financial institutions. There were never more than one hundred issues listed on either of the exchanges during the 1890s, and the majority of these were banks, savings and loan companies, building societies and to a lesser extent insurance companies. During the last years of the century the character of the stock market began to change slightly, but until the beginning of the recovery investors showed a marked preference for these relatively secure stocks (see Tables 2 and 3).

Banks and savings and loan companies accounted for more than 80 per cent of all stock listings in 1896 on both exchanges, a dominance that was only slightly diminished in 1900. Utilities, mainly the Bell Telephone Company, Montreal Gas, Montreal Street Railway, Consumers' Gas, Toronto Railway, and Toronto Electric Light, had already made their

TABLE 2
Toronto Stock Exchange Listings by Category
1886–1901

	1886	1891	1895	1901
Banks	11	10	10	12
Building societies	34	39	38	30
Savings and loan				
Bonds and debentures	2	1	1	2
Miscellaneous	11	10	10	36
Total	57	60	59	80

SOURCE John F. Whiteside, 'The Toronto Stock Exchange to 1900: Its Membership and Development of the Share Market' (MA diss., Trent University, 1979) 127

TABLE 3
Montreal and Toronto Stock Exchanges Compared, April 1896, 1900
(number of listings as a % of total)

	April 1896		April 1900	
	M	T	M	T
Banks	40	43	41	34
Savings and loan	41	38	38	27
Insurance	0	9	0	8
Railways and navigation	1	3	1	8
Utilities	10	7	10	8
Industrials	8	0	9	4
Land companies	0	0	0	2
Mines	0	0	0	9
Total	100	100	100	100

SOURCE *Journal of Commerce* 3 Apr. 1896, 6 Apr. 1900; *Monetary Times* 3 Apr. 1896, 6 Apr. 1900[15]

appearance by 1896 and were among the most actively traded securities. Industrials (mainly cotton mills) had made their presence felt in Montreal by mid-decade; promotion of industrial issues in Toronto (Canadian General Electric, Commercial Cable, Canada Cycle and Motor, Carter-Crume, and Luxier Prisms) came later in the 1890s. Toronto investors also took up various Kootenay mining stocks with greater enthusiasm than their Montreal counterparts. On the Toronto market in 1896 the most actively traded stocks were the Toronto and Montreal street railways and the Bank of Commerce. Local utilities and banks also led the generally 'dull' Montreal market as well.

The stock exchanges became more important instruments of capital formation at the turn of the century. A general recovery leading, as we have seen, to several years of sustained economic growth contributed significantly to the revival of the stock market. As Canadian aggregate income rose, more of it was saved and invested to replace and expand the national capital stock. Estimates of gross domestic capital formation as a percentage of gross national product ranged around 14 per cent for the 1890s rising to approximately 27 per cent between 1906 and 1910. At the turn of the century more than 20 per cent of national output (or about $1.2 billion) was being channelled back into private residential and commercial construction, new plant and equipment, additional land and livestock, and public works or used to build inventories to accommodate expanding trade. At about this same time estimates of the ratio of gross domestic capital formation as a percentage of gross national product were in the order of 8 per cent annually for Great Britain. In the first half of the twentieth century only the United States posted comparable rates of capital formation.[16]

This unusually high rate of domestic saving and capital formation contributed mightily to economic growth. As the Canadian economy expanded it attracted not only immigrants but also large and increasingly heavy flows of capital from abroad that in a self-reinforcing process, further augmented the nation's wealth. Foreign investment increased both absolutely and relatively between 1896 and 1915. In the early part of this period the $124 million average annual inflow was about 2.5 per cent of gross national product. The $1.5 billion at the end of the period amounted to 12.4 per cent of GNP, during which time it has been estimated that an astonishing 46.2 per cent of gross domestic capital formation was financed by foreigners.[17] An overwhelming majority (85 per cent) of this additional capital came from Great Britain in the form of portfolio investment. During this period British financiers directed a steadily increasing portion of the funds at their disposal to Canada. In 1900 approximately 10 per cent of the new foreign security issues in London were Canadian; between 1910 and 1914 the ratio rose to 20 per cent. This British and to a lesser extent US investment added considerable fuel to the Canadian domestic capital boom.

In September 1899 the *Monetary Times* devoted a long editorial to the effect 'the extraordinary tide of prosperity' had had upon banking.[18] As a result of several years of good harvests, commercial expansion, and abundant money, banks and other financial intermediaries found themselves with more income than could favourably be placed in the usual investments – commercial loans in the case of banks, and mortgages and municipal debentures in the case of insurance companies. These rapidly accumulating deposits and premiums thus created a powerful demand for additional high-class, interest-bearing securities and greatly expanded the sums available for short-term call loans. Taken together this capital 'supply push' created an extremely favourable environment to new company promotions on the one hand; on the other, it generated the call loans necessary to sustain a ready market for those securities.

Between 1890 and 1910 the assets of Canadian chartered banks increased four times over. During that same period holdings of securities as a percentage of total bank assets rose from 3 per cent to 9.3 per cent in 1905, falling off to 7.6 per cent in 1910. Fragmentary statistics indicate that approximately half of this portfolio consisted of stocks and bonds of railways and other private corporations. Call loans, mainly to brokers and other stock market operators, increased from 5.1 per cent of total assets in 1890 to 13.3 per cent in 1910. Taken together this relative expansion of the banks' investment portfolios and growth in the call loan business pumped an additional $221 million into the nascent Canadian securities market between 1890 and 1910.[19]

Life insurance companies were growing even faster than the banks (though from a much smaller base), and they too redirected large quantities of Canadian savings towards the securities market. In 1890 insurance companies accounted for 8.6 per cent of the assets of all Canadian financial intermediaries. By 1900 brisk policy sales increased that proportion to 13.1 per cent, and in 1910, though insurance companies had begun to slip back relative to banks, they still accounted for 11.9 per cent of assets. In effect the two largest companies, Canada Life and Sun Life, were free to put their money into any combination of public and private bonds, mortgages, and loans that prudence might dictate. In 1899 the other companies, which had slightly more restrictive federal charters, were given the same freedom.

With premium income rising relative to the traditional demand for these funds, the insurance companies were able to absorb sufficient mortgages and municipal debentures to meet the requirements of those markets and still increase their portfolios of corporate securities and expand their collateral and policy loans. Corporate securities rose from 6 per cent of the assets of life insurance companies in 1891 to 19 per cent in 1901 and then settled back to 17 per cent in 1911.[20] It has been estimated that between 1900 and 1905 insurance companies may have purchased 20 per cent of all domestic bond issues and 11 per cent between 1906 and 1914. Insurance companies quickly learned that utilities provided the regular interest, substantial capital gains, low risk, and long-term security their business required. As early as 1900 Robertson and T.B. Macaulay, the chief executive officers of Sun Life in Montreal, and George Cox, president of Canada Life (newly moved from Hamilton to Toronto to be closer to this investment market), had shifted their companies away from mortgages into street railway, light and power, and other utility investments.[21] Thus both directly, by purchasing the bonds and stock of new Canadian companies, and indirectly, by providing loans to private individuals, policy holders, directors, shareholders, and brokers also wishing to purchase securities, the banks and insurance companies substantially widened the market for Canadian securities in general and utilities securities in particular.

Some of the newly created stock issues aroused a broader interest in the market. Urban utility companies, at the leading edge of technological change, were then being consolidated into monopolies and recapitalized. The steady capital gains – as well as the impressive dividends – recorded by these new securities attracted considerable attention. Besides the utilities, a small market opened up for a few industrial securities, cotton mills, electrical equipment manufacturers, and bicycle makers. Considerably more uncertainty and price volatility characterized these newcomers, but in good times there were always people willing to take a chance. In each case the Canadian markets were following trends observed in the major US stock markets.[22] The credit instruments of these new companies increased the quantity and broadened the range of paper for sale in this secondary market. The old clientele had more to choose from, and the remarkable performance of some of the new issues attracted entirely new business.

Unquestionably, however, the event that drew much wider public interest in the stock market and helped make a popular market for the paper of the financial village was the Kootenay mining boom, which began in the summer of 1896. Technically this investment craze started, and to a large extent remained, outside the existing stock exchanges, but it necessarily affected them. In August various British Columbia mines published large display advertisements in the financial press. This happened at the very moment the *Monetary Times* observed a 'remarkable' outburst of investment enthusiasm all over the Atlantic world. Editorialists as well as the Toronto Board of Trade warned the public against 'the prevailing craze' for extremely risky mining investments.[23] The public, drawn by golden dreams, ignored the well-intentioned advice.

The listing of mining quotations in the financial papers on a different page from other stocks and bonds and the separation of mining brokers' advertisements from those of the established brokers indicated the considerable distance between the mining market and the stock market at the beginning. In Toronto, completely separate Standard Mining and Toronto Mining exchanges were established to promote trading in these new and slightly disreputable stocks. This Kootenay mining bubble did not burst immediately. A dozen or more mines actually did come into production, and some of the leading financial men in Toronto as well as Montreal assumed control of several of the chief producers. At this point the established exchanges could not afford to ignore the excitement, and several of these mines promoted by Cox, Mackenzie, Ross, Ames, and others were listed.

If the *Monetary Times* is to be taken literally, in 1899 hundreds of young Toronto men followed the mining quotations as avidly as the sporting news. In Montreal, it was said, a generally older crowd kept track of developments in far-off Spokane and Rossland. The *Journal of Commerce* called on the banking community to put a stop to the hysteria that had even their own clerks gambling on stocks.[24] Thus the investment enthusiasm, which reached extreme form with BC mines, carried over into the new industrial and utilities stocks that arrived on the market at about the same time. This, then, was a propitious moment for some exotic, foreign utility flotations.

Curiously a persistent 'mercantile' outlook on the part of the financial press obstructed this full flowering of Canadian capitalism. In fact both the *Monetary Times* and the *Journal of Commerce* were more commercial papers than financial papers. They followed the monthly and annual bank returns with what amounted to an obsession, and in their editorial columns they kept merchants up-to-date with the business cycle and politics as they affected commercial life. Advertisements from wholesalers and information about wholesale markets dominated their layouts. Both the *Monetary Times* in Toronto and the *Journal of Commerce* in Montreal viewed these developments on the stock exchanges with mounting alarm. The buying and selling of paper claims upon dubious assets seemed like pure speculation. Merchants and manufacturers who borrowed money to build up inventories in anticipation of demand were merely going about their business. They made real things, dealt in real goods, served straightforward needs, and therefore earned a legitimate profit as they turned over their capital. Businessmen who squirrelled these profits away in secure, steady-earning bank stock were merely prudent, saving against the inevitable reversal of fortunes. Legitimate businessmen made things and served customers, knew their business inside out, and made clear-headed calculations of risk. These neophyte investors knew nothing of the businesses into which they were throwing their money, nor were they in full possession of the facts. They were simply *gambling*, the most censorious word in the Victorian Protestant lexicon.

The very papers that conveyed the information about the stock markets were, in their editorial columns, the principal critics of them. However wise their advice or accurate their appraisal of market conditions, the financial papers stood self-consciously in the way of the broadening of a market for industrial paper. Perhaps this attitude of the two leading papers created an opening through which a third paper, the *Financial Post*, launched in 1907, could quickly rise to prominence. And however much the *Monetary Times* and the *Journal of Commerce* might deliver sermons to them, the starry-eyed clerks and unwary merchants were not the problem. The biggest stock operators and most aggressive speculators in what was now *the market* were also the guardians of the largest and most respectable treasuries in the country.

III

Thus at the turn of the century the two major Canadian stock markets emerged from the relative obscurity of earlier years, a coming of age reflected in new buildings and a greater public curiosity about the arcane rites performed in them. On the floor of the new Montreal Stock Exchange building, opened in 1904, the sixty members gathered around four cylindrical Art Nouveau trading posts. In Toronto an older regime still prevailed in somewhat dingier circumstances. 'Lost in the heart of the National Trust Building is a square chamber which has been seen by few of the thousands of people whose interest is centred in it daily,' began a reporter who passed half an hour on the exchange in 1902. 'This is the Toronto Stock Exchange where the fevered pulse of speculation beats at considerably above normal during these days of national exhilaration and individual delirium.'[25]

The story went on to describe the work of this 'little band of forty men who sit in yellow swivel chairs at yellow desks.' In a decayed colonial imitation of beaver-hatted specialists on the London Exchange, the future-oriented Toronto traders all wore hats – fedoras and derbies of the latest design. In contrast to the gaudily attired brokers, the room looked drab. The desks seemed cheap, the wainscoting cheerless, the wallpaper (green lions rampant shooting out curving green tongues) out of place, and the ceiling dirty, but no one seemed to pay much attention to the decorations. The game was the thing.

The individual desks were arranged in a square facing a raised podium where a grey-bearded patriarch with an English accent called out the names of the stocks. From the desks arose a babble of bids that he silenced with a 'sweet little bell,' after which he recorded the transaction in a ledger. Raucous cries, words and phrases chopped and clipped for speed, and jovial humour characterized this curiously easy-going mêlée. 'One or two of the members of the Stock Exchange have the lean and hungry look of the anxious speculator,' the reporter observed upon parting, 'but the vast majority are fat and forty and jolly in the bargain.'[26]

Both the Toronto and Montreal exchanges were secondary markets rather than theatres of primary distribution. New issues were underwritten privately by syndicates, usually various combinations of the financial chieftains introduced earlier. They and their institutions took large blocks of bonds to which bonus stock was attached. Once the promotion was a going concern with earnings to report, the stock could be listed and the bonus stock eased onto a carefully managed market. In this way the promoters realized their gains and freed capital for another round. The bonds, earning interest, usually remained in the portfolios of the institutions or the individuals associated with the primary distribution.

Financing for both the initial underwriting and the later market operations was arranged through compliant banks and insurance companies. A royal commission investigation of the Canadian life insurance industry in 1906 revealed the extent to which George Cox and others used the life insurance premiums at their disposal to underwrite and accommodate stock market operations in Dominion Coal, Twin City Traction, Toronto Railway, Imperial Rolling Mills, Union Electric, São Paulo Tramway, and Shawinigan Power securities. George Cox did business with himself, usually through his own savings and loan company or bank, or his son-in-law's investment house. The commissioners noted with surprising restraint: 'In many of these transactions the conflict of Mr. Cox's interest with his duty is so apparent that the care of the insurance funds could not always have been the sole consideration.'[27]

A close examination by the commission of the affairs of the Cox group's Manufacturers' Life indicated that 'In the years 1902 and 1903 the management seems to have become more adventurous, and the dealings in stocks and bonds during those years exhibit a pronounced attraction towards the more or less speculative securities of the companies in which the directors had large interests.' The company also made large call loans to brokers and other market operators, primarily Henry Pellatt, William Mackenzie, Donald Mann, and William Strachan. It also made large unauthorized loans on the collateral of São Paulo Tramway and Mexican Light and Power company securities. In Montreal it was discovered that the Royal Victoria Life Insurance Company, an element in the Bank of Montreal constellation, loaned money to brokers on the strength of CPR, Canadian Coloured Cotton, Twin City Railway, Detroit United Railway, Dominion Iron and Steel, and various other securities in which members of the group had an interest.

In this way the savings welling up within the chartered banks and the major insurance companies flooded onto the stock market around the turn of the century. Bank and insurance company executives played a leading role in financing new ventures; they then used company funds to make a market in the securities they promoted. There was nothing sinister or devious about this process. Indeed, given the small size of the Canadian market and the rather narrow band of investors, something like this kind of socially sanctioned conflict of interest was necessary for a wider market to come into being at all.

Under this forceful stimulus the volume of transactions on the two exchanges soared upwards. The fact that after 1901 a systematic annual record of stock transactions began to be published is itself an indicator of the maturing of this market and of broadening public interest in it. By 1902 the majority of the transactions on the two exchanges (excluding penny mining shares) occurred in the stock of non-financial companies, a marked shift from the 1890s. In 1902 financial institutions accounted for only 4 per cent of all transactions on the two exchanges. On the other hand steam railways recorded 28.8 per cent of all deals, utilities at least 19.5 per cent, and industrials 31.2 per cent. As the two exchanges did not classify their listings in the same way, these should be taken as only approximate figures.[28] The general picture that emerges is quite clear, however. With the appearance of credit instruments from railways, utilities, and industrial companies, the stock exchanges registered a substantial increase in business, and trading was most active in these new issues.

Thus the turn-of-the-century Canadian adventures in investment overseas occurred against a background of extremely rapid domestic economic growth, unusually high levels of capital formation, large and increasing capital flows from abroad – primarily Great Britain – and a concentrated set of financial institutions whose assets were growing more rapidly than the economy as a whole. Real incomes of Canadians were rising; large portions of these income gains were saved; some of these savings in turn were pooled by a branch banking system and an extremely aggressive insurance sector where, after 1905, they were joined by heavy imports of savings from abroad. A booming economy and a well-developed system of financial intermediaries brought a flood of domestic savings onto the metropolitan capital market. Banks, insurance companies, and savings and loan companies were suddenly awash with cash. The system needed new investment opportunities.

Moreover, the institutional guardians of these funds had developed a predilection for a certain type of investment, the relatively new but astonishingly sucessful public utilities monopoly. Since the Canadian savings institutions were both centralized and highly concentrated, investment decision making fell to a small group of individuals, perhaps as few as forty, the active directors of the largest banks and insurance companies. The *market* was far from free; it was as closely controlled as was socially possible. The social cohesion of these individuals–the fact that they were already assembled in two main groups – facilitated this complex business of investing savings. Social connections and mutual business interests created the credit and climate of confidence upon which such a nascent market depended.

That is why such company promoters as F.S. Pearson, William Mackenzie, and the young Max Aitken were able to command the rapt attention of the country's leading men of finance with their schemes to build street railways, hydroelectric utilities, and telephone companies in such unlikely places as São Paulo, Mexico City, and the Caribbean islands. They brought new ideas to a Canadian financial community desperately searching for new vehicles for idle capital.

2

Going Abroad

In the middle of a bitterly cold January in 1900, the press noted the departure from Montreal for Cuba of Andrew F. Gault (the 'cotton king' of Canada) and Miss Gault, William Hanson (Montreal's leading stockbroker) and Miss Hanson, where they expected to join Sir William Van Horne who had gone on ahead.[1] This trip by prominent Montrealers might be taken as the beginning of what has since become an annual mass migration of Canadians to the Caribbean.

It is not recorded whether the Gaults and Hansons took their bathing suits with them or whether Sir William had a pair of trunks. In any event tourism then was not their primary concern. Andrew Gault would officiate at the opening of a tramway, of which he was president. Sir William Van Horne was in Cuba trying to figure out how to build the first trans-island railway. Latterly his entourage would include the artist J.W. Morrice, and in this curious fashion foreign investment inspired a florid, exotic, palette-brightening chapter of Canadian art history.

Just a month before the Montrealers' excursion, a group of prominent Toronto capitalists, including William Mackenzie, George Cox, J.W. Flavelle, E.R. Wood, Henry M. Pellatt, and A.E. Ames, had agreed to finance the reconstruction of the tramway, light and power utilities in São Paulo, Brazil. They had been persuaded to underwrite this speculation without the benefit of a personal tour of inspection. Over the next few years Canadian entrepreneurs from Halifax, Montreal, and Toronto would exploit similar franchises in such places as Rio de Janeiro, Mexico City, Monterrey, Camagüey in Cuba, Georgetown in British Guiana, Puerto Rico, Bermuda, Trinidad, and Barcelona in Spain.

Such ventures were far from being a mere sideshow; almost twice as much capital was invested in these foreign companies as in similar utilities at home. In 1905 the fourteen or so major companies abroad represented an investment of $276 million, or something in the order of magnitude of one complete transcontinental railroad (in 1905 the CPR was capitalized at $228 million). These Latin American and Caribbean utilities involved the major financial institutions and most of the leading figures in Canadian finance and were something of a school for budding capitalists, whose graduates included William Maxwell Aitken, James Hamet Dunn, and Izaak Walton Killam.

The Montrealers followed their aging lion, Sir William Van Horne, to his winter lair where they too got caught up in his investment recreations. A century of seafaring had familiarized Haligonian capitalists with the prospects presented by Caribbean urbanization. Torontonians, never straightforward, would rebound unexpectedly into southern utility investments after having been rebuffed in a direct assault upon the heart of empire.

I

Beginning in 1895 Canada's most aggressive utility entrepreneurs and financiers began looking abroad. Not that they neglected the remaining opportunities at home, but these were relatively few in number and the cities to be served were comparatively small. Men like William Mackenzie and James Ross, who already controlled street railways in Montreal and Toronto, calculated that their technical and managerial skills would generate a much higher return outside Canada. Initially they took positions in the Minneapolis, Detroit, and Toledo promotional syndicates organized by their US associate H.A. Everett. But the United States proved to be a challenging business environment in which to operate, for competitors were numerous, aggressive and often litigious. Since Canadian investors did not control the US enterprises they received only minority shareholders' returns. Like most self-respecting entrepreneurs they wanted to build, manage, and profit from companies of their own. Thus Canadians turned away from the adjacent but overcrowded US utilities marketplace in favour of other countries where the electric trolley was a greater novelty, and where the expertise they had acquired at home would reap comparatively greater rewards.

William Mackenzie and James Ross led the way. Both men had started their business careers as railway contractors, prospering on the construction of the main line of the Canadian Pacific Railway during the mid-1880s. In the latter years of the decade Ross settled in Montreal while Mackenzie moved to Toronto, where, early in the 1890s, he became interested in the acquisition and electrification of the street railway whose franchise was due to expire. He invited Ross to become a member of the syndicate organizing the new Toronto (street) Railway Company, and the following year Ross reciprocated when a new trolley company was floated in Montreal. Shortly thereafter the two men undertook a similar promotion in Winnipeg, and before long their joint affairs became so numerous and complicated that they hired Charles E.L. Porteous to act as their secretary and executive assistant. As they moved about from place to place overseeing their interests, Porteous co-ordinated communications back in Toronto or Montreal.[2]

Bluff and straightforward, William Mackenzie proclaimed himself simply a 'capitalist.' In his late forties by 1895, he looked every inch the part of the restless, self-made corporate empire builder. Youthful, ever alert to the main chance, his mind bristled with schemes for oil-shale projects, patented railway cars, mines, sawmills, land companies, and of course railroads. His formal education had ended in public school; all his knowledge of technology and business had been acquired on the job. With the enthusiasm of the self-taught he saw only possibilities, never obstacles; a relentlessly optimistic promotional outlook drove him forward. This he leavened somewhat with a gloomy Calvinist evaluation of possibilities in the afterlife. An evangelical Presbyterian who had carted a piano around his Rocky Mountain construction camps to sing Sankey hymns to his workmen, Mackenzie later sought spiritual comfort and social respectability as a member of St Andrew's congregation in Toronto. Mackenzie's ragged but fashionable Prince of Wales beard and moustache could not hide the rough edges of his character, just as his twinkling eyes and impatient manner betrayed a driving ambition.

Behind a patriarchal set of full whiskers James Ross was by comparison a rock of sober calculation. Son of a Scottish sea captain and an engineer by training, Ross had ranged over much of the northern United States and western Canada since coming to North America in 1870. After supervising construction of the CPR main line west of Winnipeg, Ross developed the railway's Maritime and Quebec network from his base in Montreal. His talents, temperament, and instincts complemented those of his headstrong co-religionist, Mackenzie. Ross possessed an engineer's understanding of technology and he took a more cautious view of business prospects than

Mackenzie. His Scottish reticence notwithstanding, however, he respected Mackenzie's promotional ability and fully shared his partner's eagerness to take quite remarkable risks – with other people's money – where there was a reasonable prospect of striking it rich. And both men wanted desperately to be rich.

By the middle of the 1890s Mackenzie and Ross had begun casting about for other propositions in the street railway business where they might take over a horsecar system and replace it with a trolley system powered by a thermal generating plant. The prospects for gain lay not only in what might be earned from construction but also in the ability to secure control of rapidly growing new companies with a very small outlay in cash. The Toronto Railway Company, for instance, was authorized to issue $1 million worth of stock and $2 million worth of bonds, whose interest was guaranteed by the municipal authorities. The money from the bond sales went to finance the reconstruction, but the company initially issued only $100,000 worth of common stock on which only a 10 per cent call was paid up. Mackenzie took his commission for reconstruction not in cash but in additional stock so that he became the major shareholder although he and his associates had put up a mere $10,000 in cash.[3]

Mackenzie and Ross carefully examined other Canadian cities, and in 1895 embarked upon a similar scheme in Saint John, New Brunswick; but the city had fewer than 40,000 people and obviously offered much smaller scope for their talents than larger centres.[4] As a result Mackenzie and Ross began to look farther afield. In the summer of 1895 Mackenzie reported from England that he was considering entering the street railway business there. As an experienced street railway man he was immediately struck by the relative slowness with which the new technology of the electric trolley was being adopted in Britain, and he scented the chance for an ambitious colonial to show the mother country a thing or two.

Once Frank J. Sprague had demonstrated the practicality of the overhead electric trolley system in Richmond, Virginia, in 1888, it swept through North American cities, rapidly putting steam locomotives, cablecars and battery lines to rout. By mid-1890 one-sixth of the 9,300 kilometres of US street railways were already electrified, nearly double the length of steam lines and more than three times the length of cable routes.[5] Thus the trolley car became, in the words of one historian, 'one of the most rapidly accepted innovations in the history of technology.'[6] Mackenzie and Ross oversaw the electrification of Canada's largest cities in the early 1890s; they were also the leading agents of the US 'stock watering' financial techniques in

Canada. In this way financial innovation piggy-backed upon technological change. By 1901, when the federal government first collected full returns from all electrified lines (including about 290 kilometres of interurbans), there were 1,086 kilometres of line in Canada altogether.[7]

In Europe, however, the spread of the trolley encountered serious obstacles at first. Despite its comparative cheapness and efficiency compared to the horsecar, the trolley car aroused serious aesthetic criticisms. As one English engineer put it in 1892, 'Our American cousins ... do not stick at forming a network of wires over their streets, so long as it facilitates locomotion, but in Europe we proceed more cautiously, and there is little doubt that these objectionable overhead wires have considerably interfered with the progress of electric traction on this side of the Atlantic.'[8] In larger US cities, such as Boston, New York, and Philadelphia, where conditions more closely resembled those in the older built-up areas in Europe, serious objections were raised to the introduction of trolleys.[9]

Nonetheless, the trolleys gradually established themselves in most European cities, owing to their economic advantages, particularly after battery cars, surface contact plates, and systems combining trolley wires with conduits in certain areas had all been tried and found less reliable than the overhead wires. Germany led the way in this with half of all the electrified lines in Europe by 1894, while progress was slowest in Britain, which had just 6 per cent of its routes electrified by the end of 1895 and only 38 per cent by 1902. Local municipalities there continued to resist the introduction of the trolley, despite the finding of the prestigious Institution of Electrical Engineers as early as 1894 that there was 'almost unanimous feeling among the members of the Institution in favour of the overhead trolley system as being by far the best and cheapest in every way.' The *Electrical Engineer* expressed some of the frustration the experts felt, because 'it is just this particular method or system which has the hardest battle to fight – the battle against foolish and ignorant prejudice ... There seems a by no means remote possibility that the building and equipment of electric lines will only begin to afford profitable occupation for our children's children, after the generation of today has vanished into dust or senility.'[10]

Gradually, however, popular demand for cheaper, speedier transportation, helped along by Glasgow's successful experiment with municipal ownership beginning in 1894, wore down some of the resistance to the spread of trolleys in Britain. Obviously London was the gem that every ambitious promoter yearned to control, and in the mid-1890s the twenty-one-year horsebus franchises in various districts were beginning to expire, opening the way for consolidation, rationalization, and electrification. In the spring of 1895 the London County Council received a proposal from the County of London Tramways Syndicate, which offered to acquire the twelve different operating companies and hand them over to the LCC, with the system to be leased back to the syndicate to manage as an integrated system.[11] William Mackenzie arrived in town while the LCC was considering this proposition. Surveying the scene, he observed,

There is a big change since I was over here three years ago, and I believe the time is opportune to make a strike. At least I think so, and I am going to look into things as far as I can while here.

... London, of course is the big field, but there are a great many outside places that can be handled much easier [sic] than London. It will require a very big syndicate to handle London, but I believe it can be accomplished if the right parties were got together.[12]

While the LCC deliberated over the syndicate's offer (which was not accepted in the end),[13] Mackenzie concentrated his attention upon the 'outside places.' He went first to visit Birmingham, a city of 500,000, where he discovered that there were seven different traction companies operating 193 kilometres of track by means of horse, steam, cable, and battery power. Local residents were particularly keen to see the noise and dirt of the steam locomotives replaced. The city engineer advised him that he thought the time 'ripe to make a deal with the [municipal] corporation.' '[L]ook what a saving it would be if the whole of these companies were acquired and amalgamated,' wrote Mackenzie to his Canadian associates. 'The cost of the separate management would pay a good dividend if put under one management, and all the extra expenses saved.'

Mackenzie was even prepared to bow to the quaint objections to overhead trolley wires on the part of the citizenry, which had already brought about unsuccessful experiments with cable and battery cars on several of the lines. '[Y]ou can see,' he wrote to Charles Porteous, 'the chances of doing business by turning the lines into electric [trolleys] and possibly partly cable, as it might be necessary in the heart of the city to put in some cable, which I think would be no detriment to the scheme. Of course, it would be better if the whole were electric, but there may be difficulties in the way of overhead wire in the centre of the city. I believe there is money in it by making the right combination which I think I can do.'

Since Mackenzie's associates often flinched at his bluntness and boldness, he sought to reassure them, albeit rather unconvincingly: 'Now don't jump to the conclusion that I am going to rush right in without due precaution, because I am going to be very careful and very cautious and won't go too fast unless I am thoroughly convinced of the position ... [P]roperly worked there is a very big field in this country in the electric line, and the people here are just beginning to open their eyes to the advantages of electric street railways, and the people that get the start will have things pretty well their own way.'[14] It was quintessential Mackenzie; shrewd, cocky, dismissive of risk, and consumed with a childlike desire to steal a march on the stuffy British.

In fact, Mackenzie was so taken with the opportunity from the outset that he ordered Porteous to sell three or four thousand shares of his stock in the recently organized Toronto Railway Company, so that he might have the money on hand if required. A larger sale would have produced a severe price break in the narrow Canadian securities market. 'I will be satisfied with whatever it will fetch,' wrote Mackenzie, 'as I believe I can go in here and make up any loss that will be made on the sale of the stock ten times over.' Meanwhile, he requested copies of the franchise agreement with the city of Toronto and the street railway's financial statements, so that he could demonstrate his bona fide to any interested parties. While he waited for these he passed the time meeting with some of the horse railway operators in London to advertise the virtues of the electric trolley and learn as much as he could about the long-term possibilities in the capital.

Even Mackenzie's bumptious push proved insufficient to bring about a deal at once, but he did not lose interest in the British situation when he returned to Canada. In the spring of 1896 he and James Ross descended upon Birmingham with the announced intention 'to wake things up.' They offered to buy control of the Birmingham Central Tramways Company from its shareholders and formed a new City of Birmingham Tramways Company to acquire the other firms and seek a new and extended franchise from the city.[15] Mackenzie's optimism remained undimmed: 'I am well satisfied that it will turn out a big thing if we can get it. Of course, the only difficulty is that we have so many things to look after that it will be very much [of an] addition and will require a good deal of personal time.'[16]

Purchasing control of Birmingham Central would obviously cost a good deal of money, and Mackenzie's first priority was to persuade the banks to lend it to him on the security of the stock. Might it be possible to interest

London financiers in the securities of some of the syndicate's other enterprises in order to improve its reputation? he wondered. The problem was that Toronto Railway stock was trading below par, which put off investors, while Montreal stock was at such a premium that it seemed over-valued to British investors. That would have to wait for the future, Mackenzie concluded: 'I do not think there is much chance of placing [Toronto Railway stock] here by itself, but if [sic] we are talking of making an arrangement whereby we can take in Toronto, Montreal and probably Birmingham if we get the business into shape, but in this matter, of course, [we] are only feeling our way.' Meanwhile, he could only wait for the Birmingham Central shareholders to approve the deal.[17]

Fortunately for Ross and Mackenzie their past reputations remained cloaked in colonial obscurity as far as Birmingham politicians were concerned. Their chief difficulty was with their bankers, who 'thought we were not able to cope with the people there [in Birmingham], and wanted the privilege of approving our arrangements with the Council before they would agree to advance us what money we required.' Eventually, though, that was sorted out: 'We have had a good deal of trouble and annoyance with one of the banks, but they have finally agreed to our terms. If they had not agreed we had a better bank ready to take the matter up, but it would have been rather awkward to have changed our bankers as they know all our plans.' A consortium of three banks, the London and Midland, the British Linen Company Bank, and the Bank of Montreal, finally agreed to supply equal portions of the £500,000 needed to swing the deal.[18] The shareholders of Birmingham Central were bought out and the company wound up, the new City of Birmingham Company replacing it. James Ross observed somewhat regretfully that while some of their friends in Canada might be offered the opportunity to subscribe for stock in the new company, the 'only profit to anyone in the transaction will be in the increase in value in the capital stock.'[19] By which he meant, of course, that English company law was less lenient than Canadian so that large amounts of bonus shares could not be given away to insiders fully paid up as was the practice at home.

Now all that remained was to procure a favourable report upon the syndicate's offer from the Public Works Committee of the Birmingham council. That came early in July 1896, although not without further vicissitudes, as Ross recounted: 'I cannot begin to tell you the trouble we have had over arranging the Birmingham matter, but many times it looked as if it would not come about. However, there is this to be said that we have settled now many important points that we expected would have to be settled afterwards. They are very clever people in Birmingham, they say the cleverest in England.' That was one reason why the bankers had been so eager to make their loan conditional on the terms of the franchise offered.[20] But the councillors were now ready to go ahead. Although they gave careful consideration to a municipally-owned tramway like that in Glasgow, they concluded that the offer by the Canadians to proceed at once, abolish all steam lines, reduce fares, shorten the workers' hours, and increase rental payments to the city was sufficiently attractive to go ahead. The full council approved the committee report despite a strong lobby for municipal ownership.[21] Canadian entrepreneurs appeared set to establish a major presence in the utility field in Great Britain.

Mackenzie and Ross each pledged $365,000 worth of securities in order to secure the loans they had received to acquire the Birmingham company[22] and began organizing their new undertaking. By November Mackenzie could report that 'Things are in very good shape here. We are settling details of construction and other matters in connection with the business. It looks as if this Birmingham business was going to turn out very well; the increases are about £300 a week so you can imagine what there will be when we get the road converted to a modern system.'[23] That, alas, proved to be the snag: the council and the Canadians could not agree upon a 'modern system.' The former still wanted to avoid cluttering the downtown streets with overhead wires, while the latter wanted the cheap and efficient trolleys so familiar to them.

In the spring of 1897, the city council decided to dispatch a subcommittee to the continent to examine alternative methods of operation. That visit strongly reinforced the hostility of the councillors to the trolley. Their report noted that

the unsightliness and otherwise objectionable features of the overhead wire are recognized in many of the places they have visited. The municipal authorities at Paris, Vienna and Berlin stated that in no case would they permit overhead wires in the central portion of those cities. At Brussels several miles of conduit are being laid to avoid them; at Dresden and Budapest they are not allowed in the principal streets, and even in some of the outer districts, where permission has been given, it is conditional, and the wires have to be removed upon notice being given.

And they recommended 'strongly that no consent be given for the erection of overhead wires in any part of the city.'[24]

As ill feeling mounted on both sides the Canadians remained naïvely optimistic that they would be able to break into the British market in a big way. In mid-July Porteous noted, 'I hear that Liverpool is going through, but that Birmingham sticks. Perhaps after the [Queen's] Jubilee matters will be smoother for Colonials.'[25] He was mistaken, however, as a majority of Birmingham city council dug in its heels and decided to oppose legislation that the company was seeking from Parliament to broaden its powers. In mid-1898 the aldermen voted, though only by the narrowest of margins, twenty-eight to twenty-seven, to cease all further negotiations with the colonial syndicate. Ross and Mackenzie were left in desperate circumstances, with only the equipment and the soon-to-expire franchises they had acquired at such great cost from the predecessor companies. Because of the stubborn refusal of the Birmingham city council to countenance overhead wires, the syndicate stood on the brink of losing everything.

Nevertheless they nursed the operation along, doubtless hopeful of a change of heart as the local citizenry came to recognize the way in which they were lagging behind other municipalities. But in the end the city council stood firm. With the council on the verge of opting for municipal ownership the two colonial financiers were fortunate to be able to sell out in 1902 to the British Electric Traction Company, which stepped into the breach, the impasse still unresolved.[26]

This first overseas venture by Canadian utility entrepreneurs ended, therefore, in a humiliating failure. Mackenzie and Ross discovered, as did others who attempted to introduce electric service into the United Kingdom, that political bodies placed awkward barriers quite foreign to North Americans in the way of the technology.[27] Regulation also ruled out some lucrative us financial practices. Whereas in Toronto Mackenzie's company had succeeded in persuading city council to adopt trolleys rather than battery-powered cars (albeit with the help of some bribes to the aldermen, put up by the Edison Electric Company, which hoped to supply the trolley motors),[28] in Birmingham the council stuck to its guns and refused to permit the stringing of overhead wires. North American councils were more pliable, perhaps because they were more eager to change their cities, to join in any effort that would make them more up-to-date and modern. There were fewer past glories to mar in North America, and much less sensitivity to them if they did exist. Thus, despite the familiarity of the legal and political environment, Britain, like the United States, did not prove an entirely hospitable environment for these Canadian financial pioneers abroad.

II

Nevertheless, Canadian entrepreneurs continued to look for opportunities overseas. But now they looked to less-developed areas where the desire for modern urban services might make political leaders more accommodating. The next venture, in which James Ross and William Mackenzie were again the principals, was a plan to build a small hydroelectric plant to supply light and power and to electrify the tramway in Kingston, Jamaica, undertaken late in 1897. The West India Electric Company was incorporated in Canada to take over a thirty-year tramway franchise granted by the colonial government that same year. The company proposed to electrify the forty-two kilometres of track using eight hundred horsepower produced at Bog Walk on the Rio Cobre, some thirty kilometres away. The lighting and power business, however, remained in the hands of another company, despite an unsuccessful attempt to purchase it in 1902.[29]

The West India Electric Company was the first utility company chartered in Canada to do business overseas. The funds for this relatively small project were to be raised by issuing $600,000 par value worth of bonds, plus $800,000 par value worth of common shares, most of the latter doubtless being given away to the insiders. The board of directors was well stocked with familiars from the Mackenzie-Ross orbit.[30] The only obstacle in the way took the form of opposition from a member of the colony's advisory council named Stearns, a shareholder in the rival lighting concern, who contended that the company lacked authority to use the waterpower or build a generating station. Porteous noted that on the latter point the councillor was correct, but an application for the necessary legislation was already in the works: 'The terms of the Bill have been approved by the authorities, and we are advised it is certain to pass. I, however, trust that proper representation from London through the Colonial Office has been made. It is very important we should be understood to be competent and responsible, and that the Governor (who is omnipotent) is safe in our hands. Mr. Stearns does not amount to much, but he is loud-mouthed and active.'[31]

With that obstacle safely out of the way, Canadian engineer Henry Holgate was dispatched to oversee the construction of the new plant, while Charles Porteous took responsibility for procuring the $320,000 worth of materials and equipment needed for the job.[32] By mid-1900 the work was substantially complete, and Holgate was recalled to Montreal to take on other tasks for the syndicate. The company prospered sufficiently that its stock was listed on the Montreal Stock Exchange in the spring of 1902.

Although the Jamaican economy was damaged by a hurricane in 1903, which reduced utility earnings, and an effort to purchase the rival Jamaica Electric Light Company was not successful, demand for power and lighting grew steadily, necessitating the expansion of the plant. Beginning in April, 1908, West India Electric started to pay a 4 per cent dividend on its common stock; this was increased a year later to 5 per cent.[33] All in all, it proved quite a satisfactory little promotion, enough to encourage others to imitate it.

At about the same time Sir William Van Horne, who had earned his fame and fortune through the Canadian Pacific Railway, also began to look abroad for opportunities. Born in the United States, he had been brought in to oversee construction of the first Canadian transcontinental railways and was made president of the company in 1888. As one of Canada's best liked and most respected business leaders his name lent great weight to any proposition.[34] (William Mackenzie and James Ross were doubtless delighted when they secured his participation in the Toronto street railway syndicate in the early 1890s.) A big, swaggering boastful man who could outdrink and outlast most of his contemporaries at the card table, Sir William (he was knighted in 1894) also possessed an artistic, more refined side – perhaps an inheritance from his Knickerbocker ancestors – that attracted artists, authors, and scholars to his circle of admirers.

By the end of the century Sir William had grown bored with the day-to-day management of a transcontinental railway. Perhaps he had burnt himself out building the CPR in the 1880s, or perhaps in saving it from bankruptcy during the bleak years of the early 1890s. In 1899, with the railway safely back in a profitable condition, he relinquished the presidency to become chairman of the board.

Though formally retired in 1899 Sir William was not ready to retreat in smoking jacket and carpet slippers to his cavernous studio to catalogue his fossils or privately savour his large collection of oriental vases, Middle Eastern sculptures, and French (though, alas, pre-Impressionist) paintings. At fifty-six, full of vigour and still a man of gargantuan appetites, Sir William sought new challenges and new parts of the world to roam. Montreal winters made him think seriously about warm places. In his new-found ease he could no more put his old life behind him than give up smoking cigars. Even in the midst of a Cuban holiday, sitting on the veranda out of the noonday sun, Sir William fretted that the richest island in the Caribbean still lacked a comprehensive railway system.[35] The conquest of Cuba by the United States quickened his interest.

Not only was Van Horne familiar with the Cuban situation through his friendship with such prominent us politicians as Elihu Root and General Russell Alger, but he seems also to have discussed possible ventures with Gonzalo de Quesada y Arostegui, at one time Cuban minister in Washington. Some years later Van Horne wrote to Quesada: 'It was really through you that I was first attracted to Cuba, and although this has involved me in vastly more care and hard work than I expected I have been amply rewarded with the thought that I have been some use in helping the people of that lovable island. I have not yet had any return on the large amount of money I have invested there during the past nine years, but I am confident that the return will begin to come before long.'[36]

These Cuban, and later Central American, ventures occupied Sir William's ample energies during his Caribbean winters following his 1899 retreat from the CPR. But his us partners never fully shared his enthusiasm. The Cuban affairs were amiable amusements, but surely they were not worthy of his undivided attention. Thomas Fortune Ryan, who knew both Sir William and the possibilities of North American capitalism intimately, could never understand why Van Horne was 'turning his back upon an empire and chasing a rabbit.'[37]

As soon as the Spanish-American War ended and shipping service to the island was restored, an agent representing Van Horne (who had also invited William Mackenzie to participate) set off for Havana in an effort to gain control of the three mule tramways in the city with the intention of electrifying them.[38] The Canadian syndicate soon discovered that several other groups of investors were interested, including the American Indies Company, backed by the New York tramway men William C. Whitney, William Elkins, P.A.B. Widener, and Thomas Fortune Ryan. Another American, Percival Farquhar, was also in the field, and he eventually succeeded, with the backing of French financiers, in securing control of most of the properties in conjunction with local Cuban interests. Farquhar had sent a young engineer, F.S. Pearson (about whom much more will be said later), to examine the properties in Havana, but the competition was so hot Farquhar had to go ahead and take them over while Pearson's yacht was still storm-bound off Cape Hatteras. One jump ahead of his rivals, Farquhar obtained a vital franchise from the departing Spanish administration in December 1898 and set up the Havana Electric Railway Company. He then made peace with the later arrivals by purchasing in conjunction with Van Horne and William Mackenzie the one franchise that the American Indies Company had obtained. Farquhar then offered Van Horne a seat on the board of directors, and Van Horne accepted.[39]

Van Horne was immediately attracted to the much younger Farquhar, who had, after all, bested some of the sharpest entrepreneurs in America. Farquhar perhaps reminded Sir William of a younger version of himself. Though not a self-made man, Farquhar had turned his back upon security several times already. After graduating as an engineer and serving a successful apprenticeship as a minor speculator in the New York stock market in the 1890s, Farquhar had set off to seek his fortune and adventure in the tropics, much as Van Horne had done earlier in the old North West. Intrigued by the possibilities of further investment on the island of Cuba, Van Horne allowed Farquhar to persuade him to make a grand tour in January 1900, along with his friends Root and Alger. Farquhar was now working on plans for a railway to serve the eastern part of Cuba, running from Santiago through Camagüey to Santa Clara, where it would connect with the rest of the island's rail network. Van Horne became thoroughly enamoured of the possibilities of this scheme, and in the spring of 1900 accepted the presidency of the Cuba Company, incorporated in New Jersey. To raise the $8 million required to build the line, Van Horne secured the participation not only of the tramway men Whitney, Elkins, Widener, and Ryan, and his old railway rival, J.J. Hill of the Northern Pacific, but also of his Canadian Pacific associates, R.B. Angus, T.G. Shaughnessy, and C.R. Hosmer of Montreal.[40]

The greatest obstacle the new company had to overcome was the Foraker Act, passed in 1899, which, in an effort to protect the Cubans from exploitation, forbade the US military government from granting any franchises or concessions. Faced with the problem of trying to build a railway without power to expropriate lands, Van Horne decided to buy a private right of way. Fortunately for him local landowners, convinced of the benefits that would flow from rail service, donated most of the property required. Construction commenced in the fall of 1900 and was pushed forward as rapidly as possible by a workforce totalling six thousand men. But when construction costs outran estimates in 1902, Van Horne was forced to ask syndicate members to put up an additional 40 per cent in funds. Elkins, Widener, and Ryan refused, but Van Horne was able under the Cuba Company's charter to force them to sell their shares, and he persuaded the Scottish investment banker Robert Fleming to take over their interest and put up an additional $3 million. Thus in December 1902 Van Horne alone presided over the opening ceremonies at railway headquarters in Camagüey. As he later remarked, 'I never had to do with a railway that started off so well.'[41]

Despite a certain amount of inspired puffery in the press, the Cuba Railroad Company (as it was renamed in 1902) failed to live up to its early promise.[42] Investment in the sugar industry came only slowly, owing to the maintenance of a protective tariff by the United States. The recession of 1903 further retarded development, and a new insurrection in 1906 necessitated another intervention by the United States to restore order and created more problems.[43] Yet the railway did help to arouse Canadian interest in Cuba, along with the Havana Electric Railway Company and the Port of Havana Docks Company, on whose boards Van Horne served. He brought his old allies from the Canadian Pacific into his railroad, and later a group of younger men followed him with a utility promotion, in which he took a share, in the city of Camagüey.

In 1899 Van Horne also joined a group of Halifax men who were interested in installing an electric lighting and trolley system in George-town, British Guiana. The most prominent of these Maritimers were Senator David MacKeen and lawyer and newspaper proprietor B.F. Pearson, both of whom were well known to the central Canadian business elite through their participation in the reorganization of the Nova Scotia iron and coal industry during the 1890s. The syndicate evidently sent a couple of scouts down to the British colonies in the Caribbean to search out likely prospects, and they recommended the establishment of a Canadian-chartered firm, the Demerara Electric Company, to undertake the task.[44]

Capitalized at $850,000 and financed by a $600,000 loan from Sir William's friends at the Bank of Montreal, the company constructed a steam-powered plant to generate its power and laid down the tramlines.[45] Here, too, the Canadians encountered unexpected obstacles. Owing to electrolysis, their rather primitive wiring seriously disrupted the local telephone system owned by the provincial government. The small under-taking limped along and eventually had to be reorganized towards the end of the decade.[46]

III

Predictably, publicists reported these moderately successful southern ventures in the most glowing terms; they were seen as a perfectly 'natural' thing for North American capitalists to be doing. The *Journal of Commerce* observed, of 'the Canadian Magician' (Sir William Van Horne) and his associates, that they 'seek fresh fields and pastures to prove that neither snows nor tropical suns could check the onward march of well-directed energy.'[47] Southern business served to stoke the flames of northern vanity and nationalist self-assurance. It was as if the development of the tropics could be undertaken on a part-time basis in retirement, as exotic comforts rewarded and complemented northern enterprise. A decade later a fawning journalist left Van Horne's vast sugar estate in Cuba thoroughly enchanted with the Lion in Winter: 'He finds the country fascinating, the climate ideal. With a home in the stern, hard and enterprising North, and with great interests to call him often to mild and lovely Cuba, where the thermometer rarely falls below seventy and rarely rises above eighty, and where even oranges grow wild, his life is rounded out.'[48]

Some, like Sir William, went south to find amusement in their semi-retirement. Others saw it as simply another place, albeit more agreeable than most, in which to make money. They were all drawn by an eagerness to make their mark upon a world wider than just Canada. Besides, Canadian opportunities in these lines of endeavour had dried up.

Mackenzie and Ross, in particular, were incessantly scouting for opportunities. In August 1899 Charles Porteous travelled across Canada with Mackenzie and his railway-building partner, Donald Mann, and learned that they had a concession in China to build a 1,000-kilometre railroad from Shanghai to Hankow, along with a 400-kilometre branch south from Hankow along the Yangtse. The partners confided that they had extracted an offer of a subsidy from the Chinese imperial government worth 'as many Pounds [sterling] per mile as they would get in dollars in this country.'[49] Late in 1901 Mackenzie and Ross learned that they might be able to secure a tramway concession in Shanghai, although again there seems to have been no result.[50]

In 1900 they were also offered a chance to take control of the electric lighting plant at Santiago de Cuba, the terminus of Van Horne's Cuban railroad. A few months later engineer Henry Holgate, who had been employed by the West India Electric Company, was inquiring about their participation in a scheme to build electric railways in the Malaga district of Spain that some Torontonians were trying to float.[51] And in 1905 a friend of Charles Porteous, then working in Mexico, wrote to reproach him for not showing an interest in an electric company in Aguascalientes about which the friend had alerted Porteous: 'There are many schemes in this country that unquestionably would make large returns for the money invested. I wish you could find time to pay us a visit as I feel sure that you would enjoy all you would see.'[52]

Many schemes there might be in all parts of the world for those with the will to take the risks involved, but the sad truth was that the first ventures by Canadians overseas in the field of utilities were not notably successful. In general entrepreneurs laid the blame upon the uncooperative attitude of the foreign politicians with whom they had to deal. Porteous, for instance, complained to a doctor in Jamaica that the West India Electric Company had been 'a pioneer one for the people of Canada, and we all hope that we will get a fair return and do some patriotic work in cementing the two colonies. I may tell you privately that we have not been satisfied with the attitude of the Island authorities; they are inclined to stand on the limit of their extreme rights and to enforce them in an arbitrary manner. Now the Company's intention is to do right, and we think that we will not fail of its [sic] reward.'[53]

West India Electric was, after all, one of the more successful early ventures. Those who had their money tied up in the City of Birmingham Tramways Company, the Cuba Railroad Company or the Demerara Electric Company must have felt even harder done by. But believers are seldom deterred by initial setbacks. The promoters never doubted their judgment; success was only a matter of time as long as their credit was good. So when Mackenzie got wind of an opportunity to get in on a big utility promotion in São Paulo, Brazil, he did not hesitate for one minute before plunging in with all his friends.

PART TWO

Foreign Affairs

3

Success in São Paulo

Canadians owed their involvement in Brazil to an engineer from the United States, Fred Stark Pearson. Driven, almost obsessed, by his desire to live the life of a capitalist baron, he would shuttle restlessly around the Atlantic world in the years after the turn of the century in search of more and better opportunities to apply his technological know-how and make his fortune. A rare photograph of him in middle age shows a thin, almost drawn face, with staring eyes lifted only momentarily from the papers lying before him. He acquired the trappings – a mansion in the Berkshires of Massachusetts and a country estate in England – but the constant worry, frenetic pace and ceaseless travel of company promotion took their toll on his health and severely interfered with his enjoyment of these rewards.[1]

Pearson achieved his early success in classic fashion by dint of apparently limitless energy. When his father died while he was still in his teens, the young man went to work for the railroad as a station agent in Medford, Massachusetts, but was soon combining his duties with scientific studies at the town's Tufts College. Upon graduation he immediately joined the Tufts faculty and, taking advantage of the creation of one of the earliest programs in electrical engineering in the United States, quickly mastered the rudiments of that subject. He was overseeing the design and management of electric lighting systems serving several nearby towns when in 1889 Henry M. Whitney approached him to become chief engineer of his West End Street Railway in Boston.

Pearson successfully tackled the problems of installing an electrified trolley line in the Massachusetts capital, including the design and construction of a powerhouse of unprecedented size. In 1892 he made his first contact with Canada when Whitney sent him to Cape Breton Island to investigate the potential of its coal mines for supplying the West End company. On Pearson's advice Whitney joined with William Mackenzie and James Ross in forming the Dominion Coal Company for this purpose. While in Nova Scotia F.S. Pearson also met the prominent Halifax lawyer and entrepreneur B.F. Pearson when, as the apocryphal story has it, they received each other's mail. The two Pearsons worked together on the electrification of the Halifax street railway, in which the Massachusetts engineer took a financial interest.

In 1894 William Whitney persuaded F.S. Pearson to leave his brother Henry Whitney's Boston utility and join the Metropolitan Street Railway in New York as chief engineer. Pearson's growing reputation as a tramway expert was severely tested by the refusal of the city government to accept overhead trolleys. He struggled to design an underground conduit system with which the cars could make contact through a slot in the roadway, although this never operated very satisfactorily. By 1897 Pearson had advanced about as far financially as he could as an engineer in the employ of other men. He wanted to become another Whitney.

I

During a trip to Montreal an opportunity of the sort Pearson had been looking for offered itself when he ran into a former Italian naval officer named Francisco Gualco. In 1896 Gualco had visited São Paulo at the invitation of a prominent Paulista family, and the following year procured from the municipal government a concession to establish a trolley system and supply electricity. Gualco had already travelled to Europe and the United States in an effort to raise the necessary capital to build and equip the utility, but had met with no success.[2]

Pearson had visited Brazil on his honeymoon a decade earlier to study a mining venture and seems to have been impressed by the country's prospects. He decided that Gualco's proposition was worth investigating and at once dispatched a street railway engineer to examine the situation in São Paulo. The initial report was evidently favourable, for Pearson then recruited a former subordinate, R.C. Brown, to go to Brazil and make further inquiries at the end of 1898. Knowing that imported coal was expensive, Pearson also sent along a young hydraulic engineer, Hugh L. Cooper, to see whether there was a source of waterpower near São Paulo that could easily be developed.

Having spent three weeks in São Paulo in December 1898, Brown reported that the situation looked promising. The city, which was the centre of the growing Brazilian coffee trade, had a population of more than 240,000.[3] The business district stood upon a hill separated from the main residential quarters by deep ravines. There was a mule tramway, but it was forced to follow slow, roundabout routes. Nevertheless, the cars enjoyed a good ridership, especially in the summer when the weather was hot and humid and the patrons preferred to ride even a short distance rather than toil up and down hill. Brown was confident that electric trolleys could negotiate the slopes without difficulty, while out in the suburbs there were broad avenues that would permit the cars to run as fast as in North America. All in all, concluded Brown, 'Such a city as São Paulo should give excellent returns to a street railway, especially one operated by electricity, and one that is managed with a view to giving its patrons convenient, quick and cheap service.'[4]

An important key to profitability, of course, was low-cost power. Utility managers had come to recognize that while street railways were highly valuable customers for electricity and absorbed a large, predictable base load, the most satisfactory results could be obtained by adding a light and power supply business that utilized equipment more fully and helped to flatten the load peaks. Experience also showed that demand would rapidly increase if lighting rates were reduced. If production costs declined as output increased, revenues and profits would show a gratifying rise within a short period.

Fortunately, Hugh Cooper's explorations of the territory around São Paulo revealed that there was a good waterpower site just forty kilometres from the city on the Tietê River near Parnaíba. Building a run-of-the-river hydroelectric station that could turn out between 16,000 and 18,000 horsepower annually would be a comparatively simple matter despite the primitive equipment and unskilled labour available. Even before Brown and Cooper's visit ended, Francisco Gualco had, on their advice, acquired the hydraulic rights at Parnaíba and was ready to approach the government of the state of São Paulo for the right to develop the power and transmit it to the city. Brown anticipated that, as well as lighting customers, businessmen now generating their own power at a cost of between $100 and $125 per horsepower unit would form a sizeable clientele. The only other good waterpower site in the vicinity was twice as far from the city and would cost much more to develop, valuable protection for a local monopoly if it could be established.[5]

But if monopoly was the key to success for a promotion of this kind, Pearson's was neither the first nor the only company in the São Paulo utilities market. Before the turn of the century, British and German entrepreneurs had been particularly active in organizing such ventures along with some Latin Americans. At São Paulo, for instance, the gasworks had originally been built by an English company (now controlled by prominent Paulistas) to supply coal gas for street and domestic lighting.[6] In addition the Companhia Água e Luz provided water and also enough electric current to light about 5,000 incandescent lamps and 100 arcs in the city centre.[7] A third utility, the Companhia Viação Paulista ran the ninety kilometres of muletram lines in the city.[8]

By the time R.C. Brown submitted his final report in the spring of 1899, F.S. Pearson had already begun his efforts to find financial backing for the takeover and reorganization of the utilities in São Paulo. Unfortunately, the New York capitalists to whom he first turned were not impressed, so Pearson considered offering it to some French investors connected with Percival Farquhar, who had retained him to examine the Havana street railway. Before leaving for Europe, however, F.S. Pearson consulted his Canadian associate, B.F. Pearson of Halifax. The Nova Scotian concluded that he and his fellow Maritimers would not be able to raise the large sums of money required but was eager to see the scheme taken up and suggested that William Mackenzie of Toronto be approached, for he was a man willing 'to take a chance on a promising new enterprise anywhere.'[9]

Mackenzie, with his large portfolio of utility investments, recognized the profits to be gained from amalgamating all the utilities in one city into a single entity, as he was doing in Winnipeg at that very moment. Mackenzie already knew F.S. Pearson through Pearson's work for the Dominion Coal Company in Nova Scotia and his subsequent service as consulting engineer for the Royal Electric Company of Montreal in which Mackenzie's partner, James Ross, was heavily involved. So, when F.S. Pearson came calling, Mackenzie was prepared to lend a friendly ear and to recommend the proposition to his cronies in the Toronto financial community – George Cox, Joseph Flavelle, Frederic Nicholls, and E.R. Wood.

The plans that R.C. Brown had mapped out for São Paulo were costly by the standards of the day. Pearson needed to raise at least $5 million initially, and he knew that the ultimate investment was likely to be much higher. He later reminded one of the other insiders:

As you are aware the $5,500,000 did not by any means furnish sufficient money to do this job in a proper way, but as it was evident that this was the maximum amount of money that could be obtained at that time we were obliged to carry out our work in São Paulo in view of the amount of money available. A great deal of work which was absolutely necessary could not be attempted.[10]

All the members of the original syndicate recognized that Pearson's proposition was 'very speculative' and that only the opportunity to earn extraordinary profits would induce people to risk capital in an unknown venture in a far-off country. Nonetheless, Mackenzie and his friends in Toronto agreed to back it. That did not mean, of course, that they would put up the money out of their own pockets, for they all had a multitude of other calls upon their resources. Instead they adopted a method that was to become standard for the underwriting of ventures of this kind. A company was incorporated with power to issue bonds with a par value somewhat greater than the sum required to carry out the necessary works along with common stock of equal par value. A syndicate of underwriters took the bonds and sought to market them at about 90 per cent of par. In order to make the deal more attractive the common stock was given away with the bonds as a bonus, ranging from stock with the same par value as the bonds for investors on the 'ground floor' to much smaller percentages for outsiders. Since the Canadian capital market was too narrow and volatile to accept an issue of even $5 million all at once without inducing wild price swings, the bonds had to be fed out onto the market over a period of time by syndicate members and their associates. In order to make it easier for purchasers, the bonds were paid for in instalments over a period of months, and banks and insurance and trust companies had to be persuaded to lend money with the securities of the new undertaking pledged as collateral, so that funds were available to commence construction. If all went well the company's operations would begin to generate enough revenue to pay the bond interest and to commence dividends on the common stock before long. That, in turn, would make the remaining securities all the more saleable and render subsequent financing easier.

The syndicate that agreed to back Pearson in the São Paulo venture made one important decision at the outset: the utility would be incorporated in Canada. There were several reasons for this. With the exception of F.S. Pearson, all the insiders were Canadians, familiar with Canadian company law and aware that nervous investors would not accept Brazilian incorporation. Moreover, there were real advantages to using Canada as a legal domicile because of the laxity of its securities and corporation law as well as the latitude permitted to controlling shareholders in the event of difficulties.

In Britain, by contrast, any publicly traded company had to undergo careful scrutiny from the stock exchange in order to secure a listing. The Companies Act contained a number of restrictions on such matters as the allotment of stock and the issuing of prospectuses, and it did not provide for the granting of powers of expropriation, which were of crucial importance to utilities. Listed companies were required to file annual accounts and lists of shareholders with the registrar of joint stock companies. 'This is a feature that has no counterpart in the Canadian Act,' noted a report to the Canadian minister of justice in 1901.[11]

A Canadian charter meant that nothing need be said about the amount of common stock given away as bonuses. No accurate prospectus need be filed and no accounts submitted, even to the shareholders, until it suited the board to reveal what was happening. Moreover, these experienced businessmen were aware that Canadian companies were usually regarded as British firms in all but name. British investors might be persuaded to put money into them in due course, and the companies might expect to enjoy whatever diplomatic and commercial protection the government of the United Kingdom could provide in foreign parts. Hence the decision to domicile all the utilities organized by these entrepreneurs in Canada.

In the spring of 1899 William Mackenzie's lawyer, Zebulon Lash, applied to the province of Ontario for the letters patent of the São Paulo Railway, Light and Power Company. (When the company began operations in Brazil it soon discovered that there was a long-established British firm called the San Paulo Railway (the 'San' was a Britishism), and, in order to avoid confusion and antagonism, the new company was renamed São Paulo *Tramway*, Light and Power.) Authorization was obtained to issue 50,000 $100 par value thirty-year bonds bearing 5 per cent annual interest, plus 60,000 common shares with $100 par value. The underwriting syndicate agreed initially to take $3 million par value worth of these bonds at 90 per cent with instalments of 10 per cent due every sixty or ninety days as the money was required in Brazil. The entire issue of common stock was given away to the insiders in order to compensate them for their risk.

On these terms the company had little difficulty floating its securities in the good times then prevailing in North America. B.F. Pearson took on $1 million worth of the bond underwriting, $300,000 of it being re-underwritten by a group of wealthy Haligonians, while the remainder was taken over by the Montreal stockbroking firm of Hanson Brothers. The other bonds were acquired by William Mackenzie and George Cox and distributed in batches of $100,000 or more among such friends and associates as James Ross, J.W. Flavelle, A.E. Ames, W.B. Ross, Frederic Nicholls, and Patrick Burns, the Calgary meat-packer. Twenty-two smaller fry connected to this group received allotments ranging from $80,000 to a mere $1,000. The more powerful and influential the individual the larger the percentage of bonus stock received. Most people received a 100 per cent bonus (one share of stock with each $100 bond), but Senator Cox and others, including William Mackenzie and F.S. Pearson, got a 130 per cent bonus.[12]

II

With the syndicate successfully formed, F.S. Pearson set off for Brazil in the middle of 1899 to oversee the transfer of the various franchises to the company, to seek additional privileges from the city and state of São Paulo, and to discover on what terms the existing utilities there might be purchased. He took with him not only R.C. Brown and Hugh Cooper, who had performed the initial investigations, but also a young lawyer named Alexander Mackenzie from Zebulon Lash's firm of Blake, Lash and Cassels. In time Alexander Mackenzie was to become as important a figure in the world of Canadian utility companies abroad as Pearson himself. Mackenzie went along to arrange the legalities of the transfer of franchises from Gualco and his associates in exchange for 10 per cent of the common stock, and to consult with Brazilian lawyers to make certain that the company had all the necessary certificates and licences required to operate its business. Of utmost importance was to make sure that the trust deed securing the bonds with the National Trust Company (controlled by George Cox and Joseph Flavelle) was ironclad, if possible by procuring legislation in Brazil confirming its existence, as was normally done in corporate charters in Canada.[13]

When Alexander Mackenzie and F.S. Pearson reached Brazil in late June 1899 (mid-winter there, of course), they immediately entered into intense negotiations with São Paulo's prefect, Dr Antônio Prado. Language, the first obstacle, was overcome partly through hiring an Englishman to act as intermediary and interpreter. Mackenzie reported home that, 'The English spoken by one or two of the lawyers is of the "pigeon" variety, and it is most difficult to carry a discussion very far.' On the other hand Pearson's powerful charm more than compensated for any linguistic deficiency. 'Mr. Pearson is as good as a staff of lawyers and I think his judgement can be relied upon to keep us out of any great mistakes,' Mackenzie confided. At first Prado believed that these were merely a gang of speculators, part of an 'American bluff' to manipulate the local utility franchises for a quick profit. Eventually, however, Pearson and Mackenzie got through to him and convinced him of their bona fides, and subsequently he endeavoured to assist them as far as possible.[14]

Pearson and Mackenzie arrived in Brazil at a propitious moment. Owing to the moratorium the country had recently declared on its foreign debt, the value of the milréis had dropped sharply against other foreign currencies, which made it relatively cheap to purchase assets there. But local entrepreneurs would have found it difficult if not impossible to raise the large sums required for electrification; hence the lack of progress made up to the time the Canadians arrived on the scene. Moreover, the Brazilian federation was both weak and decentralized, leaving the city and state of São Paulo, as the centre of the export trade in coffee, relatively powerful and autonomous. Thus, once Prado threw his support behind the Canadian syndicate, the other obstacles in its path could be swiftly cleared away.

Nonetheless, it became clear that the proprietors of the existing utilities were not prepared to give way to the interlopers without a fight. Alerted by the arrival of the investigators sent from Canada the proprietors of the Viação Paulista had recently succeeded in having its muletram franchise extended for another forty years with exclusive rights to all the streets where its tracks ran; they were letting it be known that they would not sell out for less than $1.3 million. The company also entered into negotiations with the French Thomson-Houston organization concerning the purchase and financing of new electrical equipment. The gas company, too, had procured a renewal of its exclusive franchise for a thirty-year period in 1897, although that did not debar competition from electric lighting, but efforts were being made to lock up a long-term street lighting contract with the city. The Companhia Água e Luz likewise protested the plans to erect poles and wires on the streets.[15]

Alexander Mackenzie reported to his partners that care was going to have to be exercised, as all three rivals were 'powerful enemies and have friends in high places, so that notwithstanding that we are supposed to have the Municipal Chamber with us, much can be done to delay and thwart us in completing our business.' He and Pearson worked away, and gradually the arrangements with the city were formalized and the licence to operate was procured from the federal government. In the fall of 1899

Pearson departed for North America leaving Mackenzie to handle future dealings with officialdom.[16]

Cooper, meanwhile, oversaw the start of construction on the dam and powerplant at Parnaíba, while in São Paulo R.C. Brown supervised the laying of trolley tracks and the canvassing for electricity customers. (The plan was to supply both for the time being from a temporary steam plant until the transmission line from Parnaíba was completed and ready to operate.) The hydraulic plant was eventually built by the company with local day labour under the supervision of seven Americans using twelve derricks, three pumps, an aerial cableway, a rock crusher, eight steam engines, one air compressor, and five boilers, all imported for the purpose.[17]

Back in Toronto, cut off from Brazil by a three-week sea voyage out of New York, the syndicate of insiders waited anxiously for news. Construction costs required the payment of regular instalments of principal on the bonds, and the underwriters were eager to launch a public flotation of the securities with a prospectus designed to induce outside investors to put up money. But George Cox and William Mackenzie believed that it was first imperative to secure a local monopoly in the electrical field in São Paulo by coming to terms with the Viação Paulista and the Água e Luz. Near the end of 1899 the two men informed F.S. Pearson that they were 'strongly in favour of buying them in the near future, as they feel it would make it much easier to float the securities and be worth considerable to us for this reason.' Pearson therefore urged Alexander Mackenzie to try to work out a deal, 'even if we paid a little more than they are actually worth.' At the same time he pressed Mackenzie to try and get permission to break the gas company's hold on street lighting and secure the right to light some of the streets in São Paulo electrically,

as it is very important for us to have a portion of this public lighting on account of the moral [sic] effect of placing the bonds in London later. I shall be very sorry if we do not get this. I should think that with the influence our friends have that we should be able to swing this. Perhaps some of the 'Mans' will have to be seen.[18]

In São Paulo, however, matters proceeded at a leisurely pace that the Canadian sometimes found very frustrating. By early 1900 the Viação Paulista people seemed ready to sell out, but then gained new heart when they persuaded a judge to hold that the work undertaken by the Canadian company violated their franchise. Brown was served with summonses whenever the trolley lines were laid across the old muletram tracks, and it was feared that the electric cars would be prevented from running until all the litigation was sorted out. Mackenzie was convinced that the judge in question had been bribed and eventually secured his removal from the case. Meanwhile, he brought a counter-suit for damages in an effort to scare off investors from putting any money into the Viação Paulista with the intention of electrifying it.[19]

The Toronto insiders champed at the bit as they waited to launch their promotion upon the public. Early in 1900 the provisonal directors were replaced, and in February William Mackenzie became president, with Frederic Nicholls as vice-president.[20] The underwriters formed a pool managed by the National Trust to keep bond prices at 95 per cent of par, an essential precaution in a narrow market where 'bear' raids were all too common. Hopes ran high: B.F. Pearson wrote optimistically to Hanson Brothers in Montreal: 'I am more than ever convinced that this enterprise, unless something very unforeseen should happen, is bound to succeed fully as well as ever has been anticipated.'[21]

At long last things began to sort themselves out in São Paulo. By April, Alexander Mackenzie was able to report that he had finally been able to purchase 86 per cent of the outstanding stock of the Água e Luz at 85 per cent of par along with 60 per cent of the company's debentures for a total of $240,000. If the rest of these securities could be had at the same prices, the total cost would be $300,000, or $180,000 less than asked the previous summer and only $50,000 more than Pearson had originally been prepared to pay. Evidently the Brazilians had found it impossible to raise the additional capital required to modernize their plant in order to compete with the Canadian company. Pearson observed:

I consider this a very satisfactory purchase as we will take over their business at once, and at the same time it removes their opposition, which I have always regarded as of more danger than the mule road, inasmuch as all of the people live in São Paulo and have a much greater local influence. Furthermore, they are very nice people of good standing, and I have always felt that it would be a mistake to squeeze them to such an extent in buying them out as to make them feel sore. At these figures I have no doubt that they feel friendly and will cooperate with us in future.[22]

Gaining control of the Viação Paulista proved to be more difficult. The owners persisted in their opposition to the new trolley company, and scuffles broke out in the streets between rival work gangs. To avoid issuing further injunctions, the judge whom the Viação had allegedly bought ordered the posting of a $100,000 bond while the lawsuits between the two parties were fought out. Alexander Mackenzie remained confident, however, that the Viação would lose in the end. The track-laying work was pursued vigorously, and in May 1900 the running of the first trolleys was greeted with general public celebration.[23]

Behind the scenes the Canadians continued their efforts to gain control of the Viação Paulista, whose internal affairs proved to be almost impossibly complicated. Eventually F.S. Pearson concluded that it was useless to try and settle the matter in Brazil and set off for Paris with William Mackenzie and Zebulon Lash to seek an agreement with the company's three French bankers. The São Paulo Tramway, Light and Power Company's banker, Edmund Walker of the Canadian Bank of Commerce, also turned up in Europe, so Pearson could report to Alexander Mackenzie upon arrival, 'We have the whole Toronto contingent.'

The negotiations, however, did not go smoothly. Pearson wrote ruefully:

We have had a monkey and parrot time in Paris for the last month, and I am at a loss to decide which are the worst to deal with, McKenzie [sic] or the Frenchmen. Between the two there has been trouble of the most varied hues, and one could not tell from day to day what would happen next. As a rule, however, the trouble commenced whenever Mr. McKenzie appeared on the scene from London.

Without reflecting on his merits at all it is clear to me that he is not a success as a negotiator with the French, and I shudder when I think what would have happened if he had been in São Paulo last summer dealing with our friend Prado.[24]

In the end an agreement was arrived at in June 1900 by which a loan of $175,000 from the Banque française du Brésil to the Viação Paulista was repaid by São Paulo Tramway, which also handed over $385,000 worth of its bonds in exchange for the 40,880 shares of Viação stock held by the bank. Despite a promise by all three French banks to use their influence to support a complete takeover, a controlling interest in the mule tramway remained lodged in the hands of the Banco Nacional do Brasil, which was still determined to exact a high price.[25] Meanwhile, São Paulo Tramway's employees were cooling their heels in idleness, waiting to start laying trolley lines on the routes still served by the mule cars. Mutterings of discontent began to be heard from Toronto as profits from the street railway failed to appear as fast as anticipated. R.C. Brown could only point out that, 'During the first two months of operation the electric street car was a novelty, and people were fairly crazy to ride them. Now we have gotten down to the standard conditions on the lines now operating and these show constant increases.'[26]

On the day after Christmas in 1900, Alexander Mackenzie sat down and set forth all the problems that still had to be ironed out. By then the Viação Paulista's creditors had forced it into bankruptcy, and there was intense manoeuvring to secure the appointment of a receiver favourable to one party or the other. In addition, Mackenzie was still trying to persuade the municipal government to give him a monopoly on the supply of electric lighting in the city and making an effort to acquire all the potential waterpower sites in the vicinity to outflank any competition. Perhaps, wrote Mackenzie, another visit by Pearson might break the logjam and, within a couple of months, 'You could make hundreds of thousands for the company, I am sure.'[27]

The directors in Toronto were getting a bit edgy, too; they had just been forced to approve an increase in the size of the company's authorized bond issue from $5 million to $6 million in order to meet the cost of acquiring the rival utilities. two million dollars' worth of bonds were promptly pledged to the National Trust Company for a loan of $1 million to cover construction charges. At the end of January 1901 Pearson announced that he would arrive in São Paulo in March with the hope of tying up all the loose ends of the negotiations with the Viação Paulista and the city. Meanwhile, Alexander Mackenzie was instructed to continue buying up both the shares and the debts of the mule line whenever possible so as to strengthen his hand when it came to a hostile takeover.[28]

In typical fashion, Pearson descended upon his staff in Brazil with something of the force of a tropical storm, juggling several different projects at once. The wife of Leslie Perry, an engineer from the United States employed in São Paulo, wrote of Pearson's whirlwind visit: 'Pearson and his wife came two weeks ago. They expect to stay but a short time and he is rushing the men all the time. Leslie has taken very little time to sleep & some days to eat.' And later she added, 'Pearson goes this week and I hope then there will be less work. He has kept Leslie crowded with "estimates" ever since he came. Last week he worked at the office nights until eleven and after nearly every night.'[29]

By the time of Pearson's arrival Mackenzie had succeeded in acquiring such a degree of control over the Viação Paulista that, as the largest creditor and shareowner, the São Paulo company could expect to get back about 75 per cent of any sums it paid to the Viação Paulista receiver. Not only that, it was clear that the earnings of the mule lines could easily be improved in the short run and, when they were eventually replaced by electric trolleys, the resale value of the rails and mules would also be considerable. The receiver was asking $1.5 million for the property, but Pearson was confident that if they held out and refused to submit a bid until the last moment they could get it for a third of that sum. In fact, he and Mackenzie did even better than that, securing control in May 1901 for a mere $220,000, less than the value of the physical plant. Patience and toughness had paid admirable dividends.[30]

Now the way was clear for the negotiation of a comprehensive 'unification contract' with the city covering the entire street railway operation. Yet care still needed to be exercised, for the old Viação Paulista franchise contained some decidedly unpalatable and unprofitable conditions. In particular there was a requirement to operate cheaper, second-class cars and some onerous provisions regarding the paving of the streets. Pearson and Mackenzie were both determined that in taking over the Viação Paulista they should not be burdened with these obligations. Everything rested upon Pearson's renowed charm and skill as a negotiator.

The personal magic worked. Ultimately Pearson did hammer out a deal with Prado, the prefect, which then had to be shepherded through the municipal council. By July 1901 the company had acquired an exclusive tram franchise for a forty-year period under which the city was divided up into three concentric zones whose boundaries lay three, six, and nine kilometres from the city centre. The maximum fare within each zone would be 200 réis (five cents) for adults and 100 réis for children, with special rates for workers and students to be introduced within a year. The company was given the right to expropriate the lands it required to operate, and all municipal taxes were commuted to a single annual payment of $10,000 beginning in 1905 and rising after five years to $20,000 for the remaining thirty years of the concession. At the end of the franchise the company would continue to own and to operate its lines as it wished, though the city would have the right to build other routes if it desired to do so. The one defect in this otherwise admirable agreement, so far as the company was concerned, was that it provided a system of fines for failure to comply with municipal regulations. But in view of the stiff fight that had been required to get the agreement with the prefect through the municipal council, Mackenzie and Pearson judged it wise to give in on that issue.[31]

All in all the São Paulo company had accomplished a remarkable amount in just a couple of years, not only in its construction program, which had surmounted difficult working conditions,[32] but also with the rearrangement of its relations with the civic authorities and the elimination of competition in the tramway and electricity supply fields. Looking over the situation in mid-1901, F.S. Pearson could pardonably express pride:

The situation at São Paulo is very satisfactory, and I feel confident that our enterprise there is going to be very successful from a financial point of view. The City Government is very friendly to us, and we also stand well with the public, which, as you can appreciate, are important points for any new corporation. The income from the cars operating is very large, much above the average in this country [the USA], and our contracts for light are steadily increasing. As soon as we have the power from Parnahyba [sic] we shall add to these contracts at a very rapid rate. For the next year I think that the growth in the lighting business will be limited by our ability to install lamps. We also have contracts for quite a number of motors, and there is no doubt of our getting an income fully equal to what we originally estimated.[33]

Their tasks successfully completed R.C. Brown[34] and Alexander Mackenzie prepared to leave Brazil and return to North America.[35]

III

Such smooth sailing as F.S. Pearson hoped for did not lie immediately ahead, though he was essentially correct about the long-term success that lay in the São Paulo company's future. The service provided by the Viação Paulista had to be replaced with trolleys while the mules were disposed of and the other company's employees gradually let go. This, however, proved a slow business, for men could not be suddenly dismissed in large numbers without provoking an outcry, so that it had to be done carefully. In an election year, as 1901 was, the prefect refused to let some muletram lines be discontinued for fear of provoking the electorate, and the remaining mule routes were naturally the less-travelled ones and so earned little, or even lost money.[36]

Gradually, though, the trolley network was extended, and by the spring of 1902, sixty-six kilometres of track were in service with six more under construction. Together with twenty-four kilometres of mule lines, this gave a system extending ninety-seven kilometres altogether, a good part of it single track snaking through the narrow downtown streets. And, as anticipated, ridership rose in a gratifying fashion from 15,721,261 in 1902 to 19,199,202 in 1903, reaching a peak each year in the hot summer month of

December. The gross earnings of the railway department went from $630,000 in 1901 to $880,000 by the end of 1902, while the operating ratio declined steadily (see Table 4) and profits rose.[37]

In September 1901 the generators were turned on in the powerhouse at Parnaíba, reducing the need to import coal at fourteen dollars per ton. Unfortunately the two turbines supplied by General Electric did not function properly at first and frequently had to be shut down for adjustment in the early months, arousing public doubts about the reliability of the company's service.[38] Yet demand for electricity rose steadily, and more money was soon required in order to install additional generators and to duplicate the transmission line, as well as for the work on the tramway.

Financially, however, the company only narrowly averted a crisis. By the summer of 1901 the São Paulo company's bankers in Toronto, the Commerce, were balking at the size of its overdraft and threatening to cut off further credit. With the powerhouse on the verge of completion, F.S. Pearson, melodramatic as always, complained bitterly that this might mean the discharge of the labour force employed in São Paulo, creating

a general mess down there. It would mean bankruptcy as far as the people in Brazil are concerned, and the news would be cabled to London and Europe and our standing financially would be ruined. I can't understand the attitude of the bank as they must know that Mr. Cox and Mr. Mackenzie with other large interests are not going to let this company be ruined for the lack of $100,000 more when they already have over $4,000,000 invested.[39]

However short-sighted it may have been, the Canadian bankers were worried. The extent of the bank's concern may be judged when it is remembered that Senator Cox was actually its president at this time. In the end (and perhaps for that reason) everything got sorted out, ruffled feathers were smoothed, and the work in Brazil went forward. All Pearson could do was to urge James Mitchell, who had taken R.C. Brown's place in São Paulo,

to build up our business as fast as possible, in order to get a large gross and net income to aid us in raising the additional money required. Our people here have already invested a very large amount of money and naturally want to see some result before going in still deeper. It is perhaps wholly unnecessary for me to request you to spare no pains or expense in keeping this plant in continuous operation during the first few months of its history and until good reputation is well established for us.[40]

If necessary, Pearson counselled, run fewer cars to save on expenses: 'In our northern cities where everyone is in a hurry it very often happens that a company will make the mistake of operating too few cars, thus diminishing riding and educating people to walk, but in Brazil I do not think there is much danger of this as the people are more indolent and not in any such great hurry, and with reasonably frequent service we would probably get all the business there is.' Poor Mitchell could do little, however, about the faulty turbines, and his problems were compounded when the plant had to be shut down, causing a general blackout during a political meeting called to discuss the re-election of the prefect in December 1901.[41]

Mitchell was also left to deal with the machinations of the company's single remaining rival in the utilities field, the San (another Britishism) Paulo Gas Company, whose management secretly approached the minister of agriculture to seek modification of its street lighting contract in order to maintain its monopoly. The minister tried to rush the amendments through, leading Mitchell to conclude that he had been bribed. An effort to block the changes failed, but Pearson remained hopeful that it might be possible to persuade the state Congress to overturn the new decree, 'without antagonizing the politicians who were concerned in making this contract to influence Congress to disallow it, but anything we do should be done in a very careful way and without having it appear on the surface that we are doing anything in connection with this business to influence Congress.'[42]

By the time the company held its first annual meeting in Toronto in April 1902, Vice-President Frederic Nicholls had only good news for the shareholders. During the fifteen months when the company had operated with coal-fired generators it had earned a mere $139,823, but in the last four months of 1901, after Parnaíba came into production, earnings had reached $151,333. News like this buoyed up the price of the company's stock, which had begun to trade publicly in February 1902. Having commenced trading at as low as $50 per share, the stock rose steadily upwards past $108 by April, a wonderful capital gain for the insiders who had received free bonus stock. Nicholls told shareholders that during the first four months of 1902 earnings had reached a level of 6 per cent on the common stock after paying all the bond interest and that from 1 April dividends would be paid at an annual rate of 5 per cent.

In light of that news the more than two hundred investors present readily approved an increase in the amount of capital stock from $6 million to $7 million. Now that earnings were sufficient to valorize the stock, it could

TABLE 4
São Paulo Tramway, Light and Power Co., 1901–9

Year	Gross revenues $	Operating ratio %	Annual dividend %	Stock prices High $	Low $
1901	749,676	64.9	nil	—	—
1902	1,123,285	37.2	5	109	50
1903	1,303,175	31.0	5	100	74⅞
1904	1,419,338	32.4	6	110	87
1905	1,908,405	33.0	8	142⅞	107
1906	2,018,405	32.2	8	146	125
1907	2,111,523	33.9	8	138¼	98¾
1908	2,287,410	34.2	9	157	113
1909	2,439,485	34.7	10	160	142½

SOURCE São Paulo Tramway, Light and Power Co., Annual reports, 1902–10; *Annual Financial Review (Canadian)*, 1902–11

readily be sold, and the current shareholders were happy to be given the right to subscribe for 1.5 additional shares at par for each 10 shares held, to be paid for in three installments up to October 1902. With this money coming into the company treasury for capital spending, along with rapidly rising earnings, the financial difficulties of the previous year evaporated.[43]

By the time the results of operations during 1902 were revealed to the second annual meeting in the spring of 1903, the full extent of the success of the São Paulo Tramway, Light and Power Company was becoming clear. Not even the financial panic of June 1903, which caused one of the company's original underwriters, A.E. Ames, to suspend his stockbroking business, could seriously break the price of the stock (see Table 4). Although share prices dropped from par in January 1903 to below seventy-five dollars six months later, F.S. Pearson still brimmed with confidence:

The reason that it did not fall more is due to the fact that the stock is owned by a few people who did not care to sell it, and that very little of it is held on a margin. The company is doing an enormous business at very profitable rates, and I have no doubt that this stock will go back to 120 at least.[44]

Pearson's confidence proved well founded. Within a year of the slump of 1903, share prices had climbed back above par and, once the dividend was increased to 8 per cent at the beginning of 1905, values moved upward through $140 by the fall of that year. Although the severe recession of 1907 once again knocked values below par in the fall, they soon recovered to all-time highs of $157 in the summer of 1908 when the dividend reached 9 per cent. The market hovered just below these values for the succeeding two years while the dividend was eventually put up to 10 per cent. This handsome rise, which clearly most benefited those insiders who had received their stock for nothing, naturally attracted a large number of hopeful outsiders. From about two hundred shareholders when dividends started the number reached nearly seven hundred by the start of 1905.[45] The investment was made more attractive in the fall of 1904 when an additional $500,000 was raised from shareholders by offering them five thousand new shares at par at the rate of one new share for every fourteen already held, to be paid for in four equal instalments by February 1905, by which time the shares were selling at between $142 and $146.[46]

As a result of its success, one of the major concerns of the company's management became the desire to release as little information about its affairs as possible in order to prevent embarrassment in Brazil on account of its profitability. F.S. Pearson warned the corporate secretary in the summer of 1903 that

It is of great importance for us to conceal as much as possible from the public the facts concerning our business in São Paulo, particularly from the Brazilian public, and I would suggest that you make your reports containing the most meagre details, leaving it to the president at the annual meeting to state the additional information which it may be considered advisable to give to the stockholders in Canada.

Any public report that we make up here is sure to go back to Brazil, and both on account of the question of taxes and for other reasons you can understand we should see that no information is made available in a printed form which we do not care to have the Brazilian officials know.[47]

This became a recurrent theme as the local management frequently reminded the head office in Toronto of the problems the release of such information caused in dealing with the Brazilians. And the company's success was such that envy and antagonism were bound to develop. At the end of 1905 Pearson reported to the board of directors that,

There is a feeling among the Brazilians that we are making a great deal of money which naturally gives rise to various demands, the most dangerous of which is that we should introduce second-class cars for the accommodation of the poorer classes. This would be a serious innovation, as it would make a great reduction in the gross income of the tramway department ...

It is fortunate that we can legitimately expend a large amount on the improvement of our property during the next two years, as otherwise there would be certain to arise a feeling of jealousy against the company as a foreign corporation, which, sooner or later, would affect us in some prejudicial manner. This is especially true as I feel that in a very short time, perhaps two or three years, the net earnings of our company will be from 15 to 18% on the stock and I should not be surprised if the company was showing 20% before the end of five years.

As the dividends that we pay are known it is far better for us to spend a large portion of our net earnings on the development and improvement of the property rather than increase the dividend at an unduly rapid rate.[48]

The company was especially keen to conceal from the Brazilian authorities that the entire capital stock had been given away for nothing to the insiders. With the exception of the six thousand shares handed over to Gualco and his associates for their franchises, the rest represented no tangible assets received and was carried on the books against goodwill and engineering services. As Pearson confided to Alexander Mackenzie, 'If the people of São Paulo should ever think they had given us something for nothing which we value at $6,000,000, there would be some explanations to make.'[49] Hence management's acute embarrassment in 1905 when the London Stock Exchange (which took a less benignly neglectful attitude towards such matters than its colonial counterparts) demanded a sworn statement regarding the disposition of the first sixty thousand shares. In the end, however, the governors of the exchange were persuaded, to the relief of the company to accept a vague affidavit that glossed over the truth.[50]

The rapid and quite spectacular success enjoyed by the promoters of the São Paulo Tramway, Light and Power Company was of great importance in propelling the group of investors surrounding F.S. Pearson into a whole series of utility ventures in Mexico and Spain as well as Brazil (see Appendix). The relative ease with which this promotion had been carried out convinced these men that it could be duplicated with similar gratifying results in other places. Indeed, it might be argued that the largest Canadian-incorporated utility ventures abroad were simply efforts to repeat the same results. Those who had got into São Paulo on the 'ground floor' could hardly afford to ignore F.S. Pearson's entreaties when he came calling with yet another promotion in mind, wherever it might be. The São Paulo Tramway, Light and Power Company became the cornerstone upon which the entire 'Pearson group' of utilities rested.

4

Blame It on Rio

Even before the São Paulo Tramway, Light and Power Company paid its first dividend in the spring of 1902, F.S. Pearson was well advanced with similar plans for utility promotions in Mexico City and Rio de Janeiro, Brazil's largest city. Everything had seemed so simple and gone so smoothly in São Paulo: surely that success could easily be duplicated elsewhere.

Yet the American promoter and his Canadian backers soon discovered that doing business in Rio was an entirely different proposition. They were not, after all, alone in the field. Other foreigners and powerful Brazilian interests had already begun to take an interest in Rio utilities. To secure the local monopoly so crucial to profitability they would have to eliminate these rivals, either by acquisition or merger. That would cost money – a lot of money in a city the size of Rio – and the Brazilian authorities would also have to be persuaded to grant a suitable franchise. The pursuit of this objective would prove frustrating, time-consuming, and above all expensive for Pearson and his associates.

With large sums of money tied up in the acquisition of properties in Rio and heavy commitments for the reconstruction of the plant there, the Canadian company found itself faced with the need to raise large amounts of additional capital in 1907 at the very time that a severe recession gripped the Atlantic world. For months the Rio de Janeiro Tramway, Light and Power Company teetered on the brink of bankruptcy. In the end European investors were induced to put up more money, though only at a heavy cost to the company, and the Brazilians grudgingly granted the necessary concessions.

Then the various subsidiaries had to be reorganized and the physical plant put into proper shape. As a result of Pearson's cavalier attitude towards cost control, more and more money had to be raised in order to provide satisfactory tramway, electrical and telephone service. And the threat of competition never disappeared altogether. Experience in Rio taught F.S. Pearson and his associates that it would not be as easy as they had imagined to repeat their São Paulo success.

One great advantage that the Canadian syndicate enjoyed in its Rio promotion was the permanent presence in Brazil of Alexander Mackenzie. Born in 1860 of the tough Scottish stock of rural Ontario, Mackenzie had been called to the bar in Toronto in 1883 and joined the prestigious firm of Blake, Lash and Cassels. In 1899 his partners chose Mackenzie to go to São Paulo and oversee the legal formalities required to found the utility there. A tall, serious, unflappable man, Mackenzie quickly demonstrated his talent for getting on with Brazilian officials. He gradually began to master Portuguese and to conceal any irritation and impatience he might have felt when documents were demanded in five copies, each in a different colour of ink. With the São Paulo venture well launched, Mackenzie had returned to Toronto in 1901 to resume his law practice.

But Pearson could not get along without someone on the scene in Brazil who both understood the legal and financial side of affairs and was competent to deal with officialdom. In 1902 Mackenzie was persuaded by the very generous offer of a $20,000 annual salary, 250 shares in the company, and an option on 50 more for each year he stayed, to return to São Paulo for another five years to head up operations there.[1] Mackenzie managed the Brazilian enterprises for more than a decade until his wife's perennial ill health led him to quit the country once more, but he was induced to return again in 1914 to cope with new problems. Thereafter he stayed on until his retirement in 1928.

I

By 1903 F.S. Pearson had decided that the time was ripe to take on Rio. A US citizen named William Reid had obtained a concession giving him the sole right to develop and supply electricity for power purposes up to 1915, but no work had been done. The Belgian-controlled gas company possessed a monopoly on domestic lighting, both gas and electric, until 1915 and on street-lighting until 1945. Its financial affairs were in chaos, and there was no possibility that it could raise the funds needed to build an electric generating station. Yet both the Reid concession and the gas company would have to be acquired to secure an electrical monopoly.[2]

The tramway situation was equally complicated, with different districts of the city being served by separate muletram lines, each with an exclusive franchise. Four companies accounted for about 75 per cent of the city's transit business, but a hodge-podge of other steam- and mule-powered vehicles criss-crossed the rest of the metropolitan area. None of these concerns had installed electric trolleys, although one German-controlled firm had begun making plans to electrify.[3]

If most of these existing enterprises could be brought under a single corporate umbrella on satisfactory terms, the prospects for electrification looked promising. Seventy kilometres inland from the city lay the escarpment called the Serra do Mar, down which a small stream, the Ribeirão das Lajes, plunged 300 metres, almost half of that in a single vertical leap. Although the flow was a mere three cubic metres per second in dry seasons, engineer James D. Schuyler reported that building a dam thirty metres high on the granite ledge at the lip could permit the storage of a hundred million cubic metres of water. A flow of seven metres per second conducted down the face of the scarp through penstocks would generate 20,000 horsepower of electricity annually. Schuyler advised that the initial development would not be too costly and that, if the flow of water into the reservoir could be increased, the capacity of the plant could easily be expanded.[4]

Here was a scheme that seemed tailor-made for F.S. Pearson's promotional and technical talents, and in the spring of 1903 he advised Alexander Mackenzie to begin the preparations. Unfortunately, this decision coincided with a severe recession on North American markets. Pearson was unable to persuade his Canadian backers even to put up $30,000 to cover the initial expenses, and the project had to be relegated to the back burner until times were more propitious.[5]

The following year a feeler was extended by the powerful Guinle family in Brazil to see if Pearson would be interested in a joint venture. The plan was to take over the Reid concession and apply to the authorities for broader powers. Pearson was intrigued, as the Guinles' control of the Port of Santos Dock Company in the port city serving the prosperous state of São Paulo had already made them one of the wealthiest and most influential families in Brazil. But it was not his style to share control or profits with local interests, and the opportunity was not pursued.[6]

With the return of better times in 1904, however, the Canadians brightened to the prospects. An application was made to parliament in

Ottawa to incorporate the Rio de Janeiro Tramway, Light and Power Company. Although the utility was authorized to issue up to $25 million worth each of both stock and bonds, Pearson was permitted by his bankers to spend only $75,000 up to 1 October 1904, when the whole matter was to be reviewed and a decision taken on whether to proceed further. Pearson admitted that, owing to the bad times of the past couple of years,

it has been exceedingly difficult to get Mr. [William] Mackenzie or any of the other São Paulo shareholders to take a real and enthusiastic interest in this proposition ... So far as all of the prominent and influential capitalists in Canada are concerned, it was making water run uphill to get these men to undertake the enterprise at all.

E.S. Clouston of the Bank of Montreal, for instance, was reported to think poorly of the proposed scheme, a potentially fatal problem when bankers were relied upon to make cash advances on the securities of new utilities pledged as collateral. Pearson, therefore, directed Alexander Mackenzie to 'nurse the scheme along until the capitalists of Canada become interested and believe it will make money.'[7]

Mackenzie did his best to extract a new electricity supply franchise from Brazilian Public Works Minister Lauro Müller at no cost. He soon discovered that the Guinles, having been spurned, were using their influence to block this, and decided that he would have to buy up the Reid concession. By this time the financial situation in Canada had brightened sufficiently for Clouston to signal his approval. Duly blessed by the Bank of Montreal the venture could proceed. In November 1904 the provisional directors were replaced by E.R. Wood, Zebulon Lash, Sir William Van Horne, New York investment banker W.L. Bull, and Pearson himself; William Mackenzie was installed as president.[8]

With the syndicate committed to going ahead, Alexander Mackenzie moved from São Paulo to Rio in the spring of 1905 to handle negotiations with the authorities and the owners of the existing utilities. The decision was taken to market an initial offering of $5 million worth of bonds at 90 per cent, $2 million worth being set aside for acquisition of properties, $1.8 million for the electrification of the tramways, and $1.2 million for a temporary thermal generating station while the hydroelectric station was being built. That project would obviously require the raising of large additional sums. The usual generous stock bonuses were granted to insiders and, in addition, the syndicate set up another company, called Brazilian Securities, to handle marketing to their benefit.[9]

Mackenzie discovered that he would have a far less easy time obtaining the desired concessions than had been the case in São Paulo five years earlier. There industrialization had begun fairly recently with the rise of the coffee economy. São Paulo was a boom town with lots of room for everyone as the economy grew by leaps and bounds. By contrast Rio, with its home-grown nucleus of entrepreneurs and technicians who wanted Brazilians to own and control development as far as possible, was already well advanced towards industrialization. The Clube de Engenharia, for instance, was an important nationalist organization linking those who opposed foreign investment in areas where Brazilians possessed their own capabilities. Powerful interests like the Guinle family had close connections with the Clube. Once the federal government floated its international funding loan in 1905, the value of the milréis advanced against other currencies and opened the possibility that Brazilians might be able to borrow abroad to finance new investments. At the very least, already entrenched interests would be more costly for foreigners to acquire than had been the case when the São Paulo enterprise got off the ground.

And such interests could operate through a variety of political institutions. Not only was there the municipal council in Rio, but the federal district that encompassed the city was under the control of national politicians. The governor of the state of Rio de Janeiro had authority over the waterpowers to be developed, while the central government had granted some of the key concessions that needed to be changed. Mackenzie would find during the next few years that political and business rivalries made it difficult to sew up the kind of local monopoly on the favourable terms that he and Pearson considered so vital to the success of the promotion.[10]

Under pressure from the Guinles, Public Works Minister Müller refused to grant the new company permission to develop waterpower. Eventually Alexander Mackenzie sought the backing of the US ambassador and obtained a hearing from the entire cabinet. Fearful of the dangers of favouritism, Müeller's colleagues forced him to drop his objections to the company's plans. With Müller 'pretty well on his knees,' Mackenzie could turn his attention to gaining control of the major tram companies and soon had a controlling interest in the Carris Urbanos and São Cristóvão lines.[11]

In order to acquire the Villa Isabel company Pearson dealt directly with the Deutsche Bank, which had gained control by lending money for the purchase of electrical equipment. E.R. Wood and Walter Gow (a partner in Blake, Lash and Cassels) went to Berlin in the summer of 1905 and arranged the purchase of the tramway and its telephone subsidiary for $5 million.[12]

Next came the troubled gas company. The creditors of the Société Anonyme de Gaz de Rio de Janeiro had collected nothing since 1902 in the hopes of restoring its profitability, but the investment required to replace the forty-year-old gas retorts and install new electrical equipment was so great that the future looked exceedingly bleak. When the Belgian bondholders and shareholders were offered the chance to swap their securities for Rio de Janeiro Tramway bonds most of them accepted eagerly.[13]

While the subsidiaries already earned enough to pay the interest on new Rio bonds with a par value of almost $20 million, large profits and common stock dividends were dependent upon the company's procuring revisions to the franchises. With construction getting under way on the powerplant at Lajes, more securities would obviously have to be sold in the near future. Increasing the cost of acquisitions was a demand from the prefect of Rio for a payment of $2 million to consolidate all these concessions into a new, uniform tramway franchise. Unlike the helpful officials in São Paulo, the authorities in Rio showed no disposition to assist the Canadians by granting such a unification contract. The prefect, reported newly arrived General Manager F.A. Huntress, 'seems to be in a position where he is pleased to put every obstacle in our way, and grant us no concession whatever which would be either for our benefit or the benefit of the public.'[14]

The profitability of the São Paulo company made obtaining concessions in Rio all the more difficult. With the older concern now paying an 8 per cent dividend on stock trading as high as $145 per share, the authorities were quite understandably determined to drive a hard bargain. When F.S. Pearson visited Rio in the autumn of 1905 to assist in the negotiations, he cabled Toronto that the 'great success' in São Paulo had seriously hampered operations in Rio: 'You must prevent increase of dividend or any proposal regarding increase of capital or in any way giving shareholders advantage at present as [this would be] suicidal [for the] future success of both Rio, Saplo.'[15]

Still, Pearson was confident that once the Lajes plant was completed all the issues in dispute could be settled. The city was currently paying the exorbitant price of $640 per year for each arc light on the Avenida Central, but when hydroelectricity was available the company would offer to cut that to $200, provided the gas company's exclusive lighting franchise was extended beyond 1915. Rates would then be sharply reduced:

We are apparently making great concessions to the Minister in reducing our prices to so great an extent, which is his justification for granting to us the changes in the concession. In reality, the reduction in the price is no hardship to us, however, as it would be impossible for us to secure much, if any, business at prices in excess of those we propose.[16]

Pearson's irrepressible optimism was not, however, balanced by any appetite for careful supervision. This lack of tight managerial control over costs was to be the major weakness of all the utility enterprises with which he was connected. Having arrived somewhere – Rio, London, Toronto – he would rapidly assess the situation, propose a solution, and be gone almost before his plans could be fully analysed and discussed. The case of the Santo Amaro dam near São Paulo, intended to increase the capacity of the Parnaíba plant, was all too typical. In the fall of 1905 a consulting engineer estimated that it would cost $150,000. The board approved the work, but by the summer of 1906 Pearson was reporting from Brazil that triple this sum would be required. No accurate surveys had been made of the Pinheiros River valley, and it was found that to store sufficient water the dam would have to be far higher than anticipated. Already nearly $200,000 had been spent; but, characteristically, Pearson argued that the advantages to be gained were so great that the board would have approved it even at a cost of $500,000. In fact, in the end it cost nearly that much – or triple the original estimate.[17]

Pearson had his finger in too many pies to keep a close enough watch on any one of them. A member of the accounting staff in Toronto pointed out

the absolute necessity of Head Office having full knowledge of all undertakings. Of course, were Dr. Pearson at New York always and personally passed upon everything it would be different, but he is not ... and we at Head Office have more interest in São Paulo than outsiders on Dr. Pearson's staff ... The only question will be to devise a suitable method of keeping us informed.[18]

Pearson always ignored this kind of criticism and refused to mend his ways. He insisted that any capital invested in a highly successful enterprise like the São Paulo Tramway could be counted upon to earn 15 per cent per annum, and additional capital could easily be raised if the dividend on the common stock were increased to 10 per cent and ultimately to 12 per cent. To members of the São Paulo board who persisted in questioning his judgment, he replied that their caution might wreck everything: 'Unless we are ready to take all business offered [at] São Paulo, we certainly shall have competition within [a] short time.'[19]

Despite the success of the São Paulo enterprise, its heavy spending made its bankers nervous. In the spring of 1906 the corporate secretary reported that, 'the Bank of Commerce ... cannot understand what is being done with the enormous profits. So far as the bank is concerned we have an overdraft at the present time of between one hundred and two hundred thousand dollars.' Pearson simply refused to listen and blithely drew up plans for further security issues by the São Paulo company that would, he claimed, finance all the necessary works and leave the overdraft at a mere $145,000 at the end of three years. Even the demonstration that his erroneous assumptions meant that the overdraft would actually total $915,000 failed to dent his confidence.[20]

Some of Pearson's associates began to worry about this casual attitude. E.R. Wood, for instance, fretted about the amount of money that had to be raised to complete the Rio plant; he harped upon the need to keep a close check upon spending in Brazil by careful preparation of and adherence to estimates. Pearson, however, was constitutionally incapable of concerning himself with such details. Since the Rio company did not release its first annual report until mid-1906, two years after it was organized, management did not even have to bother keeping shareholders informed about what was going on. When one Nova Scotian, who had had a small share in the original underwriting, wrote to enquire how the work was going, he received only a brief outline of what had been done in Rio, to which the company secretary added forthrightly, 'We have been doing very little other than spending money so that there is not very much to write about.'[21]

Throughout 1906 and 1907 Alexander Mackenzie continued to seek the extension of the gas company's exclusive private lighting franchise beyond 1915 and a unification contract for the tramway. As the Lajes plant neared completion he sought permission to increase the size of the reservoir by diverting the waters of the Pirái River through a tunnel. Brazilian politicians maintained their unfriendly attitude towards the company, doubtless urged on by the Guinle interests who had not given up hope of entering into competition with the Canadians. The federal government refused to extend the electricity concession, and both the prefect and the governor of the state of Rio de Janeiro insisted that only upon condition of large cash payments could the other two requests be granted.[22]

Not even F.S. Pearson's legendary powers of persuasion proved able to extract what the company sought from the federal government. During a two-month visit to Brazil in the spring of 1906 he repeatedly told the ministers that the gas company would not live up to its commitment to build new gas retorts unless the private lighting franchise was extended, since ten years was not enough time to recoup such a massive capital investment. An exasperated Pearson complained that 'this Rio crowd is about the worst I have ever had anything to do with as far as getting anything settled in a businesslike way.' Alexander Mackenzie agreed. He had discussed all these issues with the president of Brazil, with his ministers, with the state government, and with the local prefect before acquiring the Reid concession. Though all had conceded that the franchises needed to be changed, they now refused to act.[23]

Uncertainty was compounded by the election of a new Brazilian president, Afonso Pena, in May 1906, to take office in November. This, in turn, would mean the replacement of the prefect of Rio. Any change could only be for the better so far as the Canadians were concerned. They had long been working to persuade the current prefect to grant the company a single sixty-year tram franchise with a fixed level of taxation, because 'the present concessions make it impossible to operate the lines in an intelligent and economical manner or with a view to the best accommodation of the public.' Even switching cars between the various subsidiary lines required municipal permission. But the prefect was a man of 'arbitrary, violent decisions,' deaf to all entreaties. Pearson concluded that his behaviour was 'inexplicable except on the theory that he is generally opposed to any corporations occupying the streets of the city, as often publicly stated by him.'[24] Nationalist resentment and quite justifiable suspicions about Pearson's financial methods aroused opposition in Rio that had not been present in São Paulo.

Mackenzie did his best to reach an agreement in the fall of 1906, because he knew that at least six months would elapse after the new prefect took office before an understanding could be achieved. But he reported gloomily that 'immense pressure had been brought to bear by the Gaffrée-Guinle people,' who were determined to prevent the Canadians from locking up another monopoly like that in São Paulo. Working through the press the Guinle interests adopted 'a plan of campaign which is to be violent, persistent and a determined opposition all along the line to anything and everything we propose in the city.'[25]

Mackenzie had no luck either in persuading the government of the state of Rio de Janeiro to permit the company to divert the entire flow of the Piraí River into the Lajes reservoir. Here, too, the Guinles were actively opposed, seeing the supply of scarce water as crucial to their plan to enter into competition in the hydroelectric business. The governor demanded $1,660,000 in exchange for the privileges, and in a bid to keep them out of hands of the Guinles Mackenzie actually offered to pay $300,000. But the governor continued to waver and eventually left office without issuing the necessary decree.[26]

Despite a last-minute lobby by Mackenzie, Lauro Müller also refused in the end to carry out his oft-repeated pledges to amend the gas franchise. Pearson expressed astonishment at his duplicity, but noted contemptuously that Müller was 'a politician first and always and about as near an invertebrate as it is possible to be.' Perhaps they could look for better treatment from the incoming administration. The president, after all, was known to rely upon friends of the company for advice, the new minister was full of assurances of goodwill, and the new prefect was, in Pearson's words, 'a man of modern ideas who has lived in the U.S. and must sympathize with our plans which are in the line of progress and will benefit the city.'[27]

Management continued to tell investors that all was going as planned. At the first annual meeting in July 1906, Vice-President Frederic Nicholls reported that prospects looked favourable.[28] In the fall Pearson advised the board that the mule trams were returning 14 per cent on the funds invested in them, so that the company could hold on as long as necessary to secure the unification contract. He predicted that the operating ratio in Rio would soon decline to levels like those in São Paulo, and that even a ratio of 45 per cent would earn 'enormous' returns. By the end of the year the temporary generating station at Lajes was nearly complete, and work was well under way on the main dam and powerhouse.[29]

Despite his frustration, Alexander Mackenzie allowed himself to feel more optimistic as 1906 ended. By refusing to electrify the tramway the company would eventually force the municipality to give in: 'I am sure that by waiting a little longer we can get something much better than we could obtain by accepting what the council might be prepared to give us at the present moment.' And his hopes seemed justified when the new prefect proved more co-operative and the municipal council quickly granted the prefect the authority to negotiate a unification contract with the company.[30]

The Rio company could not look to Britain's diplomatic representatives for help in dealing with the Brazilians. Pearson had earlier complained that, 'The English ambassador at present in Brazil is useless, as he apparently takes no interest in any industrial or business questions concerning English corporations, but is rather an ornament and confines himself largely to [the capital at] Petropolis.' When stories favourable to the company were planted in British newspapers in 1907, the British consul in Rio denounced them as 'advertizing puffs,' full of 'inaccuracies and misrepresentations calculated to mislead ... persons with little knowledge of business.' The Rio company, added the consul sourly, had acquired its position in the city largely through the support of the United States Embassy during the wave of pro-us sentiment that had followed the meeting of the Pan-American Congress and the visit of Secretary of State Elihu Root in July 1906: 'By much push and lavish expenditure the company have overcome opposition and have acquired many concessions, and now virtually control the tramway, lighting and telephone systems of the city.' He feared it was 'over-capitalized,' its word 'not to be taken solely on trust,' since the citizenry had 'only a vague idea of the financial condition of the Company, and in the absence of published accounts their very American methods do not inspire confidence.'[31]

The ambassador fully endorsed the consul's views. He, too, was critical of the company's managers for playing up 'their American connection to the utmost' during and after the Pan-American Congress. The newspaper publicity he denounced as 'pure and simple paid advertizements, although not usually admitted as such ... [which] may deceive innocent investors.' And he reminded the foreign secretary that he had never favoured Brazil as a field for British investment. Beneath the glitter of Rio's recent modernization the ambassador discerned only 'rottenness and corruption.' With a recession ending the recent wave of foreign lending to Brazil, he concluded bleakly, 'I venture to assert it as my conviction that there are no elements of truth in the newspaper representations ... as to this country being a desirable field for investment.'[32]

Within a few weeks, however, this diplomat had radically revised his opinions, perhaps because Alexander Mackenzie was able to meet his request for £1,000 worth of Rio stock on favourable terms. The ambassador now observed that the Canadian manager 'may indeed, both metaphorically and actually, be said to have overcome – if not removed – mountains.' The highly successful operation in São Paulo showed that for foreign entrepreneurs Brazil was 'virgin soil, and Canadian vigour has already – and that during the span of a very few years – made a deep impression on it.'[33]

Nonetheless, the Rio company continued to look more to the United States mission to Brazil, as us diplomats had long displayed a friendly interest in its activities. In 1904 the chargé d'affaires was reported to have said that there was 'absolute certainty' that the federal government would grant any concession asked for, as Brazil was

exceedingly anxious to propitiate the American government, because of prospective boundary differences with other South American countries, which must be settled during the next ten years, and that as the United States might be in a position to intervene in the case of Brazil, bringing pressure to bear upon some of her weaker neighbours, the government officials are anxious to do everything they possibly can to stand in the good graces of the Americans.[34]

The chargé, therefore recommended incorporating the utility in New Jersey so as to make its US pedigree clearer, but this advice was ignored.

In 1906 Pearson noted that the ambassador, Lloyd Griscom, had intervened with the Brazilian government on several occasions on behalf of the company, on the grounds that most of its equipment was imported from the United States and some of its largest shareholders were US citizens. Secretary of State Root spoke warmly of the undertaking to the president of Brazil and to other officials during his visit for the Pan-American Congress. As a result of Root's visit, observed Pearson,

there has been an entire revolution in the feeling as regards the United States. The jealousy and suspicion which formerly existed have entirely disappeared. The American ambassador in Brazil has had for many years much more influence with the government than the British ambassador and this is certain to be accentuated in future.

Lloyd Griscom agreed to see several federal ministers for the company even without instructions from Washington. 'The interest that he evinced in our enterprise,' Pearson noted, 'has already had a very good effect.'[35]

Alexander Mackenzie recognized that there were limits to the value of diplomatic intervention. Seeking help too often made it less effective, particularly because the opposition to the company, orchestrated by the Guinles, could easily use such incidents to arouse xenophobia. In the spring of 1907 the Guinle newspaper, the *Jornal do Comércio*, charged that the US ambassador was doing the company's dirty work in seeking franchise revisions. Not so, reported Mackenzie to Pearson. He had deliberately avoided seeking such assistance, 'because it is a sort of two-edged sword; while [officials] may give effect to it, they certainly do not like it and some of them are extremely susceptible because of it.'[36] But that was splitting hairs; Griscom certainly had been involved up to his elbows.

Painstakingly, Mackenzie worked away at hammering out an agreement with the Brazilian authorities on a unification contract for the tramway and new concessions for electricity and water supplies. One bright spot was the start-up of the temporary powerplant at Ribeirão das Lajes in the spring of 1907, which ended the company's dependence upon expensive imported coal for steam generation and permitted it to begin canvassing for new electricity customers. In May he finally procured permission for a limited diversion of the Piraí River into the reservoir.[37]

At the same time Mackenzie believed that he had at last reached agreement with the prefect of Rio on the unification contract, granting the company a tramway franchise until 1990 with exclusive rights through 1945. All the lines would be converted to a uniform gauge over the next three years and operated as a single system, while taxation would be consolidated into a single annual payment. Unfortunately, these terms had to be approved by the municipal council, and the press, fired up by the Guinles, raised a violent outcry against the deal. The council began a secret debate on the contract that dragged on throughout the entire summer of 1907. Unlike the friendly Dr Prado in São Paulo the prefect had difficulty persuading the political bosses in Rio to go along with this deal. Mackenzie laboured on, seeking promises of support, but it was not until September that he was finally able to obtain approval. In November the new concession was finally signed into law, leaving only the new electricity franchise for the gas company to be settled.[38]

II

By that time, however, bankruptcy loomed. As early as the spring of 1906 F.S. Pearson had estimated that $3.75 million was still required to complete the hydroelectric station, $2 million for the transmission line, $4.4 million for the reconstruction of 160 kilometres of tramways and 400 trolleys, along with $700,000 for administrative expenses, or nearly $11 million in all. By the fall of that year the figure had increased to $14 million, while the entire $25 million bond issue was expected to have been sold by early 1907.[39]

Raising such sums far outstripped the capacity of Pearson's backers in Canada. Already Belgian investors in the gas company who had exchanged their securities for Rio bonds had created a secondary market in Europe. Such expatriate Canadians as James Dunn and E. Mackay Edgar were now busy trying to distribute the securities of Canadian companies in Britain. After 1905 the major responsibility for raising capital for the Brazilian ventures shifted to London and came to rest in the hands of R.M. Horne-Payne, an old associate of William Mackenzie's who had helped to finance his Canadian Northern Railway.[40]

In 1902 'Monty' Horne-Payne had set up the British Empire Trust Company 'mainly for the purpose of facilitating the placement of British capital in desirable Colonial investments.'[41] To publicize these companies, however, Horne-Payne required a steady flow of information, in particular monthly 'traffics' (earnings and ridership figures), to release to his clients 'with the object of strengthening the market in the securities of the companies in which we are mutually interested.'[42] This marketing technique, of course, ran directly counter to the desire of insiders to reveal as little as possible about the affairs of the Brazilian companies, a practice strongly endorsed by Alexander Mackenzie who had to cope with the repercussions whenever buoyant figures were released. The board, therefore, decided that the unsettled situation in Rio made it inadvisable to release such information at present.[43]

From this date forward, however, the ultimate success of the enterprise in Rio depended upon the ability of Horne-Payne and his associates in Britain to dispose of the additional securities required to finance construction and amalgamation. By the fall of 1906 the company's bankers were complaining that its overdraft was too large. William Mackenzie set off for London to try to sell the $4 million worth of bonds remaining in the treasury but could not secure an underwriting on acceptable terms. Soon he was back in Canada, the bonds pledged to the bank for a loan of $2 million to permit work on the dam at Lajes to continue. These problems were compounded by a rise in the value of the Brazilian milréis against other currencies, which meant that the properties and construction would cost more than originally estimated.[44]

At that very moment F.S. Pearson's doctors pronounced him unwell owing to overwork and ordered him to stay at his Massachusetts home and rest. Pearson blamed his exhaustion upon worries created 'by the interference of others who have hindered work without helping, which has made the work doubly hard.' To Alexander Mackenzie he complained that

As I feared in Rio we have suddenly run short of money and Mr. [William] Mackenzie and the other directors have just realized it. I have been writing and telling Mackenzie for the last eighteen months that we should be out of money this fall, but apparently he has never realized the situation.

'My great fear,' he added, 'is that with the procrastination we shall suddenly find ourselves without money and be obliged to stop work in Brazil.'[45]

Could Horne-Payne raise the funds required? At long last he persuaded the board to allow him to release regular earnings and traffic figures. British investors were no longer willing to be fobbed off with the excuse that providing such information would create problems in Brazil. James Dunn reported that, 'They have taken this answer for a long time but are getting tired of it, and if this market is to be made active and the confidence of our clients maintained, we must have better intelligence.'[46]

In February 1907, Horne-Payne negotiated an agreement with Dunn and his Belgian associate, Alfred Loewenstein, to take up the remaining $4.2 million worth of Rio bonds at 90 per cent for sale in France and Belgium. Unfortunately, they found themselves flying in the face of an ever-worsening recession, which led to a decline in security prices and a tightening of credit as the year advanced. As a result of slow sales Dunn and Loewenstein defaulted on the third instalment of the bond underwriting. Dunn and his associates eventually had to return $480,000 worth of the underwriting owing to their inability to sell or pay for the bonds, and they also defaulted upon a loan secured by $473,000 worth of bonds. By the end of September Horne-Payne was reporting that 'a panic prevails in Brussels and threatens to kill sales.'[47]

Even the normally optimistic F.S. Pearson feared the worst:

our financial situation is very critical, as we are practically out of money, and until the unification [contract] is settled it is going to be very difficult to get additional funds. There is a general feeling in Europe that our concessions are valueless, and that it is impossible for us to get new concessions, and this, of course, makes it very hard to get additional funds.[48]

As early as April 1907 the Bank of Commerce had refused to permit the Rio company to increase its overdraft, 'owing to the extreme money stringency.' In June the bank threatened to cancel chequing privileges unless further collateral was pledged.[49] When Dunn and Loewenstein defaulted on the final instalment of their underwriting, the company tottered on the brink of bankruptcy. William Mackenzie suggested trying to raise $1.5 million in London with short-term notes secured by the assets of the gas company, but Horne-Payne was convinced that British bankers would immediately scent danger and refuse to renew existing advances if this was even suggested to them. By midsummer the company and was completely out of funds, and its creditors were becoming restless.

Westinghouse was already owed $100,000 for electrical equipment, and another $200,000 worth of materials was about to be delivered.[50]

In July the Bank of Commerce did suspend the Rio company's chequing privileges, leaving it with nearly $500,000 worth of materials on hand that it could not pay for. Pearson's only suggestion was that they seek a loan in Brazil, but Alexander Mackenzie reported that there was little hope of arranging this. Horne-Payne's confidence finally cracked; he denounced Pearson's glib conviction that the money markets might soon recover, telling William Mackenzie, 'I am not a croaker and I am not a rat, and I will fight under your orders to the last, but I do not want any aspect of the matter to escape your attention, and I do want you, no matter what Pearson and Alexander Mackenzie may think or say, to shut down tight before it is too late.'[51]

This suggestion enraged Pearson: 'his attitude ... is perfectly childish, as it is simply impossible to shut down construction in Brazil without putting the company into a receiver's hands.' So much did Horne-Payne's proposal rankle with Pearson that he later blamed the English financier for having 'practically ruined' the standing and prestige of the Rio company in Europe, because he had done 'nothing of value' to raise money during the past year. Pearson considered it a great mistake to have handed over the responsibility for financing to Horne-Payne, who was 'a sick man and ... not ... absolutely right in his mind.'[52]

The board of directors finally concluded that it had to gain control over spending in Brazil. R.J. Clark was sent from Toronto in the autumn of 1907; to his astonishment he discovered that even the prosperous São Paulo company faced problems owing to poor financial planning. In his report to the board a year earlier, Pearson had outlined work there estimated to cost $755,000 over five years, that it was now clear would require $3.5 million to complete. Much of this could not be postponed. Many of the original wooden power poles were discovered to be rotten and in danger of collapsing. If the authorities learned of this they were certain to order all of them replaced at once with iron standards, so that the only solution was to remove the old ones as rapidly as possible and hope that no disasters occurred. Some of the older trams were so decayed that their bodies were in danger of breaking in two, but taking them out of service would create a serious shortage of rolling stock. Meanwhile, the prefect had returned from Europe, having floated a loan to finance a series grandiose of street improvements that would require the company to relocate tracks and wires under its concession.[53]

By the end of 1907 São Paulo operating expenses had risen 20.1 per cent to 36.7 per cent of gross revenues, which were up a mere 12.3 per cent. Capital expenditures exceeded estimates, notwithstanding the budgetary stringency, by 28 per cent. Far from assuming responsibility, Pearson, pleading pressure of other business, now attempted to distance himself from the affairs of the São Paulo company.[54]

In Rio the situation was far more serious. To stop work made bankruptcy inevitable, however, so the board of that company decided reluctantly to authorize creation of a new issue of second mortgage bonds to rank behind the existing $25 million in first mortgage bonds. Since these Rio 'seconds' could not be sold at present except at sacrifice prices, William Mackenzie persuaded the Bank of Montreal to lend the company $250,000 on the collateral of $350,000 worth of the new bonds. In Britain Horne-Payne induced the Bank of Scotland to give him $1 million for six months by pledging the new bonds and some Rio gas company securities. Meanwhile, Pearson and the engineering staff were instructed to go through their plans with a fine tooth-comb.[55]

Beyond a certain point Pearson was insistent that spending could not be reduced. The company was obliged by its franchise, for instance, to keep a three-month supply of essential materials on hand, and it had already been fined $1,000 for failing to do so. Corporate Secretary J.M. Smith and the staff of Pearson's engineering firm were left to juggle the demands of the largest and most insistent creditors, sending some of the dwindling supply of funds to pay accounts owing when absolutely necessary. Big companies like us Steel and Western Electric were offered part payment and asked to take a note from the Rio company for the balance.[56]

By late October Smith's assistant was asking for advice as to what to do if a receiver in bankruptcy came calling. With North American stock markets in chaos following the financial panic in New York in early October, the only hope of raising new money to complete the $8 million worth of work still unfinished lay in Europe. E.R. Wood and Percival Farquhar joined Pearson in London to see what might be done. At a meeting of directors there it was decided to convince the financial community that management had a firm grip on the company by installing Pearson as president with Horne-Payne as vice-president. William Mackenzie was kicked upstairs to become chairman of the board and, for the next eight months, however uneasy their personal relationship, Pearson and Horne-Payne took control. To ensure instant action the board of directors met in London rather than Toronto as they struggled to stave off bankruptcy by selling the Rio second mortgage bonds.[57]

The first effort proved abortive when an attempt to borrow $3 million in Brussels had to be abandoned owing to panic on the bourse, and the Belgian underwriters had to be relieved of the final instalment of their first mortgage bonds when they failed to meet their commitments. Even the news that the tramway unification contract had finally been signed into law in November 1907 did not rescue the situation. William Mackenzie and Zebulon Lash now joined the others in London for an all-out effort to borrow $2 million to tide the company over until the Rio seconds could be offered to the public at 85 per cent of par. Pearson complained, however, that Horne-Payne had let slip the plan to issue short-term notes earlier in the year and that nobody would lend the company funds when it was in such dire straits. Characteristically, Pearson assumed an air of martyrdom and laid all the blame on his associates rather than admit that his over-confidence and inattention to cost control lay at the root of the problem.[58]

In Toronto poor Smith was complaining that there was 'practically nothing' left in the bank, and the major creditors were threatening to file a bankruptcy petition. Ironically, in the depths of this financial crisis, the company's affairs in Brazil suddenly took a turn for the better: it had a large backlog of power orders to be filled as soon as the main station at Lajes went into service; the telephone company was growing steadily and the tram system could now be rationalized. All that was left was the revision of the gas company's lighting franchise, and Alexander Mackenzie was even confident that, 'if I live long enough I think we will get more or less what we want. Should we fail to do this our present contracts are good enough to enable us to hold the fort and make a lot of money. It is only that we can so easily make more that I am anxious to round up these matters also.'[59]

Eventually, Pearson and Percival Farquhar succeeded in persuading a group of French bankers and brokers to participate in underwriting an issue of Rio second mortgage bonds. The par value was raised to $16.5 million in the hope that this would supply all the money needed to complete the works in Rio. The new securities were to be denominated in either French francs or pounds sterling to make them more attractive to European investors, and it was hoped that initially $9 million worth could be sold, half in the English series, half in the French series.[60]

Snags developed. One of the leading French banks got cold feet and dropped out of the underwriting at the last moment, which threatened to wreck the whole deal. Only when Pearson and Farquhar stepped in and personally assumed responsibility for the bank's position did the syndicate agree to go ahead. And the money did not come cheaply: for each 6 per cent bond in the French series the company netted only 66 per cent of par.[61] Still, by the spring of 1908, new funds were flowing into the treasury for the first time in many months.

Pearson also induced the London merchant banker Robert Fleming to take out a series of options on the $950,000 worth of first mortgage bonds that still remained in the company's treasury, at prices rising from 77 per cent to 83 per cent of par, which gave him a strong impetus to create a rising market for them. Pearson also persuaded the Deutsche Bank, which was owed $3.5 million, to complete the Villa Isabel tramway purchase in order to lend the Rio company part of the money required; Fleming put up the rest.[62]

But the Rio company was not out of the woods yet. The French brokers were able to place only 80 per cent of the first continental issue of Rio seconds (less than a quarter of the total planned), and some of the banks withdrew from the deal. Once more, Pearson and Farquhar were forced to assume personal responsibility for a large portion of the issue and, when the Belgian firm of Stallaerts and Loewenstein announced it could not absorb all its bonds, the two men had to take one-third of those, too. Back in Toronto Smith was still juggling $268,000 in overdue bills, paying a bit here and a bit there on account, and facing a bond interest payment of $600,000 on 1 July for which no funds had been set aside.[63]

Gradually, however, the good news from Brazil began to help along sales of securities in Europe. With the tramway contract settled the Rio de Janeiro Tramway, Light and Power Company ceased to function as a holding company and received the entire earnings of all its subsidiaries, further brightening up the balance sheet. Moreover, the Lajes powerplant opened in May 1908 with considerable fanfare and favourable publicity, and the company began to take on new electricity subscribers, which meant a further boost in income. The board approved the start of work on the electrification of the tramway, and that summer Pearson even placed a secret order for the new retorts needed by the gas company in anticipation of reaching a satisfactory agreement on the revised lighting contract.[64]

As a result the English series of Rio second mortgage bonds was over-subscribed, and Pearson was successful in disposing of the remainder of the French series. In recognition of the importance of European investors in funding the company, the board was expanded to include one Belgian and two French directors at the annual meeting in September.[65]

III

By mid-1908 the financial problems that had plagued the Rio promotion seemed on the way to solution. Even before the second mortgage bonds of the Rio company had begun to be taken up by European investors, F.S. Pearson's customary optimism had fully revived. The directors had authorized the issuing of $16.5 million par value worth of Rio seconds, which Pearson declared would produce sufficient funds 'for cleaning up the Rio enterprise.' Even without any further investment he calculated that the company could earn all its bond interest plus enough to pay a 7 per cent dividend on the common stock.[66]

As usual Pearson was far too optimistic. Large additional sums soon had to be raised for both the Rio and the São Paulo companies. In São Paulo as well as the $1 million spent in 1908, $770,000 would be needed in 1909 and $1,180,000 in 1910, and a study by the board in the fall of 1910 showed that an additional $4,125,000 would be required over the next few years. Despite its buoyant earnings the São Paulo enterprise remained seriously undercapitalized. The original $6 million bond issue had not produced sufficient funds to complete the plant, and before the recession of 1907 only $1.5 million worth of additional common stock had been issued to raise more capital.[67]

A pressing need for additional funds forced the São Paulo company to offer shareholders another $1.5 million worth of stock during the recession of 1907. Still, São Paulo Tramway was such a solid earner that Alexander Mackenzie remained unworried:

If there is any trouble at all, it is that those in charge of the finances in Toronto forgot to take in time the needful steps to provide additional capital for the construction work and were caught napping when the big smash took place. The company can easily pay its dividends on its present stock and the stock now being offered and still show a surplus.[68]

Moreover, relations with the authorities in São Paulo created few problems because the franchises needed little modification and the prefect, Dr Antônio Prado, was well disposed towards the company. To ensure good relations Mackenzie and Pearson had volunteered to reduce the higher fares on some suburban lines in São Paulo to the standard 200 réis in 1906. The company also had no objection to reducing electric lighting rates, calculating that higher demand would more than restore the lost income in short order, although a perennial shortage of power made it reluctant to encourage consumption. Work on a third generator at Parnaíba had been started as early as 1902, followed by a fourth in 1904; even so the company was unable to keep up with demand, and this complicated negotiations with the civic authorities. Still, the attitude of Paulistas towards the utility, noted Pearson in a report to the board in 1906, was 'remarkable in view of the fact that the company is a foreign corporation with no local share-holders, conditions which generally induce ill-feeling and antagonism.' In 1909 Mackenzie was able to negotiate new franchises that extended the term of the tramway concession and the electricity monopoly in exchange for cuts in fares and rates.[69]

As usual the situation in Rio de Janeiro was more complicated. The tramway unification contract received approval in the fall of 1907; the franchise, good until 1990, was exclusive through 1945. At the same time the exclusive right to supply power throughout the federal district under the Reid concession until 1915 was confirmed and extended on a non-exclusive basis from 1950 to 1990. But the revison of the gas company's lighting concession (exclusive until 1915), which also covered electricity, remained unsettled, as did the telephone franchise, which was due to expire in 1929.[70] In the spring of 1909 Pearson succeeded in negotiating a new gas franchise while in Brazil, but the governor of the state of Rio died two weeks later without having signed it. Not until November of that year was the gas concession finally passed, opening the way for the reconstruction of the worn-out plant.[71]

Visiting Rio a little more than a year later, F.S. Pearson could report that business was growing in all departments. The electrification of the tramway was nearly complete; the telephone company (which had been acquired along with the Villa Isabel tramway) was booming, having reconstructed its plant following a disastrous fire in 1906; demand for electricity was strong. That posed a problem, however, since the Ribeirão das Lajes plant, opened in May 1908, had no more capacity. Once two additional generators were installed to bring its rating up to 82,000 horse-power, the only way to secure additional power was by diverting the waters of the Piraí River through a tunnel into the reservoir, an elaborate and costly undertaking.[72]

A dry spell during the winter of 1911 increased the pressure to expand the powerplant, but Alexander Mackenzie was unable to gain final approval from the governor of the state of Rio for the diversion project. The Brazilians insisted that the construction of the Lajes reservoir in 1908 had provided a breeding ground for malarial mosquitoes and that infected employees had spread the disease through the region causing an epidemic that affected 8,000 people, half of whom had died. The company denied all responsibility for this, but the governor refused to consider the expansion of the reservoir unless compensation was paid.[73]

The Guinles still lurked in the wings, seeking to break into the Rio utility market. In 1905 the family had obtained a perpetual concession for generation and distribution of electricity in the state of Rio de Janeiro, and in 1909 got a concession from the city of São Paulo to distribute energy there.[74] Alexander Mackenzie and Pearson did their best to avert competition in both cities even if it necessitated spending more money.[75] An accelerated program of construction of underground wiring conduits in São Paulo was approved on the grounds that nobody else was likely to go to the expense of duplicating it, nor would the city agree to permit further excavations. Thus wherever the conduits were laid the company would have 'a practical monopoly for all time to come.'[76]

When the new São Paulo concession was finally approved in 1909, the Guinles went to court to block it. Ultimately their suit was dismissed but they continued to scheme against the Canadians. While the Guinles failed to obtain any franchises that posed an immediate threat to either of the Canadian companies, much energy had to be devoted to keeping an eye upon them because of the political influence they were able to wield.

Utility promotion in Rio de Janeiro thus proved to be a much more difficult, time-consuming, and expensive proposition than anyone had anticipated at the outset. And the insiders did not profit to the extent they had expected. Unlike São Paulo, where existing enterprises and potential competitors had been quickly neutralized or easily swept aside, in Rio they proved difficult and expensive to purchase. The tramways and the gas company exacted a high price to surrender their franchises to the interlopers, and even when they did so there were domestic interests, principally the Guinles, who continued to erect obstacles. The pressure from the Guinles and a desire to exploit anti-foreign sentiment caused Brazilian politicians to drive a harder bargain with the outsiders than had been the case in São Paulo.

All these problems were eventually overcome through the patience and diplomacy of Alexander Mackenzie, whose role was crucial to the success of the venture. But the amount of time taken and the sums of money required (in part owing to Pearson's over-casual attitude to planning and cost control) left the Rio company needing to raise very large sums of money just when a serious recession had gripped the economy of the Atlantic world. Unable to raise the necessary funds in the small, volatile Canadian capital market, the company had to turn to British and eventually European investors to save the day. The utility was fundamentally sound and profitable. However Pearson's high growth monopoly strategy via rapid expansion and expensive acquisitions placed almost unbearable burdens upon his financiers in the best of times. And Rio de Janeiro Tramway, Light and Power Company needed a massive infusion of capital in the very worst of times. That bankruptcy was avoided in 1907 owed as much to good luck as to good management.

5

Falling Out in Mexico

With that tone of easy condescension that has always been the mark of Foreign Office men, the British minister to Mexico noted his gratification at the conspicuous arrival there of Canadian businessmen and capital in 1906. 'The Canadian colony here is not a numerous one, but its members make up in enterprise what they lack in numbers,' W.G. Muller informed Sir Edward Grey, the foreign secretary. 'They seem to combine the push of the Yankee with the recognized commercial integrity of the Englishman.'[1]

Ironically, they were led by a Yankee. Fred Stark Pearson, the same nervous, peripatetic technical genius who had shown Canadian business-men how to modernize their own domestic utilities and then led them to even more profitable opportunities in Brazil, also discovered the commercial possibilities of hydroelectric development in Mexico. While attending an international engineering convention in Mexico City in the fall of 1901, the impulsive promoter accompanied Dr Arnoldo Vacquie on a rough, overland trek to view the remote and picturesque gorge in which the Necaxa River fell more than 730 metres in less than half a kilometre. During the rainy season water roared and plunged through this gorge, but in the long dry season the cataract was reduced to a trickle. Of course Vacquie and Pearson were not mere sightseers in pursuit of the sublime; they were developers. Up to that point the erratic waterflow and the isolation of the waterfall had confounded Vacquie's plans to build a carbide plant at the site.

Tramping through the country snapping pictures with his bulky pano-ramic box camera, Pearson conceived a much more grandiose scheme. He would impound the rainy season floods in a series of upstream storage dams, divert the nearby Tenango River into the Necaxa watershed via a tunnel, and thus supply enough year-round water to a powerhouse at the foot of the gorge to generate electricity for transmission to Mexico City almost a hundred miles away. Additional storage reservoirs and further diversions would greatly increase the hydroelectric potential of the site and provide for future growth requirements. Impressed by the possibilities, Pearson took an option on Dr Vacquie's waterpower concessions on 11 March 1902.[2]

I

Pearson family lore has it that the timid Canadians balked at the size of the project, dragged their feet, and eventually reneged on their first agreement. In view of their heavy commitments to Pearson's project in São Paulo, the Canadian financiers may well have tried to restrain him. Certainly Pearson did have to negotiate two extensions of the time limit on his option before he managed to kindle some interest among his associates.[3] Nevertheless, in October 1902 a group of Halifax lawyers, consisting of B.F. Pearson and G. Fred Pearson, Robert Harris, Charles Cahan, and Henry Lovett, incorporated the Mexican Light and Power Company. F.S. Pearson and Cahan were dispatched to Mexico with joint power of attorney to examine the title, confirm the concessions with the government, and close the sale of the property for $150,000.

The roots of subsequent differences between Pearson and Cahan probably stretch back to this first joint mission to Mexico. The two men possessed quite different temperaments and talents. Pearson, the impulsive promoter-builder, excited by the intriguing technical problems of development, had probably overlooked or discounted the equally important financial and commercial aspects that were apparent to Cahan, the cautious lawyer who had been sent, after all, to enhance the security of the Canadian investors. Pearson had acquired a reputation for technical audacity, relative indifference to financial considerations, and a frustrating habit of neglecting important details. Grandiose conception and engineering virtuosity were his strengths; he tended to lose interest and become bored with the nagging difficulties of construction and operation.

Cahan was not satisfied merely with an up-country waterpower concession, however picturesque the setting or ingenious the engineering solution proposed. He wanted to make certain the company could sell its power after investing a lot of money in dams and turbines. An impatient Pearson could easily imagine this to be a lack of confidence. In any event, Cahan came away from his discussions with Mexican officials with a much broader, more generous concession, which not only granted the company exclusive rights to develop the waterpowers of the Necaxa, Tenango, and Catapuxtla rivers, but also conferred upon it authority to build power lines anywhere in Mexico, expropriate land for this purpose, and operate distributing systems in Mexico City and elsewhere. Most importantly, to ensure that it could not be held to ransom by obstreperous local authorities en route, the company received an indefinite exemption from state taxation on its lines.[4] With this the Mexican Light and Power Company obtained permission to transform itself from a wholesale primary producer into an integrated hydroelectric utility. Pearson would most certainly have approved of this – it followed the usual pattern – but it was undoubtedly of Cahan's doing. The press reported it that way and, more to the point, the company considered the contribution sufficiently important to pay Cahan $14,383.59 for a few months' work.[5]

When everyone approved this new agreement, Dr Vacquie would receive $135,000 in cash for his original concessions; Pearson would be paid a $47,500 finder's fee, and Messers Del Río and Company of Mexico City were to be paid $25,000 for legal and other services (the firm was also kept on a $5,000 annual retainer). A further sum of $50,000 was to be deposited in Mexico City to cover various unspecified disbursements – probably bribes – that Pearson and Cahan had made on behalf of the company. In total the Mexican Light and Power Company paid $257,000 in cash to obtain the basic property and franchises necessary to commence operations.[6]

If São Paulo and Rio were primarily Toronto promotions, Mexican Light and Power was to become a predominantly Montreal property. As soon as the Mexican government signed its part of the revised concession, Montreal capitalists took over and moved the head office to Montreal from Halifax. This had probably been the plan from the beginning, but there is no way of knowing. All that can be said for certain is that on 20 January 1903 the Halifax directors resigned, to be replaced by E.S. Clouston, president of the Bank of Montreal, George Drummond, its former president, James Ross, the wealthy contractor and utilities magnate, F.L. Wanklyn, general manager of Ross's Montreal Street Railway, Sir William Van Horne, of the CPR, and four Torontonians familiar from previous promotions: George Cox of Canada Life, William Mackenzie of the Canadian Northern Railway, J.H. Plummer, assistant general manager of the Bank of Commerce, and

E.R. Wood, stockbroker and president of the Central Canada Loan and Savings Company. Ross was elected president and Plummer vice-president, and F.S. Pearson and his firm were retained as engineers and prime contractors for the Necaxa project.[7] C.H. Cahan was to remain general attorney for the company in Mexico City, performing there the role carried out in Brazil by Alexander Mackenzie. The division of authority between Cahan and Pearson was never spelled out, however, an ambiguity that led inevitably to conflict between ambitious, determined men.

Once Mexican Light and Power metamorphosed from a marginal speculation into a property controlled by the leading men of Canadian finance, construction could begin. During 1903 Pearson and his chief assistant, Hugh Cooper, set up a field headquarters at Necaxa and took command of the extraordinarily difficult excavations. Roads had to be cleared through mountainous country; later these would be replaced by narrow-gauge railroads. Villages had to be laid out to house the army of skilled workmen and labourers. Millions of cubic metres of earth had to be moved to the dam sites, a problem Pearson solved with a clever system of sluices. Diversion tunnels had to be blasted through the hills and penstocks run over the rapids and down the sheer face of cliffs. And most difficult of all, the powerhouse had to be constructed and generators installed at the bottom of the deep gorge.[8]

While Pearson marshalled men and equipment, Cahan and the Montreal directors worked out other designs. As in São Paulo and Rio, the several well-established utilities already serving Mexico City had also to be dealt with if the promotion were to succeed. These companies mainly depended upon expensive coal, some of which had to be imported from Great Britain. Hydroelectric power from Necaxa would be much cheaper, which accounted for the optimism of the Canadians, but it still had to be delivered and sold. The preferred solution was to buy out the existing companies, then create an integrated distribution monopoly.

The newest, largest, and most efficiently managed utility, the Mexican Electric Works, held the franchise for lighting the city streets. Owned by Siemens and Halske, the German electrical equipment manufacturer, and the Dresdner Bank, it had been in business only a few years. Anthony Gibbs and Company, one of the oldest Latin American trading and banking houses in Britain, owned the older Mexican Gas and Electric Company, which had formerly lit the city streets but was now confined to commercial and industrial service by the aggressive German competition.[9] The third major power distributor, the locally owned but Swiss-financed La Compañía Explotadora de las Fuerzas Hidro-Eléctricas de San Ildefonso, operated a small, isolated hydroelectric station in the region.

In April 1903, Pearson and Cahan jumped at the chance to purchase the Mexican Electric Works from its German owners. Long-distance negotiations went on over the summer among Montreal, Mexico City, London and Berlin; in July the shareholders approved the acquisition, and in September Cahan sailed for London to close the deal. Mexican Light and Power obtained Mexican Electric for $990,000 in cash, $1.4 million in bonds, and an equal amount of common stock. The previous owners also obtained the right to appoint two members to the Mexican Light board: Arnold Ellert, London manager of the Dresdner Bank, and Dr Alfred Berliner, of Siemens and Halske. With this acquisition, Mexican Light thus became an operating company within a year of its incorporation.[10]

Why were the Germans ready to sell? First and foremost because the Canadians made a very good offer in cash and promising paper. Equally important, Siemens and Halske were not primarily interested in the long-term operation of utilities. That company decided that it could earn a better short-term return on its capital in the manufacturing end of the electrical equipment business. At the beginning of the electrical era that company, like many others, had perforce been drawn into the promotion and operation of tramway and electrical utilities in order to sell equipment. Some of these ventures turned out to be excellent speculations. However, the competition for franchises narrowed profits. Moreover, the ownership of utilities tied up enormous quantities of capital that might be more advantageously applied elsewhere. Thus the Canadian willingness to buy knit nicely with the Siemens' goal of tactical withdrawal.[11]

The takeover may also have been conditional upon the sale of equipment. Siemens subsequently received an order from Mexican Light and Power for six generators for the Necaxa development. This might have been either a mere coincidence or an angry response to the difficulty with the General Electric generators in São Paulo. Certainly Pearson had used Siemens equipment before in the modernization of Whitney's Metropolitan Street Railway in New York. The company made excellent generators, and the price ($97,830) may well have been the best. GE, with whom Pearson had a much closer working relationship, did however win the contract for the nine transformers required.[12]

After swallowing the Mexican Electric Works so quickly, the company moved more cautiously on further takeovers. For the time being at least, the directors of Mexican Light and Power preferred to come to terms with their remaining competitors rather than absorb them. Perhaps they feared official and public hostility if they monopolized the electrical business too quickly. Eventually the company did receive a signal that the government would welcome a consolidation of electric utilities, especially if that meant lower rates. Perhaps with Necaxa making such heavy demands the directors thought they had enough on their plate at the moment. Or perhaps the company needed the higher profits of a price-fixing combine to pay the interest on outstanding securities pending the completion of the works at Necaxa. Mexican Light and Power broadcast its aim of greatly reducing rates once hydroelectricity could be delivered – which no doubt partly explains the competitors' eagerness to sell out – but in the meantime the company chose to maintain existing rates through an agreement with its competitors. By turning down all offers for the time being, delaying takeovers, publicizing eventual rate reductions, and applying pressure with actual cuts now and then, the company strengthened its bargaining position *vis-à-vis* its rivals and maximized its profits in the interim.[13]

When the Canadian directors quite sensibly chose January and February of 1904 to examine the Necaxa hydroelectric project first hand, they took time out from a busy round of tours and official appointments – which included an impressive audience with President Porfirio Díaz – to meet with the managers of the Gas and Electric and the San Ildefonso companies to arrange 'an understanding in regard to [the] maintenance of rates.' This satisfied everyone temporarily, although offers to sell were received from both companies over the summer and declined. Pressure to break the agreement came, ironically, from Mexican Light and Power itself. In attempting to line up buyers for the large block of new power about to come onto the market, Pearson wanted to lower rates immediately as a sign of good faith, as a public relations gesture, and as a sweetener in negotiations with municipal and federal agencies over new or extended power contracts. He unilaterally lowered rates across the board in the fall of 1904, which drew an anguished protest from the Gibbs company. The board of directors could hardly repudiate the actions of their man in charge, but they urged their local representative (in a letter that went to every member of the board) to do all he could 'to act in union' with the competition 'and if possible, to avoid forcing an issue at present.'[14]

II

With optimistic progress reports on Necaxa before them at the beginning of

1905, the directors of Mexican Light and Power turned their attention once again to acquisitions. Further overtures by Gibbs and Company led to serious negotiations during one of Pearson's frequent trips to London. E.S. Clouston was also in London on business at the time, and Pearson was instructed 'to act with him in all negotiations when practicable.' The two were authorised to offer $2.5 million in bonds and $600,000 in stock with the possibility of $250,000 in additional stock if they encountered resistance. In Mexico Cahan received instructions to buy out the San Ildefonso company with Mexican Light bonds and stock. The sale was facilitated by Pearson who, on his way to Germany to inspect the generators being completed at Siemens and Halske, secured the approval of la Société Financière, which held the mortgage. All told, Mexican Light and Power would issue a further $5,666,000 in 5 per cent bonds and $1,350,000 in stock from its treasury to complete its monopoly.[15]

After options on these companies had been secured in May 1905, it was discovered that, in view of the other obligations the company faced, the creation of this much new debt would exceed the limit specified in the first mortgage trust deed. Therefore, it was decided to create a subsidiary, the Mexican Electric Light Company, capitalized at $6 million in bonds and a like amount of stock, to purchase the Gibbs and San Ildefonso companies. The securities of this new company were guaranteed as to principal and interest by the Mexican Light and Power Company, which held all the stock.[16] These companies cost so much primarily because they had both installed expensive underground conduit systems in accordance with the government ban on overhead wires in the central squares and fashionable residential districts. Thus for a minimum annual expenditure of $300,000 (in the form of interest on the bonds created) Mexican Light and Power acquired two distribution companies whose combined earnings in 1904 were, it claimed, $311,000. With savings from consolidation and the substitution of hydroelectric for thermal power it was optimistically estimated that the combined company would earn $1.9 million annually.[17]

Meanwhile, Pearson and Cahan had been busy in Mexico consolidating the company's franchises and lining up customers for Necaxa power, which was expected to be ready in mid-1905. The states of Puebla, Hidalgo, Mexico, and Michoacán were persuaded to allow the company to do business within their borders. The Mexican government, in return for a 25 per cent reduction in domestic lighting rates, enlarged the company's original Mexico City franchise to take in the entire Federal District and extended its term to the year 2012. With the company's permanent existence thus legally secured, its representatives turned their attention to the problem of guaranteeing sufficient waterpower to meet long-term needs. In May 1906, the company gained exclusive control of the headwaters of the Necaxa, Tenango, and several other nearby rivers. According to the terms of these perpetual agreements, Mexican Light and Power could store and divert enough water from all of these streams to produce 235,000 hp at its Necaxa plant.[18]

As salesmen Pearson and Cahan had been equally aggressive. In 1904 they persuaded the directors to build a transmission line into the El Oro district to supply six large mining operations. The municipal government got talked into extending the street lighting franchise – due to expire in 1909 – until 1917, at much lower rates. In 1905 the Water Commission, whose board contained several good friends of the company, awarded Mexican Light a twenty-year contract to supply power to its pumping stations. Further block sales of power were negotiated with textile companies, railroads, mines, irrigation companies and other public authorities.[19] Then in the summer of 1905 the biggest plum of all came within reach, the contract to supply 5,000 to 7,000 hp to the street railway in Mexico City.[20] By the end of 1905, with all these contracts duly signed, with the company's franchises and concessions entrenched, with a monopoly of the federal district secured, and with Necaxa power due to be delivered any day, the Mexican Light and Power Company directors could at last list the company's stock on the Toronto and Montreal stock exchanges and perhaps realize some profit from their speculation.

As usual the demand for power greatly exceeded the immediate supply. The promoters raised expectations that they then had to scramble furiously to fulfil. By the fall of 1905 the company was contracting to sell power it did not have and as a result had to face the necessity of expanding its yet-to-be-completed plant. By 1906 a total demand of 46,655 hp had already been connected, divided up as follows: public lighting, 2.9 per cent; private lighting, 42.9 per cent; industrial power, 33.5 per cent; tramway, 1.3 per cent, and the El Oro mines, 19.8 per cent. By the end of 1907 existing contracts would raise the total to 64,000 hp as the tramway claimed its full quota. To meet this the company had a hydroelectric generating capacity of only 41,000 hp from its Necaxa and San Ildefonso plants combined, supplemented by 16,000 hp from its three steam plants.[21]

To complicate matters further, the Necaxa power station was not ready in June 1905 as promised.[22] Heavy rains during the construction of the storage and coffer dams, unexpected flooding during the cutting of the two diversion canals (which required concrete lining of the tunnels), and problems with the narrow-gauge railway delayed completion of the project a full year. Then, when power was finally delivered in July 1906, the Necaxa station could operate at only a fraction of its capacity on account of a shortage of water. Since systematic streamflow measurement had begun only in 1902, no one could predict how much water to expect in any given year. The wet weather that had plagued construction gave way to unusually dry weather during 1905 and 1906, which slowed the filling of the storage reservoirs. No water could be stored at all in 1906, as it turned out, which cut hydroelectric production drastically. Consequently, the steam plants of Mexican Light and Power's subsidiaries, which had been scheduled for stand-by duty, had to be run more or less continuously, with a resulting increase in operating expenses and decrease in profitability. Much to the embarrassment of the hydraulic engineers, two steam plants had to be purchased second-hand from American utilities to maintain output in the interim.[23] Thus, as the company's promoters waited anxiously for rain to fill the reservoirs, even before the first turbines had turned the decision was taken to embark upon phase two of the development, which would double output from the Necaxa powerhouse.

All of this cost money, much more than expected. The prospectus for the Mexican Light and Power Company, published in May 1903, implied that the $5 million raised by the sale of the first instalment of bonds would build the dams, powerhouse, and transmission lines, and put the company on an operating footing. A second installation, involving the expenditure of $3.5 million would add 40,000 hp when the need arose.[24] These optimistic estimates were rapidly obliterated by inflated expenses, cost overruns, expensive acquisitions, the prolonged operation of the steam plants, and, especially, the constant revision and enlargement of the original plan. Characteristically, Pearson himself kept modifying the design of his storage dams to increase their holding capacity. Construction tie-ups added a year to the wage bill. Strategically placed landowners demanded exorbitant prices for property along the transmission line right of way. The cost of the El Oro line, for example, originally estimated at $475,000, ended up at more than $1 million. Salaries and legal expenses were generous and company funds were diverted into loans to third parties. It all added up.

As a result of these increased expenditures a further block of $2.5 million in bonds was issued in 1903 and another $2 million worth had to be sold in February 1905 to pay for the El Oro line, for extending the distribution system in Mexico City, and for raising the height of the storage dams and lining the diversion tunnels. Another $1.3 million in bonds was disposed of in October 1905 to meet the company's growing cash requirements, and in the spring of 1906 a further $1.2 million worth. Thus by the end of 1906, the entire $12 million worth of authorized bonds had been exhausted and the second phase of the Necaxa power development had just begun – and this did not include the $6 million in bonds created and guaranteed for the Mexican Electric Light distribution subsidiary.

Nor did the rapid increase in the company's bonded debt completely meet its cash requirements. In June 1905 the company obtained the first of what would be a series of loans from the Bank of Montreal, loans that by the end of 1906 would total more than $4 million. The bonds issued in 1905 and 1906 were intended to pay off this floating debt. Late in 1905 the company took the unusual step of issuing common stock to raise additional money, but this was undersubscribed in a soft market. At the height of the financial panic in 1907, with no more bonds left in the treasury, the directors faced the unenviable necessity of raising more than $2 million to finance the expansion program. The bank refused further loans; the usual underwriters were pinched as well by their bankers. Reluctantly the company created $2.4 million in 7 per cent preference stock, which Messrs Sperling and Company of London agreed to place. But that was expensive money, raised at no profit to the directors themselves.[25]

The Clouston, Ross, Pearson, Plummer, Wood circle had managed the first $5 million offering and also handled the subsequent issues of $1 million in July 1903 and $2 million in February 1905. E. Mackay Edgar and Company of Montreal acted as the principal underwriter for the October 1905 sale of $1.3 million, $300,000 of which was taken up by H. Scherer and Company of Mexico. E. Mackay Edgar and Company and Dominion Securities of Toronto divided the spring 1906 issue of $1.2. In each case the bonds were taken up by the underwriters at 90 per cent of par with 100 per cent bonus stock. These parcels were, of course, further subdivided among associates who received a proportionately diminished stock bonus. In 1904, for example, when Max Aitken, newly arrived on the financial scene, was in line for $40,000 worth of bonds sold to finance the Mexican Electric Works takeover, he received only a 40 per cent stock bonus. A year later he secured $250,000 of Pearson's underwriting with only a 25 per cent stock bonus.[26]

By the end of 1907 the Mexican Light and Power Company had been in existence for five years during which it had created securities with a book value of $39,985,000. With this capital the company had monopolized the distribution of electricity in the Federal District, extended its lines to the cities and mining regions of neighbouring states, and completed the first stage of its ambitious hydroelectric development – though it was still not running at peak efficiency because of the shortage of water. In 1906 the company earned a total of $1,188,609 on its investment and aimed at $1,760,000 in 1907. Notwithstanding the rapid increase in the bonded debt, interest charges had been readily met from the growing business (67,353 hp connected in 1907). In 1908, as the hydroelectric plant took on more of the base load and the thermal stations reverted to stand-by duty and the peaking functions for which they had originally been intended, it appeared likely that a dividend on the common shares would be justified.[27]

The unexpectedly heavy capital requirements of this project had taken their toll, however. Some Montreal backers had begun to cry 'enough.' At this point, the Pearson family's traditional perception of Canadian resistance rings true: some Montrealers lost their patience and refused to put up any more money.

III

The trouble could be traced back to F.S. Pearson's appetite for acquisitions. In the summer of 1905 Pearson had called on the owners of the Mexico Electric Tramways Company, Wernher, Beit and Company of London, with a proposal to replace that company's high-cost thermal power plant with a long-term contract for cheaper hydroelectric power from Mexican Light. During these negotiations it transpired that the street railway itself might be for sale.

The merchant bank of Julius Wernher and Alfred Beit had been built upon the legendary wealth acquired by the principals in the South African diamond trade and gold rush. In the 1890s the partners began to diversify their portfolio by moving into the promotion of railroads and public utilities in South Africa and elsewhere. Their purchase of several horse and mule tramways in Mexico City in 1898 was only one of several such speculations, which included as well the Cape Electric Tramway, the Lisbon Electric Tramway, and the Chilean Electric Tramway and Light Company.

By the time Pearson appeared on the scene in 1905 Wernher and Beit were aging bankers, not street railway operators, and were interested primarily in the rate of return on their invested capital. Every Wednesday at twelve noon sharp, Colonel Sir Charles Euan-Smith, president of the utility company, met with directors Vice Admiral Albert H. Markham, Ludwig Breitmeyer, Lionel Phillips, Alfred Parrish, and Rutherford Harris in offices at 55–6 Bishopsgate that the company shared with other utilities in the Corner House stable. There the board worried over the weekly reports of the resident engineer, A. E. Worswick, and the company's roving engineer-troubleshooter, Chandos S. Stanhope.[28] Their Mexican property had proved to be something of a disappointment. The conversion to electricity had been plagued by political complications, bickering among the members of the management committee, troubles with local managers, adverse exchange rates, accidents, construction delays, and engineering problems. If the truth were known the company had lost a great deal of money from 1898 to 1904 and had just begun to turn the corner. As a result the company remained heavily indebted to Wernher, Beit and Company, the group's merchant bank.[29]

Wernher and Beit were prepared to entertain offers if, of course, the price was right. Pearson obliged by offering extremely generous terms to the controlling shareholders in May 1906.[30] The British consul in Mexico, for one, thought the £600,000 profit garnered in the deal by the Corner House crowd outrageous and likely to hinder the new owners.[31] But Pearson saw tremendous opportunities which in his view justified making a quick, clean deal. The tramway had a franchise with the city lasting until 1982 and owned a perpetual franchise in the suburbs. It was in excellent condition, with 148 kilometres of electrified lines, 69 kilometres of muletram routes, and 16 kilometres of steam railroad. Under the previous management the company produced a net operating profit of 1,345,000 pesos in 1905 despite the fact that operating expenses were much higher than they ought to have been. With cheap power and more effective management Pearson predicted an operating surplus of $4,250,000 within two years even allowing for $200,000 on renewals and expansion. On the street in Montreal it was rumoured that Pearson's coup was simply 'too good to hand over to the Mexican Light and Power Company.'[32]

The truth is Pearson tried and failed to effect a merger with the Light and Power Company. He proposed issuing $8 million worth of bonds to acquire the tramway, putting all of its common stock in the power company's treasury. The power company would then lease the tramway and guarantee the interest on its bonds. But in view of the agonizingly slow and expensive development of the Mexican Light and Power promotion it is not surprising that some of the directors – James Ross, in particular – became impatient with Pearson's proposal to load them up with more bonds at this time. Some thought that the power company should be put on a paying basis before further acquisitions or expenditures were entertained. On the other hand, E.S. Clouston could see merit in the proposition; the cash flow of the tramway would help pay for light and power extensions.

Resolution of this problem created some misunderstanding and some lingering ill will within the Montreal financial community. Having failed to gain the support of the Mexican Light board, Pearson then turned to individual directors and some outsiders with a view to financing an entirely separate company. E.S. Clouston of the Bank of Montreal and Sir William Van Horne agreed to support the venture. Clouston in turn invited James Dunn, E.R. Wood, Mackay Edgar, and Sperling and Company of London to participate. In this new venture, Max Aitken in Montreal reported to C.H. Cahan in Mexico, 'the Montreal people will occupy the same pen with the Toronto,' by which he meant E.R. Wood's associates, William Mackenzie, Donald Mann, Henry Pellatt, and Morris Bryant. Nominally this was a Toronto promotion that shared head office quarters with the Rio and São Paulo companies. The Bank of Commerce in Toronto provided financial accommodation. But behind this Toronto façade English capital predominated, represented by James Dunn, Sperling and Company, and Mendel and Myers. This arrangement raised quite a few eyebrows in the small Canadian financial community. James Ross, who opposed the original merger, resigned from the Light and Power board soon afterwards. However, the involvement of the Bank of Montreal in the underwriting of both companies signified that, for the time being at least, these resentments would be contained.[33]

The Parliament of Canada was petitioned to expand the powers contained in the charter of the dormant Yucatán Power Company owned by this group. Approval of this legislation was facilitated by the offer of $500,000 worth of the underwriting to the Forgets and a further $250,000 worth to religious organizations in Quebec.[34] The Canadian-incorporated Mexico Tramways Company raised the money to buy Wernher, Beit's Mexico Electric Tramways Company by issuing $7.5 million in bonds and 60,000 common shares with a par value of $100. According to James Dunn the insiders received their bonds at 90 per cent of par with a 25 per cent stock bonus and immediately re-underwrote their portions with a 12.5 per cent stock bonus and a 2.5 per cent stock commission. E.S. Clouston and the Bank of Montreal took one part of the underwriting; E.R. Wood and Sperling shared a second, and James Dunn, who was in the process of moving from Montreal to London, took a third. For his part Dunn agreed to place $1,450,000 in bonds and contracted for an additional $500,000 each for his associates, Alfred Loewenstein of Belgium and Robert Fleming of

London. Brokers taking large blocks of bonds received slightly better terms from the syndicate.[35] But on this deal the insiders kept a fairly sizeable portion of the bonus stock for themselves.

The Mexico Tramways promotion went to the market at a particularly good time. Earnings from São Paulo were so good that accurate results could not be published without embarrassing the companies in Brazil. The troubles in Rio remained hidden from public view. In Mexico earnings increased as expected in early 1906, permitting the promoters to promise a dividend of 7 per cent by year's end.[36] Notwithstanding the fact that Pearson had major hydroelectric projects under construction in Brazil, Mexico, Ontario, and Manitoba, he nevertheless took a direct personal interest in reorganizing the Mexico Tramways Company, of which he was the president. By June 1906 Pearson had the property well enough in hand for Dunn to organize a syndicate to make a market in Mexico Tramways common stock. With the stock buoyed by rumours of high earnings, Dunn was able to float the shares up to sixty dollars for most of the summer (on the basis of his privileged access to weekly traffic statistics from Mexico) and had hopes of being able to get it to eighty dollars before long. The main difficulty was once again satisfying the stock exchange in London with hard and verifiable data concerning company affairs.[37]

Over the next several years Pearson as president and Harro Harrsen, his general manager, continued the program of modernization begun by Wernher, Beit and Company and greatly expanded the system. Pearson had begun his engineering career in the street railway business, and he knew from experience how to make a street railway profitable. The trick was to get expenses down to less than 50 per cent of income, a task that could be accomplished by rapid electrification, prudence with extensions, and careful attention to service to maximize receipts per car kilometre. He was doing the same thing in São Paulo and Rio as well.

In Mexico City over the next three years under Pearson's management the number of passengers carried increased; but more important, through better scheduling, maintenance and routing, average daily car earnings and average receipts per car kilometre rose as well. Pearson and Harrsen made the system more efficient. The net result was a 12 per cent reduction in the amount of income required to meet expenses (including extensions) and a 47 per cent increase in total erarnings, which converted into a 73 per cent increase in profitability. The company paid a 1 per cent dividend on its common shares in 1907 and a 4 per cent dividend in 1908. This improved performance was not immediately reflected in share prices on account of the general recession in 1907, but in the spring of 1908 Mexico Tramways stock bounded up from $59 to $97 on the strength of rumours about 1908 earnings and reached a high of $139 in the fall. Thus by the end of 1908 the Mexico Tramways promotion could be considered a resounding success (see Appendix).[38]

For the Mexican Light and Power Company, on the other hand, life did not present as rosy an aspect. The drought in the Necaxa region persisted through 1907. Lacking sufficient water to operate its hydroelectric generators at full capacity, the company had to run its less-efficient thermal plants full time. This increased expenses and lowered the company's capacity to meet its financial obligations alarmingly. Gross receipts rose fairly steadily, but net earnings remained constant at around 250,000 pesos per month, which was barely enough to meet interest payments and not enough to pay a dividend.[39] Moreover, the company had been compelled to raise money at the very worst time in 1907, and it faced the prospect of having to borrow heavily again in 1908 to complete the reservoirs and hydroelectric installations at Necaxa. The price of the company's stock fell from a high of seventy dollars at the beginning of 1906 to a low of thirty-five dollars at the bottom of the recession in November 1907, and rose only slowly to around fifty dollars at the beginning of 1908. The financial statement prepared for the annual meeting in February 1908 produced 'keen disappointment' on both sides of the Atlantic.[40] The prospect of operating the costly thermal plants while waiting for rain discouraged a large number of impatient shareholders who had been counting on dividends and capital gains to salvage their speculation. To still these troubled waters the directors voted a 1 per cent dividend in July 1908, but it was apparent to everyone that this was not warranted by the company's performance.

Although F.S. Pearson remained a director of Mexican Light and Power as well as chief consulting engineer, he had more or less severed his connections with the company. Board members associated with the Bank of Montreal handled financial affairs, while Charles Cahan managed the company in Mexico. When Pearson visited Mexico he devoted himself completely to the affairs of the rapidly growing Mexico Tramways and paid only scant attention to the trouble-plagued Light and Power project. His conspicuous neglect of Mexican Light affairs perturbed the Montreal directors; Pearson's prominent role in the ascent of Mexico Tramways particularly annoyed Charles Cahan and rekindled the rivalry between the two men that had been latent since the beginning.

So rapid had been the growth of Mexico Tramways that, early in 1908,

Pearson needed to secure large quantities of additional power to accommodate future expansion. With characteristic impertinence he chose not to buy more power, but rather to buy the power company. Joint management offered modest operating economies. More importantly, the two companies could finance one another from retained earnings and thus command much better terms on the bond market. For example, the cash-rich and credit-worthy tramways company could loan its surpluses or borrow on behalf of the weak but promising light and power company. This would lift some of the interest burden on the weaker partner. Conceivably at another time the process might be reversed. Certainly in 1908 the Light and Power Company needed additional funds, and a merger with Mexico Tramways provided one solution.

An amalgamation made sense, but several obstacles stood in the way. Those who had rejected a merger before would have to swallow their pride. Secondly, the resentment of some of the Mexican Light directors against F.S. Pearson, who many thought was the main source of the company's troubles, would have to be overcome. And finally Charles Cahan in Mexico adamantly refused to submit to Pearson and his friends. The rivalry between the two men and their companies assumed comic proportions in the spring of 1908. Cahan publicly exposed Pearson as the culprit responsible for hiring a private detective to report on anything disreputable in his private life. Meanwhile he busied himself slandering Pearson in Mexico City and Montreal to prevent a merger. Such behaviour caused sufficient damage to foreign business generally as to occasion an anguished dispatch by the British minister.[41]

Early in the summer of 1908 F.S. Pearson met E.S. Clouston in London. Clouston had been authorized by the Mexican Light board to negotiate a lease of Mexico Tramways. Pearson countered with an offer to lease the light and power company, and the two of them, with the assistance of Z.A. Lash, worked out a plan for presentation to their respective boards. According to the terms of this draft agreement the tramway company would lease the light and power company, assume its interest and sinking fund liabilities, supply funds to complete the second phase of development, pay a dividend of not less than 4 per cent on the common stock, and liquidate the floating debt. If any money remained after meeting these obligations it would be divided equally between the two companies, except in the first two years, when the tramway company had a claim to $150,000 for assuming these obligations. Clouston's interest, as banker to the floundering light and power company, was palpable. Accordingly

Pearson was quite confident the deal would go through despite Cahan's resistance.[42]

Cahan rushed back to Montreal to scuttle the deal. He was present on 5 August 1908 when Sir George Drummond, E.S. Clouston, F.S. Pearson, F.L. Wanklyn, and E.R. Wood considered the matter, and a majority of the board voted to continue negotiations towards a lease of the company to the tramway. Cahan was instructed to draw up a suitable lease and report back. But at this point things fell apart. Cahan's draft proved unacceptable to Zebulon Lash, acting for the tramway. Then on 22 September 1908, Sir George Drummond resigned as president of Mexican Light and Power, to be succeeded by E.S. Clouston. Drummond and Cahan, who had been the minority voting against the lease on 5 August, then formed a lobby to defeat the proposal.[43]

With Drummond out of the way (Cahan stayed on the board to fight), the remaining directors of Mexican Light moved towards an agreement with the representatives of the tramway company. But at this point other objections arose, especially from directors who held bonds of the underlying Mexican Electric Light Company. Under pressure from the Drummond faction the Light and Power board backed away from the tentative agreement. On 12 October in Pearson's absence, the directors of Mexican Light and Power voted to increase its capital and explore the prospects of selling more preferred shares, presumably on the assumption that the two companies would remain separate. By 25 November Pearson admitted that there was 'no prospect of being able to arrange [the deal] amicably at present.'[44]

Yet Pearson fought on. After circulating a statement showing the advantages of the lease – which drew a stinging rebuke from the directors – Pearson managed to force a general meeting of shareholders to consider it on 30 December. For at least a year Pearson and his supporters on both sides of the Atlantic had been quietly buying up Mexican Light and Power stock in case a collision could not be avoided. He was reasonably confident by December that if push came to shove he would prevail. On the other hand the Drummond–Bank of Montreal group assumed it had a majority. If not, Max Aitken reported, rumour had it that the bank would call its $3 million loan.[45]

Conflict reached a head over Christmas 1908 as the two rival groups courted the shareholders. In the press the dispute assumed nationalistic overtones. Pearson's colleagues were represented as pushy Englishmen, barging in upon a perfectly contented Canadian company. As seen by the papers, the conflict pitted Sperling and Company, the British merchant banker, against the Bank of Montreal. The Montreal shareholders cast themselves in the unlikely role of the Guinles of Brazil stemming a foreign invasion. By way of defense the Pearson people simply offered the shareholders a much higher dividend than they had been receiving along with less risk. Pearson himself did not lead the attack, but rather operated through surrogates – Lawrence Macfarlane, Sir Edward Stracey, and Mackay Edgar.

The extraordinary 30 December shareholders' meeting in Montreal ended in an infuriating stand-off. Sir George Drummond denounced the proposed lease and challenged its legality. When a resolution calling for a shareholders' committee to negotiate the lease was presented, E.S. Clouston, caught in the middle as president both of the company and of the Bank of Montreal, ruled it out of order. Round one went to management. However, when the board recommended the creation of 36,000 additional preferred shares the insurgents voted this down 89,966 to 22,849. The Montreal group had retained control of their company, but the writing was on the wall. They had stopped the lease but at the cost of not being able to raise the money necessary to complete the second phase of the project. The company's affairs were in a terrible mess, the opposing factions in a deadlock, and the unsettling controversy among the leading men of the Canadian financial community was now a matter of sensational gossip.[46]

On 4 January 1909, the Mexican Light and Power directors raised the dividend on the common stock. The financial press charitably interpreted this move as being justified by the company's improved performance. However, at the time the directors were borrowing money to pay the bond interest.[47] An angry Pearson then resigned in a huff, followed by E.R. Wood, Arnold Ellert, and Dr Alfred Berliner. With this Pearson revoked his offer of a lease and declared his intention to seize direct control of Mexican Light and effect a merger. He offered eight Mexico Tramways shares for fourteen Mexican Light and Power shares, which, of course, the Drummond group regarded as a rank insult. In reply the Montrealers claimed that Mexico Tramways stock had been artificially inflated in value.[48] This unseemly and unusual public quarrelling set the stage for a final confrontation at the regular annual general meeting on 17 February 1909.

Emissaries criss-crossed the Atlantic to see if terms could be worked out privately. In Montreal the management began to reconsider its position; clearly it could not hold onto power indefinitely against a majority. Rather than force an ugly scene the directors chose the course of prudence and decided to capitulate in advance. 'Tomorrow Mex Directors Will Walk the Plank,' the Montreal *Star* headline announced on Tuesday, 16 February. 'The splendid fight against the English interests made by the directors, together with Sir George Drummond, Mr. James Ross and Senator MacKay, has apparently been unfruitful, and they have failed to convince the English shareholders of the folly of the exchange of 14 Power shares for 8 shares of Tramways.'

In the absence of what the *Star* called 'the English crowd' the annual meeting went forward with elaborate and dignified formality. The old directors presented the annual report, apologized for an additional $100,000 in steamplant expenses, and then quietly resigned. They were eloquently thanked for their services, and a new board was voted in consisting of F.S. Pearson, president, Walter Gow and Miller Lash, vice-presidents, and directors R.C. Brown, George Flett, Zebulon Lash, J.M. Limantour, E.R. Wood, and Sir William Van Horne. Charles Cahan and J.H. Plummer stressed the importance of advancing the interests of the company while at the same time defending the honour of the former management and conceded without rancour that the majority must rule. In public, all was decency and civility.[49]

The recriminations followed later that afternoon in private when the new directors met. Charles Cahan was fired as general counsel and his power of attorney revoked and, just to rub it in, his fees were challenged. The Bank of Montreal did in fact call its $3 million loan that very day, but Mexico Tramways was ready with the funds necessary to meet these notes. With that, Mexican Light and Power severed all its connections with the Bank of Montreal and to a large extent with the city of Montreal, moved its head office to Toronto, and opened an account with the Bank of Commerce.[50]

Pearson and his engineering company threw themselves into the task of completing the Necaxa works. In London James Dunn and his colleagues schemed to make the takeover a profitable speculation as well. On 5 October at the first board meeting held in the Toronto offices of Blake, Lash, Anglin and Cassels, it was reported that the company had not been required to use steam power since the end of August and that earnings for September and succeeding months would be very largely increased.

Thus after six years and the investment of many millions of dollars, Mexican Light and Power had finally become a fully hydroelectric system. At the same time the management of Mexico Tramways and Mexican Light and Power had been completely integrated, although the two companies retained their separate legal identities. F.S. Pearson reigned as president of both companies, and the boards were virtually identical. Integration had been achieved, however, at considerable cost, including a rare (for Canadian capitalism) open proxy battle and the alienation of some key Montreal financiers.

Given Pearson's appetite for capital, a break of some sort was probably inevitable. Promoters and bankers were locked in a golden embrace. To bankers, promoters meant loans and new opportunities for capital gains. But prudence demanded that bankers should not take on too much of one company's securities at a time. If the directors of the bank were also promoters and underwriters, prudence could be stretched – but not indefinitely. Further concern arose when a promotion failed to measure up to expectations. Here, too, opinion divided between those who had bought (bankers) and those who had sold (promoters). The promoters offered plausible explanations and begged for patience; people who had paid real money for paper demanded dividends and capital gains at the earliest opportunity. Along these fault lines a rupture eventually occurred in the affairs of the Mexican Light and Power Company. In the crunch Pearson, however, held the upper hand. When some of his Montreal backers quailed, he readily lined up others in Toronto and London to take their place.

By 1909 the essential construction and managerial reorganization in Mexico had been completed. The hard part was over. Now, F.S. Pearson mused during a moment of peace at his estate in the Berkshires, it was time to plant some articles in the financial press describing the wonderful prospects of both companies and begin the work of placing this stock 'as a permanent investment' among shareholders who 'won't sell when the prices rise.'[51]

PART THREE

The Promoters

6

The Money Spinner

While Canada's leading financiers invested in utility promotions on a grand scale in São Paulo, Rio de Janeiro, and Mexico City, other Canadians were on the lookout for smaller propositions that suited their more limited capacity to raise money. A group of Nova Scotians began aggressively seeking opportunities throughout the Caribbean and Central America, a region with which Atlantic Canada had longstanding commercial ties based upon the trade in sugar and fish. The Demerara Electric Company's venture at Georgetown in British Guiana in 1900 was the first of these; by 1907 similar enterprises had been founded in Trinidad, Cuba, and Puerto Rico.

These men soon discovered, just as their counterparts in central Canada were doing, that their personal wealth and the accumulated reserves of the financial institutions they controlled were not sufficient to provide all the funds required, modest as those requirements might be by comparison with the Brazilian and Mexican ventures. They had to sell securities, mainly bonds, to raise the money for the capital investment needed while the insiders retained enough of the common stock to exercise managerial control over the utilities. To arrange these company promotions and to raise money by selling bonds the Nova Scotians established the Royal Securities Corporation to develop a clientele of 'real investors' among the doctors, lawyers, ministers and sea captains of Atlantic Canada.

I

Halifax, Nova Scotia, had long been the entrepôt for Canadian trade with the Caribbean. This trade was confined to a very narrow range of items: in the mid-1890s Canadian imports from the West Indies were valued at $1,240,000 annually, 90 per cent being sugar and molasses. The $1,850,000 worth of Canadian exports was 90 per cent fish.[1] Nevertheless, this modest commerce was sufficient to underpin the expansion of Canadian banks to service the trade. The Bank of Nova Scotia opened a branch in Jamaica as early as 1889 while the Merchants' Bank of Halifax (later the Royal Bank of Canada) opened the first of many Cuban branches in Havana in 1899. Others like the Union Bank of Halifax soon followed to Port of Spain in Trinidad and elsewhere.[2] The banks provided introductions and commercial information to Canadians seeking to do business in the region.

Thus it was only natural that it should have been Haligonians who first moved to take control of utilities in that area as part of the shift from the old staple trades to new lines of endeavour. Early in 1900 the same group of entrepreneurs who had floated the Demerara Electric Company petitioned the colonial administration in Trinidad for the right to operate in Port of Spain.[3] The British governor proceeded cautiously, referring the application to a select committee of his legislative council for study. Doubtless he was aware that British colonial administrators in other islands had already been approached by foreign electrical promoters, and that London had displayed little enthusiasm about these schemes. For instance, early in 1899 the Foreign Office had vetoed F.S. Pearson's plan to electrify the island's railway on the grounds first that he was a Yankee and second that 'he knows nothing about electricity.'[4]

Perhaps the fact that the applicants for privileges in Port of Spain were loyal British subjects helped to smooth the way for them. In any case the select committee soon reported in favour of the plan, and the governor passed it on to London with his backing, noting that the same syndicate was already operating in Georgetown. The Colonial Office approved the proposal, which was in the same terms as the Guianese concession granted the previous year, although it did query the very high rates the company proposed to charge.[5]

The new Trinidad Electric Company began operation on 1 June 1901, reconstructing the thermal electric station and converting the old mule lines to trolleys, a process expected to take about two years. To aid in selling securities a board of directors was recruited composed of a number of prominent Nova Scotians – J.F. Stairs, B.F. Pearson, Robert E. Harris, Charles Archibald and W.B. Ross. The strength of this group, one insider observed, was that, 'The Trinidad interests are synonymous with the Nova Scotia Steel [and] Coal Co. interests.'[6] John F. Stairs, president of both companies and the most important entrepreneur and financier in turn-of-the-century Nova Scotia, also headed the Union Bank of Halifax. He and his associates commanded the respect of businessmen and bankers throughout Atlantic Canada, and their names in a company's annual report automatically earned it the respect and interest of prospective investors.

If plans to undertake a whole series of such promotions were to be successful, some means was necessary to raise money from a much wider circle of investors. Here fate smiled upon an elfin twenty-three-year-old, William Maxwell Aitken, the future Lord Beaverbrook. The ambitious Aitken had somehow scraped an acquaintance with John Stairs,[7] who decided in 1902 to put him to work raising money for the companies that he and his friends controlled. The unlikely child of a Newcastle, New Brunswick, manse, Max Aitken bowled everyone over with an indomitable will to succeed, a salesman's counter-jumping enthusiasm, and a rare zest for life. In his youth both his raffish manner and arresting physical appearance invariably impressed the people he met. His round head was, by universal agreement, far too large for his body. A huge Cheshire-cat grin permanently creased his cheeks; and outlandish ears, a tight collar, and a porkpie hat perched casually atop his head did nothing to diminish the first impression of a boyish mischief maker.

The middle child of the Reverend and Mrs William Aitken's nine, Max fled the patriarchal rectitude of the Presbyterian manse and its preordained career in the church, banking, or law. The truant of Newcastle set out for the west to make his fortune selling insurance, running a bowling alley, selling real estate, and delivering meat. Drink and disappointment carried him home to Atlantic Canada contrite, more sober, but all the more determined to make his mark. It was at this point that John Stairs sought to harness the young man's abundant energy; Max Aitken made the most of his opportunity. One way or another he made certain that no one would forget him, and no one ever did. Legend has it that the brash twenty-five-year-old 'financier' from Halifax failed to sell a deal to E.S. Clouston, president of the Bank of Montreal, on their first meeting. But not long afterward Clouston, reflecting upon this astonishing encounter, ordered his secretary to 'Send me back the little fellow with the big head.'[8] Max made himself useful to the powerful, all the time angling to make *them* useful to him.

Aitken threw himself into the promotion of Trinidad Electric. By that time he was already corresponding with several scouts to see if they had uncovered any likely prospects for tram franchises in the United Kingdom.[9]

Aitken proved to be sufficiently resourceful that Stairs and his friends decided to create a permanent institution through which he could seek out promising propositions and willing investors. In the spring of 1903, C.H. Cahan and R.E. Harris joined with Stairs to sign a memorandum of association with the young man, setting up the Royal Securities Corporation. Capitalized with $50,000 worth of $100 shares, the new undertaking was endowed with power to act for its founders as 'investors, capitalists, financiers, concessionaires, brokers and agents,' doing all sorts of financial business.[10]

The success of Royal Securities depended a great deal upon the Trinidad Electric promotion. The company's bright prospects provided Aitken with an auspicious debut. The Trinidad manager of the Union Bank reported in the spring of 1903 that he was convinced that the utility would do a 'large business.' Fears that black Trinidadians would not ride the cars in any numbers had evaporated; recent riots had not hurt the company, and the cars seemed fuller than those on the streets of Halifax. All in all, a large rise in stock and bond prices might be anticipated once the electrified system entered full operation. By mid-1903 Aitken was able to report that the company was already earning enough to pay the 5 per cent interest on its $720,000 par value worth of bonds and 7 per cent on $1,032,000 par value worth of common stock.[11]

Before any broad public sale could take place, however, Aitken and his associates took the precaution of forming a pool to manage the prices of the securities. So long as the underwriters who had received the shares as bonuses held the stock closely, they could (by and large) be relied upon not to try to reap quick speculative profits or to sell short in anticipation of a decline. But as soon as public trading began, particularly if the stock were listed on the exchanges in Montreal and Toronto, such predatory temptations could be contained only by a pool manager willing to enter the market and steady the stock. The task of the manager was to maintain an orderly market, gradually to feed the securities to those who would not dump them back onto the exchange at the merest hint of an advance, and to push up prices when the company's earnings would sustain such an increase. Such tactics were required to attract the attention of 'real investors' ready to salt the securities away in their portfolios.

Thus in the spring of 1903 Aitken asked A.E. Ames, the Toronto stockbroker, to take on the management of the Trinidad pool. The Torontonian was interested but worried by the current state of the market.[12] Ames's premonitions proved well founded. Within a month his firm would be swept away in a sharp market downturn. Gossip swiftly circulated that other brokerage firms like McCuaig and Company of Montreal and Pellatt and Pellatt in Toronto were in trouble, but by mid-June Max Aitken was able to report from Montreal that 'the danger to these firms is for the moment over.'[13]

Gradually the recession lifted, and Aitken's plans for a public flotation of Trinidad Electric were finally set in motion. In the fall of 1903 he announced that Royal Securities had 'decided to carry on the business of buying and selling high grade investment securities such as government, municipal and corporation bonds, with special attention to steam and electric railway securities and first class industrial bonds.'[14] At the same time Aitken made contact with a transplanted Nova Scotian in Toronto who was to be vitally important to his success over the next few years. W.D. Ross (not to be confused with W.B. Ross, a director of Trinidad Electric) had spent twenty years with the Bank of Nova Scotia before moving to Ottawa as chief clerk of the federal finance department in 1901. In 1902 he was recruited as assistant general manager of A.E. Ames's Metropolitan Bank. When financial embarrassment forced the stockbroker to resign from the presidency of the bank in 1903, Ross was promoted to the general managership.[15] Aitken's links to the chief operating officer of this small, aggressive bank in Toronto, and through him to the city's business community, were to prove immensely valuable.

In September 1903 Aitken advised W.D. Ross of his plans to float a public issue of Trinidad Electric Company bonds. Royal Securities had on hand $100,000 par value worth of them and options on a like sum from those controlling the company.[16] Aitken busied himself collecting further options from the other bondholders of Trinidad Electric, offering to pay 95 per cent of par with the aim of selling at 97 before 1 July 1904 once the bonds had been listed for public trading on the Montreal Stock Exchange. His letter to one insider was typical:

As the bonds are held entirely in large blocks, and by persons who do not wish to retain them for permanent investment, we think it highly in the interests of the bondholders themselves, and in view of the prevailing prices of securities of this nature, that some systematicized effort should be made to place the bonds in the hands of permanent investors.

We are asking holders of bonds who do not desire to sell to not sell at less than par and accrued interest before the first of July, 1904.[17]

Aitken could, of course, point out that the bonds should be highly saleable, as the company was now earning enough to pay the 5 per cent interest on its entire authorized bond issue of $720,000 plus 7 per cent on the $1,032,000 of stock. He predicted that the company would begin to pay dividends on a 5 per cent annual basis from the fourth quarter of 1903. As a result many of the bondholders were only too happy to grant him the options requested, though some preferred to hold on and enjoy the income. Trading began on the Montreal exchange on the day before Christmas 1903.[18]

In preparation for this, Aitken endeavoured to arouse interest in Trinidad Electric by feeding titbits to the Toronto press through W.D. Ross. At the same time Aitken was careful to see that stockbrokers would have an opportunity for some return on this flotation:

I would just like to say that to make a successful culmination of this Trinidad venture we have to give a little profit to those brokers who make the market for us. If we don't have any support from the brokers, we cannot have purchasers to absorb that amount of stock which is offering for sale. If the market is over-supplied, and there is no protecting hand at work, and the stock once begins to fall, every broker on the Exchange will go short of it. Also if the upward progress of this stock is permitted to be too rapid, it must of necessity come down again, and the result is just as disastrous as if there was no upward tendency at all.[19]

Simultaneously Aitken was busy organizing a pool in the common stock of the corporation, urging the insiders to grant him options of their holdings at prices on a graded scale rising from 70 per cent to par, up to 1 July 1904. 'You will understand no doubt,' he wrote to industrialist D.W. Robb, 'that it is our intention to judiciously handle this security with a view to distributing it as much as possible in the hands of investors. We desire to avoid speculative holdings.' All the directors agreed to enter this pool and not to try to sell their stock outside it during the next six months.[20]

For its services as pool manager Royal Securities would claim a 1 per cent commission on all sales, one-quarter of which would be paid over to the stock exchange. Heavy though this charge might seem, Aitken defended it by arguing

that we will have to pay several commissions before we have safely landed the stock in the hands in which we desire to place it.

Also bear in mind that we are keeping the company well before the public in the newspapers, and that this cannot be brought about without considerable expense.[21]

The Trinidad Electric bond flotation went off very successfully. All the pooling agreements and options were put in place, and at a directors meeting in Halifax on 11 December 1903 a dividend of 5 per cent per annum was declared. The press took a gratifying interest in the new company, and the public proved eager to take on its securities.[22]

During 1904, therefore, while Max Aitken busied himself in organizing security flotations for such important regional industrial concerns in Atlantic Canada as Nova Scotia Steel and Coal and the Robb-Mumford Boiler Company, he also moved to reinforce the control that Royal Securities exercised over Trinidad Electric by obtaining more of the common stock from the company treasury. That autumn he signed an agreement with the board by which he agreed to pay off its $85,000 debt to the Union Bank and furnish $40,000 in cash as well as four additional trolleys and some other equipment. In exchange he would receive a small number of bonds plus common stock with a par value of $138,000, which he got at 60 per cent.[23]

When his own holdings were pooled with those optioned to Royal Securities, Aitken could control almost all the company's stock, and he immediately commenced negotiations to dispose of a block of $500,000 par value worth at prices ranging from $75 to $85. His friend Clarence J. McCuaig, the Montreal stockbroker, agreed to take on the task provided that Aitken would give him the stock on 10 per cent margin so that the smaller brokers might participate without having to put up much capital.[24] Meanwhile, Royal Securities continued to sell Trinidad Electric stock in Atlantic Canada, pushing out three thousand shares at 77\frac{1}{2}$ during November. Aitken could report with pride that, 'The market is getting broader for this stock all the time,' noting that $300,000 worth of the company's bonds had been disposed of altogether during 1904.[25]

In later years Max Aitken often looked back wistfully to this first successful utility promotion by Royal Securities. In the spring of 1905 he wrote to C.H. Cahan, 'I wish we could get some little proposition like Trinidad, and I feel very much like doing nothing else but looking for one, which I think would be better for Royal Securities than anything I could do here.' The corporation, he added, had many satisfied purchasers of Trinidad Electric securities 'who would gobble up anything new in quick shape.'[26]

II

There was the rub. Having built up this distribution network Aitken had to try to keep it furnished with new wares so as to hold his existing clientele and attract additional buyers. Even in a recession there were security-holders who wanted to change their portfolios, as well as others who had savings to invest if something attractive came along. Hence the importance of scouting out likely propositions for Royal Securities to develop. At the same time, though, an eye had to be kept upon past ventures to make sure that management was competent and that the bears on the stock exchanges did not decide to mount some sudden, disastrous raid that would mean a heavy price break.

His dealings with Clarence McCuaig in Montreal reflected Aitken's realization that the size of the underwritings in which Royal Securities was participating was rapidly outgrowing the demand of investors in Atlantic Canada for securities. He therefore began discussions with a Toronto stockbroker to form a partnership to acquire a seat on that city's exchange. That plan, however, was aborted by the untimely death of John Stairs in September 1904, which left Aitken with sole executive responsibility for the affairs of Royal Securities.[27]

The young man proved entirely equal to the task, and by the end of the year could write proudly: 'During the last three months it has become apparent that the corporation has built up a provincial clientele which will be most desirable in absorbing securities.' But it was also clear that Royal Securities should expand further in order to prosper, and the directors decided to increase its capitalization by issuing new stock when a good opportunity offered. Aitken told W.D. Ross, 'We do not feel that we need the money very much because our resources seem to be sufficient, but we are sometimes regarded as being a bit smaller than we really are, by the [Nova] Scotia [Steel and Coal] underwriters in Toronto for instance.' To provide the corporation with more presence in the nation's financial capital, Aitken moved to Montreal in 1905 to open an office there as the new managing director (at a salary of $4,000 per annum).[28]

The major problem was that the corporation had, for the moment, no proposition in hand nearly as attractive as Trinidad Electric. Not that Royal Securities did not continue to earn profits: in November 1905 the directors voted themselves a 100 per cent stock dividend, doubling the capitalization from $50,000 to $100,000.[29] But simply selling already-established issues or participating in underwritings arranged by others did not hold the same kind of promise as instigating one's own projects. Aitken advised C.H. Cahan, who had gone off to work on F.S. Pearson's big new venture in Mexico City, that he had been making money on the securities of the Canadian utility companies in Mexico and Brazil, buying and selling as the market rose and fell. What he needed, though, was a big deal: 'There is no profit in our making a local market and filling our own clients up. I wish you would get us something like Trinidad and come home again.'[30]

For an entire year, through the spring of 1906, Aitken investigated and discarded a whole series of propositions in Latin America. Indeed, he was constantly in touch with a roving band of entrepreneurs and engineers who were criss-crossing Latin America in search of prospects. Cuba was the first target. After all, Van Horne's Cuba Railroad and his interest in the Havana tramway made it familiar territory for Canadians, and the Royal Bank had been established there for several years. Halifax businessman B.F. Pearson visited Matanzas for Royal Securities in the spring of 1905 and arranged to have the US engineer H.P. Bruce go down and look over the city. A syndicate was organized including Aitken, B.F. Pearson, W.B. Ross, and R.E. Harris, and Aitken made plans for a visit accompanied by F.S. Pearson. In the end Pearson could not get away, and the project was consigned to the back burner for a while.[31]

Next Pernambuco in Brazil was scrutinized. The two Pearsons, B.F. and F.S., got together and discussed the idea. The tramway could be purchased and revamped for $2.5 million, or $4 million if the gas and the electric company were included. Insisting that his estimates were 'very conservative,' B.F. Pearson concluded that such a merger could earn a 5 per cent return on $4 million worth of bonds as well as 5 per cent on a like amount of common stock. Yet these returns were not generous enough to persuade him to put up $10,000 to secure an option on the properties. Instead, he sought a sixty-day option so that chief engineer F.W. Teele could be dispatched from Trinidad Electric to look over the situation in detail: 'this thing should not be neglected for a little trouble.'[32] Once again nothing seems to have come of this plan.

Finally, Aitken got enthusiastic about Barranquilla in Colombia. Advice was sought from the US minister to Venezuela (who had just been transferred from Colombia) as to what he would advise in view of the fact that 'Of course, Colombia is recognized as a revolutionary country of the first class.' Would the government be prepared to abrogate the existing franchise, which still had thirty years to run or make a similar concession to a competing concern? Again arrangements were made to send somebody to look at the situation first hand from a legal and engineering point of view.[33]

Aitken's way of handling this venture also indicated that he and his associates had been paying careful attention to the Brazilian enterprises. In imitation of what had been done in the case of Rio de Janeiro Tramway, Aitken prepared to add another rung to the corporate ladder by setting up a holding company, controlled by the insiders, that would acquire the properties and in exchange receive the securities of the operating company, thus permitting an additional round of profit taking. 'The basis of proceeding,' wrote Aitken to W.D. Ross in Toronto,

is similar in many respects to the Rio mode of procedure. The entire proposition will probably necessitate the expenditure of $2,000,000 roughly. A first issue of $1,000,000 of bonds with 100 per cent stock will be made to the Colombian Securities [Corporation], who [sic] will have the right to take up the second million dollars of stock [i.e., bonds] with 100% [of bonus stock] and sell on the best basis possible, making what profit it can.[34]

Matters proceeded slowly, however, and it was not until October that the syndicate's legal scout, A.K. McLean, reported from Barranquilla. Apparently the local parties with whom the syndicate was dealing had misrepresented their position; they did not possess an option on the tramway, which had been sold a few days before McLean's arrival. Worse still, yellow fever broke out at that moment, and McLean found it difficult to escape from the city with a clean bill of health. All in all he formed a decidedly unfavourable impression of both city and country, and he advised against any thought of seeking a concession in Bogota: 'It's a dead city at present.' Far better to consider Caracas, which was 'much like an American city.' McLean's report was sufficient to induce the syndicate to drop its interest in Colombia and to rule out a project in Panama, which he also visited on the way home to Canada.[35]

As one after another of these propositions failed to pan out, Max Aitken's need for a promising venture, any venture, intensified. In the end he could hit upon nothing except a scheme to take control of the Demerara Electric Company, the first of the Halifax ventures, and reorganize it. The firm had always suffered from problems because its thermal power station with reciprocating engine, located right in the city of Georgetown, had aroused complaints from neighbouring property owners about severe vibration. Eventually the neighbours sued and the local courts found in their favour. By 1905 the property was in dilapidated condition, and the company needed to raise a substantial sum of money to refurbish it. One of the original investors, iron and steel tycoon George Drummond, even grumbled, 'We should not be in these foreign enterprises. There are enough good things in Canada.' R.E. Harris, Aitken's partner in Royal Securities, reported that, 'the Montreal crowd were pretty sick of Demerara, and that it should not be hard to make a dicker with some of them, perhaps to buy out the whole business.'[36]

Such a deal was what Aitken was seeking, if he could buy up the stock at bargain prices, rebuild the plant, and turn it into a profitable undertaking, in the process impressing the élite of Montreal financiers – Drummond and Van Horne, for example. By doing so, the feelers he was already discreetly putting out to such men as the Bank of Montreal's Clouston about investing large sums in Royal Securities might get a favourable response. With that sort of backing he would be on his way to a leading position in the Canadian financial world, well before the age of thirty. Because his relations with R.E. Harris had become strained after Royal Securities opened up in Montreal, Aitken was all the more eager to carve out an independent position in Quebec, freed from the influence of his original backers in Halifax.[37]

Max Aitken failed to persuade Clouston to buy into Royal Securities, but Canada's leading banker did listen intently to the other proposition presented by the 'little fellow with the big head.' By mid-October Aitken had convinced Clouston and Van Horne, as well as the original promoters of the Demerara enterprise, Hutchinson and Chapman, to sell two-thirds of their shares to him at only $12 each. Meanwhile, Aitken agreed to take on from Demerara Electric $100,000 par value each of new 6 per cent second mortgage bonds at 60 per cent, the money to be used to reconstruct the plant. Engineer Fred Teele would travel from Trinidad to oversee the reconstruction of the plant in order to restore profitability. Ultimately Aitken was able to acquire about four thousand shares (or half the total) at a cost of around $50,000 (or 25 per cent of par). This stock and the new bonds would be formally held by Dominion Trust, a paper concern controlled by Aitken, Clouston, Van Horne, and the Halifax insiders who had put up the money to buy the shares. If Teele could put the plant in Demerara on a sound basis and start to pay dividends on the common stock, the syndicate stood to make a small killing.[38]

In structuring this deal Aitken displayed his customary skill and adroitness; he also revealed a cunning desire to garner extra profits for himself by not telling certain people what they were entitled to know. Since he controlled a majority of shares through Dominion Trust he could compel the board of Demerara Electric to do his bidding if he wished. But since engineer Teele was loyal to him personally rather than to the management,

Aitken was able to conceal certain things from the board. Almost his first act was to order Teele to communicate vital information to him alone rather than through the corporate secretary, F.H. Oxley.

In particular Aitken was determined to hide from the board the precise cost of the repairs and reconstruction required. The Demerara company had already commissioned a report from US consulting engineer H.P. Bruce, who found that $60,000 would be needed to put the plant in proper shape; hence the size of the second mortgage bond issue. But Aitken was convinced that Bruce had been far too pessimistic and that Teele could do the job for much less, using the $12,000 already in the treasury plus current earnings, combined with rigorous cost-cutting. 'Don't make any estimate of probable money required to re-equip Demerara except to me,' he warned Teele. 'I don't want Directors to get to [know?] that it will cost less than $60,000. This might result in a reduction of the issued 2nd Mortgage Bonds and a consequent loss of profit to the holding company.'[39] If the company could soon start to earn its bond interest and pay a 3 per cent dividend on the stock, he wrote to Teele with endearing candour,

then we can take this stuff up to the last notch. But you and I do not want to burden ourselves with slow stuff. It is all right to go in a little bit, but do not let us get too much. On the other hand if this is going to be good stuff and if our chance looks well [sic], then let us dip in deeply and make a decent profit.[40]

At the same time Aitken was determined to conceal from his principal backers, especially from the most influential of them, Clouston and Van Horne, any bad news that might make them nervous. When Teele reached Georgetown he found the powerplant on its last legs, the brick in the boilers going, the water feed pipe 'a wreck,' the suction pipe 'an example of some of the remarkable feats of engineering I have run across.' Though the overhead work looked all right, the cars needed overhauling and the most heavily travelled tracks re-laying. Teele pitched in to rebuild the generators and soon reduced coal needs by a ton and a half per day at a saving of $10 per day. At the same time he cut back car service and remodelled the office system along the lines used by Trinidad Electric. Yet he had to admit that the local economy was depressed, with sugar prices down and much poverty evident in Georgetown. 'Let me know frankly,' Teele asked Aitken, 'whether you wish optimistic or pessimistic reports regarding Demerara.'[41]

Aitken ordered him to be neither positive or negative in his reports to Oxley until he received instructions that the opportune moment had arrived and also warned him to make no extensions to the system unless this seemed the only key to profitability. Aitken was particularly worried that he might have to go to the board and reveal the low earnings to persuade them to permit additional investment. In the case of Clouston and Van Horne he preferred to be the sole conduit of information concerning the company. He personally delivered a progress report to Edward Clouston at the Bank of Montreal, having first excised all the references to Teele's reports to the company secretary, Oxley, so that the banker would not ask to see them. To Aitken's mind Clouston's support was vital; Clouston had told the younger man that he did not believe the Demerara enterprise could be turned into a profitable concern (though he admitted that Aitken could do it if anyone could). Clouston had agreed against his better judgment to leave his money in the venture only on account of Max Aitken's persuasiveness. Putting the company on a basis where it could earn a 3 per cent dividend could mean much to Aitken's future: 'If we succeed in this Demerara undertaking there will never be any proposition which we bring out that Mr. Clouston will not back,' he exhorted Teele.[42]

Likewise he hastened to pass on to Van Horne the news that Teele's rerouting and repairs had reduced expenses by $15 per day. If the great railway builder were sufficiently impressed he might easily be induced to join another syndicate headed by Aitken, perhaps to build tramways in Guatemala or Panama, about the future of which Van Horne was optimistic. While Clouston hung back, dourly refusing to commit money to any other venture unless Georgetown was a success, Van Horne was keen to see Aitken press ahead in Latin America.[43]

Even the insiders at Royal Securities had their doubts about whether Aitken could make a go of Demerara Electric. W.B. Ross 'only consented to take the property over because he thought it would be advantageous to the West India [Electric Company] situation.'[44] In the long run these gloomy views proved accurate. Teele did manage to get the company earning the bond interest plus 2 per cent on the common stock by the end of 1905, but he was unable to increase the rate of return beyond that level.[45] Van Horne pronounced the early results not bad considering everything, but as the months passed there was no further improvement. In the spring of 1906 Teele tried to put the best face on the situation in British Guiana: 'It is exceedingly unfortunate that they are having such a financial depression just as we have taken over the company, but the fact that we are making a showing even under these conditions should be very encouraging to those who have backed us.' Yet by the fall he was forced to report that to the economic difficulties there had now been added political unrest. With an election at hand some of the 'coloured lawyers' in Georgetown had sought to

raise the Race Question, which would certainly result in trouble, but the Government is acting very firmly, and I hope none will occur. The cruiser *Indefatigable* is in port and will remain until the elections are over, and its presence will have a most restraining effect on the rowdy element. I only wish it would remain permanently.[46]

Things went from bad to worse in the spring of 1907 when the Judicial Committee of the Privy Council sustained the verdict of the lower courts against the company in the suit for damages caused by vibration from its generator. Although Aitken was soothing to Van Horne, telling him that things were going well, in private he was urging Teele to seek relief from liability for the vibration damage from the legislature, or at least to secure a waiver of further damages should the vibration continue once the company installed new equipment.[47]

By the fall of 1907 it had become clear that Demerara Electric needed to raise $25,000 in order to finance the purchase of a new turbine to end the vibration. In a market made increasingly soft by the onset of a serious recession, Aitken laboured to sell the company's second mortgage bonds to raise the funds. A Royal Securities' salesman reported from Wolfville, Nova Scotia, however, that one Halifax broker had informed several likely prospects that Demerara seconds were 'no good.' Efforts to discover which brokerage house was being so bearish about the bonds were unsuccessful, 'but the advice seems to have been quite emphatic.'[48]

The government of British Guiana also applied pressure by threatening to amend Demerara Electric's franchise to require it to install new equipment to end the vibration. Privately, Teele admitted that the company lacked the financial resources to move the plant out of the city altogether. To prevent more drastic action, he proposed that the capital stock be reduced by half, from $850,000 to $425,000. This would wring out some of the water and make the securities more attractive to investors, since the dividend could then be increased from 2 per cent to 4 per cent.[49]

Even before the reduction in the size of the capital stock was formally approved, however, the earnings of Demerara Electric began to improve. New equipment made possible more economical operation, and the end of the recession improved business. By 1909 the company was covering its bond interest and earning over 6 per cent on the par value of its common shares. This, of course, represented a much higher percentage for the insiders, who had acquired them for an average of $25 per share in 1905. As a result the holding company, Dominion Trust, was able to pay Aitken and his associates a 6 per cent dividend in 1907 and 1908. By 1909 the trust company was in a position to meet that dividend without any earnings drawn from Demerara Electric, and Aitken was offering to exchange its stock at par for that of Dominion Trust. In view of the success of the promotion the shareholders unanimously endorsed the long-promised reduction in the capital stock in April 1909.[50]

Thus despite a rocky start, Max Aitken was able to carry the reorganization of Demerara Electric to a successful conclusion. Naturally, those on the inside reaped the largest returns, Aitken the handsomest of all. His achievement helped to win him the admiration of financial leaders who remained blissfully unaware of the guile with which he had manipulated them. By that time, however, he had many more strings to his bow, with several other highly successful promotions nearing completion.

III

Aitken had, of course, taken up the reorganization of Demerara Electric in the fall of 1905 largely because he could find nothing of a size and type that suited him elsewhere. As soon as that venture was under way he wrote to W.P. Plummer, F.S. Pearson's chief assistant, to advise him that, 'Demerara financing is all over now and our people would be in good shape for a nice little new proposition. It would need to be "little".' He even contemplated sending an agent to western Canada to look at a land deal, reasoning that, 'If he cannot get lands, he can probably get some small electric light franchises with perhaps some water works contracts in growing towns.'[51]

W.P. Plummer was, in fact, the man who steered what seemed a highly promising prospect in Aitken's direction at the beginning of 1906. Ecuadorian diplomat Luis A. Carbo had appeared in Pearson's office seeking a developer for the tramway in Quito; the project would cost about $500,000, and Carbo wanted one-fifth of the stock in a new company plus $30,000 in cash for the rights he already held. Plummer concluded that the deal was too small to interest Pearson, but recollected Aitken's recent letter and directed Carbo to him in Montreal.[52]

After intensive discussions Aitken was highly attracted to the proposal.

Carbo already had in hand a recent engineering study that showed the scheme to be quite feasible, and he made much of the political stability of Ecuador. The last revolutionary uprising had been in 1887, and Carbo contended that his country was a better bet than Mexico, since 'the Government is more stable, and the amount of foreign capital invested proportionately larger. Foreign capital has never been disturbed, and Ecuador has never had a quarrel with her foreign investors.' Aitken was convinced that the deal would be very profitable if he could find twenty underwriters to put up $25,000 each; this would permit him to build the system and begin earning the bond interest before marketing the securities. As the originator, Royal Securities would be entitled to a generous stock bonus even if it took only a small share in the underwriting.[53]

Aitken thought the Quito proposition would be even better than the Trinidad one had been. Moreover, the proposal was well suited to the financial capacity of Royal Securities, which could handle any project costing up to $600,000 or perhaps $1 million. 'We can only go into one thing at a time,' he wrote to another engineering firm that had investigated Ecuador previously; 'therefore, when we do get loaded up we want to have the very best thing going.'[54]

The deal seemed all set to go when suddenly there came the news that a revolution had broken out in Ecuador. 'I think somebody must be on my trail and incite these countries to revolution as soon as we think of putting some money in,' wrote Aitken to Teele. 'It is a curious coincidence that the Colombia experience should be repeated in this case.'[55]

Proudly surveying Royal Securities' new offices in Montreal, Aitken confided to C.H. Cahan, far off in Mexico:

The year 1906 looks very promising; the staff is getting very large in Halifax and very expensive, too, in the way of salaries, consequently our profits must grow accordingly. Unfortunately, we have not got anything on hand at the present time and I hope something will come up before long.

Aitken could think of nothing except a renewed appeal to the helpful Plummer:

I ... trust that if any proposition on the east coast of South America comes before you, that you will communicate with me. I would like you to bear in mind that propositions slightly larger than Trinidad would not be too big for us. In the meantime, if you are undertaking anything new in your office, I would very much like to be communicated with in reference to underwriting.[56]

With the need for some more attractive merchandise for his burgeoning distribution organization looming ever larger, Aitken decided at long last to carry out his oft-repeated pledge to travel to the Caribbean – on his honeymoon – to examine the situation at first hand. 'This climate is too cold in the winter,' he had written to Teele a month earlier, 'and I want to see some of those places where all my money is invested.' In February 1906 he and Teele toured Cuba in search of prospects. While there they encountered a number of fellow Canadians, including two prominent Halifax businessmen, entrepreneur John Y. Payzant and banker William Robertson. Also on the scene was Montreal utility man Herbert Holt, although 'he seemed to be inclined to criticize and make fun of anything Cuban.'[57] Aitken did not share this view and, from the first port of call, Matanzas, reported that, apart from occasional outbreaks of yellow fever, local prosperity was most impressive: 'Except for the buildings, Cuba will compare favourably with Canada in every respect barring morals.'[58]

The first proposition to which Aitken gave serious consideration was a tramway and lighting scheme for Santiago de Cuba, the southeastern terminus of Van Horne's Cuba Railroad. Teele reported favourably upon the plan, but negotiations with the local owners failed. Once again it seemed as though Royal Securities would be left without any desirable new utility offering to dangle before its clients. All that Aitken had on the table was an underwriting for the Brandram-Henderson Paint Company, which his friends in the securities business found of little interest.

But help was at hand, help that came through the well-established commercial connections of the Canadian banking system throughout the Caribbean. While in Cuba Aitken and Teele had made a flying visit to the city of Camagüey, the headquarters for Van Horne's railway, pausing only for a quick look at the local generating plant. A few days later, however, the manager of the Camagüey branch of the Royal Bank of Canada put Aitken in touch with a local businessman, Roberto A. Betancourt, who was seeking financing for a tramway and hydroelectric development there.[59]

Betancourt was one of the three owners of the Puerto Principe Electric Company, which owned the modern thermal generating plant in Camagüey, a solid concern that was earning a net profit of more than $30,000 for the current year, up substantially from the year before.[60] Betancourt had been discussing a refinancing with US interests when the Canadians arrived on the scene, but he was prepared to deliver control of his company for $300,000. What made the deal more attractive was that it also included a defunct muletram franchise, abandoned at the time of the Spanish-

American War, that might be revived and extended to permit construction of a trolley system.

In addition, there were profits to be earned through a real estate venture. On a visit to the city in April 1906, Aitken picked up an 81-hectare site that could be combined with a slightly larger area already controlled by Betancourt. Altogether the company would own about 174 hectares situated between the city proper and Van Horne's carshops, land that could be subdivided into building lots. This made the outlook especially juicy, as Aitken enthusiastically advised C.H. Cahan:

I have a Camagüey proposition in view which is in its present position a much better one than Santiago. The city is not as large as Santiago, although it has ultimately much better prospects. However, by incorporating a land trade in the proposition, we have made a pretty good thing. I think without the land trade it would be as good as Trinidad, but with the land trade I think it is much better.[61]

Aitken set about organizing an underwriting syndicate composed of the usual Royal Securities insiders to raise the necessary funds, touting the 'tremendous possibilities which exist in this real estate.' He decided upon a bond issue of $600,000 par value with $700,000 worth of common stock. The 'guarantors' agreed to take the bonds at par with a 100 per cent stock bonus, on the understanding that the bonds would be issued for sale at par with a 50 per cent bonus.[62] Aitken also received an extra $100,000 worth of bonus stock, $15,000 of which went to Betancourt, $20,000 to the manager of the Royal Bank in Camagüey and $10,000 to the superintendent of the bank in Havana for having steered the business their way. 'The rest I take for R[oyal] S[ecurities] Corporation & for general uses,' he wrote to Cahan.[63]

The initial distribution was reasonably successful, as $100,000 worth of bonds were sold immediately, leaving the underwriters to take up the remaining $250,000 at the rate of 10 per cent a month from June 1906. They were well rewarded, however, since they shared $175,000 par value worth of bonus stock for their risk.[64] Aitken's main problem was finding enough securities to go around among the insiders. Although realizing the importance of Van Horne's goodwill and support, he complained, 'I am sorry that I am committed to hold a block of the stuff for Sir William Van Horne, because it ties everything up, and makes it very hard for me to get small blocks back again for other people.' He added, 'I am very anxious to give [B.F.] Pearson a little, but do not know where in the world I am going to get it.' Doubtless, therefore, it was something of a relief when Van Horne withdrew from the syndicate at the last moment, pleading too many other demands for his funds at that particular time.[65] Aitken must surely have taken pride in the fact that he was getting along quite well now without the patronage of great men.

He certainly convinced himself that this was one enterprise that could hardly fail. As he told F.W. Teele, 'Our position is perfectly good, because we have our Electric Light Company already earning $30,000 and likely to earn $35,000 for the year ending June 30, 1907, so it really does not make much difference to us whether we get the tram franchise or not.' When Betancourt wired in mid-September to say the concession was all signed, sealed, and delivered, that merely added the icing to the cake.[66]

After the dry spell caused by the lack of good prospects to offer his clients Aitken was determined to redouble his efforts to sniff out all the most promising situations throughout the Caribbean as systematically as possible. While putting the Camagüey underwriting in final shape he had written to C.H. Cahan in Mexico City to suggest that once that was out of the way,

I would like to immediately send a young Cuban, now in Sir William Van Horne's company at Camagüey, to Mexico. I would like him to travel to all the small cities where there are at present mule or horse tramways, and send us reports according to a schedule which we would prepare for him beforehand. When he could find a good place to exploit, I would like to arrange for sending down the proper person to negotiate, if in their opinion the situation was as good as my young Cuban reported ... Can you give me any information which would be valuable in directing the itinerary of my young agent?[67]

By such means Aitken hoped to come up with a continuous series of highly desirable promotions. He had become convinced that the time had come to give up the flotation of industrials in Canada and to commit Royal Securities to specializing in Latin American utilities. As he confided to another Nova Scotia financier in the fall of 1906: 'I prefer to confine my operations to Public Utilities and undertakings of greater certainty than industrials.'[68]

From these Caribbean promotions and trips to Cuba Max Aitken derived his lifelong passion for calypso music, daiquiris (he kept a cocktail blender at hand in each of his several houses), and movies – though in the first instance his interest in films was more commercial than critical. At Camagüey he rigged up a hut out at the end of an unproductive tram line, developed a park around it, then installed a movie projector – all to lure patrons onto his under-utilized street railway.[69]

What distinguished the undertakings in which Aitken was involved from the Canadian utility promotions in Brazil and Mexico was chiefly their size. All his utility undertakings were comparatively small promotions, each involving a total investment of less than $5 million, which reflected the limitations of the promoters' access to capital. While these same men might take a share in underwriting the Rio Tramway or the Mexican Light and Power companies, their capacity to raise money was measured in hundreds of thousands rather than tens of millions. Thus Aitken and his associates had to search particularly assiduously through Latin America and the Caribbean, a region with which they already possessed some familiarity, to find smaller but promising prospects that might net a healthy return.

Max Aitken's extravagant promises sometimes made for harrowing times for the promoter (he complained constantly of the strain) and absolute hell for his underlings. There was little margin for error. The bushes had to be beaten for every likely prospect, for at any and every moment the whole house of cards threatened to come tumbling down. Aitken worked closer to the edge than most people; he used people mercilessly, and the future press lord took a proprietorial and manipulative approach to information. But in good times he enjoyed great success. On the strength of these early Caribbean utility promotions Max Aitken turned Royal Securities into a 'tremendous money spinner,' a phrase that might equally appropriately have been applied to himself.[70]

7

Making a Market

The Canadian capital market before the First World War was both narrow and volatile, afflicted with barriers that impeded the flow of funds from one part of the country to another and from one industrial sector to another. Promoters like Max Aitken had to manufacture a market for their securities by manipulating prices with one hand while beating the bushes for buyers with the other.

Speculative buyers in the banking halls and brokerage offices across Canada might eagerly take a security on margin with borrowed funds for a short time, but they disliked having to put up their personal money to own it outright. They looked to interest and dividends only to pay for their borrowings; they hoped to profit from capital gains. At the slightest sign of bad news they might unload a stock, or worse, organize a bear raid against it. In times of recession the banks were quick to call in loans, and speculators might find themselves unable to meet underwriting instalments that fell due while the securities were still in distribution. At the best of times a few hundred shares dumped on the Montreal or Toronto stock exchanges might break prices sharply.

Part of a successful underwriting was, therefore, 'making a market' for a new issue until the 'stuff' (as it was universally referred to) was reasonably safely lodged and the enterprise on a sound enough earning basis to keep it there. Manipulating prices was one side of making a market; the other was simply thumping the salesman's drum for untried companies in order to convince investors to put up some money. Prejudices (against enterprises operating overseas, for instance) and uncertainties (about the soundness of new industries, for example) had to be overcome. All manner of men fanned out across the Canadian countryside in the years before the First World War seeking buyers for securities. One Royal Securities salesman reported to Max Aitken in the summer of 1908 from the southwestern tip of Nova Scotia that 'the Coast has been infested with Investment men.' On another occasion the same man reported from Wolfville, 'There is a Baptist parson in town from Toronto pushing Sewer Pipe and other securities.'[1]

Making a market entailed risks. A promising promotion might begin to go sour on account of unanticipated expenses, governmental obstruction or unexpected competition. Having to raise additional capital before a solid earnings record had been established aroused suspicion among investors. In a recession, which frightened investors and tightened credit, promoters had to carry the unsold securities themselves or go under. The trials and tribulations of Max Aitken – greatly magnified by his contumelious style – serve to illustrate the difficulties of company promotion in the narrow and skittish Canadian market.

I

After his success with the tramway at Camagüey in Cuba in early 1906, Max Aitken had big ambitions for the future but no really good propositions. During this lull he took to nursing his grievances against his associates in the Royal Securities Corporation. In particular, he complained that R.E. Harris was trying to take too large a share of the underwriting profits for himself personally, leaving too little for the company, and, of course, for Max. This would become a recurring refrain.[2] His salary was too low and Harris and George Stairs (who had replaced his kinsman, John, upon John's death) treated him with indifference. The authorized capital of Royal Securities ought to be doubled, Aitken claimed, so that he need no longer scramble around to secure cover for liabilities of more than $1 million on a day-to-day basis. He held a trump that he hoped would force his backers to pay attention to him: J.G. White and Company, a New York firm of utility engineers and promoters, was ready to offer him a job with a hefty salary increase. 'It would be better for me,' he wrote to W.D. Ross, 'to accept the biggest salary I could get outside and begin to feather my own nest a little bit, rather than look after profits for other people all my life.'[3]

On a visit to New York to negotiate with the White firm, however, his mood shifted dramatically. He learned of a deal so desirable that he became convinced that Royal Securities would be crazy not to take it up. His many grievances against his colleagues dissolved in a frenetic campaign to enlist their support in capitalizing the opportunity.

Canadians had established some commercial contacts with the island of Puerto Rico during the nineteenth century, and the Union Bank of Halifax had opened a branch there during the Spanish regime.[4] When the United States took over after the war with Spain, it at first refused to grant any new franchises for utilities and other services. But at long last, however, opportunities began to present themselves. In partnership with a local entrepreneur, Ramón Valdés, J.G. White and Company had already purchased all the outstanding bonds of the Porto [sic] Rico Power and Light Company supplying electricity in San Juan; they were prepared to let Aitken in on this deal on highly favourable terms.[5]

The White people proposed to float a new enterprise to acquire the San Juan Light and Transit Company (which operated the trams) and to develop a hydroelectric site outside the city. Valdés and his US associates were prepared to surrender the interest they had already acquired in the lighting company in exchange for shares in the new enterprise, on the understanding that J.G. White and Company would receive the contract for the engineering and construction of the tramway and power station and would ultimately manage the system in return for 5 per cent of net earnings. Here was a promotion of the sort that F.S. Pearson had carried out so successfully in São Paulo. In fact, Pearson had already examined this Puerto Rican proposition but had rejected it as being too small. Although it was considerably larger than anything Royal Securities had previously attempted to underwrite, Aitken was convinced that Canadian buyers could absorb these securities. George Stairs, who was well informed owing to the large trade Halifax conducted with the region, confirmed Aitken's view that 'Great profits can be made out of this.'

Aitken's enthusiasm was sufficient to convince the backers of Royal Securities (Stairs, R.E. Harris, W.B. Ross), along with W.D. Ross's Metropolitan Bank, to take up the project.[6] The plan was to incorporate a Canadian company called Porto [sic] Rico Railways, and to underwrite an initial issue of $650,000 worth of bonds at 90 per cent with a 100 per cent stock bonus to provide the money to purchase the electric company and secure control of the existing tramway. A.E. Ames and Company agreed to manage a pool in the securities, taking them from the underwriters at 90 per cent with a 60 per cent stock bonus and selling them to the public ('putting the stuff out,' in Aitken's words) at $92.50 with a 50 per cent stock bonus.[7]

At the same time Porto Rico Railways also issued $220,000 worth of bonus stock to the insiders, $30,000 of which went to Aitken personally for arranging the deal, the rest being divided among the pool members – Royal Securities, Ames, and the Metropolitan Bank – in proportion to their shares of the bond issue. Meanwhile, Aitken sought to ensure himself an additional personal profit by buying up a piece of land in San Juan in partnership with W.D. Ross in the hope of duplicating his coup in Camagüey.[8] B.G. Burrill, the Halifax manager of Royal Securities, reported that, by mid-September, $186,000 worth of bonds had been sold to such luminaries as Premier George Murray, provincial Supreme Court justice J.W. Longley, and Union Bank general manager E.L. Thorne, attesting to the high regard in which the venture was held. By the fall of 1906 Aitken was boasting to an acquaintance in New York that the issue had been 'largely oversubscribed,' and he told an English stockbroker that 'we could easily have sold another half million.'[9]

When Aitken visited San Juan in company with A.E. Ames and W.D. Ross he came away even more impressed with future prospects. The city was situated on a narrow peninsula, and many residents came to work from inland on the trams. The construction of a hydroelectric plant at the forty-nine-metre-high waterfall at Comerio, twenty-five kilometres away, would provide an excellent supply of low-cost energy. This, in turn, would open the way for the construction of an interurban line to Caguas that should generate a lot of traffic. Once the whole system had been revamped, operating costs could be cut to 35 or 40 per cent of gross, which would mean very healthy earnings to pay dividends on the common stock. All in all, as the various parts of the deal fell into place in the late fall, it looked as though making a market in Porto Rico Railways was going to be a cinch.[10]

Avarice got the better of the promoters. Even before work had fully commenced on phase one in the fall of 1906 the decision had been taken to extend the tramway from the terminus at Río Piedras to Caguas, since a contract had been signed to carry tobacco on this route. Work would also be started on the hydroelectric development. Although this would necessitate a further sale of securities with a par value of between $500,000 and $800,000, Aitken was eager to go ahead at once because Royal Securities had an option to acquire this entire issue.[11] Counting upon the enthusiasm that investors had displayed for the earlier offering, he anticipated a quick and handsome profit from this underwriting. What he could not foresee was that a recession lay just over the horizon; the failure of the Ontario Bank that very month was a portent.[12]

Early in 1907 Aitken visited both Cuba and Puerto Rico, squiring some of the Torontonians most heavily interested in the San Juan venture. 'I dare not let these people go down without a guide or guardian, lest, owing to adverse tropical conditions they do not get a proper appreciation of the undertaking there,' Max explained to George Stairs back in Halifax. 'I fear it is out of the question to let them go alone [as] they might get attacks of palm fever or bad butter for breakfast, and come back with a pessimistic opinion of the Porto Rico Railways undertaking. As they are our best bond buyers I cannot take any chances.'[13]

Just before he left the arrangements were completed for the second issue of the company's bonds with a par value of $800,000, underwritten by George Stairs, D.E. Thomson, W.N. Tilley, S.J. Moore and J.G. White and Company. As previously, they agreed to take up the bonds at 90 per cent with a 100 per cent stock bonus, but Royal Securities was to receive 10 per cent of this stock as its fee for arranging the deal. The selling syndicate was again headed by A.E. Ames, although the Halifax brokerage firm of J.C. Mackintosh and Company was also admitted, to improve the prospects for retail distribution.[14]

By early 1907, however, a sharp recession had suddenly changed the climate of enterprise. Not long before the Porto Rico underwriting agreements were signed, Halifax stockbroker F.B. McCurdy observed: 'Money is tight as a drum here – no new loans and many old ones are being called. Brokers are as a rule buying only for cash.' That spring Aitken ordered his Halifax manager, Burrill, to be 'absolutely ruthless' in collecting debts and to assume 'an absolutely stony heart to everybody.'[15] Max Aitken would now have to make a market in Porto Rico Railways in the worst of times.

By early May he was bemoaning the way 'the demoralization of the market has affected the Royal Securities Corporation's sales ... I have never known our customers to be affected by Stock Exchange declines before; it would seem as though universal pessimism has affected the market.'[16] Reports from the sales force of Royal Securities only confirmed these fears. J.S. Harding advised that, in Saint John, 'The branch banks here are holding up their customers pretty severely, and it is felt very much by businessmen and investors.' After spending two days in St Stephen, New Brunswick, in June and interviewing a dozen prospects, he made not a single sale, as 'they all appear to be invested up to the hilt ... It is an entirely different proposition to sell securities now from what it has been for the past ten years.'[17]

Always quick to blame his difficulties on others and to feel that his efforts were undervalued by his associates, Aitken wrote to A.E. Ames at the end of May 1907 to demand a list of all subscribers to the first issue of Porto Rico bonds who had not paid up their instalments on 1 May. If they did not come through by 15 June, he threatened, he would sell them out:

For five years I have struggled under financial burdens in Nova Scotia and have always had all my associates turn a deaf ear to my appeals for money. Then, when the shoe would pinch, they would let me go out and borrow from banks. Hereafter, they have got to borrow, and if they don't I am going to sell their stuff.[18]

No more than an idle threat, of course, since all the insiders realized that such a forced sale would only induce a severe price break and make the task of financing the Porto Rico project all the more difficult, but whining seemed to produce psychic satisfaction for Max Aitken. In truth he was in a tight spot, caught between contractors in New York demanding their payments on time and underwriters in Canada who could not meet their obligations.

The need for funds was made all the more acute by the fact that J.G. White and Company were incurring substantial cost overruns on construction in Puerto Rico. The extension of the tramline from Río Piedras to Caguas was requiring $37,000 per kilometre or double the estimates, while the Comerio hydroelectric plant would exceed its planned cost by several hundred thousand dollars. Together these projects would require the raising of an additional $500,000. Max Aitken became so angry about this that, early in September 1907, he submitted his resignation as vice-president of Porto Rico Railways, declaring that he had too many opportunities available to waste his time sweating blood on San Juan and getting nothing except abuse from the engineers in New York about the lack of funds.[19]

His Canadian associates were not prepared to let him off the hook so easily. W.D. Ross of the Metropolitan Bank observed: 'as far as the Canadian interests are concerned the Porto Rico proposition is yours. You conceived it; you promoted it and up to date you have financed it, and whether you make a dollar out of it or not, having put your hand to the plough I cannot see how in justice to yourself you dare turn back.'[20]

Thus bluntly faced with his responsibilities Aitken reopened negotiations with the contractors, offering to raise the additional money needed if J.G. White and Company would agree to surrender its construction agreement voluntarily. He hoped to force White's hand by refusing to arrange an additional bond issue otherwise, perhaps saving up to $150,000 by renegotation and reducing expenditure by deferring the electrification of the tram system for up to two years.[21] The new plan was to build a narrow-gauge steam line to Caguas to fulfil the tobacco-freighting contract, but this, in turn, necessitated modifications to the franchise.[22]

Unfortunately some territorial officials, notably the nominee for treasurer, were markedly unsympathetic to this request, and all that the Canadians could do was to exert their influence with the Taft administration in Washington to try to block the nominee's confirmation and have him recalled: 'It will be a salutary lesson to the rest and we can get what we want with him away.'[23] Eventually J.G. White personally lobbied President Taft's secretary to have him approve the recommended franchise changes, warning that otherwise the Canadians were threatening to close down the system altogether. Aitken could only hope that this would do the trick and 'result in our path being strewn with roses.'[24]

The dispute with J.G. White and Company proved difficult and time-consuming to settle. The engineers refused to accede to Aitken's demand for a guarantee that future construction costs would stay within their estimates. In retaliation Aitken began holding back $47,500 from the monthly instalments he was forwarding to them from the underwriters and from the proceeds of bond sales. White's contract to operate the tramway was cancelled as of 31 December 1907, but not until the summer of 1908 was a compromise reached on a settlement that satisfied both sides.[25]

II

By that time panic had gripped North American stock markets. Aitken himself was present in New York in October 1907 when a run developed on the Trust Company of America, stemmed only when J.P. Morgan gave the agitated depositors his personal assurances that they would be paid off.[26] Rumours of failures gusted through the tiny Canadian financial community. Aitken reported the rumour that Henry Pellatt's Toronto brokerage house had failed, adding boastfully that Royal Securities 'has plenty of money, few liabilities and [an] optimistic state of mind.' This was hardly the news he was giving to his partner in the corporation, R.E. Harris: 'We have no money for Camaguey, our Porto Rico money is all spent; we will require $25,000 for Demerara. The Royal Bank of Canada is calling loans and no bank in Canada will advance a dollar ... We are hard pressed and financial matters loom largely in my view.' To protect the firm he concluded that it should 'not buy any more Municipal Bonds whatsoever, but confine itself solely to dealing in Public Utilities and other issues on which we make a stock profit.'[27]

When the market turned sour, the promoters fell upon each other. During the autumn of 1907, as Aitken wrangled with J.G. White and Company over the cost overruns, he persistently blamed his associates for failing to do their share. 'What is the matter with the Toronto deadbeats?' he asked D.E. Thomson. 'They are all the time keeping our prices down, and if it was not for the overloaded high financiers of Toronto, the Montreal market would be selling ten points higher.' Not surprisingly Ames resented these slurs, pointing out that Aitken had rushed into the second issue of Porto Rico bonds to finance the Caguas extension, notwithstanding an agreement that they would await a favourable moment before going to market again.[28]

Despite the gloomy outlook, the imperative need to raise more funds to complete the Porto Rico project convinced Aitken that they would have to make another flotation. Rejecting Ames's suggestion that they seek to place some two-year notes with New York brokers in the hopes that times would improve, he decided that another $500,000 worth of bonds should be issued at once.[29] The Torontonians (W.D. Ross's Metropolitan Bank and D.E. Thomson for the McMaster estate) agreed to do their share, but J.G. White and Company would take on no further obligations. Because of White's refusal to guarantee that there would be no further cost overruns, George Stairs in Halifax refused to participate either. Aitken had to step in and pick up half the total issue, 50 per cent personally and 50 per cent through Royal Securities.[30]

Faced with the need to shift this heavy burden of securities from all three issues in such adverse circumstances, Aitken could only urge on the already hard-pressed sales staff of the corporation to greater efforts.[31] Even extending an offer of a special commission of $2\frac{1}{2}$ per cent in cash plus 5 per cent in bonus stock to some dealers did little to move the stuff. Aitken's main task became cajoling the underwriters of the Porto Rico and Camagüey bonds to pay their instalments.[32] In the end he was forced to borrow the money from the Merchants' Bank by giving his personal guarantee.[33]

By December the syndicate was in default to the tune of $218,600, and the few insiders at Royal Securities who had paid their instalments had done so only by dint of borrowing the money from the Montreal Trust Company, of which they had recently acquired control. Ever ready to feel sorry for himself, Aitken wrote to W.D. Ross on Boxing Day: 'Although as you state in your letter, 'Banking is hard enough these days,' still there are harder jobs, and I am on one at the present time.'[34] Aitken was particularly bitter because the usually compliant Ross turned down his request for an additional $30,000 in credit.

The only way Aitken was able to relieve his frustration was by abusing the other syndicate members when they met. When Ames reproached him for his behaviour he was unrepentant:

I am very sorry if I was too hard at our meeting in Toronto. I have been very hard pressed in the Porto Rico business, and I can assure you that my quarrel with your firm was not half as bad as my quarrels with the Halifax underwriters. I seem to be compelled to constantly quarrel with everybody concerned in this Porto Rico undertaking. But I suppose money could not be got otherwise.

Not only did this wrangling add to the growing bitterness between Aitken and Harris, but it also left Ames aggrieved. Almost a year and a half later the Toronto broker was still annoyed at the failure of the Porto Rico underwriting, contending that the timing of the second issue had been decided upon without consulting him:

The result was we fell somewhat behind in placing our securities, due both to bad money conditions and to its becoming known to a number of investors in our territory that Porto Rico securities could be had at better than the ordinary subscription price. Some little concessions of time were made to us, but later on you dunned us unmercifully by letter and telegram and personally in my office. You arbitrarily withheld for months the bonus stock to which we were entitled.[35]

The only other thing that could be done was to try to generate some favourable publicity about Porto Rico Railways. Much attention was lavished upon the preparation of a pamphlet, to be attached to the first annual report, setting forth the work already completed 'in a manner,' as Aitken put it, 'calculated to meet our purposes in the sale of securities.' Eventually it was decided that Ames would send out three thousand copies of this production to all new bondholders, as well as to all brokers and financial institutions in Ontario. Contrary to his usual preference for concealment, Aitken now felt compelled to publish earnings.[36]

When the situation seemed at its most desperate, in January 1908, there came a sudden glimmer of hope. The underwriters of the second issue of Porto Rico bonds had so far been unable to sell a single dollar's worth of the issue. Ames could not keep up his payments, and $25,000 of his underwriting had to be transferred to J.C. Mackintosh and Company in Halifax. Yet all of a sudden Aitken was able to report that 'The market in Porto Rico is just opening up. We have sold more bonds during the latter part of December and in the month of January than in the past six months. There is every indication that this market will continue, and we hope to see all the underwriters through safely.'[37]

To promote sales Aitken set off in February to lead another party of Canadians down to the island to see what had been accomplished. Several underwriters, some security salesmen, and some recent investors were invited along in the hope that a favourable impression would be created.[38] This outing seems to have been a success and, as soon as he returned, Aitken began discussions with A.E. Ames about the possibility of putting out a block of stock at attractive prices.

Even though there were signs of economic recovery and the Porto Rico underwriting seemed to be on the road to success by the spring of 1908, the syndicate's task of making a market in the company's securities was by no means ended. Emphasis shifted from survival measures to profit-maximizing over the long term. Aitken warned that to avoid ruining the market the bonds should be kept in a selling pool and carefully controlled until the entire underwriting was disposed of. The insiders must resist the temptation to take quick profits, and instead content themselves for the present with the capital gains they had already earned from the sale of the 2,500 shares of bonus stock they had received free.[39]

The need for constant care and attention remained the basic theme over the next couple of years. All the syndicate members had large holdings, and Aitken admitted that there was no market except what they themselves worked to create. Shares might be trading at around $33, but there remained another $2 million par value worth waiting to be sold, so that this price could speedily be broken. 'Unless we handle these issues in a scientific manner we will not have a very satisfactory market for a long time,' he wrote to George Stairs. 'We must let out cheap stock and let out more expensive stock as the price goes up.' Beating the bushes for customers was vital: 'it must be borne in mind that every purchaser is worked up to the purchasing point by the amount of literature which is being sent out and the amount of canvassing which is being done.'[40]

The ever-present danger was that some underwriters might try to unload their holdings quickly by price cutting. 'Unless I am able to dictate the selling price,' Aitken complained, 'the market is lost at once.'[41] His critics grumbled that he was putting up share prices too slowly, making the stuff hard to sell.[42]

With the aim of making Porto Rico securities more desirable, the insiders discussed the listing of the securities on the Toronto and Montreal stock exchanges in the spring of 1908. What they hoped for, in A.E. Ames's words, were 'transactions in such volumes as would in a short time provide a free market. This would enable those who wish to hold for a period to borrow upon the security of their stock.' But one of the Toronto underwriters, D.E. Thomson, was strongly opposed to the idea of a listing, perhaps because of fears about bear raids, and Aitken chose to defer to him in this matter.[43]

By the fall of 1908, however, the prospects of Porto Rico Railways seemed excellent. Negotiations with the island government for an extended franchise to permit the double-tracking of the line from San Juan to Río Piedras were well advanced. Once granted, Aitken believed, 'This ensures us against further financial worries.'[44] Still, when the stock reached fifty dollars in mid-1909 he considered this entirely too high, and predicted that not two hundred shares could be absorbed without breaking that price, a prediction that proved correct, as the stock was hovering around thirty-five dollars by the autumn.[45]

With the promotional phase complete, Max Aitken planned to move on to other things. Nevertheless he continued to pay keen attention to the affairs of Porto Rico Railways. The following year, a new enterprise, the Puerto Rico Railway, Light and Power Company, was organized in response to changes in the company law of the Commonwealth that required foreign corporations to file articles of incorporation there and consent to being sued in local courts. The company, however, retained its Canadian charter and its Montreal head office as well as its association with Aitken's name in the minds of the Puerto Rican people. Over the next thirty years it continued to be a major hydroelectric producer until its properties were expropriated in 1944.[46]

III

Promoting companies like Porto Rico Railways brought financiers like Max Aitken face to face with the limitations of the Canadian capital market. In particular, they discovered the barriers between various regions of the country, the power of the banks, and the relative scarcity of risk capital. Promoters of transit and hydroelectric projects of any considerable size would have to surmount these obstacles if they hoped to raise the sums of money needed. Direct experience with these market imperfections led to attempts to restructure of the system of financial intermediaries in Canada in an effort to loosen up immobile savings. As always Max Aitken was at the centre of things, complaining.

A critical problem was the lack of capital within a region like Atlantic Canada. The obvious solution was to try to tap new sources of funds in central Canada and, almost from the time of the establishment of Royal Securities, Aitken began to explore the possibility of moving the base of his operations to Montreal, the country's financial capital.[47] By the end of 1904 the board of Royal Securities had built up a good list of buyers of industrial and municipal bonds in the Maritimes. But if the company was to continue to grow, new clients were needed. The directors finally took the decision to send Aitken to Montreal to open an office there. Aitken was convinced that even greater returns might be secured if the corporation had more capital, which led him to his first, unsuccessful approach to E.S. Clouston, general manager of the Bank of Montreal. Although Clouston refused to put money into the undertaking, Aitken nevertheless persuaded the board of Royal Securities in the fall of 1905 to double the nominal capital to $100,000 by issuing a stock dividend of $50,000 par value worth of fully paid up shares.[48]

Aitken attracted an aggressive group of salesmen to Royal Securities, including several who would one day become prominent Canadian financiers. I.W. Killam was recruited to run the Saint John, New Brunswick, office, while A.J. Nesbitt travelled throughout Quebec trying to persuade various insurance companies to take up issues that Royal Securities was handling.[49] In the autumn of 1906 the corporation decided to set up a centralized engineering and purchasing department to serve the several utilities it controlled in Trinidad, British Guiana, Cuba and Puerto Rico. This was soon spun off as a subsidiary named the Montreal Engineering Company.[50]

As more of Royal Securities' activities came to be centred in Montreal, Aitken saw an opportunity to expand his operations in the financial services field and perhaps tap new pools of capital directly. Early in 1907 he learned that the Montreal Trust and Deposit Company was anxious to open a branch office in Halifax or to make some arrangement with a trust company there. He immediately made a counter-proposal that the Nova Scotia-based Commercial Trust Company, which was controlled by W.B. Ross of Royal Securities, should amalgamate with Montreal Trust. Commercial Trust would thereby avoid competition on its home turf and at the same time gain access to new types of business in Montreal. A trust company could undertake the business of a stock transfer agency; it could establish a real estate division and undertake property management; and as a trustee it could 'control all of the Eastern [i.e., Maritime] business which is now transacted in Montreal.'[51]

Richard Wilson-Smith, the financier who controlled Montreal Trust, was attracted to the idea, and a deal was quickly worked out. A syndicate formed by Aitken acquired 2,550 of Montreal Trust's 5,000 shares at 110 per cent of par with Royal Securities putting up the $280,500 required, while the Montreal company agreed to acquire up to $65,000 worth of the stock of Commercial Trust. Once he was in control of Montreal Trust, however, Max learned that his new acquisition was not all that had been represented: 'I ... found the business in the company's charge small and of little importance outside of one estate.' The old board of directors he did not consider sufficiently influential in the business world, and they were discovered to have shared a commission of $17,500 amongst themselves on the recent sale of a new issue of stock. In a typical Aitken move Max demanded that the deal be renegotiated with the price of the shares purchased reduced from 110 to $106\frac{1}{2}$. Wilson-Smith reluctantly agreed to this.[52]

Soon Aitken pronounced himself thoroughly satisfied with his new undertaking. When the recession of 1907 struck he suggested to his Halifax associates that Royal Securities should purchase the rest of the outstanding shares of Montreal Trust. He and his friends held only just over 50 per cent of the stock, and both the Merchants' Bank and the Royal Bank were eyeing the company with a view to a takeover. This move was blocked, however, by R.E. Harris, who held a large interest in a competitor, the Halifax-based Eastern Trust.[53]

As security prices slumped further, the trust business began to look more and more promising as a profit centre, and Aitken encouraged his associates to make use of the services of Montreal Trust. Early in 1908 he moved to strengthen the firm and bolster his control over it by replacing the old directors with a new and stronger board. The addition of the general manager of the Grand Trunk Railway, the president of Molson's Bank, and a prominent Liberal senator and businessmen, Raoul Dandurand, to the board reflected Aitken's increasing prominence in the national financial community.[54]

Perhaps the most surprising move made by Max Aitken as part of his strategy of becoming a pure company promoter was the decision taken in

January 1908 to surrender control of the Royal Securities Corporation to one of its employees, G.W. Farrell, himself a few months younger than the twenty-eight-year-old Aitken.[55] The company had originally been set up because the Halifax brokerage houses would not or could not sell securities of the ventures that John Stairs and his associates wished to promote. Despite the establishment of the new office in Montreal the corporation had failed to make a profit on sales in both 1906 and 1907. 'Were it not for the money we have made in promotions,' Aitken confided to C.H. Cahan, 'we would have lost our capital long ago.'[56]

Aitken had clearly been badly burned by the Porto Rico Railways fiasco. He put his views plainly to George Stairs in the spring of 1908:

The day of the small electric bond issues in far-off countries is past. Don't let my change of heart amuse you because the change is the result of experience. I venture the opinion that no other organization in Canada could have sold the small and isolated issues which Royal Securities sold ...

I never want to engage in the bond and share business again. I don't believe in trying to tie up the bond and share business with the promoting business. I do believe in promoting large companies. I think that in the promotion of a large enterprise the market can be better left to those who specialize in marketing securities only and do not engage in promoting. My business from this time forward is purely promoting.

If the opportunity had offered itself he might perhaps have 'gathered together an aggregate of financial institutions on just the same lines as the Morton Trust Company and its allied interests,' linking the merchant banking and trust business with brokerage. On the whole, however, he was happy with the change, glad to be free of the 'decidedly onerous' business of retailing stocks and bonds. And he was certainly not unhappy to sever his close links to some of the Halifax investors, in particular R.E. Harris, with whom his relations had always been tense.[57]

Yet another feud erupted over the closure of the sale of Royal Securities. Farrell had persuaded the Bank of Commerce to lend him the money to purchase the goodwill and the inventory of municipal bonds. Aitken, therefore, set up a new concern called the Bond and Share Company to hold all the industrial and utility securities in the Royal Securities portfolio with a view to disposing of them as advantageously as possible and distributing the profits.[58]

Aitken was eager to liquidate swiftly so that he could devote himself to his new line of endeavour. However, he resented the desire of the Halifax crowd to control the new Bond and Share Company and fix the prices at which the assets of Royal Securities would be sold off. To R.E. Harris's complaint that everything was being 'cut and dried' in Montreal, he replied, 'If I do not cut and dry matters for this company who is going to do it?' All his accumulated resentment against Harris welled up:

We have never had any capital. Our shareholders, including myself, have always been indebted to us for more than the amount of stock subscriptions, with the exception of the late Mr. Geo. Stairs, Mr. Cahan and usually Mr. [W.B.] Ross. All our resources have come from our borrowing capacity. All our profits have come from promoting companies …

If you or any other shareholder will undertake the task of looking after our assets and will also assume responsibility for our loans, then I will very gladly step down in his favour. But until such a successor is found I must continue to 'cut and dry' for the company.[59]

Aitken fumed over the complaints from Halifax: 'I have never gotten any good from Harris. He has never done anything but borrow money and feast on our underwriting projects. Then when the underwriting project came up in which he had to pay a little money, he did not come to the point.' Aitken insisted that H.A. Lovett and the two Rosses (W.B. and W.D.) must back him up and 'read the Riot Act' to Harris. W.B. Ross refused to bend to this ultimatum. While he was quite happy to have Aitken oversee the liquidation, he calmly pointed out that Harris was, after all, a director of the Bond and Share Company and had a right to be concerned about what he saw as an attempt by Aitken to sell things to himself on his own terms: 'Try and view these matters calmly and not get worked up into a state where it means impairment of health.'[60]

A chronic hypochondriac, when the going got tough Max often got sick. His partners could not afford to lose him to illness, real or imagined. Eventually it was decided that they should gather in Montreal early in May 1908 and thrash everything out. Aitken's account of the meeting was that he had been fully vindicated: Harris was offered the opportunity to assume responsibility for the liquidation and declined for fear that Aitken might drop out altogether; Aitken would do the job on his own terms 'and without further letter writing.'[61]

Ironically, however, before the month was out Aitken learned that the Bank of Commerce was getting ready to call the loan it had made to young

Farrell for the acquisition of the Royal Securities Corporation. The bank had concluded that he was too erratic to manage the firm and was seeking somebody else to take over. And who should step forward to take on the task? None other than Max Aitken himself. He re-acquired a 35 per cent interest in the corporation, though the rest of his old Halifax associates stayed out of the deal.[62] Instead he persuaded Toronto financiers and railway contractors William Mackenzie and Donald Mann to convert a sizeable debt owed to them into equity.[63]

Over the next few months Aitken worked to restore his old pride and joy to its previous profitability. This did not prove too difficult, for the stock market was once again booming; early in 1909 he informed William Mackenzie that, 'Sales are very good and the amount of business we are turning over is exceedingly satisfactory.'[64] Although Aitken de-emphasized the retail side of the business to some extent, in keeping with his resolve to stick mainly to promoting in future, he soon had Royal Securities functioning smoothly again, ready for use as a vehicle in the industrial mergers and acquisitions upon which his enduring reputation in Canada was to be founded.

In mid-1909 he strengthened Royal Securities further by inducing Herbert Holt, president of both the Royal Bank and Montreal Light, Heat and Power, to invest in the company and take a seat on the board. Subsequently, he also persuaded Sir Edward Clouston, his once-reluctant mentor at the Bank of Montreal, to take an interest, too; that link, he noted proudly in the fall of the year, placed him in a position to borrow $380,000 from the bank on a single day. And the investors were well rewarded when the 1911 annual meeting passed a dividend of 16 per cent.[65] The corporation continued to prosper in the years prior to the First World War, raising its pay-out to 17 per cent per annum in 1913, and supplementing it by a bonus dividend of 300 per cent out of surplus profits in 1914.[66]

While Aitken surrendered, then regained, control of Royal Securities he continued to manage Montreal Trust, which was also a solid earner, almost too solid for his liking. With success came the expectation of dividends. As he explained in all seriousness to W.B. Ross in 1908: 'Dividends are like bad debts. You pay money away and never get anything back. The Montreal Trust and Deposit Company pays its first dividend on the 1st of April. I am sorry.'[67]

The trust business, however, quickly proved too dull and predictable for Aitken's liking. He confided to one of his board members: 'I have got very little to do in Montreal. I am almost without a job. The trust company is running along very smoothly and all the old plans are maturing. I wish you would capitalize some company and require my services as chief money finder.' All he could do was content himself with making call loans at 5 per cent interest, chafing at the fact that Montreal Trust lacked the capital to acquire entire bond issues when the principal sum was more than $150,000. Without an infusion of the additional capital that would permit larger participations and allow the company to begin seeking buyers for its securities abroad, it could not break free of the relatively narrow confines of the regional markets in Quebec and the Maritimes.[68]

Aitken demonstrated his usual quick grasp of the situation: 'I think trust companies in Canada are doing about as impecunious and uninteresting a class of business as can possibly be transacted, and in addition thereto, think those trust companies will never improve their class of business because the banks will not allow them.' From that it followed that the chartered banks were most likely to be eager to invest in trust companies, as the Bank of Montreal had already done with Royal Trust. In July 1909 Aitken sought out Herbert Holt and persuaded the Royal Bank to acquire a controlling interest in Montreal Trust.[69]

Thereafter he quickly severed his connections with the day-to-day affairs of the trust company and concentrated his attentions upon his first love, Royal Securities, of which he had so fortuitously been able to recapture control, now free of the restraining hand of his old Halifax associates. As he told an English financier in April 1909, his ambitions were bold: 'What I want is that the Royal Securities Corporation (and the Montreal Trust Company, which has to be squeezed in,) shall be the leading company in Canada, consulted and relied upon by all the banks. I do not think my ambitions are too lofty.'[70]

IV

Indeed, he had already set his sights on even bigger things. All of his problems with the narrow market and weak associates convinced Aitken that he should seek buyers for his securities in Britain. In the spring of 1906 he signed an agreement to send salesman J.S. Harding off to London for a six-month period to try to open up the London market.[71] But Harding found the going tough. The conventions of the City made for awkward difficulties: one could approach only a single broker at a time or else none of them would take a proposition on, and if one broker's clients evinced no interest, when one went elsewhere one was likely to be turned away with the disdainful comment, '"Oh, that is on the market. Other brokers have had this before," which rather gives it a black eye.'[72]

Harding laboured diligently for the remainder of 1906, but it was all uphill work. First of all, he was not alone in the field; one man had been representing a number of Canadian and US brokerage houses in Britain for more than twenty years. Another expatriate Canadian, E. Mackay Edgar, had recently left Montreal and established a close relationship with the important City firm of Sperling and Company. By the beginning of 1907, Harding reported that, owing to the eruption of revolt in Cuba the previous year and the reports of earthquakes in the Caribbean, only the most resourceful of men could sell Latin American utility stocks. He eventually concluded that for the time being Royal Securities should not try to operate in London but simply establish a corresponding relationship with a broker who might sell a few shares if the opportunity presented itself. Meantime he retreated to the French Riviera for several months to repair his health.[73]

Aitken was not prepared to admit defeat so easily. He himself began corresponding with likely buyers and prepared a glowing brochure describing the Canadian utilities in Latin America and the Caribbean.[74] Altogether these first efforts by Max Aitken to crack the British market produced negligible results. Still, the London market had irresistible appeal; as Aitken observed about the possible flotation of another utility venture in Mexico in the spring of 1907, 'I can positively say that nobody can capitalize any Mexican property at the present time, at least in this country. Of course, it might be that a property could be capitalized in England but not otherwise.'[75]

Aitken continued his efforts to interest such London firms as Sperling and Company in his latest ventures, but he also decided to recall Harding to Canada and to send A.J. Nesbitt to take up the rounds of brokerage houses in the City. Nesbitt beavered away: 'I am sure that it is only a matter of time when we shall have to open an office here or make a very close connection with some bankers which will give us an outlet for our securities, [as] the Canadian market is so narrow.' But he had to admit that progress was slow.[76] Efforts to interest the London brokers in Porto Rico Railways again proved fruitless. Nesbitt sold a few blocks of securities on his own, but eventually he, too, gave up and went back to Canada.[77]

During the panic in the fall of 1907 a desperate Max Aitken turned once more towards Britain. Briefly he even contemplated the idea of going there himself in company with A.E. Ames, but eventually decided that the combination of his ill health and the growing crisis in the financial affairs of the

Porto Rico Railways required him to remain at home. Instead he dispatched A.J. Nesbitt to resume the weary round of the brokers. Nesbitt found it frustrating to adapt himself to the mores of the British business world, where one could not even call upon a man without a letter of introduction:

The people over here are so far behind the times as regards business, etc., that I get disgusted ... Of course, the money is over here, & once you get in with them it is all o.k. but it takes a lot of time & money. A stockbroker here will not buy or sell stock for cash for a client unless he is introduced or known to him, so you see the antiquated methods they have of doing business.[78]

The London brokers proved as uninterested as ever in taking on Porto Rico Railways. Even A.M. Grenfell, who was another of those who had begun to make something of a specialty of Canadian stocks, advised that in the present circumstances 'they will not touch anything except enterprises [operating] in Canada.' And Nesbitt's efforts to arouse interest through publicity produced furious criticism from Aitken owing to the cost: 'The present advertizing contracts cannot be called extravagant, the proper term is destructive. Destruction of money hard earned at that.'[79] Nevertheless, in his financial straits Aitken had nowhere else to turn. He gave Nesbitt permission to sell Porto Rico common stock for as little as twenty-five dollars per share if he had to: 'The situation rests with you. You may sell at prices to net a profit. I have no other advice to give. Times are bad and securities in Canada are uncertain.'[80]

Nesbitt, meanwhile, had concluded that Royal Securities must make some formal arrangement with a London house if it was ever to secure wide distribution of its offerings among British investors. A natural choice was the expatriate Canadian James Dunn, who had recently arrived from Montreal and set up Dunn, Fischer and Company, which had quickly built up 'a tremendous connection both here and on the continent.' Whenever brokers and underwriters were offered something like Porto Rico Railways they immediately turned to Dunn and Fischer for advice, and, Nesbitt observed, 'as they were not interested consequently they sold them their own stuff instead.'[81]

Aitken was quite well-disposed to this idea. Dunn was a childhood friend and had earned his respect if not his complete trust while in business in Montreal:

I have a high opinion of Mr. Dunn's capacity, and although I would not be prepared to confide in him to too great an extent, nevertheless I can readily see that the course you are taking is probably the most desirable. In the event of your tying up with them, we will, of course, share our promotion stocks with them hereafter.

When he saw the actual terms of the arrangement suggested by Dunn, however, he was taken aback. Dunn, Fischer would not only receive a commission on all European sales by Royal Securities but also gained the right to sell its own stuff to all the corporation's customers. Everything was skewed too much in Dunn, Fischer's favour, Aitken growled: 'If D.F. & Co. had accomplished a great deal for us, I would be more inclined to enter into the present contract; but, until this firm has proved itself of use to us, I cannot see any reason for giving them one-quarter per cent on all sales we may make in Europe.'[82] Nesbitt admitted somewhat shamefacedly that he had allowed Dunn to dictate the terms of this agreement, and in the end Royal Securities did not make any formal arrangement with a London firm.[83]

With demand once more picking up in Canada the urgency of securing such a tie declined somewhat, but, because shares like Porto Rico Railways tended to flood onto the Montreal and Toronto market at the slightest rise, the idea of an English connection still remained highly attractive. As Nesbitt pointed out, however, a firm like Dunn, Fischer could hardly be expected to do much to push the Canadian stuff unless it was made really worth their while.[84] With more buoyant times during the summer of 1908, however, nothing more was done as Max Aitken settled in at Montreal Trust, then recaptured control of Royal Securities.

That fall A.E. Ames reported to Aitken from London: 'Their ways here, as you know, are not our ways, but I have a wholesome respect for them. John Bull is not as big a fool as he sometimes looks, and it inclines one to be humble when one realizes how quickly and well they handle big things in their own, to us, peculiar fashion.' Ames, too, gravitated to Dunn, Fischer and Company, on account of its well-established Canadian connections, and proposed that the firm take on between $500,000 and $750,000 worth of Porto Rico Railway bonds to be sold to the public at 85 per cent. Once again James Dunn drove a hard bargain with his colonial counterparts: he insisted on getting more bonus stock so that bond sales would net the company only 75 per cent of par. Again Aitken balked at the demand as too steep.[85]

The lure of the London money market remained irresistible, however. Aitken himself went over in October and November 1908, and he wrote proudly to R.E. Harris to advise him that in only a few short weeks he had sold nearly $600,000 worth of bonds in various Canadian enterprises despite the lack of a formal connection with an English house.[86] The volume of these sales after all the troubles in Canada convinced Max Aitken that the future financing of capital-intensive utilities operating overseas would lie mainly in Europe.

Royal Securities Corporation was founded in order to retail the securities of companies floated by John Stairs and his associates. Yet before long Aitken's salesmen found themselves bumping up against the constraints of the capital market in Atlantic Canada, where the supply of funds was limited and investors showed a marked reluctance to invest in ventures elsewhere. To meet these problems Royal Securities gradually shifted its base of operations to Montreal after 1905, despite reservations on the part of some of the Halifax shareholders.

In order to tap new sources of funds Aitken first engineered the acquisition of Montreal Trust and then sold off the security-retailing operations of Royal Securities. As often, when Max was involved, both transactions were cloaked in a cloud of recriminations and left a bitter legacy of damaged feelings. Max accused his associates of shirking; they suspected him of lining his own pockets at their expense. All were right.

Pressure from the banks eventually brought Aitken back to the helm of the Royal Securities Corporation, now freed of his Nova Scotia allies. Instead he formed increasingly strong ties with Herbert Holt and the Royal Bank in Montreal. Eventually, he withdrew from the trust company and concentrated on Canadian industrial mergers using Royal Securities as his vehicle. Thus Aitken not only changed the tasks that this financial intermediary performed but also shifted the geographical base of its operations and its source of financial backing to the broader, richer latitudes of central Canada.

Even so, Aitken recognized from an early date that enterprises of the type that he wished to promote would have difficulty in raising sufficient funds in Canada. Utility promotions had clearly outgrown the capacity of Canadian, much less Maritime, investors to put up the sums required. This lesson was burned upon his consciousness during the recession of 1907–8. While such new institutions as interlocking brokerage houses, trust companies, and chartered banks might proliferate in Montreal and Toronto, the real business would have to be done in Brussels, Paris, and London from now on.

8

Jimmy Dunn and His Circle

Once launched, these utility companies demanded continuous and ever-increasing infusions of capital to keep pace with burgeoning Latin American urbanization. Of course the promoters, who profited from each flotation, had every reason to issue as much paper as the market would bear. The problem was that by 1906 the regional and national capital markets in Canada could not wholly satisfy either the utilities' needs or the promoters' ambitions. To finance his fairly small promotions in Cuba, British Guiana, and Puerto Rico, Max Aitken had to move closer to central Canadian pools of capital and soon saw the need to move on to European markets. At about the same time F.S. Pearson was also exhausting the capacity and patience of his biggest Montreal and Toronto backers with his Brazilian and Mexican promotions. Scale drew promoters to the centres of international capitalism.

So did panic. When Canadian speculators dumped their Latin American utility stocks and bonds during the recession of 1907, many of these heavily discounted securities migrated to London. Thereafter the City became the main theatre of new issues and new promotions; the Canadian market fell into eclipse on account of the large amounts of money required for expansion and hydroelectric development, the narrowness and skittishness of the investment community, and the tendency of Canadian securities to gravitate to London through arbitrage in any event.

Where Max Aitken and his associates had failed to establish a London beach-head, James Dunn triumphed in spectacular fashion. James Hamet Dunn, Jimmy to his cronies, succeeded in selling the securities of the

Pearson group of companies to financiers in London, Brussels, Berlin, and Paris. Among the most active buyers was Robert Fleming, the legendary father of the British investment trust industry. On the continent Alfred Loewenstein, the larger-than-life principal of the Belgian investment house of Stallaerts and Loewenstein, supplied the various European bourses.

A gaudy flock of brokers, company promoters, merchant bankers, and trust fund managers added colour and a touch of the exotic to this intercontinental financial aviary. Scottish bankers mixed with daredevil aviators, Yankee buccaneers, theatrical European aristocrats, prime ministers, lesser politicians, and callow colonials – and they all frolicked together with their wives and mistresses at Jimmy Dunn's slightly disreputable weekend parties at Coombe Hill. The prosaic profits made by Dundee manufacturers from selling jam and jute may have underwritten these promotions, but they floated upon a sea of champagne and laughter as well.

I

The story of James (later Sir James) Dunn's rise and fall and rise again in the British social and financial world ranks as one of the great legends of Canadian history. Dunn typified the first wave of colonials, like Evelyn Waugh's Rex Mottram, who stormed the keep of empire before the First World War, blazing a path so heroic that generations of vain and ambitious provincials have been compelled to imitate it ever since. The country house with its Holbein, Goya, and Gainsborough and its stables and fleet of motor cars, the influential friends, the scandalous dalliances, the aristocratic bride, and eventually the knighthood – all these were the rewards of introducing the Pearson enterprises to the City and Europe.

Growing up on the bleak north shore of New Brunswick in the 1880s, Jimmy Dunn acquired enough drive and ambition to keep him running the rest of his life. Dunn's father died in a logging accident only a few months after James's birth in 1874. The young widow, struggling to maintain her independence as a telegrapher and then as a housekeeper, sought strength and consolation in a stern Presbyterianism. Steeled by his mother's fierce pride, young James learned one abiding lesson from his strict religious upbringing – *make money*. A somewhat literal and partial reading of the Shorter Catechism, but young New Brunswickers were not alone in that interpretation.

Dunn used to scamper about the shoreline during the summers with the

Presbyterian minister's son, Max Aitken, who was five years his junior. Lord Beaverbrook's *Courage*, a warm octogenarian tribute to his youthful mentor, captures the aching ambition of their raw youth chafing within the sabbatarian strictures and limited opportunities of their surroundings. As boy-Friday to a genial country general practitioner, Dunn found a stabilizing father figure and developed an interest in the professions.[1]

When her son was in his mid-teens, Eliza Dunn moved to Lynn, Massachusetts to join relatives. After a brief stint as a seaman on the Great Lakes, Dunn wound armatures in the Thomson Houston plant at Lynn. But that was not enough. With the prize money from a boxing match James invested in some lessons with and eventually fell into the employ of an itinerant 'Professor of Memory.' As the advance man for Professor and Madame Loisette, Dunn travelled the east coast and, in 1893, made his first Atlantic crossing. He returned from England to New Brunswick with a clear view of what lay beyond the horizon and a determination to become a lawyer. Max Aitken, the awestruck youth who met this prodigal son at the station, never forgot the seeming urbanity of the well-tailored swell stepping down from the train in his gleaming patent leather boots into the Bathurst slush.

Clerking in the local lawyer's office, Dunn acquired the necessary recommendations to get into Dalhousie University's law school. Afterwards he more or less forced himself upon the Halifax firm of Pearson and Covert as an articling student. B.F. Pearson was then at the peak of his powers as a company promoter and lawyer. He had introduced Henry Whitney to Cape Breton coal and iron opportunities; advised by Whitney's young engineering genius F.S. Pearson, B.F. Pearson took over the Halifax street railway system. By the time Dunn arrived the Pearson and Covert offices were abuzz with schemes for Maritime industrial incorporations and western Canadian railways.[2]

Dunn ventured west to Edmonton in connection with B.F. Pearson's railway interests and with an eye to setting up practice on his own. In Edmonton his path briefly crossed that of Max Aitken, and the two debated the merits of finding their fortunes in the west. Max waxed enthusiastic; Dunn demurred. 'The West must pay tribute to the East,' Aitken recalled his saying, 'And I'm off to the East where I can collect tribute.'

He arrived in Montreal in 1900 – his timing, as usual, was very good – and found employment with Greenshields, Greenshields and Henniker, one of the leading law firms in the city. His star rose quickly. Within a year he had become a junior partner. At the same time marriage in 1901 to

Gertrude Price, daughter of Herbert Molesworth Price, one of the wealthiest lumbermen in Quebec, confirmed his arrival in Montreal society.

Characteristically he was not satisfied to remain a black-coated minion, a draughtsman of other people's trust deeds or pleader of other men's briefs. Borrowing $20,000 from his father-in-law, Dunn bought a seat on the Montreal Stock Exchange in 1902 and threw himself into market operations. After a humiliating failure to establish a 'corner' in already existing Nova Scotia steel stocks, Dunn decided it would be better to get in on the ground floor of a new promotion. That chance came in 1905 when F.S. Pearson arrived in town looking for more backers for his ever-expanding Mexican interests. Max Aitken later insisted that Dunn was one of the most enthusiastic Pearson promoters in a somewhat sceptical investment community. But as we have already seen, by 1905 F.S. Pearson needed new friends; he had gone through quite a few of the old ones.

At that time Dunn's Montreal brokerage house specialized in arbitrage, the buying and selling of securities on different stock exchanges where there were small price differentials. In New York he dealt with Laidlaw and Company. In London Dunn employed C.L. Fischer, a Swiss merchant banker. During 1905 this business of buying Canadian stocks in Montreal for sale in London assumed such importance that Dunn opened a London office, Dunn, Fischer and Company, at 85 London Wall.[3] In 1906 Dunn took on a large block of Mexico Tramways bonds for placement on both sides of the Atlantic. Then in 1907, perhaps nudged by the collapse of the Canadian stock market and the embarrassment of the Sovereign Bank – to which he owed a large sum of money that ultimately led to the suicide of his Montreal partner – Dunn made London his permanent home.

Up until this time R.M. Horne-Payne of the British Empire Trust had been the principal connection between these Canadian promotions and the City. However his troublesome fastidiousness actually created an opening for an ambitious rival like James Dunn. Horne-Payne financed William Mackenzie's transcontinental railroad ambitions and himself presided over the flourishing British Columbia Electric Railway empire. While a director of Sperling and Company, Horne-Payne had made himself the most knowledgable British financier on Canadian investment matters –which perhaps explains his caution.[4] Through Mackenzie's influence Horne-Payne had taken a position in some of the early Latin American underwritings; but, as we have seen, F.S. Pearson tired of Horne-Payne's constant requests for full disclosure and insistence upon playing by the stock exchange rules. Pearson wanted a committed, promotional under-writer in London, not a critic. And that is the role in which James Dunn cast himself.

Horne-Payne and Sperling continued to underwrite portions of Pearson's issues (Horne-Payne even served as an officer of one of the companies), but by degrees Dunn insinuated himself into the City, opened up new sources of funds, and gradually took over as Pearson's principal representative. Guided initially by Fischer, who had an extensive network of contacts in the City and on the continent, James Dunn became the centre of a small circle of financiers who between 1906 and 1913 underwrote a new generation of much more grandiose F.S. Pearson promotions in Mexico, the United States, Brazil, Central America, and Spain.

II

The City at the turn of the century was not the snooty, exclusive, financial men's club it seems from a distance. There was always room somewhere in its winding lanes and back alleys for outsiders – as long as they had something to offer. With luck, private knowledge, the proper style, and the right 'stuff,' ambitious colonials could make it on Threadneedle Street. If they were cocky enough, they might herald their arrival by parking a gleaming Daimler at the front door – James Dunn's trademark.

Apart from a native wit and considerable charm, James Dunn did have something substantial to lay before the London financiers when he came calling: extremely promising, cheap, American securities, from a reliable source, for portfolio managers and brokers with a surplus of funds. He also offered an attractive bonus to large purchasers and repeat customers. It was a compelling combination. Not surprisingly, he flourished.

In London at this time a new venture could be financed in one of three ways. The issue could be underwritten by one of the great merchant banking houses such as Rothschild. Or smaller, more specialized finance or trust companies could take up the security issue singly or in combination. However, most industrial flotations were handled by 'ephemeral syndi-cates of promoters,'[5] small merchant bankers, jobbers (who could trade on their own account), brokers (who theoretically could not), and financial houses that formed around individual issues. The principals would then either hold the securities, or collect a commission and mark-up on the resale to other financial institutions, brokers, or clients.

Over time James Dunn developed a small coterie of merchant bankers and brokers who eagerly sought participation in his new issues. Most but not all of Dunn's syndicate members were drawn from a group of financial houses known by Fischer – such houses as Mendel and Myers, Bierer and Company, Bauer and Blundell, A. Biedermann and Company, and Drucker, Morris and Company. Dunn also cultivated Ellis and Company, Ernest Davies and Company, A.M. Grenfell and Company, Robert Escombe and Company, J.S. Morgan and Company, and the Bank of Scotland. Sperling and Company, well connected to Canadian markets, had previously taken portions of the Mexican Light and São Paulo underwritings. When E. Mackay Edgar joined the firm as a director from Montreal these connections to Canadian promotions were strengthened.

But Robert Fleming, the principal of Robert Fleming and Company, was by far James Dunn's most valuable contact in the City. Fleming not only had millions of pounds to invest, but he also had a special interest in precisely the kind of securities Dunn and Pearson were offering. It was a perfect and ultimately mutually beneficial match. Later, when Dunn hung on the brink of disaster, Robert Fleming saved him. Business aside, he might have felt some affinity for an ambitious, rising young man; he had once been one himself.

Fleming got his start at the age of thirteen as a bookkeeper in the employ of Edward Baxter and Son, of Dundee. During the 1860s the Baxter firm had invested its substantial profits from the manufacture of linen and jute in American securities. By the age of twenty-one young Robert had risen to being private clerk to the senior partner of the firm, a position in which he received instruction from Edward Baxter himself on the proper management of an investment portfolio. In 1870 Baxter sent Robert Fleming on an inspection tour of company holdings in the United States. Fleming returned with firsthand information about American possibilities and a conviction that with post-Civil War economic growth the greenback would rapidly appreciate in value.

The Baxters, of course, were not alone. By the 1870s the 'juteocracy' of Dundee and the bankers of Edinburgh had already begun to invest in western us railroads, land, and mortgage companies.[6] Scottish income doubled between 1850 and 1885, and doubled again before 1910. This rapid accumulation of wealth provided surplus funds seeking profitable investment. Competition from India had already dimmed future prospects for manufacturers of jute and other coarse-fibre textiles. Capitalists diversified out of these declining industries into other activities (jams and preserves in the case of the Baxters of Dundee) and sought other means of capital accumulation. The early success of individual investors, such as Edward Baxter, Thomas Nelson (the publisher), and William J. Menzies, an Edinburgh lawyer, attracted wider public attention. Menzies and Fleming did not invent the investment trust, but they were primarily responsible for popularizing and adapting it to tap this Scottish capital reserve.[7]

In 1873 Fleming, with the backing of Baxter and several other jute manufacturers, organized the Scottish-American Investment Trust. Investors purchased shares upon which they were promised a 6 per cent annual dividend.[8] Fleming and the trustees reinvested these funds in American securities, providing professional portfolio management. As the value of the portfolio increased, from the reinvestment of income in excess of the 6 per cent dividend and from net capital gains, the value of a share in the trust increased as well. Both the unit trust, as perfected by Fleming, and the investment company, favoured by Edinburgh investors, proved enormously popular. During the 1870s the Fleming and Menzies groups inspired English and other Scottish competitors (most notably William Mackenzie of Dundee). Investment trusts proliferated during the boom of the late 1880s, and again after 1909. Frequently these new trusts specialized in particular kinds of investments – railroads, mortgage companies, mines, ranches, industrials, cables and utilities, government bonds – each with different risks and likely rates of return.

The investment trust movement traded upon the knowledge and reputation of the trustees and directors. Investment companies reduced the risk to small investors by sharing (for a price) the market knowledge of the managers. Centralized control over large pools of capital gave the trust a certain leverage in the securities market that individual investors lacked. Such funds could also borrow large additional sums for investment at favourable rates of interest; in the parlance of the trade the funds could be geared through borrowing, thereby enhancing the benefit to shareholders in rising markets. The unit trust also captured some economies of scale: several funds could easily be managed from one office; volume purchases at favourable rates could easily be subdivided among the family of trusts, thus raising the yield to each. Investment trusts reduced transaction costs and improved the overall rate of return by combining high risk and more secure investments. But they depended above all upon the judgment and skill of the portfolio manager. In this realm Robert Fleming established an enduring reputation.

During the 1870s and 1880s Scottish savings mobilized in this way financed railroads, cattle ranches, silver, copper, and gold mines, loan and mortgage companies, real estate ventures, and telegraph companies, primarily in the American far west – but also in Florida, Hawaii, western Canada, and Mexico. The Mackenzie and Menzies groups concentrated upon land and mortgage company investments. The Fleming group of trusts specialized in the stocks and bonds of US railroads. Through shrewd buying and selling and repeated trips to the United States (128 in all) to size things up for himself, Fleming was able to pay dividends in excess of 8 per cent on his first and second Scottish American-trusts and only slightly less on the third. Moreover the unit value of the shares advanced appreciably. The land-based trust and investment companies performed almost as well. By the late 1880s these Edinburgh and Dundee trusts between them had channelled more than £5 million pounds into American land and transportation investments.[9]

Fleming moved to London in 1890 to be closer to the large lenders and the market in American securities. Because Scottish trusts tended to outperform their English counterparts, and because the Fleming trusts survived the Baring crisis in flourishing condition, Robert Fleming developed an avid following. On the strength of the 'astronomical'[10] founders' profits that flowed from the promotion of these trusts and his growing financial reputation, Fleming was able to establish his own financial house in 1900, Robert Fleming and Company. From this base in the City he continued to manage the Dundee trusts; he also launched new vehicles of his own to take advantage of the rising turn-of-the century market and took on the management of portfolios for insurance companies and private individuals, as well as for several other already established investment trusts. When James Dunn made his acquaintance in 1906–7, Robert Fleming controlled the investment portfolios of thirty-seven separate trusts (five from Dundee, eight from Glasgow, two from Edinburgh, twenty from London, and two small private funds).[11] By 1913 Fleming probably managed between a third and a half of the £82 million worth of capital tied up in the various British and Scottish funds.

The partners of Robert Fleming and Company generously allowed us to examine the surviving syndicate books and box files of the company for the years 1909 to 1913.[12] On the basis of these documents it is possible to piece together a comprehensive picture of the Fleming portfolio during this period, of his methods, and of the relative importance of the Dunn-Pearson securities among the firm's acquisitions. Typically Fleming signed up for a large participation in the flotation of a particular issue and then subdivided the underwriting among the many portfolios he managed for trusts,

TABLE 5
Percentage Distribution of Fleming Portfolio by Region and Type

Region	Com	Gov	Ind	Lnd	Rly	Utl	Mis	Total
Afr	0.0	0.0	0.12	0.0	1.36	0.0	0.0	1.49
Asia	0.35	0.15	0.09	0.0	0.78	0.39	0.0	1.76
Can	0.83	0.36	2.27	0.46	0.93	0.26	0.0	5.11
Eur	0.37	0.08	1.36	0.0	0.45	2.48	0.72	5.46
LatAm	1.36	1.27	1.55	0.16	11.72	7.01	0.04	23.13
USA	2.10	0.0	15.71	2.29	28.77	14.05	0.13	63.05
Total	5.01	1.86	21.11	2.92	44.01	24.20	0.89	100.00

SOURCE Robert Fleming and Co., box files and syndicate books, 1909–13
ABBREVIATIONS USED IN TABLE Com – Commercial; Gov – Government bonds; Ind – Industrial; Lnd – Land companies; Rly – Railways; Utl – Utilities; Mis – Miscellaneous; Afr – Africa; Can – Canada; Eur – Europe; LatAm – Latin America; USA – United States

insurance companies, and his numerous private clients. Each of the trusts was identified in the syndicate book by a code: for example, 1st Lily (First Scottish-American Trust); 2nd Lily (Second Scottish-American Trust); 3rd Lily (Third Scottish-American Trust); N. American (North American Trust Company); Lobo (Low and Bonar Group); Swico (Scottish Western Investment Company) and so on. Robert Fleming and Company normally took an underwriting commission, or a handling charge of between $\frac{1}{2}$ and $2\frac{1}{2}$ per cent. Frequently the company retained a portion of the purchase as a principal in its modestly expanding role as a merchant banker.[13]

The Fleming syndicate books record 315 separate purchases between 1909 and 1913 totalling $157,612,610 US or £32,497,445. Most of the purchases (63.05 per cent) involved US securities, primarily the stock and bonds of railways (28.77 per cent), industrials (15.71 per cent) and utilities (14.05 per cent). Second in geographical importance were Latin American securities (23.13 per cent of the total portfolio), mainly railways (11.72 per cent) and utilities (7.01 per cent).[14] Table 5 indicates the complete distribution of Fleming's portfolio by type and geographical region.

Thus when James Dunn began marketing his Latin American promotions, Robert Fleming was well disposed. Of course, if Dunn had had a flock of US railroad or industrial prospectuses Fleming would have been even more interested. Nevertheless Latin America represented the second most important geographical specialization of the high growth 'American' funds Fleming managed and, within that region, utilities were preferred. Up to that point Fleming's Latin American interests had been concentrated in Argentinian railroads and tramways. Fleming also evinced an interest in

TABLE 6

Dunn, Fischer and Co. Securities as a Proportion of Robert Fleming and Co. Purchases, 1909–13 (in US dollars)

Year	(A) Fleming Purchases	(B) Dunn Sales (possible)	(C) Dunn Sales (certain)	A / B High %	A / C Low %
1909	6,343,000	4,212,500	1,212,500	66.4	19.1
1910	36,231,215	6,534,370	3,346,870	18.0	9.2
1911	46,361,100	15,631,779	5,328,250	38.7	13.2
1912	46,047,846	4,855,445	3,505,195	10.5	7.6
1913	28,629,449	6,128,928	4,866,678	21.4	17.0
Total	157,612,610	37,363,022	18.259,493	23.7	11.6

SOURCE Robert Fleming and Co., box files and syndicate books, 1909–13

promising Canadian industrials and railway and government issues, some of which Dunn also had for investment. The Fleming name helped enormously in recruiting other merchant bankers and financial houses to the underwriting 'tombstone.'

It is impossible to identify precisely the proportion of these 315 purchases sold by Dunn, for he participated in many syndicates with Fleming without acting as principal underwriter. Indeed, over time, as a regular pattern of promotions developed, the distinction between promoter and purchaser disappeared. Nevertheless, knowing the range of Dunn's interests and the nature of Fleming's purchases, it is possible to indicate a high and low estimate showing the upper limit of their possible collaboration and the lower limit of Dunn's sales to Fleming over the five-year period. Robert Fleming and Company relied upon Dunn, Fischer and Company during these years for at least 11 per cent of its total subscriptions, and the two firms together participated in perhaps as many as 23 per cent of these flotations. The lower limit is the most likely, the difference between the two being created by the uncertainty surrounding Dunn-Fleming collaboration in speculative raids on various US railroads in 1909 and 1911.

Fleming had previously been involved with the Canadian utility men at an early date. As we have seen he supplied a large chunk of the financing for Van Horne's Cuba Railroad at a critical moment in 1902.[15] Although that was not a particularly successful venture it provided Fleming with additional trans-Atlantic connections and excellent inside intelligence for further investments. It was probably during the course of the Cuba Railroad flotation that Fleming learned about Van Horne's other Latin American companies. He also met Percival Farquhar, Van Horne's remarkable protégé, who would subsequently bring a whole host of Brazilian railroad and industrial properties to the London and continental money markets.

By the time Jimmy Dunn arrived in London in 1906 Fleming was well acquainted with many of the principal Canadian promoters of these Latin American utilities. Moreover, he was eager to get in on what he understood to be exceptional opportunities. With a huge portfolio behind him, Fleming could afford to take chances, spreading the risk over a number of funds. The bonus stock supplied to insiders in promotions of this sort rapidly swelled the asset values of the funds. A high-growth portfolio manager needed precisely investments of this sort: Pearson, Farquhar, and their like supplied these needs through brokers such as Dunn.

Fleming seized the opportunity, for instance, to obtain ground-floor terms in Pearson's new Mexico Tramways venture in 1906. He took $500,000 worth of bonds at 90 per cent with a 25 per cent stock bonus and a $2\frac{1}{2}$ per cent underwriting commission.[16] The next year, with European and North American markets in the full grip of a panic, Fleming came to the aid of the floundering Rio venture by purchasing almost a million dollars' worth of heavily discounted first mortgage bonds. This timely intervention not only helped save the company, it probably also helped save James Dunn's skin. In the credit squeeze Dunn, Fischer and Company had been unable to take up its full participation in a Rio seconds flotation.

After the market recovered in 1909 and the trust industry entered another boom phase, Robert Fleming and Company became a regular participant in the numerous underwriting syndicates put together by Dunn to finance Pearson's new projects and expansion in Barcelona, São Paulo, Rio, and Mexico. In all, Fleming probably assumed about 30 per cent of the total Dunn-Pearson issues taken up between 1909 and 1913 by British financial houses.[17]

Fleming stood by the Pearson group of companies during the embarrassing recession of 1907 and the punitive bear raids on Pearson securities in 1909. Fleming's faith survived the collapse of part of Mexican Light and Power's Necaxa storage dam in 1909 and the Mexico City earthquake in the next year. During the early stages of the Mexican Revolution Fleming steadied the market by lending substantial sums to Mexico Tramways. It is quite likely that Fleming was a silent partner to Pearson and Farquhar in their daring attempt to corner the Rock Island and Wabash railroad stocks in 1910.[18] If the initial terms were sweet enough, insiders could tolerate a good deal of trouble before things began to pinch.[19]

The expanding role of Dunn and the rise to prominence of Robert Fleming as a major financier of these promotions tended to shunt some former allies to the background. R.M. Horne-Payne, for example, complained bitterly during the panic of 1907 of his treatment in the Rio seconds offering at the hands of the upstart James Dunn. Threats of legal action were exchanged before Pearson intervened to calm things down.[20] Mendel, Myers and Company protested that it was not obtaining as favourable a position on the new underwritings as it had in the past.[21] Eventually Sperling and Company, one of the first friends of Canadian enterprise, sensed that it was being frozen out of the Rio second mortgage flotation.

Everyone suspected – with good reason – that other syndicate members and secondary underwriters were being given better deals. Success imparted its own internal tensions. The rapidly expanding new market for these Latin American utilities and railway promotions inevitably raised jealousies. It took considerable skill to chivvy so many egos and conflicting ambitions and so much greed into a lasting combination. Nevertheless, somehow the ever-so-suave Jimmy Dunn managed to keep conflict among the parties within tolerable limits. Notwithstanding many difficulties – exaggerated in the surviving correspondence –there was a great deal of money to be made from commissions, resales, market operations, and arbitrage on these promotions, especially for insiders. As Dunn told a Boston investment dealer with pardonable exaggeration in 1910, 'Money in England is easy and there is a good market here for investment issues.'[22]

Dunn's progress in the city was paralleled by an equally remarkable rise in the political and social realms. Inspired by his boyhood friend Andrew Bonar Law, Dunn took an active interest in Liberal politics, providing funds, advice, and – inevitably – - motor cars whenever needed. Through a close friendship with Lady Violet Asquith, Dunn played the role of raffish guest at various country weekends.[23] His own lavish entertainments at Coombe Hill in Surrey attracted a sizeable social following. In short Jimmy Dunn sought to make himself as indispensable on the Liberal side of politics and society as he had made himself in the City. And to an astonishing degree he succeeded. The Prime Minister could send Venetia Stanley off discreetly in 'a Dunn motor car,' and inevitably the question arose as to whether 'the much debated Dunn' deserved a knighthood.[24]

III

Even the London money market was not big enough for these expensive Latin American ventures. French, German, and Belgian promoters and investors had long been active in Latin America. Pearson acquired the Mexican Electric Works from German owners; the Rio gas and telephone companies were acquired from European syndicates. Percival Farquhar's early Cuban investments in utilities and railroads had been backed by French merchant bankers. Thus a significant market already existed in Europe for investments of the sort Dunn and Pearson were promoting. C.L. Fischer and Percival Farquhar independently forged links to various continental pools of capital.

C.L. Fischer was indispensable to Dunn in these complex negotiations with continental bankers. Not only did Dunn lack the languages, but also he needed a guide to the complex protocols that governed the management of sterling-franc syndicates. Fischer's most valuable contact on the continent was Alfred Loewenstein, founder and managing director of the merchant banking and brokerage house of Stallaerts and Loewenstein. As early as March 1906 Fischer visited Loewenstein in Brussels and interested him in 10,000 Mexico Tramways shares. Loewenstein also held shares in the Rio gas company, shares that Pearson and William Mackenzie needed to secure the Rio promotion.[25]

Loewenstein was every inch the film-maker's notion of a European financier: haughty in bearing and mercurial in negotiations, petulant and threatening when things did not quite work out as planned, always difficult to get along with, proud to a fault, and never quite trustworthy. Nevertheless, he had great flair, impeccable taste, and the means to indulge his passion for flight in the newly developed airplane. (This enthusiasm for the latest technological gadgets on the part of financiers, to the point of incorporation of the technology into their personalities, deserves separate psychosocial analysis.) Loewenstein invented (or so he claimed) the bearer share warrants that allowed Belgian and French investors to avoid paying taxes on these off-shore investments.[26]

Loewenstein put Dunn and Pearson in his permanent debt in 1908 when he joined in to help salvage the disastrous flotation of the Rio second mortgage bonds. In the panic the previous summer he and Dunn had been forced to back out of an earlier underwriting, but early in 1908 Loewenstein and Dunn combined on a $9-million issue of deeply discounted 5 per cent second morgtage bonds denominated in both francs and pounds. Loewenstein, with the assistance of Farquhar, managed to place his portion with the Banque de Paris et des Pays Bas and the Deutsche Bank. In London Robert Fleming supported the operation with timely loans and a commitment to take a large portion of the English underwriting. Loewenstein never let the promoters forget that 80 per cent of this flotation was taken up on the continent and only 20 per cent in Britain, thereby conveniently taking credit for the efforts of Farquhar and Pearson himself.

Percival Farquhar, the expatriate American promoter of Latin American railroads, played an equally essential but ambiguous role in these latter promotions. Farquhar abandoned a successful career as a Wall Street speculator to capitalize on opportunities in Cuba in 1898. When various groups consolidated their interests following the Spanish-American War Farquhar, an engineer by training, emerged as Sir William Van Horne's second in command in the promotion and construction of the Cuba Railroad. In this promotion he met Robert Fleming and Minor Keith, the founder of the United Fruit Company. Keith was also interested in railroad construction to further the enlargement of his rapidly expanding fruit-growing empire. Subsequently Farquhar and Van Horne teamed up to build the Guatemala Railway, and the three formed a loose syndicate to finance Minor Keith's International Railway of Central America.

Along the way Farquhar acquired the backing of the Deutsche Bank, which in 1904 sent him to Brazil to revitalize its flagging utilities company in Rio. There Farquhar served the useful purpose of forcing the Canadians to expand their activities in Rio to counteract his advances, a feint from which he and the Deutsche Bank withdrew counting their money.[27] Nevertheless a close association between Farquhar, Pearson, and Dunn developed around the Rio promotion. Farquhar, who made his headquarters on Rue Louis le Grand in Paris, chose to concentrate upon railroad promotion and construction. His Brazil Railway ultimately developed transcontinental ambitions backed by Parisian and German merchant bankers and in a much smaller way by the familiar Robert Fleming in London.[28]

In Brazil it was assumed that Farquhar and Pearson formed a single interest, a 'trust.' This was not the case. Farquhar, who was fluent in French and Portuguese, played the roles of both helpful fixer and meddlesome intruder in Paris and Rio. Farquhar and Pearson respected each other's promotional abilities, and Farquhar especially valued Alexander Mackenzie's subtle grasp of the Brazilian political situation. But Farquhar was not part of the management group of Rio, nor was Pearson an active participant in Farquhar's Bahia, Pará, Madeira-Mamoré, and trunk railroad enterprises.

Rather an elaborate constellation of Latin American promoters took shape, held in orbit by mutual interests and driven by competitive ambition. In this international financial galaxy, independent centres of activity formed around Minor Keith in Boston with his Central American and Caribbean railroad and dock promotions; Farquhar in Paris, with his Brazilian railroad and Amazon River port and shipping interests; and Pearson and Dunn in New York, Montreal, Toronto, and London, with their Mexican and Brazilian utilities and railroad ventures.[29]

Each promoter had a client group of merchant banker quasi-partners who regularly subscribed for new issues. Moreover, each promoter agreed to take the 'stuff' of the others, and in turn subdivide it among his associated underwriters. No formal alliance bound these men together except the unwritten code of mutuality that required them to give each other ground-floor terms, to stay out of each other's territory, and to make common cause in supporting each other's promotions in the market (up to some indefinable limit of self-interest). They rallied together to fight off bears and float new ventures and, if conditions were right, in a twinkling they could pool their stock to create lucrative bull markets on the bourses and exchanges of two continents.[30] They differed considerably on matters of timing and market tactics, and frequently sent each other confusing signals, buying when they ought to have been selling and vice versa – that being the subject of a good deal of their surviving correspondence. But beneath it all they stuck together, united by a grudging respect for one another, a desire to be in on the next good proposition, and a knowledge that they could not escape each other's grasp without courting general disaster.

Thus through this informal network of mutual obligation the Dunn-Pearson promotions in Brazil and Mexico acquired a broad base among merchant bankers in Berlin, Paris, Brussels, Berne, London, and to a much smaller degree Boston and New York. Robert Fleming in London and Alfred Loewenstein in Brussels took the largest share in these latter promotions, along with the Banque de Paris et des Pays Bas and A. Spitzer and Company in Paris.[31] All around a cloud of old and new 'friends' fluttered, eager to grasp what they could of these golden promotions.

The majority of the bonds of the Pearson group of companies were held by Europeans, mainly Belgian, French, and British investment houses. Indeed, as the centre of gravity shifted gradually to the continent, James Dunn was reduced to pleading with Dr Pearson not to neglect the English market.[32] Canadians held small and declining amounts of bonds and a slightly larger proportion of common stock, an inheritance from the promotional phase. During the summer of 1910 Pearson proposed selling some bonds with a 25 per cent stock bonus in Canada. Dunn protested violently by cable insisting that Canada was a borrowing country whose securities always came to London in bad times; London had provided the money for the enterprise and would provide more if necessary, and loyal London supporters would deeply resent a bond sale in Canada. Pearson failed to convince Dunn that the principal Canadian directors were entitled to a share of the profits. Dunn fumed indignantly to Robert Fleming (no doubt to scotch dangerous rumours): 'I do not see that Canada has done anything for this enterprise and the directors he has there, outside of Blake, Lash and Cassels who are paid for their work, are mere figureheads and are of no possible value to the Company in this country.'[33]

IV

The inner workings of this complex international financial system that connected Europe, Great Britain, and North and South America can best be seen in the 1911 flotation of Pearson's most audacious undertaking of all, the Barcelona Traction, Light and Power Company. Capital markets in general were in a buoyant mood, and the securities of the Pearson group in particular had rebounded (under the influence of the Anuahuac Syndicate)[34] after the market reverses of 1910. The time was ripe for a new promotion.

Pearson visited Spain in September 1911 apparently at the behest of the Deutsche Bank and the Swiss Bank, the principal owners of the Compañía Barcelonesa de Electricidad. The intention in the first instance was to combine a host of small thermal electric companies into one utility linked by long-distance transmission lines to a high-head hydroelectric site in the mountains. As with all Pearson ideas it grew. In fairness, his backers offered him every encouragement.[35] In a short time the promotion flowered into a scheme to develop an integrated hydroelectric system and electrified transportation system for the city of Barcelona and the Catalan region.

After several months spent examining the available hydroelectric sites, Pearson reported that he was 'very well satisfied' with the situation in Barcelona but that he anticipated considerable delay in settling the hydraulic concession with the government. He estimated (as ever optimistically) that it would take about £2.5 million to acquire the necessary underlying properties.[36] By November the promotion had developed sufficient momentum to enable the deal to be packaged for sale.

Old familiar methods were put to use once more. The Barcelona Traction, Light and Power Company was organized in Canada, authorized capitalization being $25 million, with a roster of Canadian financiers known to European investors from previous flotations. Initially £4 million worth of first mortgage bonds were to be issued at 90 per cent with a 50 per cent stock bonus, divided as follows: £1.2 million for Canada, £1.5 million for Europe, and £1.3 million for Britain. Members of the underwriting syndicate bound themselves to stay in the venture until 15 December 1913. Loewenstein in Brussels and Arnold Spitzer in Paris took the entire European offering between them for division among their clients. Fleming in London took only £200,000, but so many other houses were clamouring for a place at the table as to oversubscribe the London issue. E.R. Wood had no difficulty finding buyers in Canada for his portion.[37]

Proceeds from the sale of these securities (£3,238,300 after the discounts and bankers' commissions had been deducted) went towards purchasing the Barcelona Electric Company and various other small companies in the suburbs and the region. Pearson's Barcelona Traction acted as a holding company, financing the purchase of these subsidiaries – most of which retained their legal existence – and undertaking construction of the three hydroelectric installations and the transmission lines, the reconstruction of the distribution system, and the electrification and standardization of the railways once they had all been acquired. Needless to say all this cost a good deal more than Pearson expected, and a further issue of £3.5 million in bonds was needed in 1913 (£2.5 million for the continent, £350,000 for Canada, and £650,000 for Great Britain) – plus some preferred shares – to complete the job.[38]

In most respects the Barcelona promotion went forward like the others. The underlying properties cost more than anticipated, as well-placed owners sensed their strength and drove a hard bargain; more companies were gathered in than was originally intended, and unexpected technical and political delays held up the hydroelectric development. As Dunn explained to an inquiring M.M. Warburg, Pearson 'has found it impossible to proceed with the same rapidity as in the Latin American countries in the settlement of questions with the various departments of the Government of Spain.'[39] Despite these irritating delays, hopes remained high, buoyed by extremely favourable stock markets. And it remained a proposition that even the most cautious of Canadian bankers might recommend to their most valued clients.[40]

Warburg's questions had been prompted by some disturbing rumours. As with all such deals, some people had emerged with less than they considered their due. The principals began fighting with one another as to who was doing the most to maintain the market value of the common stock. Some underwriters suspected others of surreptitiously dumping their securities onto the open market. The Deutsche Bank proved surprisingly difficult: it refused to accept common stock in part payment for the tramway company unless the promoters guaranteed to buy it back at forty dollars per share whenever the bank proposed to sell. Agonizing questions about the relative size of the commissions given continued to go the rounds. There were suggestions that Pearson's construction company was skimming off cream through cost overruns and inflated commissions. When the time came to raise new money there were problems in settling the type, discount, and ranking of the new securities. London failed to hold its own in the eyes of the Europeans. Dunn as usual blamed everyone but himself, insisting that he had taken on the risk of the Deutsche Bank stock and received neither profit nor credit in the transaction. Loewenstein let it be known that though he was doing all the work, Dunn was getting better terms. And so it went.[41]

These were the normal sorts of tensions in any complex underwriting. What set Barcelona apart was the taint of scandal and more than a whiff of blackmail. The facts are by no means clear, but something along the following lines seems to have happened.[42] Led by the Demmé family, the owners of a Spanish waterpower concession (who were also dissident bondholders) demanded an extortionate price for their property; they had grievances of their own against the Jewish financiers who had not offered them insiders' commissions.[43] Spitzer and Loewenstein refused. R.A. Demmé then threatened them with blackmail; either they paid up or he would expose the whole promotion as a swindle. To make matters worse, Loewenstein himself suspected Pearson of fraud. His proposed rejoinder to Demmé threatened to be more damaging than the previous accusations. Dunn tried to restrain the headstrong and increasingly aggressive Loewenstein: 'From what I have heard of the charges of the blackmailing group which you are so bitterly pursuing, I do not find that any of them hold such unfavourable opinions regarding Dr. Pearson as your letter will indicate you do yourself. As in their hands your letter to me would be excellent evidence of the justice of their contention that the Barcelona Traction Co. is a fraudulent organization, I would advise you to keep the copy under lock and key.'[44]

Nevertheless in October 1913 the blackmailers went public. The Paris newspaper *L'Humanité* published on its front page a series of articles on 'a financial scandal which they try to hush up' alleging that officials of the

Paris Bourse had begun to investigate certain Canadian companies operating in France. 'Canadian companies' legislation is particularly elastic, permitting combinations of chance,' the lead article explained. 'Owing to this legislation, financial men can drain French savings to the profit of enterprises operating abroad which are more or less illusory.' The article contained disparaging references to 'internationalist capitalism' operating under a veil of patriotism. Various French ministers were accused of attempting to cover up the scandal or interfering with a full investigation.

It has been necessary to go as far as Canada to find a legislation which permits the formation of a Company with 125 million, of which not a single share has been subscribed in cash and the founders and promoters of which have themselves taken without any scruples Frs. 125,000,000 of shares. Now where do those 125 million go, to the foreign promoters, to the sharpers of international finance, under the shelter of a plenipotentiary minister.[45]

Loewenstein and Dunn struggled to explain to those who were not in the know that these curious financial practices were common and above-board.[46]

Loewenstein, Spitzer, and Dunn organized a frantic damage-control mission. Co-ordinated efforts were mounted in Paris, Brussels, and London to ensure that the newspaper attacks would not have a depressing effect upon the company's securities. A wounded Pearson worried less about the publicity than about Loewenstein's demand to see the books and have an independent engineer examine the property. A proposition could not be evaluated properly in mid-stream, he protested. Moreover, French engineers were 'too theoretical and not practical,' and few had any experience with high-head hydraulic work. They were too rigid and plodding to appreciate the brilliance of his design. Besides, he warned, it was likely that any French engineers would be connected to the company's enemies or competitors.[47]

For the time being a trip to Barcelona and a guided tour by the good doctor himself temporarily mollified Loewenstein. Yet one can sympathize with the hard-pressed financier. It was the old story with Pearson. Loewenstein complained: 'one could reproach the Doctor for having undertaken so many different works at the same moment, because it would probably have been wiser to develop first one hydroelectric power and only afterwards commence the second one, to do the Sarria business at a much later date, and to acquire, on the contrary, much earlier the operation of the Tramways de Barcelona.'[48]

Clearly by 1913 the promotion was falling apart from within. Such troubles were fatally magnified by the sudden onset of a worldwide business recession. As the syndicate scrambled to forestall further damaging revelations in Paris, stock markets came crashing down around them. Tightening credit shifted a punishing burden of obligation and debt upon the insiders, who had just had to take up a new issue of Barcelona preferred shares. The breezes of optimism and easy money that had filled the promoters' sails and order books in 1911–12 gave way to gloomy skies and threatening gales. The principals struggled to meet the carrying charges on unsold, over-valued securities even as they had to go into the market to buy more to stem the downward slide. Bankers became nervous. Insiders once more began accusing one another of not doing enough.[49]

Then at the height of the storm James Dunn suffered the ultimate disaster. C.L. Fischer broke under the pressure and simply ran away. His mysterious disappearance further heightened the strain on Dunn and lent credibility to charges that all had not been proper with his flotations. Dunn claimed publicly that in financial terms Fischer's departure was no great loss.[50] Nevertheless, financial embarrassment was compounded by scandal and a loss of confidence. At the peak of his power the dashing colonial financier became 'the much debated Dunn.'

By late 1913 Barcelona and the numerous Latin American ventures might as well have been a million miles away as far as James Dunn was concerned. He was fighting for his life in the City. In this moment of trial several people stood beside him as he struggled manfully to pay his enormous debts. Robert Fleming loaned Dunn, Fischer and Company £235,000 from his several trust accounts in June 1913. This loan was not in fact repaid, but rather liquidated by Fleming's purchase from Dunn of $1.7 million worth of bonds of Minor Keith's International Railway of Central America.[51]

But that was not enough. A year later Dunn was desperate. The knighthood had now slipped temporarily from his grasp. So, the trappings had to go. Henry Clay Frick was approached for a loan of £150,000 secured by some mundane stock and some extraordinary paintings by Holbein, Goya, El Greco, Gainsborough, and Manet.[52]

As Dunn floundered, so too did the Barcelona venture. A victim of the usual cost overruns, Dr Pearson's incurable experimental engineering impulses, and the inexplicable optimism and lack of managerial control of its promoters, the Barcelona company now became one of the first casualties of war. On 30 December 1914, Barcelona Traction, Light and Power was placed in the hands of a receiver.[53]

Seemingly undented by all this controversy and entrepreneurial failure, Dr F.S. Pearson retreated from the war-torn continent with a new gleam in his eye, a proposition more in tune with the tenor of the times. What a world at war needed badly, he reasoned, was nickel to make armour plate and armour-piercing shells. Gathering up the unfortunate James Dunn – who by now had nothing to lose – Pearson reassured his old partner that this was a sure thing. The two inveterate plungers picked themselves up, dusted themselves off, polished up the Daimler, and like old stagers threw themselves into financing an electrolytic nickel refinery located back where they had started – in Canada.

Main street of the financial village, St James Street, Montreal, circa 1900.
The head office of the Bank of Montreal is on the right.

The architecture of finance,
main branch of the Bank of Montreal,
1905

OPPOSITE

Men who habitually wore their hats indoors,
traders on the Toronto Exchange
in the late nineteenth century

A modern Temple of Vesta, the Montreal Stock Exchange,
opened in 1904

William Mackenzie, capitalist

Zebulon A. Lash, of Blake, Lash and Cassels, master draughtsman of charters, contracts, and trust deeds

James Ross, William Mackenzie's partner in overseas ventures

Early Canadian visitors to the Caribbean,
A.F. Gault and family

After the CPR Sir William Van Horne moved on to Cuba and Central America.

E.S. Clouston, the president of the Bank of Montreal, gave his blessing to these
early promotions abroad.

Clouston's Toronto counterpart at the Bank of Commerce,
Edmund Walker, here surrounded by his picture collection,
is seen talking with the Arctic explorer Shackleton.

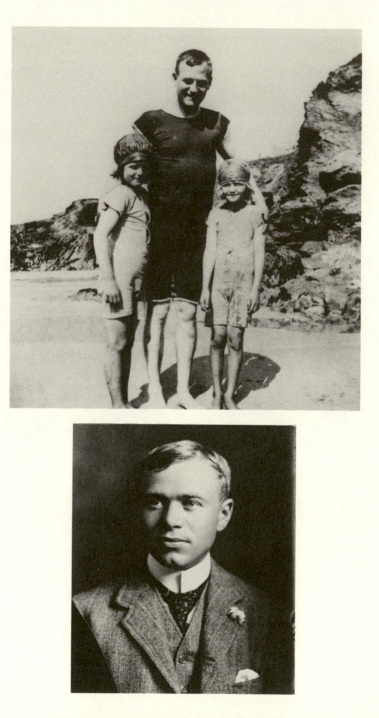

The little man with the big head, Max Aitken

The much-debated James Dunn
at the seaside with his daughters about 1913

F.S. Pearson,
electrical engineer and inveterate promoter,
in a rare moment of repose

Building the São Paulo Tramway, Light and Power dam
at Parnaíba, January 1901

Brazilian labourers at Parnaíba

Feeder pipe to the powerhouse at Parnaíba

Falls of the Ribeirão das Lajes, the hydraulic foundation
of Rio de Janeiro Tramway, Light and Power Company

Drawing of the Lajes powerhouse
showing feeder pipes on the right and
incline railway on the left

View of the Serra do Mar, site of the Lajes hydroelectric development

Avenida Central, Rio de Janeiro, in the gaslight era

An electric tram on the Carioca line
crossing the old aqueduct (1740),
Rio de Janeiro

OPPOSITE

Villa Isabel mule trams on Uruguayana Street, Rio de Janeiro

Alexander Mackenzie,
the indispensable Canadian in Brazil

Dignitaries at the opening of the
Lajes power station, May 1906,
President Nilo Peçanha of the State of Rio
seated right of centre;
Alexander Mackenzie centre rear

José Limantour, leading cientifico
and Diaz's finance minister

Porfirio Diaz, president of Mexico,
whose regime accorded liberal
treatment to foreign investors

The rugged landscape at Necaxa transformed by F.S. Pearson

Construction of the main control dam of the Mexican Light and Power Company,
Necaxa, 1909

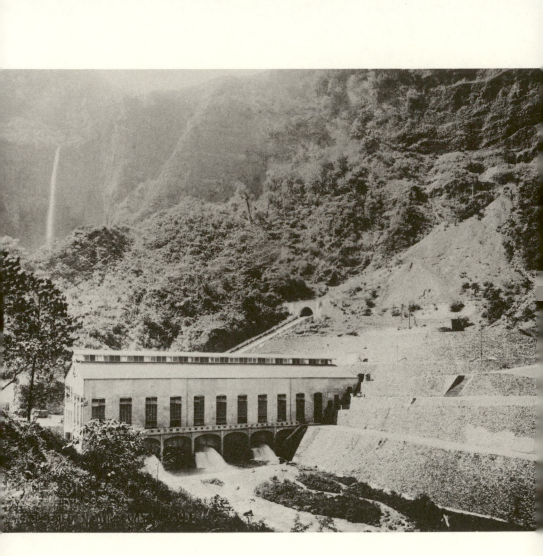

Powerhouse of the Mexican Light and Power Company, Necaxa

OPPOSITE

Pancho Villa temporarily occupies the presidential chair
with Emiliano Zapata on his right.

Foreign-owned trolley cars and electric lights transform Mexico City.

British diplomat Thomas Hohler who acted as go-between for the companies during the Mexican Revolution

Alfred Loewenstein descends upon Toronto in May 1928.

THE EVENING TELEGRAM. TORONTO, WEDNESDAY, MAY 2, 1928

ritish Women Rejoice Over Flapper Vote

ndon, May 2—Fully 1,000 dele-
are attending the convention
n Women's National Liberal
tion, which opened here yes-
y. Mrs. Margery Corbett Ashby,
esident of the Federation, is
president of the International
ry Suffrage Alliance.
r Banister Fletcher, a doughty
er for female enfranchisement
before the word "suffragette"
coined, moved a resolution re-
g that women had now come
er rights through the exten-
of the franchise to women 21
of age. This resolution was
ed with enthusiasm by the con-
n. Amongst the pioneers in
men's suffrage movement, the
s of two were specially men-
Josephine Butler and Mrs.
rton, the latter being near
th birthday.

it Other Teams. But Insist on Local Softball Players

MPTON, May 2.—The organ-
meeting of the Peel-York
ll League was held at Wild-
ast night. Alec Houston, hon-
president in the chair. Several
rs were made in the constitu-
n opening being made for the
ce of other teams into the
being one, the present league
ting of Wildfield, Humbersale
ne and Nashville. It was

BELGIAN MILLIONAIRE FINANCIER HERE

CAPT. ALFRED LOEWENSTEIN,
who is in the city to-day for a series
of conferences with Toronto business men arising out of complaints
of Belgian sharcholders in the Rio
de Janeiro Tramways, now controlled by Brazilian Tractions.

COMMITTEE TO REVIEW IT
ST. JOHN'S CHURCH TROUBLE

Toronto Presbytery Hears of Controversy in Private—"Divisionists"
Came in For Criticism.

omplaints and disagreements in
St. John's Presbyterian Church,
Broadview avenue, were dealt with
at last night's meeting of Toronto
Presbytery, held in St. Andrew's Institute, and the whole matter was
referred to a special committee of
Presbytery, consisting of Rev. Dr.
J. G. Inkster, Rev. Dr. D. T. L. Mc-
Kerroll, Rev. Dr. Wm. Rochester.
Messrs Wm. McKenzie and Samuel
Wallace, six additional ministers and
an equal number of elders to be added by the Moderator and Clerk. The
ress and those who were not official members of the Presbytery
were asked to leave the meeting during the discussion of the controversy

Doubtful l Egypt's R Satisfa

London, May 2.— W
Egyptian reply to the
matum would lessen the
tween the two countri
garded as questionable
The Egyptian reply
consideration of the Ass
had been postponed, w
British had demanded
drawal of the measure.
ber of the cabinet was o
saying that postponeme
bill would not satisfy
ment.
The Earl of Birken
tary of State for India,
speech that it was usel
pone the action "for n
country with imperial
ties, with obligations to
pean nations and the vit
of maintaining com
agree to legislation lik
never, in my opinion, wi
try under any governmen
BILL CANNOT BE WIT
The Egyptian reply,
delivered at the British r
Cairo, said that Egypt b
she constitutionally cou
poning examination of
blies Bill until the next
tary session for the sa
understanding between th
tries and in response
matum. The reply regre
tervention of Britain ir
legislation.
The Daily Mail to-day
personal statement fro
Mahas Pasha, cabled fr

PART FOUR

War and Revolution

9

Rates of Exchange

Brazilian Traction was a creature of the last bull market before the First World War. In order to distribute some of the large profits being earned by the São Paulo and Rio companies, Pearson, Dunn, Loewenstein, and William Mackenzie decided to create a holding company called Brazilian Traction, Light and Power. This corporate reorganization also permitted the authorized capitalization of all the Canadian utilities in Brazil to be doubled. The grouping of all the assets under one corporate umbrella was designed to facilitate the raising of additional capital to permit the expansion and development of gas, electrical, transit, and telephone services in the Brazilian heartland.

The Rio and São Paulo companies faced problems common to public service corporations in many jurisdictions: rapidly increasing demand for their services required almost continuous expansion of their plant. As E.R. Wood observed, 'In this respect the São Paulo company is no doubt having the same experience as all other public service corporations operating in rapidly growing communities.'[1] Profitability attracted the envious attention of potential competitors and required careful negotiation about franchises and concessions in order to maintain a hold on local markets. Both expansion and negotiation required great tact.

This financially driven reorganization increased the pressure upon Alexander Mackenzie, the Canadian managing director on the spot in Brazil. First he had to wring more income out of the underlying companies and at the same time satisfy the Brazilian authorities that no undue profiteering was taking place. Secondly, just as he began this difficult

TABLE 7
Population of Brazilian, Mexican, and Canadian Cities, 1900–20

City	1900	1910	1920
Rio de Janeiro	691,000	—	1,157,873
São Paulo	239,000	—	600,000
Mexico City	344,721	471,066	600,000
Montreal	267,730	479,480	618,506
Toronto	208,040	376,538	521,893
Winnipeg	42,340	136,035	179,087

SOURCES R.E. Boyer and K.A. Davies, *Urbanization in Nineteenth-Century Latin America: Supplement to the Statistical Abstract of Latin America* (Los Angeles: Latin American Center, University of California, 1973); George A. Nader, *Cities of Canada*, vol. 2, *Profiles of Fifteen Metropolitan Centres* (Toronto: Macmillan, 1976)

juggling act, the First World War overturned the international financial system under which these ventures had been promoted and organized. The impossibility of long-term borrowing and the fluctuation of rates of exchange created particular problems. When the international capital flows that had given rise to Brazilian Traction dried up after 1915 and the company still needed additional funds to grow, management had to look inward to retained earnings for investment funds. Then its overcapitalization became a burden.

I

By 1909 Mackenzie had succeeded in settling franchise problems with the Brazilian authorities; but the lower electricity rates that had been offered in exchange for extending the term of the concessions only increased the demand for power. All the major cities of Latin America were growing steadily at this time, and by 1910 the largest ones had outpaced their Canadian counterparts (see Table 7). Rio was almost twice the size of Montreal (and Mexico City), while São Paulo was considerably larger than Toronto and far bigger than Winnipeg, the next largest Canadian city. Although real income and consumption of electricity and telephone service per capita were much higher in North America than in South America, the rate of urban growth still meant that utility systems there would have to undergo continuous expansion to meet demand.

This problem was exacerbated by a drought at São Paulo in December 1910 that forced the company to cut off several large power consumers.

The Parnaíba plant's capacity would be exhausted within two years, so F.S. Pearson concluded that the time had come to commence construction of a new hydroelectric development. When some German interests offered to construct a powerplant on the Sorocaba River to supply current, the São Paulo company discovered that a 50,000 horsepower plant could be built there. By acquiring the German interests, an initial investment of $4 million would produce 20,000 horsepower within eighteen months, leaving the way open for further expansion later.

Because the São Paulo company was going to need to raise up to $10 million over the next decade, it was decided to incorporate a subsidiary to develop the Sorocaba called the São Paulo Electric Company. Chartered in Canada this company would raise the money to build the dam by selling $5 million worth of bonds, while all the common stock would be retained by the parent firm.[2]

During 1911 while this project was still in the planning stage, Pearson acquired a substantial interest in the San Paulo Gas Company from British interests. That year saw further capital spending of $1.8 million, and the board approved the expenditure of $3.5 million during 1912.[3] Great as the earning power of São Paulo Tramway was, large amounts of additional capital would have to be raised in the near future.

Near the end of 1910 the directors considered replacing the existing $6 million worth of São Paulo bonds with a new issue of $10 million, the additional funds to be used for construction. From Brazil Pearson tried to convince them that the time had come to triple the bond issue to $20 million, since half that sum would be needed during the next five years alone. He failed to persuade the board, however, and the idea of a new bond issue was eventually dropped. Instead the directors decided to create a new series of perpetual debentures denominated in sterling that could be sold in London as money was required. A first instalment of these worth $1.5 million was sold with great success early in 1911 and an equal amount later that same year.[4]

So well were these debentures received that two further issues totalling $2.5 million were sold over the next year or so. Since the dividend rate on the common stock had been raised to 10 per cent in the fall of 1909 and the stock continued to trade at a premium, the São Paulo company seemed in a very healthy state.[5] Even with the costly new hydroelectric development at Sorocaba spun off into the São Paulo Electric Company in 1911, however, it was clear that further substantial sums would have to be raised before long to improve the tramway and develop the telephone system.

In Rio the reconstruction of the tramway system that commenced in 1908 proved much more costly than had originally been anticipated. Nonetheless, in 1909 the board of directors approved the acquisition of a fourth tram company, the Jardim Botânico. Originally expected to cost $3.5 million, this purchase ultimately required $5 million. And the following year the Rio company also took over the Interurban Telephone Company, which had the exclusive right to string lines throughout the state of Rio, so that its long-distance lines complemented the urban service.[6]

The need for funds continued to mount relentlessly, and the authorized capital stock of the Rio company was raised from $25 million to $40 million in the spring of 1909; 62,500 additional shares were immediately offered to the current stockholders at par. To make the shares more attractive, a 4 per cent dividend was commenced at the end of the year.[7] By the spring of 1910 another 62,500 shares and more second mortgage bonds had to be sold to finance acquisitions and construction. Even the raising of the annual dividend to 5 per cent, however, failed to persuade most of the stockholders to subscribe for more shares.[8]

By mid-1910 the company's bankers were once more complaining about the size of its overdraft, and in the autumn the board authorized F.S. Pearson to dispose of the remaining 25,000 shares of treasury stock in London. When buyers showed little interest, the shareholders were once more offered a chance to subscribe, and this time responded much more enthusiastically, influenced by favourable earnings figures. All $40 million par value worth of common shares had then been issued.[9]

Another $7.5 worth of Rio second mortgage bonds were sold during 1911. Some of the funds were used to set up the European-Brazilian Shipping Company and purchase a fleet of four colliers to carry gas coal to the reconstructed Rio gas plant. Later three more vessels were acquired.[10] But there still remained expensive projects to complete, such as the Piraí diversion tunnel to increase generating capacity at the Lajes plant. At the end of 1911 the board decided to authorize the creation of another $10 million worth of common stock and immediately disposed of $5 million worth to the annoyance of some European investors who resented the dilution of their equity.[11]

By early 1912 Rio de Janeiro Tramway had outstanding $45 million worth of common stock and $25 million each in first and second mortgage bonds. The São Paulo company had issued $10 million worth of common stock, $6 million in bonds and $4 million worth of perpetual debentures. And still Pearson's plans were far from being complete. As a result the interlocking boards of directors reached a decision to restructure the whole enterprise in order to create capital gains for the shareholders and to facilitate the raising of funds in the future. Market conditions in London and Europe seemed especially propitious for such a move, and the formal transfer of assets took place in October 1912.

Through a share exchange a new holding company was set up. Brazilian Traction would control the three underlying companies (including São Paulo Electric) and create common stock with a par value of $110 million, nearly double the total amount previously issued by the three subsidiaries, upon which a 6 per cent dividend would be paid. In exchange for allowing net earnings to flow through to Brazilian Traction, the Rio company would receive over the next five years $8 million to discharge its debts and $15 million to extend its plant, while the São Paulo company would get $4 million for debt and $10 million for expansion, and São Paulo Electric would receive the funds needed to complete the Sorocaba plant.[12]

Unfortunately, the buoyant markets upon which this massive recapitalization was floated did not last. Within a few months of its creation Brazilian Traction returned to the capital markets in London to raise funds for projects like the Piraí diversion tunnel by offering shareholders the chance to subscribe for $10 million worth of 6 per cent preference stock. Almost from that moment the price of the common stock began to decline from par to about $88. In part that drop simply reflected the impact of another downturn in the business cycle that began in 1913, but on the London exchange the price of such so-called Canadian stocks as the Brazilian and Mexican utilities slid more than most. One Englishman observed that, 'It really appears that some who have inside knowledge must be pressing the shares continually for sale.' He was quite correct, of course, for men like F.S. Pearson and James Dunn were doing their utmost to dispose of their holdings in order to avert bankruptcy as the prices of the shares of the companies they controlled tumbled.[13]

Worse was in store in 1914, when the stock fell as low as seventy-seven dollars before recovering to about eighty dollars. Why, asked one Englishman, should Brazilian Traction shares be selling for only five dollars more than those of Mexico Tramways, which was operating in a city embroiled in a revolution? *Le Comptant*, a Paris financial newspaper, charged that the company's concessions were shaky and that the management consisted of shysters: 'Brazilian Traction was organized in Canada for the purpose of carrying on business in Brazil with French money according to North American financial methods.'[14]

None of the optimistic expectations that had led to the creation of Brazilian Traction had been realized by 1914. Although the need for additional capital remained very great, the depressed state of the stock markets made any new flotation impossible except at a high cost. About the only thing from which investors could draw some comfort was the return to Brazil of Alexander Mackenzie. Early in 1911 he had expressed a wish to resign as chief operating officer. Owing to his skill in dealing with the Brazilian authorities, Mackenzie was as nearly indispensable as any one person could be. For more than a year the board ignored his request to leave, but eventually bowed to the inevitable and accepted his resignation as vice-president and director. His duties were divided between W.N. Walmsley, the general manager in São Paulo, and F.A. Huntress, Walmsley's counterpart in Rio.[15]

Early in 1914, however, Mackenzie was persuaded to return to Brazil temporarily to deal with a number of urgent problems. Rumours were circulating that the Guinle family might be ready to come to terms. After discussions with Mackenzie, the Guinles demanded $14 million for their generating station and their numerous concessions. Mackenzie, however, considered these worth no more than $8 million. When an agreement could not be reached, Mackenzie left Brazil as prearranged.[16]

Continuing problems in Brazil, however, convinced the board of directors that only Alexander Mackenzie possessed the talent needed to handle this difficult situation. F.S. Pearson turned on his charm and, with the utmost reluctance, Mackenzie agreed to return once more in 1915. The Reid concession was due to expire that June, ending the Rio company's exclusive franchise to supply power in the Federal District. In September the gas company's monopoly over private lighting would also expire. The hope was that Mackenzie might secure extensions of these in exchange for lower rates. Unfortunately, an agent of the Guinles was president of the Rio city council and well placed to block any such deal. An effort to secure an extension of the São Paulo company's monopoly on light and power past 1919 had also recently been blocked by the Guinles. Still it was hoped that Mackenzie could now achieve some sort of settlement.[17]

The other major item of business concerned the telephone system. Brazilian Traction controlled local service in Rio through the Brazilianische Elektricitäts Gesellschaft (acquired with the Villa Isabel tramway). The BEG franchise would expire in 1929, at which time the municipality could acquire the property for half the cost of the lands, buildings, and exchanges plus one-third the cost of all other equipment. Not only did the Canadians want an extension of the franchise to protect their investment, they also wanted to use the Interurban Telephone Company's franchise to build trunk lines to São Paulo and other centres and to acquire the São Paulo Telephone Company and the Bragantina Company, which served many parts of the state of São Paulo.[18]

Negotiations for the acquisition of the Bragantina Company from its British owners had begun in 1914, and the São Paulo system was taken over from its local owners that fall. If Mackenzie could arrange a satisfactory franchise, all these properties would be folded into the new Rio de Janeiro and São Paulo Telephone Company, which would borrow the money needed to modernize and extend the service. Mackenzie was now prepared to offer the Guinles $10 million for their interests provided they would accept one third of the purchase price in bonds:

We finally believe now is the opportunity to liquidate the only menace we have in Brazil, placing ourselves in a position much stronger than before. With Guinles eliminated, or rather connected with us, there is no other financial group who would be so rash as to try to compete, especially in view of our monopolies.[19]

While these delicate negotiations were under way in the spring of 1915, the managements of the Mexican and Brazilian companies were rocked by shocking news. Still struggling to recoup his damaged fortunes and battered by the recession that had begun in 1913, F.S. Pearson had continued to shuttle back and forth across the Atlantic in search of business opportunities. Once the war began, Fred Pearson and Jimmy Dunn fixed their hopes upon establishing a new nickel refinery in Canada and selling this vital strategic material to the Allies. Both of them pestered the Canadian and British governments incessantly for the loans and guarantees that would make it possible to float the new venture. Eventually the Canadian prime minister, Sir Robert Borden, met Pearson in Ottawa and told him he would provide no aid without some firm commitment on the part of the British to purchase the output of the new refinery.[20]

Like the born salesman he was, Pearson immediately set off for London to peddle his latest wares to the British Admiralty. He and his wife booked a passage on the Cunard liner *Lusitania*, sailing from New York on 1 May 1915. They enjoyed themselves on board, dining at a table with the flamboyant wine merchant George Kessler, the 'Champagne king' of London, and playing bridge with the well-known Irish art collector, Sir Hugh Lane, and the wife of Canadian shipping magnate Sir Montagu

Allan. In quieter moments Fred Pearson talked with New York playwright Charles Klein about their shared passion for collecting church organs. If the British American Nickel Company proved to be the success he and Jimmy Dunn hoped for, Pearson could treat himself to an addition to his large collection of these instruments.

Around two o'clock in the afternoon of 7 May 1915, with the Irish coast in plain sight, a torpedo fired by a German u-boat struck the *Lusitania* amidships. A huge explosion plumed skyward, and the liner listed sharply to starboard and sank bow first within just eighteen minutes. More than 1,100 passengers and crew were drowned. The bodies of Fred and Mabel Pearson were among those retrieved within a few days while they could still be identified.[21]

The news sent a shudder through those involved in what had come to be known as the 'Pearson group' of companies. Sir William Mackenzie told a meeting of the Rio board, with pardonable exaggeration, that it owed its very existence to Pearson's genius, while

the personal aspect [of] the tragedy would be felt keenly by all who had been privileged to be associated with Dr. Pearson and had felt the charm of his personality. Considering his death from a purely impersonal point of view it was hard to overestimate the loss. Dr. Pearson's mentality was of such a high order that he had attained an almost unique position in the engineering world while still quite a young man, and for many years he had been recognized as one of the world's greatest engineers.[22]

The only person who could take Pearson's place in the affairs of Brazilian Traction was Alexander Mackenzie. In order to calm nervous investors he was immediately named president of the company and its major subsidiaries.[23] From that time onward he occupied much the most important role of any single person in the affairs of the Brazilian utility conglomerate.

II

After taking over in 1915 Mackenzie had to deal with the turmoil within the international financial system caused by the First World War. In a way the war was something of a blessing, for the general disarray of stock markets masked the particular difficulties of the Brazilian enterprise and created a state of indefinite financial limbo. That was all to the good. However, the most acute problems involved the rate of exchange of the Brazilian milréis

TABLE 8
Brazilian Traction Earnings, 1913–16 (year ending 31 Dec.)

	1913	1914	1915	1916
Gross earnings (000 milréis)	71,912	73,185	77,119	84,942
Net earnings (000 milréis)	39,313	41,880	44,177	46,526

SOURCE Brazilian Traction, Annual Report, 1916

TABLE 9
Brazilian Traction Revenues, 1913–16
(year ending 31 Dec.)

	1913	1914	1915	1916
Approximate rate of exchange	16d.	15d.	12d.	12d.
Net revenue (000 $Can.)	8,421	8,059	5,613	6,019
Surplus revenues (000 $Can.)	8,112	7,667	5,395	5,675

SOURCE Brazilian Traction, Annual Report, 1916

with the pound and the dollar and the closure of European capital markets to all foreign borrowers.

In neutral Brazil itself the fighting in Europe seemed to have only a minor impact. For Brazilian Traction business not only continued as usual but grew handily (see Table 8). Problems became evident, however, when these earnings were exchanged into the pounds and dollars needed to pay dividends and bond interest. As Alexander Mackenzie and the board of Brazilian Traction watched with dismay, the number of British pence that the Brazilian milréis would buy (which was how the rate of exchange was always stated) slid downward 25 per cent from pre-war levels by 1915 (see Table 9). The 6 per cent dividend on $110 million worth of common shares required $6,250,000 to service, the preference shares another $600,000 annually. This required the company to dip into its reserves by 1915.

Coping with a fluctuating exchange was not, of course, something unknown for companies operating in Brazil. When the republic succeeded the empire in 1889 the value of the milréis was fixed at an official rate of exchange of 27d. sterling. The economic depression and political turmoil of the 1890s, however, pushed the milréis as low as 5½d. by 1897, when the government declared a moratorium on interest payments on its foreign debt for a three-year period. A rise in the exchange commenced in 1899, and by the time the São Paulo company began construction the milréis had reached 7½d. As the end of the moratorium approached, an orgy of speculation propelled it as high as 14⅜d., though it later slid off to around 12d. There the rate remained for the ensuing five years, until a burst of economic growth, fuelled in part by foreign loans to Brazil including the investment in utilities in Rio, helped to propel it as high as 18d. by 1905.[24]

The appreciation of the milréis after 1899 naturally aided foreign-financed companies already operating in Brazil: the burden of interest and dividend payments abroad became less onerous than had been anticipated. Alexander Mackenzie noted, 'For the São Paulo company the rise is, of course, pure gain.' The Rio company, which was only getting under way when the milréis moved upward from 12d., benefited less: properties and capital goods cost more than expected. Not only that but Brazil's prosperity induced inflation, which pushed wages upwards sharply after 1904, increasing labour costs for construction by 50 per cent according to F.S. Pearson's estimates.[25]

The rising exchange also produced falling coffee prices, a problem exacerbated by persistent over-production, and in 1906 the Brazilians embarked upon the valorization of coffee and the stabilization of the milréis at 15d. This rate remained fixed until 1910 when further upward pressure led to its revaluation to 16d., the rate at which it stayed until war broke out in 1914. At that time Brazil again suspended payments on its foreign debt and issued large amounts of paper currency, and the milréis skidded downward to little more than 10d. Subsequently it recovered to about 12d., but this 25 per cent decline in exchange posed a severe challenge to Brazilian Traction.[26]

Experience with Brazil's chequered financial history had long since led foreign lenders to try to insulate themselves from such fluctuations. Customs duties were collected on a basis that blended the paper value of the milréis and its gold value at the official rate of 27d. to ensure the ability to service the foreign debt. The Belgian-based Rio Gas Company, which had struggled through the financial chaos of the 1880s and 1890s, required its customers to pay rates fixed on a similar half-paper, half-gold basis and, when the gas company was taken over, all lighting consumers, whether gas or electric, were made to pay on the same basis. Most electric power users in Rio paid on a paper basis alone, but a few large accounts were payable on a gold basis with the rate of exchange fixed at 15d. The Rio telephone concession fixed rates on a sliding scale that permitted the company to levy a 20 per cent increase if the exchange fell from 15d. to 12d. Only tram riders in Rio, who paid fares solely on the basis of the paper milréis, were unaffected by the rate of exchange.[27]

The São Paulo company had much less protection against falling exchange rates. As in Rio the tram fares were fixed solely on a paper basis, and so were the electricity rates. Aware of the danger, management sought to secure some insurance against a decline. The largest power consumer, who took nearly 20 per cent of output, was made to pay on an exclusively gold basis. Arguing that the interest payments on private foreign debt ought to be given the same kind of protection as those on Brazilian government borrowings, the company claimed that rates should be fixed on the part-gold, part-paper basis used by the San Paulo Gas Company (control of which was not acquired until 1911). São Paulo Electric (which sold wholesale power to the tramway) also fixed its rates in this way when it began operation.[28]

When war broke out in 1914 Brazilian Traction soon felt the impact. Remitting funds overseas became almost impossible for a brief period. The company purchased bills of exchange for coffee, drawn on London, but these were simply not available at first and later realized only 10⅝d. per milréis. To meet the hugely increased burden of dividends on $110 million worth of common stock issued by 1912, F.S. Pearson resorted to the ingenious expedient of using the company's fleet of colliers to ship bags of coffee, which could still be sold to net nearly 14d. per milréis. This tactic had to be largely abandoned in 1915, however, when the French government banned the import of coffee to conserve foreign exchange, thus seriously depressing prices.[29]

With the milréis hovering at around 12d., the board of directors decided in mid-1915 to cut the dividend from 6 per cent to 4 per cent. Shareholders, themselves just beginning to feel the pinch of wartime inflation, reacted angrily; 'drastic,' 'appalling,' and 'horrible' were among the terms used by one person. Others expressed doubts about the competence of management when it became clear that the company also needed to borrow more money to finance new investment. From Hertfordshire a man complained that,

This is despicable if true. I do not like to think what you are doing to the value of the common shares. Perhaps you do not mind what people think, but I can assure you that the method of dealing with this great matter are [sic] making people on this side very shy of any more companies run from Canada.[30]

By the start of 1916 the situation seemed to have improved somewhat. Gross and net revenues in milréis were up handsomely, and the exchange had stabilized at 12d. The dividend was continued at 4 per cent, but more trying times lay ahead. In October 1916 an influenza epidemic in Rio killed 4,000 people and left the utilities struggling to provide service with a skeleton workforce. 'It does seem,' wrote General Manager F.A. Huntress, 'as if we played in rotten luck during the last six months.' A few days later the British Admiralty requisitioned all but two of the ships on the Rio–New York run, leaving insufficient cargo capacity to supply the coal required by the gas works. If the gas was cut off the franchise, in which $30 million had been invested, would be forfeit. 'In [the] best of circumstances we cannot make any profit,' moaned Alexander Mackenzie, '[and the] most we can hope for is to avoid ruin.'[31]

By the close of the year he was in London for consultations with British board members and investors. Mackenzie had come to the conclusion that the common stock dividend would have to be suspended altogether at a saving of $4.25 million annually. These funds could be used to repay bank loans totalling more than $8.6 million that had financed new investment during the past three years and to pay for $1.7 million worth of projects planned in 1917. The consolidation and expansion of the telephone system was proving particularly costly, and Mackenzie had been forced to the conclusion that the war had rendered the sale of long-term bonds impossible for the time being.[32]

Visiting North America en route to Britain he had sought to arrange the telephone financing in New York. The financiers whom he consulted agreed that the property was a desirable one. An expert recruited from the Bell Telephone Company of Canada noted that the expiry of the Rio franchise in 1929 was a cause for concern, but reported that linking the major urban centres with trunk lines should ensure dominance:

the acquisition of the long distance system is of great value in itself, for the telephone experience in North America has shown that the greater part of the earnings of the telephone companies comes from the long distance system, and, in fact, the tendency is now to regard the local systems mainly as feeders to the long distance system.

This, of course, was the strategy Bell Canada had followed with such success. Only 1 per cent of the urban population (and just 0.25 per cent of the total population) in Brazil had telephone service, while in the United

States there were already ten phones per hundred people. Brazilian toll revenues amounted to just four cents per capita versus seventy cents in the United States. Mackenzie pointed out that, 'We remove powerful possible competitors in the territories of the Brazilianische and Interurban companies, and by connecting their various systems and improving them we create a large volume of business.' He predicted that within two years the telephone system could be generating net earnings of more than $1 million.[33]

Unfortunately, Brazilian Traction required permanent financing of the $5 million for the purchase of the São Paulo and Bragantina companies, plus $2.6 million for new construction. But nobody was willing to underwrite the kind of long term mortgage bonds upon which the utilities had relied prior to the war. In the end all that Mackenzie could achieve was the sale of $7.5 million worth of three-year notes to the New York merchant banking firm of W.A. Read and Company at 92½ per cent.[34] This discount plus the 6 per cent annual interest and the commitment to repay in gold made these funds very costly and convinced Mackenzie that henceforth investment must be financed from retained earnings; that, in turn, entailed cancellation of the common stock dividend.

The rest of the directors in Toronto could not yet bring themselves to accept the logic of the situation. Mackenzie's insistence that optimistic predictions about a rise in the rate of exchange were unfounded was ignored, even though he pointed out that the situation was likely to get worse rather than better as Britain had now joined France in banning coffee imports. But the board persuaded the Bank of Commerce to grant further accommodation, and the dividend was continued for the first quarter of 1917 at the rate of 1 per cent (or 4 per cent annually). Eventually, however, the grim reality of the situation could be ignored no longer. In April, 1917 the dividend was finally suspended – to predictable cries of anguish from the shareholders, who watched stock prices tumble to about forty dollars per share while they fumed at the realization that steadily rising revenues in Brazil were being used to retire debt and extend the plant.[35]

The years after 1914 brought testing times for Brazilian Traction, created at the height of pre-war optimism in 1912. Millions of dollars' worth of additional common stock was issued, but under the conditions prevailing at that time the earnings in Rio and São Paulo seemed more than enough to meet the 6 per cent dividend promised to the shareholders. Bankers and investors then were eager to lend the company long-term funds to build powerplants and extend telephone service, with the probability of increased profits in the future as an incentive.

By mid-1917 all that had changed dramatically. Pearson himself had perished in the Irish Sea, and Alexander Mackenzie was grappling with the most difficult times encountered since the Rio company had teetered on the verge of bankruptcy in the recession of 1907. Earnings in milréis might be rising steadily, but they could no longer be exchanged for enough pounds and dollars to pay the thousands of shareholders in Europe and North America. Share prices tumbled once the dividend was suspended. Financiers refused to make long-term loans to the company and extracted a heavy price for short-term funds. Nor could Mackenzie count on much assistance from his namesake Sir William Mackenzie, who was increasingly preoccupied as his Canadian Northern Railway empire collapsed into bankruptcy and was taken over by the government. As he set off for Brazil from London in the spring of 1917, Alexander Mackenzie must sometimes have wondered whether Brazilian Traction would ever recover the reputation for profitability it had enjoyed among international investors prior to the outbreak of the war in Europe.

10

In Extremis

The president of a Canadian bank once advised a British investor disappointed with the performance of his Canadian securities to look into São Paulo, Rio, and Mexican utilities. 'They have, on the one hand, the advantages of being based upon charters given by countries very anxious indeed for development to take place and not having socialistic views or envy of those who may make money out of such charters,' Edmund Walker reminded his correspondent. 'On the other hand, some people are afraid of investments in those countries because of the possibility of political revolutions, etc. You are in England a better judge of these points than we are here.'[1] Nothing could have been further from the truth. The Mexican Revolution caught everyone by surprise in Great Britain, the United States and Europe, as well as Canada.

As Robert Freeman Smith has observed: 'The Mexican Revolution was the first important challenge to the world order of the industrial-creditor, and capitalistic, nations made by an underdeveloped nation trying to assert control over its economy and reform its internal system.'[2] In Mexico after 1911 all the fundamental underpinnings of international commerce were swept away. Mexico Tramways, Mexican Light and Power, and a host of other foreign enterprises had to come to terms with the bewildering, totally unfamiliar world of violent revolution.

At first the major problem posed by the Mexican Revolution was that of restoring some form of political and legal order. Later, as the Revolution became a more open class conflict and a nationalist government sought to alter the rules of the international game more in Mexico's favour, these companies confronted the possible confiscation of their damaged property. When the Revolution turned against foreign enterprises and the threat to property came not from bandits but from the government itself, mere survival became the primary goal.

What the Revolution began the First World War completed. Corporate objectives had to be pursued against a larger backdrop of Anglo-American rivalry for predominance in Mexico, the strategic concerns of belligerents and neutrals during a protracted world war, and finally the unpredictable convolutions of revolution, counter-revolution, and continuous rebellion. In Mexico the Canadian utilities were plunged into a revolutionary maelstrom; as elsewhere they demonstrated remarkable buoyancy.

I

International capitalism rested upon certain fundamental ideological and institutional presuppositions. First and foremost the creditor-industrial nations assumed that the markets of underdeveloped countries should be as open as possible to business, which meant in effect to the trade, investment, and entrepreneurship of Europe and the United States. To enhance the progress of underdeveloped countries and, not incidentally, the power and profits of developed ones, the natural resources of the poorer countries ought to be freely exportable, their domestic markets open to imported goods, and foreign investors given full and secure sway to unleash development. Under President Porfirio Díaz, Mexico was from this perspective a model regime: duly respectful, pliant when called upon, effectively authoritarian, monetarily orthodox (it went on the gold standard in 1905), economically liberal, friendly to foreign investment, and tolerably corrupt. For such good fortune one must necessarily pay.

Capitalism also required if not the rule of law, at least some kind of enforceable local order. It followed that foreign investment was protected not only by the laws and authorities of the host country (which might be arbitrary or suspect), but also by the combined moral force and military might of the industrialized countries. Capital demanded not national treatment but rather home treatment. Further it was believed that the greater wealth and power of the developed nations endowed them with a moral right, perhaps even a duty, to police the underdeveloped world to ensure the stability and order upon which a mutually beneficial international capitalism depended.

The economic corollary to this ideology of commercial imperialism was a reasonably stable rate of exchange, in this instance based upon the gold standard. The benevolent forces of trade and investment would then graft the developing countries permanently onto the trunk of western economic development. In due course international capitalism and foreign tutelage would give rise to prosperous, law-abiding, progressive societies that knew their place in the international order. And in the event that this flattering Eurocentric image and transcript failed to appear, that merely confirmed the moral inferiority of the underdeveloped countries and justified the taking of stern measures. As President Woodrow Wilson bluntly summarized us policy towards Latin America in 1913: 'I am going to teach the South American republics to elect good men.'[3]

The Canadian utilities abroad depended as much as any other foreign ventures upon this international capitalist system. Although Canada itself remained an insignificant colony economically and politically, its businessmen nevertheless had the advantage of operating under the informal but clear hegemony of two great empires, Great Britain and the United States, without necessarily suffering the obloquy of power. Capital intensive utilities were especially vulnerable to local depredations. They could not operate without access to foreign capital and imported capital goods. The fragility of their concessions and franchises made their managers fetishistic on the subject of the sanctity of private property. Utilities, as much as oil companies, mines, and railroads, placed unswerving faith in free commercial intercourse and the protection of private property backed by the lightly veiled threat of force in the event of serious interference with either.

Under the leadership of President Porfirio Díaz (in office from 1877 to 1880 and again from 1884 to 1911), Mexico launched an ambitious program of economic development based upon exports of raw materials, foreign entrepreneurship, capital imports, and the consolidation of aboriginal lands into large-scale commercial haciendas.[4] During his long tenure as president, Porfirio Díaz established political stability and preserved order in the countryside with ruthless efficiency. Foreign businessmen were attracted to Mexico by the richness of its natural resources, the size of its domestic market, and especially the security and liberal encouragement provided by the government in the form of subsidies, tax exemptions, tariffs, exclusive concessions, and loans.[5] Led by American, British, Canadian, and European entrepreneurs, foreign capital flooded into Mexico after 1896 to finance, in order of importance, railroad construction, mining, the public debt, utilities, land companies, banks, and manufacturing.

TABLE 10
Foreign Investment in Mexico by Country and Category in 1911
(percentages)

Sector	United States	Great Britain	France	Germany	Holland	Other	Total
Public debt	4.6	8.4	36.1	3.0	48.2		14.6
Banks	2.7	1.8	11.0	18.3	3.7		4.9
Railroads	41.4	40.6	12.8	28.5	43.2	40.0	33.2
Public utilities	1.0	21.4	1.1		4.9		7.0
Mining	38.6	11.8	19.8			23.9	24.0
Land	6.3	9.2	1.8	9.1			5.7
Industry	1.6	1.1	7.9	41.1			3.8
Commerce	0.7		8.8			36.1	3.6
Petroleum	3.1	5.8	0.7				3.1
	Value of Investment ($ millions)						
Pesos	1,292.4	989.5	908.7	65.7	53.5	91.1	3,401
US $	646.3	495.0	454.4	32.9	26.8	45.6	1,700

SOURCE H.K. May and J.A.F. Arena, *Impact of Foreign Investment in Mexico* (New York and Washington: National Chamber of Commerce and Council of the Americas, 1972) 10, 61–2, calculated from *Historia moderna de México, la vida economica* (Mexico: Editorial Hermes, 1965) vol. 8, 1150–6

Rising exports and heavy capital investment, most of it foreign, fuelled economic expansion estimated at an average annual rate of 2.7 per cent between 1900 and 1910 – almost as rapid as Canada's own growth. Like Canada, too, foreign capital accounted for fully two-thirds of all investment in the country outside the agricultural and handicraft sectors. Moreover, the Díaz administration showed a marked preference for British and European investment to counterbalance the pervasive presence of US capital.[6]

A rough international division of labour seems to have characterized the flow of foreign investment into Mexico (see Table 10). French and Dutch capital financed the public debt, Germans invested in manufacturing, US capitalists dominated mining, Britons controlled public utilities. Railroads, which accounted for the greatest amount of capital invested, depended mainly upon US and British finance. In these calculations Canadian capital is included in the totals for Great Britain, a pardonable confusion as we shall see. In 1911 Great Britain and Canada combined were responsible for 89 per cent of all foreign investment in telegraphs, telephones, water, light, and power systems; the United States accounted for 6 per cent, France 4 per cent, and Holland 1 per cent. Overall, according to the most conservative estimate, the United States supplied 38 per cent of total Mexican foreign investment before 1911, Great Britain and Canada 29.1 per cent, France 26.7 per cent, Germany 1.9 per cent, and the Netherlands 1.6 per cent.[7] Public utilities, a Canadian specialty, ranked fourth in importance in the list of foreign-dominated sectors after railroads, mining, and the public debt, but they represented more than twice as much capital invested as oil.

Mexican Light and Power and Mexico Tramways were thus typical creatures of the Porfiriato. The generous franchises and concessions under which the companies operated had been granted by the Díaz government during the period in which foreign investment had been given special encouragement and understanding treatment by his científico advisers. To signify this political debt Julio M. Limantour, brother of the finance minister, was elected to the boards of both companies in 1909. Upon Julio Limantour's sudden death from typhoid later in the year, Pablo Macedo, one of the most prominent of the científico advisers to the president, was appointed in his place to cement relations with the regime.[8] The Mexican utilities also retained the adept and well-connected Mexican attorney Luis Riba y Cervantes, at a cost of $12,000 per year, to provide legal and political advice and to open administration doors whenever necessary.

Accordingly it might be expected that these companies stood to lose a great deal by the overthrow of the government by the forces of Francisco Madero in May 1911. In fact they suffered comparatively little. Indeed the collapse of one of the Necaxa storage dams in 1909 did more to damage the reputation and stock of the companies in London markets than the Revolution in 1911.[9] Mexico Tramways and Mexican Light and Power had virtually all the franchises and concessions they required by 1910. The principals were busy rushing construction to completion and organizing stock market syndicates to maximize gains for the insiders in 1911 and beyond, when earnings were expected to soar. As the property passed beyond promotion to day-to-day operation, Pearson, Dunn, Loewenstein, and their associates turned their talents to the finance and promotion of a combined railroad and lumbering operation in the northwestern state of Chihuahua.[10] Having got what they wanted, they did not greatly care who formed the government so long as it left them alone, preserved some semblance of law and order, and abided by the well-understood rules of the international game while they cashed in.

Mexico Tramways' takeover of Mexican Light and Power in 1909 created a situation in which the cash-rich tramway provided relatively cheap money to the power company to finance the completion of its elaborate hydroelectric development. The five storage reservoirs, interconnected tunnels and canals, plus river diversions would increase the company's Necaxa plant's year-round generating capacity to 100,000 horsepower. Between 1909 and 1911, for example, the tramway loaned in excess of $6 million at 7 per cent for this purpose.[11] During 1911 the gross and net earnings of both companies improved to the point that this debt could be capitalized through the issue of £2 million worth of second mortgage bonds, which netted $9,733,333. The light company carried its interest burden and paid 7 per cent on its preferred shares and 4 per cent on its ordinary stock from net earnings that rose from 3 million pesos in 1909 to more than 6 million pesos in 1912. At the tramway, business was booming as well. In 1910 management reduced the operating ratio below 50 per cent where it stayed for the next two years (see Appendix). As a result the company was able to raise the dividend on its common stock from 6 per cent to 7 per cent. Even in a revolution people used the streetcars, turned on lights, and apparently paid their bills.

Pablo Macedo retired from the board with the change of government, but otherwise it was business as usual. A few arc lamps were smashed by unruly crowds during some of the revolutionary disturbances, but the distribution system and generators were untouched. The streetcars maintained their schedules except for a brief strike in July 1911 inspired by the release of pent-up worker frustration and heightened labour expectations brought on by the legalization of trade unions. Company officials remained calm throughout, according to diplomatic dispatches. Thomas Hohler, the British chargé d'affaires, appealed to the revolutionary leader, Francisco Madero, who used his influence to have the company cars protected and, when the strikers persisted, to have the organizers arrested.[12] British diplomats and company officials became convinced that the Madero government would do everything in its power to protect foreign capital.

External evidence suggests that Dr F.S. Pearson and his managers adjusted readily to the change. Pearson could charm anyone, it was said, and the Madero government proved no exception. John B. Body, factotum for Lord Cowdray, who controlled the largest amount of British capital in Mexico, boasted confidentially to his superior in August 1912: 'You will be glad to know that we have reestablished our good name in Gov't circles and this without outside help. I have made arrangements with persons to champion our cause when needed, and Riba [Luis Riba] secured the *B in L of the P* for us [brother-in-law of the president, possibly General José González Salas, the minister of war, but more probably Rafael Hernández, a first cousin who was the minister of development], he has been of great assistance to Dr. Pearson's interests.'

When militants in the regime tried to tax electrical utility companies, almost all of which were foreign owned, Body reported to Lord Cowdray that Ernesto Madero, the president's uncle and minister of finance, had been in touch with Luis Riba to gather evidence of the damage such a tax might do to the interests of the Pearson companies. F.S. Pearson declined to co-operate in a Cowdray scheme to finance a government newspaper at the request of the minister of finance. According to Body the Pearson group had already put $100,000 into the *Imparcial* and that was deemed to be enough.[13] Relations between the Pearson companies and the revolutionary regime were sufficiently secure by early 1912 that Harro Harrsen, the manager, reported to Francis Stronge, the new British minister, that he had been instructed by his principals in London 'to refrain from making any formal application for protection to this Legation but to appeal directly to President Madero.'[14]

Pearson probably realized that the Revolution represented not so much a fundamental change in the direction of Mexican policy as a change in government leaders. The Maderists basically accepted the científico plan of development, based primarily upon hacienda agriculture and foreign investment. They were theoretically more pro-American than pro-British, but that did not concern F.S. Pearson so much, since he could plausibly fly either flag when it suited him. Thomas Hohler, who as we shall see had a very low opinion of Americans, believed Dr Pearson to be a 'genius of a Canadian.'[15] Madero and his key ministers were as determined as their predecessors to resist radical social and economic change, even if it was inspired by the expectations of the revolution itself. On the whole the government proved itself capable of dealing with the threat from its left. Where it proved fatally inept was in discounting the extent of the menace from the right, the deposed Porfirians and the army.[16]

II

Rebellions flared up almost continuously in the regions during the twenty-month Madero regime. Emiliano Zapata rose in revolt even before Madero assumed the presidency, declaring that the revolution had been betrayed. In 1912 Pascual Orozco organized a stubborn insurrection in the rugged northern state of Chihuahua. General Bernardo Reyes and Félix Díaz, nephew of the deposed president, launched abortive counter-revolutions, from the northern border and Veracruz respectively, aimed at restoring the personnel of the Porfiriato to power.

The hard-pressed federal army under General Victoriano Huerta managed to contain Zapata, defeat Orozco in the field, and snuff out the insubstantial rebellions of Reyes and Díaz. Notwithstanding this military success, the damage to property and especially to the prestige and authority of the Madero government was considerable. For example the roadbed and rolling stock of Pearson's Mexico North Western Railway suffered severely as first rebels then federal troops commandeered trains and blew up bridges and tunnels to cover advances and retreats. The Zapata rising threatened the Mexican Light and Power property at Necaxa until Luis Riba outfitted a private army to defend the hydroelectric works and the principal street railway and power installations in Mexico City.[17]

Opponents of the regime and foreign diplomats, headed by the US ambassador, Henry Lane Wilson, quickly lost confidence in the ability of the government to maintain order. For a time the Pearson group of companies followed a policy of avoiding the appearance of seeking diplomatic protection so as not to offend the sensibilities of friends in the Madero administration.[18] However as the damage to their properties mounted late in 1912, an embarrassment that coincided awkwardly with the attempted flotation of £1.6 million worth of Mexico North Western Railway prior lien bonds in London, F.S. Pearson and James Dunn threw caution to the winds. 'I think the time has come when we must get the English Government to intervene,' Pearson advised Dunn from Paris in September 1912. 'I would suggest you see your friend at the Foreign Office and tell him the conditions, and point out that unless our property is protected it means bankruptcy and a loss of £5,000,000 or £6,000,000 sterling to English holders, and ask him what he would suggest. We do not, of course, want to antagonize the Mexican government any more than we can help, but at the same time we cannot allow this to go on.'[19]

The question thus became whether these capitalists could influence British policy, and if so what – if anything – the government of Great Britain could do to aid them. On 1 October Dunn petitioned Sir Edward Grey through Sir Arthur Nicholson, the undersecretary of state for foreign affairs, to use the influence of His Majesty's government to persuade the authorities in Mexico to maintain a permanent federal presence in the area served by the Mexico North Western Railway. Dunn also wired his friend Sir Robert Borden, the prime minister of Canada, to do whatever he could to get action from the British government.[20]

Nobody at the Foreign Office apparently knew who James Dunn was at first, and the stock exchange directory proved unhelpful. Some diplomats were profoundly sceptical of the usefulness of any such exercise. As one official minuted: 'The request comes in such a curious form that one is led to suspect that the controlling interest in the company must be American in spite of its Canadian domicile. I do not think anything would be gained by telegraphing; the gov't would be only too willing to protect the line if it could.' Nevertheless, Whitehall finally agreed to send the telegram requested, declining Dunn's offer to pay the costs.[21]

The task of delivering the message fell to the slightly mad Sir Francis Stronge, newly arrived as British minister to Mexico. Among Sir Francis's more noticeable eccentricities was his parrot, invariably perched on his shoulder and chattering a discordant accompaniment to the ambassador's hesitant stammer. Late in his undistinguished diplomatic career Stronge had 'gone native' and adopted a (supposedly) white poncho-type outer garment, which was made all the more remarkable by the stains and stench of the parrot's droppings. The likeable but eccentric Stronge was entirely miscast as His Majesty's minister, Hohler confessed, 'though he would have made an excellent University Don.' His wife, not to be outdone, baffled and bemused guests at the legation with her conviction that plants could think.[22]

Shortly after taking up the Mexican posting the detached and disillusioned Stronge complained of being beset by 'Canadian lawyers and others [who] pour out their woes at enormous length.' This was especially inconvenient because he and his dotty wife were still 'camped out in the Legation,' coming to terms with its bugs, and just recovering their composure after a severe earthquake. While they might cope with natural hazards these scions of the British upper classes remained beset by other worries: 'Of course I was in terror lest all the English servants should give warning [i.e., notice] but they have behaved very well.' Dutifully, however, Sir Francis, parrot on his shoulder and reeking to high heaven, set off for the chaotic presidential palace to lodge a formal protest.[23] What the Mexicans made of him one can only wonder.

By this time the Madero government was in no position to help the Pearson interests, or anyone else for that matter, because it could no longer help itself. In January 1913 the counter-revolutionaries co-ordinated their efforts with the army. The diplomatic community, especially Henry Lane Wilson, collaborated openly to undermine the regime in the hope that some strongman like Porfirio Díaz would restore a semblance of order. Then in February, during ten tragic days of bombardment, bloodshed, and treachery, Francisco Madero was deposed and the ruthless General Victoriano Huerta installed in his place. Thomas Hohler, the chargé at the British

Legation during the bombardment, commented on the behaviour of his eccentric superior in the midst of the dangerous confusion: 'Poor old Stronge came in for the most violent criticisms by the British colony, and indeed he must have been a quaint spectacle in the midst of the firing, walking about with his head as usual through the middle of a white poncho and his vile parrot perched on his shoulder dropping excrement and nibbling his ear.'[24]

As calm returned to the capital the body of the murdered president was carried to the French cemetery in one of Mexico Tramways' famous electric funeral cars. The Pearson utilities in Mexico City emerged from the carnage of the ten tragic days more or less unharmed. The street railway cars had been withdrawn from service at the first sign of trouble. Apart from a few downed wires and broken street lights, the light and power systems remained in working order. But foreign management personnel experienced a harrowing time while caught in the crossfire between the two sides. On the whole they feared the federal troops more than they did the rebels. In panic Harrsen wired on 16 February 1913 calling for US intervention to prevent a loss of foreign lives. Dunn and Pearson echoed the message.[25]

But three days after the shooting stopped, business resumed as if humdrum routine had never been interrupted. 'All but two lines running,' Harrsen telegraphed laconically. 'Slight increase yesterday earnings over corresponding period last year. Nothing new.'[26] Moreover, the company discovered to its pleasure that old friends were once again in charge. 'Col. F. Diaz sends greetings,' a greatly relieved Harrsen wired from Mexico City. 'Asked him to use his influence for benefit of MNW [Mexico North Western Railway]. Death of F.I. Madero Pino Saurez must not be taken as act vengeance but as unfortunate necessity in order to ensure peace. Mercy will not be shown anyone not in accordance with government, and I personally strongly urged Col. F. Diaz [to] adopt this course.'[27] Harrsen identified the new chief of police as a warm friend of the company, a friendship Harrsen quickly relied upon to have a number of employee 'agitators' arrested.[28]

Once again foreign capital had a government it could count on; one that was not only sympathetic but brutally strong. Most foreign observers, whether British, French, German, or US businessmen or diplomats, had come to believe that only a strongman cut from the same cloth as Porfirio Díaz could restore order and deliver stable, moderately progressive government to Mexico. As Harrsen's cable suggest the Mexico Tramways and Mexican Light and Power management welcomed the new regime with open arms. 'Revolution in Mexico over. Things settling down,' Pearson wired Dunn on 3 March 1913. 'Mexican government thanks Pearson [and] Dunn for telegram of support. New government constitutional and being recognized everywhere. Protection to company property being promised.'[29]

Pearson and Dunn therefore threw themselves into the struggle to secure international recognition for the new counter-revolutionary government. In the literature on the Mexican Revolution, which focuses largely upon the supposed influence of Lord Cowdray and the oil industry upon British policy, the much more vigorous, complementary role of these utilities companies has been overlooked. As soon as the smoke cleared the Pearson group moved heaven and earth to regularize Mexico's external relations. Dunn coached Luis Riba by telegram on the proper means by which the new Mexican government should apply for recognition from London.[30] Having been discomfited by the hauteur and indifference of the diplomats during the previous difficulties, Dunn adopted more direct methods. He reported to Pearson: 'Have finally found a man Foreign Office listens to.' For £1,000 Dunn retained the expatriate Canadian Liberal member of the British House of Commons, Hamar Greenwood, to orchestrate an effective company lobby.[31]

Greenwood interviewed Sir Louis Mallet at the Foreign Office and poured out his case for recognition on the basis of the tremendous British interests at stake in the country. He went away greatly relieved to report to his principals that the British government was awaiting a full report from its minister, but in the meantime was 'disposed to recognize the president when the final announcement of his accession is made.'[32] On the strength of this advice Luis Riba was instructed 'to bring all favourable influence to bear on Stronge so that he may cable Foreign Office that in his opinion new government is sound and permanent, but please be very careful that Stronge does not learn that you know what communications Foreign Office have made to him as he might be annoyed.'[33]

On 7 March 1913 the capitalists got half their wish. Stronge's report suggested that recognition would materially assist the new government in restoring order, and the British government complied.[34] The Mexican government probably received first word of the favourable British decision on recognition from Luis Riba via James Dunn.[35] Between 22 February and 7 March when recognition was being debated in the British Foreign Office, Dunn, Pearson, and Greenwood were by far the most pressing and persistent lobbyists. Lord Cowdray, by comparison, though extremely visible in the background, took no active part in the persuasion. If Britain hastened to recognize the new regime more quickly than the German government (which chose to wait until Huerta was duly elected), it was because, as Sir Edward Goshen acknowledged to Sir Edward Grey, political considerations weighed more heavily in Great Britain than legal niceties. 'We seem to be going faster than other Govts,' Sir Arthur Nicholson observed upon reading reports from British ambassadors.[36] That was primarily because the British government acted immediately and unequivocally in the direction suggested by the largest British companies in Mexico, its perceptions of the best interests of foreign capital, and the advice of its minister, who had played a peripheral role in the downfall of the previous regime. The utility men, rather than Lord Cowdray, pressed the case for recognition most persistently in Whitehall and seem to have assisted indirect communication between the two governments during this critical stage of Anglo-Mexican relations. That does not imply that the British government did their bidding or that the oil interests were without influence. The latter probably welcomed the cover provided by the more public protestations of their fellow investors. The British government acted upon a broad range of strategic and economic issues, of which Dunn, Pearson, and Greenwood formed only a part – though a useful and noisy part.

First indications from Mexico looked extremely promising. On 20 March Colonel Félix Díaz lunched with Pascual Orozco (the northern chieftain whose activities had been the source of so much discomfort to the Mexico North Western Railway), at which time a truce was declared between these counter-revolutionary factions. Harrsen, who claimed to be the only foreigner present among the fifty guests, reported that Díaz also convinced Orozco that the Pearson companies were friends of the new government. Orozco in return promised to do everything in his power to bring peace along the beleaguered railway. Carried away by the spirit of unity, the two leaders also boasted that the Zapata movement would soon be reconciled to the new government.[37]

With Mexico Tramways' business up 12 per cent and Mexican Light expenses down considerably over previous years, both companies continued to show healthy surpluses and to pay dividends throughout the troubles.[38] Indeed, Mexican Light and Power continued to expand, acquiring a regional electric company in the El Oro mining region during the last days of the Madero regime and an additional waterpower concession from the Huerta ministry. Now, with the promise of order throughout Mexico, it looked at last as if foreign businessmen could once again get down to the business of making money. It was not to be, of course.

III

The ten tragic days of February proved to be only the beginning of a series of troubles in 1913 that would dramatically curtail international capitalist entrepreneurship in Mexico for a long time to come. After a period of sustained economic expansion throughout the Atlantic world, a sharp recession commenced in 1913. Rising interest rates had a depressing effect upon capital markets, making it especially difficult for speculative ventures abroad to raise new money. Utilities had a notorious appetite for continuous infusions of capital. Depreciation and exchange rate instability in 1913 made it more difficult for companies to meet their interest and dividend commitments in gold.

General adversity, therefore, weakened the basis of the Pearson promotions in 1913. More particular problems relating to the partners themselves and the location of their principal investments meant that the recession hit this group perhaps harder than others. As we have seen, cost overruns and construction difficulties had damaged the financial standing of the Barcelona promotion, the last of the great Pearson ventures. Exchange rate difficulties and political instability plagued the earlier promotions in Mexico. Finally, with the markets turning, James Dunn's partner decamped and the British linchpin of the whole operation tottered on the brink of insolvency. Pearson and his friends could not hold out much longer by the summer of 1913. For a moment their hopes of recovery focused on Mexico.

Pearson wondered whether the Huerta regime might be persuaded to guarantee the bonds of the Mexico North Western Railway. Dunn doubted that possibility, since the government was having difficulty arranging its own foreign loans.[39] Loewenstein characteristically saw 'the present financial difficulties of the Government of Mexico' as an opportunity, and in the process he also became an unlikely advocate of public ownership: 'This would relieve the Doctor who is overworked, from the technical and financial worry of these two businesses and I think, on the other hand, that the Mexican Government … could justify it on the ground of unrest in Mexico requiring it to concentrate in its hands services as important for the Government as the electric lighting of the Capital.'[40] But no consensus emerged among the management group before the Revolution once again overtook them.

The newly elected Wilson government in the United States delivered the first blow to capitalist hopes by withholding formal diplomatic recognition from the Huerta regime. Repelled by its brutal methods and indifference towards constitutional practice, and suspicious of the new regime's pro-British leanings, the Wilson government proposed to teach Mexico a moral lesson.[41] The tortuous course of US policy – much of it premised upon neutralizing supposed British political and commercial power in the region – need not concern us, except to observe that it was fundamentally destabilizing.

As early as June 1913 the Revolution had broken out once again in the north and by midsummer Pancho Villa had taken control of Chihuahua. He was said to be doing everything possible to assist in the reconstruction of the Mexico North Western Railway, but not even Villa could control the region.[42] Business could live with Villa; it could live with Huerta. What it could not survive was war between them. Parenthetically it might be noted that while bribes from Pearson's railway in the north helped finance Pancho Villa's insurrection, the Mexico City utilities were simultaneously providing Colonel Félix Díaz with a 10,000-peso political contribution.[43] Meanwhile at Necaxa Harro Harrsen continued to maintain a private army at a cost of 1,000 pesos a day.[44]

Despite their precautions Pearson and his associates could only stand helplessly by as revolution once again engulfed Mexico. As the confusion mounted after Huerta's bloody dismissal of Congress in October, Pearson's best hope lay in some kind of military intervention. In New York his son, Ward Pearson, kept in touch with various shadowy US interest groups that were campaigning for intervention. Lloyd Griscom, a former US diplomat and president of the business-sponsored Pan-American Society, who had befriended the Pearson interests during his term in Brazil, was retained to lobby the State Department in Washington. There he was told that British and German pressure on the US government was much more likely to produce the desired result.[45]

Once again the Pearson group tried to exert its influence. Hamar Greenwood led a weighty deputation to the Foreign Office of 'Canadian gentlemen having large interests in Mexico' consisting of James Dunn, Sir William Mackenzie, E.R. Wood, and Dr F.S. Pearson. The Pearson delegation insisted that the continuing uncertainty over Mexico was destroying their property and asked Sir Edward Grey to persuade the US government to protect foreign investment and lives. In particular they asked for some public declaration from members of the Wilson administration, that 'they will see things through in Mexico and not merely starve Huerta out without intending to secure that Mexico eventually receives better government.' Grey agreed and transmitted this request to Sir Cecil

Spring Rice in Washington and Sir Lionel Carden, the new British minister to Mexico. But Grey held out little hope of direct US military intervention.[46] The British government itself was having no more luck than these bewildered businessmen in trying to discover the logic of US foreign policy.

Meanwhile Mexico Tramways and Mexican Light and Power were slipping quietly towards bankruptcy. Huerta's indiscriminate printing of money to finance the Federalist military operations had a devastating impact upon foreign exchange. The peso collapsed in value against the pound and the dollar and, as a result, it became increasingly difficult for these two companies to remit sufficient gold to cover their sterling, franc, and dollar interest and dividend obligations, even though both companies showed healthy Mexican peso balance sheets. Only frantic efforts by Pearson and Dunn managed to secure a large loan from the Bank of Commerce to cover imminent Mexico Tramways dividend payments and other pressing expenditures in the fall.[47]

As the forces of Zapata, Villa, Venustiano Carranza closed in on the beleaguered Huerta administration, attacks on people and property reached new heights of savagery. As the Constitutionalist armies advanced southwards, bandits operated unmolested behind them in the north. On 4 February for example, outlaws stopped a Mexico North Western passenger train, held it to ransom, and, when they did not receive satisfaction, backed the train into the flaming Cumbre tunnel, killing fifty-three people, several of whom were American citizens. No one seemed capable of stopping the carnage.[48]

In Mexico City, as the regime disintegrated the Pearson companies were victimized by their 'friends.' In January the Ministry of Communications and Public Works threatened to cancel certain of Mexico Tramway's suburban franchises on the grounds that these had been acquired in an irregular fashion. The matter could be dropped, the government officials indicated, if the company paid the requisite blackmail.[49] To make matters more awkward, Sir Lionel Carden seems to have sympathized with the official position of the government, if not its methods. However, when the ploy worked with Mexico Tramways, unscrupulous officials then tried it on Mexican Light and Power, 'a hold up pure and simple,' according to the general manager. Once again the company paid, following Riba's advice as to 'the inadvisability of turning down grafters associated with the Finance Department.'

Conditions in Mexico were beyond belief, a terrified Harrsen informed his superiors in a letter that had to be smuggled out of Mexico for fear of reprisals. Corruption was universal; no business could be done with government departments without payment. The peso had fallen to thirty-three cents (from close to fifty) and was likely to drop to twenty-five. The president was drunk and incapable of conducting any business two or three days a week; the minister of communications was not only drunk he was a 'drug fiend.' People were being murdered right and left for their participation in real or imagined plots. Companies had to make forced contributions to various factions. It seemed likely that the president would be assassinated before any order could be brought out of the chaos. (Such reports might have been exaggerated for public use by his principals.) Curiously, Harrsen noted that 'business on the other hand is exceedingly good in both trams and light,' extraordinary testimony to the ability of utilities to earn money in good times and bad.[50] Nevertheless, both companies had to cancel dividends on account of the adverse foreign exchange situation.

The poorly led and dispirited Federalist forces lurched from disaster to disaster. The Cowdray-inspired plan of us occupation of northern Mexico came to naught; nevertheless, efforts to provoke direct us military intervention succeeded to some extent with the seizure of Veracruz on 22 April. But it was a bungled, half-hearted effort, an ambiguous political gesture at best and one that was very badly received by the us press. The second track of us policy, negotiation between the combatants, also failed. On 22 April a little-known conference of all the major Mexican factions convened at the Clifton Hotel in Niagara Falls, Canada. There, the Constitutionalists, sensing their gathering strength, refused to compromise and the peace talks collapsed. It would be an agonizing fight to the finish. Eventually, when the military situation became utterly hopeless in mid-July, Huerta fled the country. After a fifteen-month counter-revolution and an almost continuous civil war, the avenging Constitutionalists under Venustiano Carranza assumed nominal control of the government of Mexico.

IV

The transition occurred without much violence or damage in the capital. And on the face of it the Pearson group had little to fear from the heirs of the Maderist revolution, as we have seen. Unfortunately the restoration did not secure the peace that the foreign powers hoped for. Moreover, the civil war had stiffened the will of all revolutionaries to assert national control over the Mexican economy and, among some, to realize the promise of social change briefly glimpsed in the initial Madero victory. After mid-1914 the Constitutionalists sought first of all to restore by force a viable national government against the wishes of the regional commanders; secondly, to alter the rules of the international capitalist order to retain more of the income generated by Mexican concessions in Mexico, and, more fitfully, to redistribute the nation's wealth. All this was overshadowed, of course, by the outbreak of a major European war, which gave the struggle in Mexico a new strategic importance.

Following the overthrow of Huerta, the triumphant revolutionary forces did not combine to form a government. Rather they remained split into three major warring factions headed by Emiliano Zapata, Pancho Villa and Venustiano Carranza.[51] Guided by Álvaro Obregón, Carranza moved closer to the resurgent labour movement in an attempt to build a mass base and occupy more of the left-centre of the political spectrum claimed by his rivals. The first few months of the disputed Constitutionalist control of Mexico City thus gave rise to a tremendous upsurge in labour militancy driven by continued high rates of inflation.[52] The street railway, with its large wage-labour force and foreign management became one of the first targets. The management of Mexico Tramways was at that moment itself in a state of confusion. Not surprisingly Harro Harrsen had fled, fearing for his life with yet another change of regime. Thomas Hohler, the British chargé, poured out his contempt for the timorous American, arguing that it was time British companies hired British managers. Englishmen were actually better at running foreign operations than Americans, Hohler contended. They were typically more honest, reliable, and sympathetic: 'They may not be quite so quick and shrewd as their Yankee brothers, but they have a certain sympathy with the native, such as they show all over the world with semi, or less, civilized races, which enables them to get on with their labourers.' Hohler concluded this hymn to British pluck and disdain for American 'cold feet' on a more practical note: 'Another great disadvantage due to the employment of Americans in British concerns is that, by a process of very natural sympathy and autonomy, valuable orders for materials are sent to the United States and not, as they should be, to England.'[53]

At this point the motormen and conductors of the street railway organized a union and demanded its recognition, a 100 per cent wage increase, a reduction in the hours of work, and a scheme of workmen's compensation for injury. The company was prepared to concede a 15 per cent increase, but on 8 October after only four hours' notice, the union went on strike. In view of the management vacuum, Thomas Hohler himself assumed *de facto* control of the company side in the negotiations, a role for which his 1911 intervention against the union on behalf of the company had prepared him.[54]

The great difficulty in reaching a settlement this time, Hohler reported, was that the authorities put themselves on the side of the strikers. In an interview with Carranza, Hohler pleaded the inability of the company to pay the wage increases demanded, much less its bond interest. Wage increases depended upon corresponding fare increases; fares had fallen to three-fifths of a penny from a penny and a half in gold according to Hohler. He noted that the refusal of the government to pay its light, power, and transportation bills for more than a year only made matters more difficult. Outright confiscation would be preferable, the implacable Hohler insisted.[55]

For his part Carranza calmly took the view that confiscation was out of the question, but he admitted that he 'might be forced to intervene to secure the running of the trams for the convenience of the public, an idea against which I strongly protested,' Hohler reported. Further interviews with the minister of foreign affairs and finance and the governor of the Federal District got nowhere in a climate of public opinion excited by what Hohler described as wild, puerile, and false press attacks on the company.

To end the impasse the government 'intervened' by taking over direct management of the company on 12 October and the strikers returned to work for an eventual 25 per cent wage increase.[56] Much has been written about the possibility of a government takeover of foreign-owned oil and mining companies. The Mexico Tramways Company was in fact one of the few large foreign-owned enterprises actually taken over during the Revolution. The Intervenor, Señor T.E. Ramos, also prevented the company from making any foreign remittances in the alleged interest of preventing a further depreciation of exchange rates, an act that brought the government in conflict as well with the Bank of Commerce.[57]

From London, Washington (via Brazil because the United States lacked diplomatic representation in Mexico), Ottawa, Brussels, and Paris a chorus of diplomatic protest arose – much of it orchestrated by the Pearson group itself – at this unprecedented seizure of foreign property.[58] The minister of foreign affairs replied that no confiscation had in fact taken place; rather, the government had acted against its wishes to reconcile the needs of the strikers and the general public. And as far as the Mexican government was concerned the company was Mexican and subject to local laws even if its shareholders lived abroad.[59] Nevertheless government intervention in the business of the tramway raised issues for the major powers that transcended the interests of the security holders of the tramway itself. If the street railway was vulnerable, what of the mines, ranches, and, above all, the strategic oilfields?

Ironically, as governments became more excited by the implications of the incident, those closest to the scene gradually recognized an opportunity in this hour of distress. Upon reflection Hohler cabled that 'if not actually a blessing in disguise,' the intervention 'may be turned very much to the advantage of the company.' By itself the company could not hope to raise fares sufficiently to meet its external gold obligations. The government action merely precipitated a crisis that was coming anyway, Hohler shrewdly observed, thereby placing responsibility for dealing with the crisis upon the government itself. The indefatigable chargé also suggested to the bondholders in various countries that they get their governments to urge Mexico to pay the Mexico Tramways bond interest for the duration of the 'intervention.'[60] Thus government seizure in Mexico and the general financial crisis associated with the outbreak of the First World War actually relieved the Pearson syndicate of an increasingly intolerable burden.

At this point the organized government in Mexico once again disintegrated. Carranza's tenuous grip on power failed completely as distrust and ideological differences among the revolutionary factions burst out into bloody civil war. First Zapata's Army of the South and then Villa's Army of the North occupied the capital city, as the Carranzista forces retreated and regrouped in Veracruz. As far as the tramway company in Mexico City was concerned, total chaos reigned. Zapata returned the street railway to its owners on 28 November 1914 only to take it back again two days later. The governor's secretary promised to restore private ownership on 2 December, but on that day he was arrested and shot. Early in the New Year Carranza supporters in the street railway union attempted to ship the all-important controllers (the handles that operated the trams) to Carranza's troops in Veracruz. Briefly, Constitutionalist forces reoccupied the capital, only to be driven out once again. A company employee informed his head office in Toronto: 'Condition of armed socialism prevails. Authorities are urging people to sack.'[61]

Villa and Zapata tried to give the street railway back to its owners. F.S. Pearson thought it a good idea to seize the opportunity, but Thomas Hohler strongly advised against acceptance without a promise of indemnification for damages and solid guarantees of protection against the union: 'Until the circumstances are far more stable than at present it will, I think, be to the advantage of the Company to endeavour to avoid, for as long as possible, taking back the business.'[62] Pearson and Dunn, it must be added, acted on this advice.

In July the Conventionists fled Mexico City taking 143 street cars to the end of the line and carrying away with them the controllers. This pattern would be repeated with each change in government. Hohler captured the summertime madness at the tramway company in an August 1915 despatch to the Foreign Office:

The Intervenors change with each change of Government, that is about once a fortnight. The present Intervenor is a man named Hesse, who was previously chauffeur to the late General Manager of the Company, who, I understand, had to dismiss him for larceny. He is now, also, a lieutenant colonel of Engineers. A stores clerk is acting as Assistant General Manager. The President of the Labour Union has assumed the remunerative post of Traffic Manager.[63]

With each evacuation and occupation, transportation in the city was immobilized until the vital controllers could be recovered or replaced.

As Carranza and Obregón gradually reasserted their control over central Mexico and the capital, the labour movement, which had contributed signally to their cause, once again seized its advantage. Rampant inflation steeled revolutionary expectations. Indiscriminate expansion of the money supply by all revolutionary factions led inevitably to a rapidly depreciating currency and spiralling inflation. Between May 1913 and April 1915 the peso had fallen from forty cents US to a mere ten cents. A year later, in June 1916 the Mexican peso was worth only two cents US. As prices soared, organized workers struggled to catch up with the cost of living by employing the only weapon at hand, the strike. In May, during a temporary Carranzista occupation of the capital, electrical workers struck Mexican Light and Power (which had not been taken over by any of the revolutionary factions because none possessed the technical ability to run it) cutting off all water and electricity to Mexico City without warning. The government pro tem admitted that it, too, was powerless 'as street fighting was not feasible.' The company and Thomas Hohler had no choice but to give in and grant the wage increases.[64]

Again in August, with a more lasting Carranzista restoration, the electrical workers struck once more, demanding payment in gold. This time the El Oro mining district was paralysed. Officials of the company claimed that bankruptcy prevented meeting these demands. General Pablo González responded sympathetically and offered to pay the 31,000-peso wage increase for one month if the company could demonstrate its insolvency. At this the directors in Toronto took umbrage. Even in the midst of a revolution, inspection of the company books was an utterly intolerable condition, they resolved. Instead the directors indelicately suggested that the government could make a more substantial contribution towards a solution to its difficulties by paying its past-due power bills. General González's mediation efforts brought the men back to work temporarily, but eventually the company had to surrender unconditionally.[65]

Affairs were further complicated by the fact that, although Carranza controlled Mexico City, the power stations in Necaxa remained in the hands of Zapata. The Revolution severed the connection between Mexican Light and Power's generators in the mountains and its customers in the Federal District. Thus the entire system had to revert to dependence upon the stand-by steam generators in Mexico City. Not until September did Obregón capture Necaxa, happily without serious damage to the works, and restore the integrity of the electric system.[66]

With the connection with Necaxa restored, the Mexico City electrical workers thus lost their bargaining power; but that did nothing to stop a wave of strikes in almost every industrial sector. By the end of December Hohler reported that government intervention had added more than $119,000 per month to the Mexico Tramways wage bill without a corresponding increase in income. Protests from the British, French, and Belgian consuls were simply ignored.[67]

In the midst of this confusion the company suffered the deepest blow of all, the loss of F.S. Pearson in the sinking of the *Lusitania*. As virtually his last act he had drafted a long sad letter to shareholders explaining that unsettled conditions in Mexico precluded the payment of dividends for the foreseeable future.[68] By this time a virtually bankrupt James Dunn had turned his hand to selling horses to the Belgian army. Captain Alfred Loewenstein had also thrown himself into the war effort with customary dash and enthusiasm.[69]

Quietly the two companies that Pearson and Dunn had largely created, along with the wreckage of the Mexico North Western Railway, passed into the hands of receivers in the fall of 1915. With Pearson dead, Dunn and Loewenstein preoccupied with the war, the physical assets of Mexico Tramways under the control of its workers and government officials in Mexico, and the corporate shells in the hands of bankers and bondholders, the soul went out of Pearson's Mexican utilities enterprises.[70] Someone else would have to preside over either their interment or their revivification.

11

Redemption

By the autumn of 1914 social unrest in Mexico had reached the point that a bedraggled band of government troops dared to pound upon the door of the British Legation, demanding entry to search for arms and ammunition – a pretext for looting the place. Thomas Hohler, as maddeningly unflappable as ever, calmly sent a message by way of his butler 'to tell them that I was at dinner, and a British Minister could never be disturbed at dinner.' It had come to that. In a cold fury Hohler telephoned Carranza's officials to order up a second detachment of troops to protect him from the first lot. He then repaired to the balcony of the Legation with a cigar to enjoy the ensuing mêlée.[1]

For the next four years the Canadian utilities in Mexico had to cope with the consequences of revolutionary nationalism in the midst of a major world war. For all practical purposes both Mexico Tramways and Mexican Light and Power had passed into the hands of their employees and customers by the fall of 1915. The British government could not act alone because of the war in Europe and its powerlessness in the face of the Monroe Doctrine. The United States would not intervene directly to restore order, though it vehemently rejected the Carranza Doctrine of national control of natural resources. US decision making by this stage was predicated almost exclusively upon the strategic situation in Europe; the United States did not want to be tied down by distractions in North America – although it did permit itself the sideshow of a punitive raid against Pancho Villa. With the great powers immobilized, the Mexican government, such as it was, thus had an unusually free hand to do whatever it wanted with the railways and utilities it had taken over.

I

The evolving Carranza Doctrine combined the claim that the state owned all minerals and natural resources (including waterpower concessions) with the assertion that all companies and individuals conducting business in Mexico did so as Mexican citizens and could not appeal to their home governments for protection against Mexican law. Moreover the Constitutionalists disputed the legality of some concessions granted under the Porfiriato and all those dispensed under Huerta. By establishing new rules and renegotiating old concessions the Carranzistas hoped to place development of the national economy more fully under Mexican control. If the revolution had a class character its object, in the words of the secretary of industry, commerce, and labor, was 'the formation and encouragement of an autonomous Middle Class.'[2]

Even before this revolutionary nationalist doctrine had been fully worked out and inscribed in the constitution by the victorious Carranzistas, Mexico Tramways along with Mexican Light and Power and several British-owned railways were, as we have seen, the first to feel its sting. In replying to Thomas Hohler's protest against the takeover of the tramway in October 1914, Foreign Minister Isidro Fabela firmly denied that the company had been seized. Rather he asserted that it had been 'intervened' temporarily because the tram-workers' strike had affected the public interest. Nevertheless, the nascent Carranza Doctrine was clearly asserted: foreign companies were subject to local laws. Companies that operated in Mexico were Mexican, Fabela insisted, and could no longer claim special rights as foreigners.[3]

Upon receipt of a copy of this note Sir Cecil Spring Rice in Washington informed Secretary of State William Jennings Bryan that the British government could not accept the contention that 'the right of diplomatic intervention is in any way affected by the above mentioned law' and inquired delicately what the US government thought. Lawyers in the State Department also rejected Fabela's contention that Mexican law could render a foreign corporation purely Mexican. The two major powers agreed on the question of principle, but could not see that anything could be done about it at that particular juncture.[4]

Oddly enough the most effective pressure to moderate the revolution came from within the government itself. Ideologically the Carranza faction hoped to create a liberal, bourgeois, capitalist society. They were economic nationalists, but definitely not socialists. Carranza sought to control foreign interests, not eliminate them entirely. Secondly, the government sought relief from the wave of strikes unleashed by its labour allies beginning in the autumn of 1915. Carranza courted labour when he needed mass support, but once in power his government sought some means to curb its influence. Business had been brought to a standstill; labour's drive towards a deeper social revolution interfered with the government's economic agenda. Thomas Hohler recorded that he had been involved in settling strikes at both Mexico Tramways and Mexican Light and Power, as well as at the utility in Puebla, the mines in El Oro, and on the railways.[5] The underlying problem, of course, was uncontrollable inflation, a phenomenon to which a militant labour movement further contributed.

Responsibility for coping with the 'First Chief,' Venustiano Carranza, on behalf of Mexico Tramways and Mexican Light and Power passed to Edward Peacock, chairman of the bondholders' protective committee. Peacock was an entirely appropriate choice, for he, like the earlier promoters, was also a Canadian, an expatriate financier in London who had risen to partnership in Baring Brothers merchant banking house. In some respects the situation was the reverse of that under Huerta. The us government had quickly recognized the Constitutionalist regime; the British held back pending a Mexican commitment to pay compensation for revolutionary damages. In this tangle, Peacock, a Canadian, might claim neutrality of sorts. And to complete the circle it was the British government that now sought to use the Mexico Tramways Company as its cat's paw.

As early as 6 January 1916 the Carranza administration signalled its willingness to return Mexico Tramways to its owners. The acting general manager sought advice from Thomas Hohler and the receiver, both of whom counselled against acceptance. Hohler regarded the move as a precedent for the possible return of other seized and badly damaged properties, such as the railways, and urged caution. The directors decided to consider taking back their property but only on stringent conditions. The tramway could not be profitably worked at present fares and wages; the fares could not be raised without government help. Similarly labour relations could only be stabilized through some co-operation on the part of the government. Moreover, a major investment would be required to get the property back into working condition, and new money could not be raised without government guarantees. The impatient Mexican authorities tried to insist that the company take back its property, but the stubborn owners refused.[6]

In March a deputation of directors consisting of F.H. Phippen and E.D. Trowbridge arrived in Mexico to undertake direct negotiations with the government. This was for appearances only, for they were explicitly *not* given authority by the board of directors to conclude a definite agreement. Phippen and Trowbridge merely explained to the authorities that the collapsing peso and militant trade unions meant that the company would in all probability not be able to meet its obligations in the very near future, and the government would thus be required to intervene once again. Moreover they privately observed: 'Property not now deteriorating more than if in our control. Also there are many advantages in operation by military authorities.' They would only agree to consider a resumption of private control if the government raised tram fares and lighting rates.[7]

While Phippen and Trowbridge were in Mexico conferring with C.D. Graves and Graham Fulton, of the tramway and the light and power companies respectively, the electrical workers at Necaxa went out on strike demanding the dismissal of the local manager, recognition of their union, and wages in gold. Phippen and Trowbridge promptly petitioned the government to raise power rates, as this was the only means of meeting the 100 per cent wage increase. The government reluctantly complied, but the workers refused to end the strike without union recognition and the dismissal of a much-hated American manager named Dunn. Their stubborn action led to the government's first serious break with its erstwhile labour allies. Carranza simply ended the strike by firing the ringleaders and ordering all labour leaders removed from the state of Puebla.[8]

Over the summer of 1916 anti-foreign sentiment reached a fever pitch, and the strike situation became intolerable. Hohler reported to Spring Rice that things were worse than ever: 'Our people have so far suffered least of any and I am trying to lie as low as ever possible.' A strike by workers at both the tramway and the light and power companies led to the arrest of Graham Fulton and sprang Hohler from cover at the end of July. Of this incident Hohler reported with glee: 'I had a glorious fight never stopping a moment for one evening and two days. I told many of them quite straight what I thought of them but with great composure and cheerfulness and they had to agree.'[9]

The street railway and electrical workers' strike, which was part of a general strike in the Federal District to restore wages to 1914 levels, blacked out the city, cutting off all public transportation and water. The receiver of Mexico Tramways and Mexican Light placed the affairs of both companies 'unreservedly' in Hohler's hands. For two days the British consul pestered the government to release Fulton and restore some semblance of order; otherwise, he threatened to withdraw British diplomatic representation within forty-eight hours. Sperling in the Foreign Office minuted the dispatch: 'Hohler long sorely tried but hesitated to recommend own withdrawal owing to damage to GB interests. If he says time has come we sh[oul]d listen.' When Lord Cowdray heard of this he called immediately at the Foreign Office urging Hohler to stay, 'as oil wells may be destroyed forever while the govt *have to* keep the power plant running in their own interests.'[10]

Cowdray was right. The Mexican government needed no encouragement from foreign powers to halt the strike epidemic. Carranza believed that his rivals were behind the movement in any event. As a first step he declared martial law. Then, through the simple act of invoking a forgotten 1862 decree, Carranza declared the strikers bandits and imposed the death penalty for anyone found guilty of disrupting work in factories and public services.[11] 'Strike over by terrorization,' Hohler wired on 2 August 1916. Eventually the jailed Fulton was released.[12]

Nevertheless the Carranza government protested the involvement of Hohler and the British government in the affairs of the company. Carranza himself refused to receive Hohler. He and his government took the position that by virtue of contracts with the Mexican government the company was Mexican and therefore had no right to invoke any foreign assistance. Hohler made himself extremely unpopular insisting upon his right to make representations on behalf of a 'British company.' The Foreign Office agreed with him, but also concluded that for the time being nothing could be done about it. As an anonymous minute on one of Hohler's dispatches observed: 'The most vulnerable and vital interest for the moment is the oil wells. If we could spare a landing force to protect them we ought to do so.'[13]

The situation was relieved somewhat by the arrival of G.R.G. Conway from the British Columbia Electric Railway in Vancouver to take charge of the tramway and power company interests. Conway had considerable Mexican experience, having served as an engineer during the construction of William Mackenzie's Monterrey Railway, Light and Power Company. Once Hohler withdrew to the background, talks between the company and the government resumed in a more conciliatory atmosphere. By the end of September Carranza had committed the government to paying its power bills, which went a long way towards meeting the 100 per cent wage increase it had granted the electrical workers. In November the government authorized both the tramway and the light and power company to charge for service on a gold basis temporarily. This, of course, was the key to the situation from a corporate point of view. By the end of a harrowing year some considerable progress had been made towards normalizing relations. The government was in a co-operative mood; organized labour had been brutally suppressed, and the income of both companies significantly improved.[14]

Under the circumstances the bondholders took a renewed interest in recovering their property. The government too evinced some interest in the subject, and Conway was given full power of attorney in March 1917 to begin negotiations. For its part the company wanted some form of indemnity for the damage to its property and its loss of earnings during the course of the revolutionary disturbances. To this the government could not agree, fearing the precedent. The company was prepared to waive this indemnity if the government raised the street railway fares and put them permanently on a gold basis. If that was to be done then the government wanted to renegotiate the entire franchise. Above all the government wanted to avoid the appearance of giving in to a large foreign corporation. Each time an agreement seemed near, senior government officials backed away.[15]

And so it went, on again, off again, for the next two years. Meanwhile it was the turn of the bondholders to become anxious. With the return of reasonably peaceful times the power and light business began to pick up. The power company in particular, with its huge, undamaged hydroelectric development already in place, was well positioned to take advantage of renewed economic growth. Before 1911 the street railway had been the big money earner, and cash flow from its operations had been directed towards completing these hydroelectric works. After 1918 the situation was reversed. Mexican Light and Power had the greater earning potential, and the tramway required substantial investment to reconstruct its much-abused physical plant. The power company had never been taken over, because of the inability of the government to run such a complex technical operation. Nevertheless, it was largely owned by the tramway company, and it was impossible to reorganize the former without also recovering and recapitalizing the latter[16]

Finally, on 7 May 1919 Carranza broke the deadlock and *ordered* the company returned to its owners. In all likelihood the return of peace in Europe figured distantly in Carranza's calculations, as did the need to arrange a large government loan. Now that the war was over he feared that the United States and Britain would gang up on Mexico. The return of the British-owned street railway was probably intended as a gesture of conciliation both to the British government and to the London capital market.

After years of frustrating negotiations the bondholders jumped at the chance. The Foreign Office considered recovery of the company without a guarantee of indemnification for losses an unfortunate precedent, but nevertheless called upon Edward Peacock's committee to make up its own mind. It did, without hesitation. The only remaining British diplomat in Mexico, H.A.C. Cummins, felt betrayed: 'Company have today accepted return from Mexican government of the whole of their tramway system on terms I consider scandalous, in view of the manner in which for a long period they have been despoiled of funds of ownership of property ruined.' The Foreign Office also questioned this sudden change of heart.[17]

What Peacock and his friends knew, and the British diplomats probably did not, was that the Mexican Light and Power Company had quietly accumulated more than $13 million in its Toronto accounts during the last phase of the Mexican Revolution. The power company had never been 'intervened.' Its owners had put it into receivership for technical reasons during the tramway company's difficulties. Under the management of the receiver the company had managed to squirrel away about $3 million in gold a year since 1915, despite an unfavourable exchange rate and after meeting all its Mexican operating expenses. This fund was almost enough to discharge the interest owing on the first and second mortage bonds of both companies, interest that had not been paid since 1915. Moreover, the tramway company had not paid for its power since 1914, an outstanding account that more than compensated for the interest owed by the power company for loans and cash advances over the years.[18] This treasure (most of it invested in Canadian Victory Bonds) lay within tempting reach, and the key to it was control of Mexico Tramways.

Besides the immediate attraction of the treasury of the power company and its obvious earning capacity, Peacock's bondholders' committee anticipated that the greatly altered international environment would lead to a much more favourable investment climate in Mexico. With the return of peace all the foreign interests victimized by the Mexican Revolution had formed themselves into the powerful International Committee of Bankers to press for compensation for losses and a moderation of Carranza's economic nationalism.[19] Since the Mexican government would soon be requiring foreign loans, a united front by the lenders would likely make credit conditional upon both reparations for revolutionary losses and good conduct. If this were the case the tramway company, having been one of the large losers, would likely be one of the big winners.

Peacock and the London financiers also hoped to increase the pressure by having the Mexican situation considered at the peace conference. This they construed to be Canada's special hemispheric role at Versailles.[20] Beyond that businessmen expected, with good reason, that the US government would finally be driven to intervene decisively in Mexican affairs.[21] The carrot of formal British diplomatic recognition and new government loans came at a high price for Mexico: compensation, conciliation, and stringent conditions. The alternative was the stick of US intervention. The overall outcome, the businessmen dreamed, would be a less nationalist regime modelled more on the lines of the Porfiriato.

II

Peace in Europe dramatically altered the situation in Mexico. The Great Powers were now free to focus their undivided attention upon the Revolution and its accumulated offences. Although conditions favoured a forceful assertion of property owners' claims after 1919, reconstruction of the Pearson enterprises proceeded haltingly. Numerous pitfalls and perils on the route had to be negotiated, not the least of which was the violent overthrow of the Carranza regime in 1920.[22]

The first problem occurred when word filtered back to the authorities about Mexican Light and Power's accumulated surplus. Naturally the government sought to recapture some of these profits, essentially through taxing the company's waterpower in the state of Puebla. This complex dispute need not detain us, except to observe that it too involved a retroactive application of the Carranza Doctrine of state ownership of all natural resources, a doctrine that both the company and the British government steadfastly refused to concede. After tense and lengthy negotiations it was finally agreed that a systematic evaluation of the utility for tax purposes would be conducted.[23]

Ultimately the Mexicans themselves removed Carranza, the man who had become such a thorn in the side of international capitalism. The increasingly unpopular 'First Chief' failed in his attempt to choose his own successor in 1920 and was assassinated in the process. The new government of generals Adolfo de la Huerta and Álvaro Obregón gave early indications of a completely changed attitude towards foreign investors. De la Huerta agreed to a permanent increase in tramway fares in return for a new method of taxing the company in which new taxes would offset payment of the government's long overdue bills to the companies, and thus be rendered relatively innocuous. The new president also disavowed the declared objective of some of his ministers to have the government acquire shares in the two companies.[24] Just as important, he also showed a determination to keep a tight grip on organized labour.

Buoyed by these heartening developments in Mexico the bondholders' committee, which consisted of Peacock, G.C. Cassels, H.F. Chamen, Robert Fleming, Malcolm Hubbard, and Sir Alexander Roger, hastened its planned reorganization. Peacock and Hubbard interviewed both de la Huerta and Obregón in the summer of 1920 and came away optimistic about both the consideration being showed to foreign capital and the likelihood of settling all outstanding issues with the new government, especially an indemnity for losses suffered during the tramway intervention.[25] All this looked very hopeful. Not surprisingly the Peacock committee lobbied the British Foreign Office vigorously for the formal recognition of the Obregón government.[26]

The bondholders themselves were undecided as to how to approach the matter of rebellion losses. Should the Pearson enterprises join all the other companies in front of the International Claims Commission set up by Mexico or should they go it alone, trusting to good personal relations with the new regime to get a better deal? Local counsel was divided. Eventually it was agreed to do both, and formal claims were submitted to the commission for 19,753,279 in gold pesos on behalf of Mexico Tramways and 8,341,784 for Mexican Light and Power. In the meantime the companies still put their faith in their ability to cut some kind of private deal with the government.[27]

The most serious danger to the reorganization and reconstruction of the Pearson empire occurred early in 1921 when an acute power shortage in Mexico City embarrassed Mexican Light and Power and briefly threatened it with a takeover by the government. By 1919 additional generators were needed to increase the capacity of the Necaxa works. The receiver and Peacock's committee agreed to spend almost $1 million to expand capacity. Despite banditry in the region and railway strikes, the equipment was in place when needed in 1921, but the company claimed that a prolonged drought meant that there was not enough water available to increase output.

Throughout the crisis the company argued that political instability, official harassment, and the failure of the government to pay its own bills prevented the investment of new capital to meet Mexico City's power requirements. Peacock insisted that the company was in a position to meet all its obligations, 'but cannot assume responsibilty in the meantime for conditions which arise from the lack of control of previous governments and from the failure of the usual autumn rains as well as the breakdown of transportation even under the present government.'[28] Since the power shortage coincided with an intensification of the dispute with the state of Puebla over waterpower taxes, the company found itself in an extremely delicate situation at an awkward time. In a display of public toughness *vis-à-vis* a foreign corporation, President Obregón ordered an investigation in April 1921 to see whether the company ought to be prosecuted for negligence.

In order to increase capacity, the utility purchased the Compañía de Hidro-Eléctrica de la Alameda, which had both an oil-fired thermal plant in the suburbs and, south of Mexico City, a partially completed hydraulic development, abandoned at the outbreak of the Revolution, that could be finished relatively quickly. For the longer term, plans were drawn up to expand production with a new station at Tepexic, downstream from the original Necaxa plant.[29] But large-scale expansion would have to await a complete financial reorganization.

In May 1921 the bondholders' committee presented its plan for the refinancing of the two companies. The announcement made much of the fact that there was not nearly enough money to meet all outstanding obligations because heavy additional expenditures were needed to increase the capacity of the power plant and refurbish the street railway. Discounting this persiflage, it was quite clear that more than enough money lay at hand to satisfy most reasonable expectations. Altogether the companies owed £8,879,000 in bond interest and sinking fund payments and £5,225,000 on the unfunded debt, a sum that included $16 million in loans from the tramway company to the power company.[30]

By the terms of the 'Agreement of Arrangement,' first mortgage bondholders received 75 per cent of the arrears of interest in cash immediately, the remainder to be paid in instalments by 1 July 1931. Coupon payments would resume on 1 June 1922, and the date of maturity of this issue was extended. Payment of installments on past-due interest on Mexico Tramways second mortgage bonds would commence, at a rate of one coupon a year, on 1 September 1921. Although the tramway had large claims for damages outstanding with the government, revenue from this source was not taken into account in arriving at a repayment schedule. The $16 million debt of Mexican Light to Mexico Tramways was to be liquidated with a $5 million cash payment, the remainder to be covered by 'Income Bonds'. To see the deal through a bondholders' protective committee would remain in existence with representation on the boards of both companies.

Everything considered, this represented a generous and reasonably satisfactory end to the upheaval of the Revolution for the bondholders, especially those of the tramway, whose payment came entirely from the electrical utility. The shareholders' equity had been trimmed by the Revolution, but it had been acquired as a bonus in the first place; moreover, the refinancing substantially enhanced the equity's present value. In June, 1921 the first and second mortgage bondholders approved the agreement without a whimper.[31]

Although the need for capital investment made it impossible for the board to resume interest payments on the lower-ranking classes of bonds, the Canadian utilities were well on the way to recovery by 1922. Mexico Tramways was able once more to lend Mexican Light and Power $1.5 million to finance part of the cost of powerplant expansion. By early 1923 heavy rainfalls were refilling the reservoir at Necaxa. That spring the power company negotiatied a ten-year contract for street lighting in Mexico City, and management devised an ingenious scheme by which some of the large debts owed by both the federal and the municipal governments would be offset against the tax payments claimed from both the electricity and the tramway enterprise.[32]

The most serious problems were in the field of labour relations. Conway reported in March 1922 that an effort had been made to shut down the entire power system. During the five-day strike the company succeeded in maintaining current to 90 per cent of industrial consumers in Mexico City as well as to the mines in Pachuca and El Oro. Although streetlights were out and some residential circuits were cut, the company was able to resist the strikers' demands successfully. Further threatened walkouts in June, July, and November were averted by negotiations.[33]

Relations with the Mexican government were greatly complicated by the fact that neither Britain nor the United States was willing to restore diplomatic relations with Mexico without some agreement on the rights, past and future, of foreigners to possess lands and natural resources. In June 1921 the American Secretary of State declared that

The fundamental question which confronts the Government of the United States in considering its relations with Mexico is the safeguarding of property rights against confiscation. Mexico is free to adopt any policy which she pleases with respect to her public lands, but she is not free to destroy without compensation valid titles which have been obtained by American citizens under Mexican laws.

The retroactive implementation of the Mexican constitution of 1917 (particularly Article 27), added Charles Evans Hughes, would be 'an international wrong of the gravest character, and this Government could not submit to its accomplishment.'[34] The Mexicans naturally resisted this effort to dictate domestic policy as a condition of securing recognition even after the Carranza Doctrine had been modified by de la Huerta and Obregón.

Private interests, US, British, and Canadian, played an ambiguous role in this process. On the one hand Canadian utility operators and US and British bankers and oilmen wished to see relations re-established so that they could appeal for diplomatic assistance when required. On the other hand they did not want the politicians to concede recognition to any Mexican regime that refused to repay the debts owed them and to promise to respect property rights in future. Hence a delicate interplay developed as foreign investors urged their governments to press the Mexicans to act, while at the same time seeking to use their influence inside Mexico to restore a due reverence for private rights.

The interests involved were substantial. In 1923 the British chargé d'affaires in Mexico estimated that foreign investment actually sunk into that country totalled £410,879,590, of which £145,817,466 was British, £134,313,288 US.[35] In an effort to protect the rights of holders of Mexican government bonds Thomas Lamont of J.P. Morgan and Company had persuaded the State Department in 1918 to support the formation of an International Committee of Bankers on Mexico; half the seats on this body were originally held by US banks, a quarter by French financiers, and a quarter by British, including Baring Brothers, Edward Peacock's firm.[36]

What the utilities still lacked was diplomatic protection against further threatened depredations of their property. In June 1922, Finance Minister Adolfo de la Huerta met with the International Committee of Bankers in New York and agreed that the Mexican government would resume service on its foreign debt after five more years in exchange for an extension of maturity dates and a waiver of all arrears of interest. With powerful business interests in the United States now pressing for recognition of the Obregón regime, Mexican and American representatives met at the Bucareli Conference in the spring of 1923, where they agreed upon two treaties: the Special Claims Convention covering losses between 1910 and 1920 and the General Claims Convention covering all other losses since 1868. In addition, there were discussions about land and mineral rights, though no firm agreement was arrived at. On that basis the United States agreed to grant diplomatic recognition to Obregón in August 1923.[37]

As many US oilmen did, the Canadian utility operators ultimately concluded that the concessions secured from Mexico in exchange for recognition were inadequate. Peacock wired from Mexico that he hoped that Britain would not recognize Obregón on the same terms. To do so without getting a firmer commitment to repay the loss and damage caused by the revolution would be to 'throw away our good card after waiting so long.' Fortunately, the Foreign Office agreed.[38]

In December 1923 de la Huerta, who had denounced the Bucareli agreements as a sell-out to the United States, led a revolt against his erstwhile associates. Fighting broke out in Yucatán, and Mexico once more seemed to totter on the brink of revolutionary violence. The utility men were especially alarmed, because the relentless hostility of President Obregón towards the British chargé, Cummins, made it almost impossible for them to obtain a hearing from the government. The situation worsened when Cummins dispatched a note to the Foreign Office on 19 December 1923 that was deemed to be insulting. Subsequently it was reported that Obregón had intercepted private letters written by Cummins to friends in England containing further derogatory remarks about Mexico and the Mexicans.

Eventually Obregón, who had quickly succeeded in suppressing the armed revolt, decided to expel Cummins from the country. The Foreign Office denied that Cummins possessed any diplomatic status, being only in charge of the archives of the British Legation, and contended that he was an obstacle to the resumption of relations on account of the false information which he had been passing to London. In May 1924 the police surrounded the Legation, and Cummins was unceremoniously bundled out of Mexico.[39]

Feeling the isolation and vulnerability of the Canadian companies, Peacock had begun to press for Cummins' replacement by some 'authoritative person' even before his expulsion and for Obregón's recognition. While observing that, 'A proposal about Mexico sponsored by Mr. Peacock is sure to deserve attentive consideration,' and noting that, 'In any case we can scarcely refuse to receive the views of the "right sort" of City men,' Foreign Office officials clearly had little enthusiasm for the idea. Five months later Peacock was still urging action upon Whitehall without success. Some thought had been given to sending Thomas Hohler (now knighted for services to His Majesty's government) out to look into the possibility of talks on recognition, but this affront by Obregón effectively scuttled any such move.[40]

In July 1924 Plutarco Elías Calles succeeded Obregón as president.

Terrified businessmen hearkened to the Marxist rhetoric of the Confeder-
ación Regional Obrera Mexicana (CROM), which led strikes against many
foreign-controlled firms, and watched in alarm as Calles revived Carranza's campaign to assert national control over resources.[41] Such a radical
shift caught the Mexican Light and Power Company at a tricky moment
when British diplomatic backing might have been particularly useful.
Despite the political turmoil, electricity demand had continued to expand
steadily, and it was clear that a new waterpower concession would shortly
be required for further development. Investigation came to centre upon a
site on the Lerma near El Oro where a dam could create a 40,000
horsepower development as well as permitting an irrigation scheme to be
constructed downstream.[42] But would the new regime be willing to make
the necessary concessions to a powerful foreign company?

In light of Cummins's expulsion, the British Foreign Office made clear
that it would not risk another rebuff by approaching the Mexicans directly.
Instead it was suggested to Peacock that he explore 'the possibility of
paving the way to recognition (on satisfactory conditions) through a
business channel.'[43] When Peacock visited Mexico in the spring of 1925 he
found the Calles government, despite its radical rhetoric, quite interested in
reopening the matter of diplomatic recognition.[44] But he and Conway
convinced themselves that the CROM ideologues completely dominated the
president and his cabinet. When a group of Mexico Tramways employees
organized a union and demanded recognition from the company, Conway
refused, claiming that the group had the support of only a minority of the
tram men. On 12 March 1925 the workers struck, and President Calles
immediately sent word (via the American ambassador) that if Conway did
not recognize the union as required by law and settle the strike within three
days he would be deported instantly.

Despite the fact that US interests were not directly involved, the
ambassador persuaded Calles to meet with Conway, arguing that his
summary expulsion would create a tremendous outcry in Britain and the
United States. Conway pointed out that automatic recognition and
immediate settlements would simply open the way for all manner of
outrageous union demands, but the president proved completely unyield-
ing. He threatened

that in case of noncompliance with this demand, on the part of the tramway
company, the government would be forced to take possession not only of the street
car company but of all the other interests of the Mexico [sic] Light and Power

Company, which are far more valuable and important, of course, than the street car establishment which hardly pays its way.

And he reiterated the warning that he would not hesitate to expel Conway from the country. Conway was forced to give way and deal with the union.[45]

As a result Peacock reported to the board in Toronto

that it seemed obvious that in view of the uncertainties in the political situation in Mexico, and the financial position of the company, the policy should be to endeavour to add to the existing supply by means of small additions and improvements to the present installations. This would enable a postponement to be made of the time for starting any large development, during which time the political situation might have clarified and more definite estimates and studies could be made covering the various projects.

Nevertheless, this short-term solution would not alter the fact that in a year's time the company would have no surplus power left and would have to face the loss of its large mining contracts unless a new development was started.[46]

The Calles regime, which believed that de la Huerta had bowed too much to the demands of the International Committee of Bankers in 1922, showed no signs of starting repayment of Mexico's foreign debts. Despite its radical rhetoric, however, the government did not intend to repudiate these debts, and negotiations with the bankers continued throughout 1925. Eventually in August, Finance Minister Alberto Pani offered to return the railroads taken over during the revolution to private control and to set aside certain oil production taxes to service foreign debt, provided that the bankers would separate railway debt from government debt and accept further extensions on repayment. Reluctantly the bankers agreed to these terms and an agreement was signed in New York in September.[47]

These negotiations and the popularity of the activist policies of the Calles regime evidently convinced the British government that it would have to come to terms with the revolutionary regime in Mexico. After discussions it was agreed that outstanding claims for losses suffered by British interests in Mexico during the Revolution would be settled following recognition. Those that could not be dealt with through private negotiation would ultimately be referred to a bilateral tribunal. On that basis recognition was extended in August 1925. The news was greeted with optimism in Toronto;

Miller Lash informed the board of Mexican Light and Power that he believed this 'should be of considerable assistance in the stabilizing of Mexico.'[48]

Some of this optimism evaporated almost immediately as Calles introduced stringent new legislation designed to implement the Carranza Doctrine by bringing Article 27 of the 1917 constitution into force. The Alien Land Law required foreign corporations to dispose of land holdings within ten years; the holdings of individual aliens were to be liquidated within five years of death. The Petroleum Law provided for new concessions even on lands acquired prior to 1917; failure to acquire these could lead to forfeiture of title. The government also created a national electricity commission to examine rates and plan future development.[49]

None of these measures, however, created serious problems for the Canadian utilities. In fact, Conway reported to the board that he had interviewed the electricity commissioners, who 'did not appear to be radically inclined, but were, so far, very reasonable in their attitude and [had] expressed themselves as being quite willing that we should earn a fair rate on our investment in Mexico, which we are not yet doing.' Because of his interest in promoting irrigation, President Calles appeared favourably inclined towards Mexican Light and Power's proposed development on the Lerma.[50]

Meanwhile, Anglo-Mexican negotiations regarding the settlement of outstanding claims from the revolutionary era proceeded. At first the British were hopeful that reimbursement for lost revenues might be included, but the Mexicans resisted and eventually the Foreign Office decided that 'we shall have to concede this point. It is anyhow not a strongly defensible position to claim for 'loss of profits' owing to revolution. People have got to take *some* chances in such countries.'[51]

The convention was formally signed in November 1926. It provided for both a period during which private settlements could be negotiated and a later claims tribunal that would deal with the remaining cases. The four Canadian-incorporated companies expected to seek compensation were Mexico Tramways (claiming 19,797,000 pesos), Mexican Light and Power (567,800), Monterrey Railway, Light and Power (5,139,351), and International Light and Power (299,500), which controlled a small powerplant. The first two, in particular, made it clear that they intended to make private deals rather than appeal to the tribunal.[52]

The board of Mexican Light and Power now turned its attention to another consequence of the revolutionary crisis: the completion of the refinancing of the company necessitated by the suspension of the bond interest and the preference dividends. Although 'the Agreement of Arrangement' of 1921 had laid out a schedule for the repayment of back interest to the holders of the first mortgage bonds, the need to retain earnings to expand capacity had left the other bondholders and the preference shareholders out of luck. Because Mexico Tramways owned the entire issue of income bonds as security for pre-war advances to fund the Necaxa generating plant, it, too, remained in default on its bonds.

In such circumstances the power company could not raise any outside funds. The interlocking boards of the two concerns decided that earnings were now sufficient to permit them to convert into funded debt more than $7 million in unpaid bond interest and $5,670,000 in accumulated preference dividends. Each holder of a £100 second mortgage bond would now receive £7 10s. in cash plus a new £50 bond in lieu of interest and, to cover the unpaid interest on the income bonds the tramway would get ten-year non-interest bearing notes that would be liquidated at the rate of $400,000 per annum. The preference dividend would be resumed and new second preference shares issued to cover the outstanding dividends that had accumulated since 1913. Gradually and laboriously all the interested parties were persuaded to give their consent to this new arrangement, and the shareholders finally ratified it in the summer of 1927.[53]

This reorganization coincided with a changing of the guard around the directors' table at the end of 1926. R.C. Brown, the last of Pearson's engineering associates to be still active, retired from the presidency of Mexican Light and Power, and Peacock stepped down as chairman of the board. Miller Lash, the new chairman, became chief executive officer, and the faithful Conway continued as chief operating officer in Mexico, where he served as both president and managing director.[54]

III

The way now seemed clear for the final settlement of all the troublesome claims left over from the Mexican Revolution. Before that could occur, however, an incident of glorious foolishness intervened that seemed to threaten all that management had been working so diligently towards during the past decade. In July 1926 the Calles regime directly challenged the power of the Roman Catholic church by secularizing education, closing seventy-three convents, deporting foreign priests, and requiring the registration of all clergy.[55] As a result, religious-based unrest developed in Mexico, leading ultimately to the *Cristero* rebellion.

What threw Mexican-Canadian relations into a turmoil with serious implications for the utilities began innocently enough. Sir Henry Thornton, president of the state-owned Canadian National Railways, had visited Mexico, with the blessing of the government of Canada, to advise about the problems facing the railroad system there. Upon Thornton's return in December 1927, Michael Fallon, the Roman Catholic bishop of London, Ontario, wrote an open letter to Prime Minister Mackenzie King sarcastically celebrating the CNR president's safe return 'after a sojourn of some weeks in the society of robbers and murderers who now form the Government of Mexico.' The prelate reminded the prime minister that 40 per cent of Canadians were Roman Catholics, and demanded to know 'what powerful, secret influence forced you to affront the Catholics of Canada by turning a portion of their taxes to the aid of the most infamous government in the world today?'[56]

At first it appeared as though the whole incident might fade away. Prime Minister King convinced himself that the open letter required no direct reply.[57] Unfortunately the Mexican consul in Toronto, L. Medina Barrón, was unwilling to let matters rest; he publicly condemned Fallon's ignorance of Mexican affairs as well as his 'blind passion and prejudice.' Barrón also contended that the Roman Catholic church, which had founded the Inquisition to torture and murder Protestants, was plotting the overthrow of the government of Mexico. The church had to be put in its place, he argued, because it had been 'a handicap for the development and progress of the Latin American countries, on account of the teaching of obscurantism to keep the masses in slavery and be able to exploit them better.'[58]

That put the fat well and truly in the fire. Angry Catholics demanded that Barrón be booted out of the country at once for his insulting remarks. In turn, extreme Protestants weighed in to support the Mexican's charges about the Inquisition and about obscurantism. Soon a storm of sectarian and political rhetoric had blown up.[59] Mackenzie King, under pressure from Catholics in Quebec, who provided much of his government's support, summoned Barrón to Ottawa in January 1928 and informed him that the controversy had ended his usefulness in Canada. He suggested that Barrón should immediately arrange to be transferred elsewhere if he wished to avoid being asked to leave.[60]

The Mexicans dug in their heels: Barrón would not be withdrawn; if he were forced to leave, the Canadian trade commissioner in Mexico City would be expelled in retaliation. The British minister, who was handling the matter in Mexico, reported that the acting foreign minister had told him plainly that the 'Mexican government might have to take certain reprisals, possibly of a commercial nature.'[61] The British government feared that the whole silly affair would lead to the breaking off of relations between Canada and Mexico, which might result in a rupture with Britain with extremely serious consequences for its large interests in Mexico. But Mackenzie King could not appear to back down, as he struggled to prevent the passage of a parliamentary resolution that might bring the crisis to a head by demanding Barrón's withdrawal.[62]

For the Canadian companies in Mexico this great brouhaha was acutely alarming. From the outset rumours had circulated that these companies had been behind Thornton's visit in the hope of promoting their own interests; this provoked them to make firm denials of any involvement.[63] The danger was that a sudden worsening of Mexican-Canadian relations might imperil the gains that Conway had so laboriously achieved in dealing with the Calles regime. As the British Foreign Office knew from painful experience, once relations with Mexico were broken off it could be extremely difficult to re-establish them.[64]

In the end the tempest blew itself out. Barrón stayed on at his post for another six months, whereupon the Mexicans agreed to withdraw him provided the Canadians did nothing to draw undue attention to his departure. That suited Mackenzie King perfectly. When Barrón himself balked at reassignment he was abruptly ordered home. Before long a new consul arrived in Toronto without attracting any notice.[65]

Political instability continued to be a problem in Mexico. In July 1928 president-elect Álvaro Obregón was assassinated, and Congress appointed Emilio Portes Gil provisional president to succeed Calles in November. Portes Gil was to serve a two-year term until a permanent president could be elected, but in March 1929 another revolt occurred. This was suppressed by Calles, acting as minister of war. In June, Portes Gil announced that he had reached an accord with the leaders of the Roman Catholic church, ending three years of conflict and permitting the reopening of the churches. In November 1929 Pascual Ortiz Rubio was elected president; with the country completely at peace for the first time in several years it was hoped that the violent disorder of the Revolution had finally ended.

During this period Conway devoted much attention to achieving, finally, a settlement of compensation for the damages suffered by the utilities during the Revolution. His aim was to reach agreement privately and avoid a formal hearing before the Anglo-Mexican Claims Commission, which he knew would arouse hostility towards the companies at a time when they had a generally good image. The Canadian trade commissioner reported in late 1928 that, 'In Mexico City the Mexican Light and Power Company is held in the very highest esteem and generally has the support of the populace, for the service it is giving is a visual demonstration of what Canadian capital has done for them.'[66]

This goodwill did not extend, however, to offering a satisfactory settlement of revolutionary claims. Reluctantly, Conway ordered Mexico Tramways to file a claim for 19,753,274 pesos with the commission in May 1929 before the deadline ran out; Mexican Light and Power simply dropped its small damage claim although it continued to seek reimbursement for the government's unpaid power accounts. At first the Mexicans resisted hearing the tramway's claim, arguing that the 'intervention' of the company in October 1914 had nothing directly to do with the Revolution but had been brought on by labour problems that interfered with service. Finally, the British government hired a special counsel to represent them before the commission in the tramway case, which was by far the largest British claim.[67]

The hearing did not take place until early 1932 and, when it became clear that the commission favoured some sort of award to the utility, the Mexicans compelled their representative to resign on the pretext that the body lacked jurisdiction over such cases, effectively paralysing the process. The Mexican government then apparently decided that it would be wise to offer private settlements in all the outstanding cases to satisfy Britain and the United States, while avoiding any formal admission that such demands were justified. The foreign minister called in Conway and offered to settle with Mexico Tramways for 2 million gold pesos; Conway refused until the offer was increased to 2.5 million but then accepted in view of the need for good relations with the authorities in future.

The legal adviser dispatched by the British government considered that 6 million pesos would have been a fair sum, and the Foreign Office grumbled that the behaviour of the Mexicans had been 'childish,' their attitude 'ludicrous.' Company officials, however, claimed that they were satisfied to have some sort of compensation at long last. Even though the payments were not to start at once, the outcome constituted a kind of vindication. As one diplomat noted, 'the moral effect is for them perhaps more important than the actual cash.'[68]

That was undoubtedly true. Conway had long since recognized that he had no alternative but to try as best he could to get along amicably with the Mexican authorities. In pursuit of good relations Mexican Light and Power had agreed in 1927 to commence construction of its dam on the Lerma River, so that the irrigation project could get under way even though there was no immediate need for the power.[69]

And Conway's strategy worked. By the end of the 1920s he had almost succeeded in redeeming the Mexican utilities from the blows suffered during the Revolution. Control of operations had been recovered, corporate finances reorganized, and expansion resumed despite the continuing political turmoil. From time to time business still had recourse to the assistance of British (and occasionally US) diplomats, just as they had during those dark days when Thomas Hohler had manned His Majesty's Legation in Mexico City. But those times were becoming more infrequent, the issues less critical. By the end, indeed, Conway was readier to make a settlement on revolutionary claims and to put the past behind him than were the diplomats.

Neither the tramway nor the power company emerged unscathed from the Mexican Revolution. However, they did escape the turmoil rather better off and more securely established than might have been expected. It had been a harrowing, unpredictable passage, but the companies survived to flourish in the 1920s and after. Like the British and US governments, they discovered to their private disgust that they would have to deal with the Mexicans more or less on Mexican terms. Much to their surprise, however, they learned that this was not only possible, but also profitable. They could not be numbered among the victims of the Revolution.

12

Growth in a Hostile Environment

Revolts. Brazil had more than its share of them – 1904, 1906, 1910, 1922, 1924, and 1930. They were always short, whether successful or not, and rarely of the same savagery and destructive violence as their Mexican counterparts. Attempted coups were not, however, the worst problems faced by Brazilian Traction during the 1920s.

In Brazil foreign entrepreneurs contended with forces as daunting as rebellion – economic nationalism and a depreciating currency. In such a hostile environment, moreover, the company faced the dual necessity of satisfying both its overseas shareholders and its Brazilian clientele; producing for the former a reasonable rate of return on their capital and for the latter investing ever larger sums in gas, electric, transit, and telephone facilities to satisfy the rapidly growing needs of Brazil's largest metropolitan areas.

I

Success created its own problems. Being a large, highly visible foreign monopoly in an increasingly nationalist and politically unstable host country inevitably made doing business more difficult. The Brazilian economy had never been dominated by foreign commercial interests to the same degree as, for example, Argentina, Mexico, or Chile. Local economic elites retained control of both staple agricultural exports and the manufacturing sector, and these elites harboured an understandable hostility towards foreign interlopers in the transportation, financial, manufacturing, and utilities sectors. Self-sufficiency imposed by wartime trade restrictions nurtured economic nationalism.

In the richest, most industrialized and most cosmopolitan state, São Paulo, economic nationalism tended to be the weakest – though the presence of the recalcitrant Guinle faction in Santos reminds us that it was not entirely absent. For São Paulo foreign investment had produced the tangible benefits of jobs in a booming economy. In the resource-rich interior state of Minas Gerais, by contrast, the regional political and economic élites stoutly resisted foreign railroad schemes and mining enterprises whose aim was the extraction of ore for shipment to refineries and processing plants elsewhere. Worried too about the relative economic decline of their region in the federation, the Minas Gerais élites sought these benefits and the profits of industrial ownership for themselves. From the state government of Minas Gerais, Brazilian Traction faced nothing but opposition. Since the Minas Gerais and Paulista political machines tended to dominate federal politics, inevitably the federal government turned against the company as well.

It was a problem that Canadians ought to have understood intuitively: foreign ownership of strategic industries in a divided and unevenly developed federation. But of course they didn't. Canadian businessmen abroad were no more or less attuned to local sensibilities than foreign investors in Canada. Sir Alexander Mackenzie, who was knighted by the British government in 1919 in recognition of his role in bringing Brazil into the war in 1917 on the side of the Allies, and his associates Asa W.K. Billings and later H.H. Couzens, placed the God-given right of Brazilian Traction to do business as it saw fit first, and all other considerations second.

The company was for the most part a victim of its own success. By the 1920s 'the Light' had risen above all its rivals to become one of the largest, most visible foreign enterprises in the country. The Brazilian government reluctantly recognized the company's importance in global financial markets and suspected that it was using that influence to thwart the domestic political agenda. Naturally the government sought to curb Brazilian Traction's power, improve its service, and capture a larger share of the profits earned – in short to bend the company to a sovereign political will.

From these same authorities Brazilian Traction needed to obtain extended franchises, building permits, and water rights to serve its growing markets. It could not stand pat and endure; it had to grow with the economy. Under the circumstances the company lacked the power to dictate to the government; at the same time the government lacked the financial resources, personnel, and ultimately the political will to national-ize the company. It did, however, possess the capacity to hinder, punish, and delay Brazilian Traction in the hope of manoeuvring it into a more compliant frame of mind. By embarrassing and causing nuisance to the company, of course, the government put at risk the utility service of its citizens. It was a delicately balanced, brutal political game, one that, for all his world-weariness, Sir Alexander Mackenzie played with considerable gusto and remarkable skill.

When the First World War came to an end the Brazilian companies had large earnings, ample reserve capacity, and no big capital projects in the immediate offing. Peacetime initially brought strong demand for such Brazilian products as sugar, beef, and beans, and even though coffee prices remained depressed Brazil recorded a trade surplus of $250 million in 1919. That created hopes for a rising rate of exchange that might permit the company to resume dividend payments, suspended since 1917, and make it much easier to refinance the $7.5 million worth of short-term notes that would fall due in the autumn. After an unsuccessful effort to arrange a refinancing loan in London, however, the company decided to renew the existing loan in New York for another three years.[1]

By the following year Brazil had slid into a severe post-war recession, and the trade surplus evaporated to be replaced by a $50 million deficit. Though the rate of exchange between the pound and the milréis remained stable, sterling slid off sharply against the dollar. The milréis, therefore, realized 20 per cent less in New York than a year previously, a serious matter for a company with one-third of its shareholders in North America. Moreover, the Brazilians tried to take advantage of this by changing the basis upon which the gas and electricity rates in Rio were calculated, cutting further into Brazilian Traction's revenues.[2]

As a result the company's finances remained somewhat shaky through-out the early post-war years. In the spring of 1920 a study by the London merchant bank J. Henry Schröder and Company concluded that any plans to issue further securities ought to be deferred and all earnings retained for reinvestment. The report noted that virtually all the funds raised to date had been by bond sales, and that an improvement in the debt / equity ratio would strengthen the balance sheet. The British periodical *Canada* put the matter more bluntly, noting that the reinvestment of $15 million in retained earnings since 1917 meant that 'a large proportion of the 'water' has been squeezed out of the shares.'[3] Wartime and post-war exchange difficulties

Exchange Rates, 1914–30
(average rates for Brazilian exchange
on New York based on remittances)

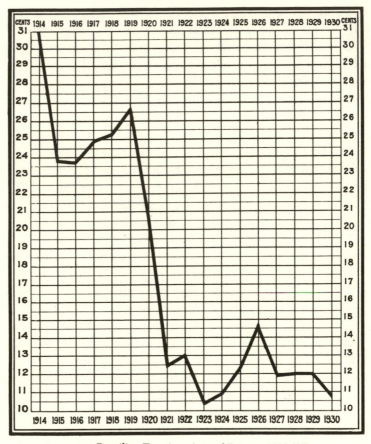

SOURCE Brazilian Traction, Annual Report, 1930 (27)

had forced the company into measures that prudent financial practice ought to have recommended earlier.

A depreciating currency and the lack of dividends plunged the company's stock into a free fall on North American exchanges. Brazilian Traction common stock dropped from a high of sixty dollars on the Toronto Stock Exchange in 1919 to a low of twenty dollars in 1921.[4] Restive shareholders, watching their capital gains vanish into thin air, began to demand that at the very least a stock dividend should be paid to them. At the 1920 annual meeting Alexander Mackenzie adopted a hard line against the idea, pointing out that a 5 per cent stock dividend would represent only 2 per cent in cash at current share prices, while permanently increasing the stock on which future dividends would have to be paid by the full 5 per cent. To complicate matters further the recession was severe enough that by the end of 1920 the head office in Toronto (in letters reminiscent of the Pearson era) was pressing the staff in Brazil to curtail plans to invest $7.6 million in 1920 and another $8 million in 1921. This caution proved well advised when the Brazilian economy continued to weaken and the rate of exchange of the milréis fell from an average of more than 14d. sterling in 1920 to near 8d. in 1921, a 'terrible blow' in Mackenzie's words.[5]

A falling rate of exchange did benefit some powerful interests. São Paulo and Minas Gerais coffee exporters who paid their bills in the local currency and sold their products on world markets in dollars and pounds had every reason to encourage a policy of devaluation. The domination of federal politics by élites from the regions dependent upon agricultural exports tended to bias monetary policy towards depreciation and fiscal policy towards expensive price-support and stabilization schemes. When world coffee prices rose this strategy worked well; but when they fell, as they did rapidly after the war, the result was inflation, budget deficits, heavy external borrowing, and further devaluation.

Such a policy seriously harmed Brazilian companies with external debts and to a lesser extent the domestic manufacturing sector. Brazilian Traction, which had to pay bond interest and hoped to pay dividends on its huge dollar and sterling capitalization, complained bitterly of the policy to the federal authorities. Curiously, the federal government was also the company's closest potential ally. For while it drew its main political support from the coffee and agricultural interests of São Paulo and Minas Gerais, the government itself was a large and rapidly growing foreign debtor. Like Brazilian Traction it too had to repay interest and principal on its foreign loans on a gold basis. And thus a subtle tension developed between the government as representative of major economic interests on the one hand, and the government as a fiscal entity with somewhat contrary interests on the other. The government might be the company's secret ally; but that did not necessarily make it a friend.[6]

The company did its best to help stabilize Brazilian finances in the spring of 1921 when it acted as a go-between with Dillon, Read and Company in arranging a $25 million loan to the government.[7] From a nationalist perspective, however, this intervention merely demonstrated the pervasive influence of foreign capital and the supine nature of Epitácio Pessoa's administration. In any event the US loan failed to prop up the Brazilian milréis. The subsequent 40 per cent fall in the rate of exchange meant that even with increased revenues Brazilian Traction was earning little more than required to meet its bond interest, preference dividends, and sinking fund requirements. When pressed about the resumption of dividends on the common stock at the annual meeting, Brazilian Traction Vice-president Miller Lash (the son of Zebulon Lash, who had died in 1919) replied that the rate of exchange would have to recover at least to the level of the previous year (14d.) to permit this. The matter was complicated by the fact that any rise in the milréis reduced the revenues received from rates which included a gold component; while a fall in the rate of exchange generated increased revenues.[8]

The need to restore the dividend was rendered acute by the fact that the company now had to finance a major project to increase its generating capacity. An unusually dry winter season in 1921 left the Lajes reservoir near Rio only half full at the very time that the authorities began pressing the company for power to electrify the Central Railroad. On a visit to Brazil in August 1921, E.R. Wood found his discussions with Mackenzie about the future so alarming that the two men wired to head office: 'It is our view that the company['s] existence [is] in peril.' As a result Asa Billings was seconded to Brazilian Traction to begin planning for expansion.[9]

A Harvard prodigy with special expertise in concrete construction, Billings had worked on a variety of projects before joining the Pearson Engineering Company in 1911. He soon found himself overseeing construction of a dam on the Ebro River for the Barcelona Traction, Light and Power Company; he stayed on until the Talarn dam, then the highest in Europe, was completed in 1916 and began planning a bigger dam at Camarasa, second highest in the world. After wartime service with the US Navy, Billings returned to Spain in 1920 and helped to plan the merger between the Barcelona company and its major rival, Compañía Energía Electrica de Cataluña. In 1921 he returned to New York as chief engineer of the Canadian and General Finance Company, which had assumed the responsibilities for engineering and purchasing once performed by Pearson Engineering it was from there in 1921 that Billings was dispatched to Brazil to plan the new generating capacity.[10]

Since the capacity of the Lajes reservoir could be increased no further, Billings proposed that a $10 million plant be constructed at Ilha dos Pombos on the Paraíba River, the border between the states of Rio de Janeiro and

Minas Gerais, a plant that would ultimately be able to turn out 160,000 horsepower. To make such a major investment largely out of retained earnings without providing some comfort for the long-suffering common shareholders seemed likely to produce a revolt against management. Noting that operating costs had declined to less than 36 per cent of gross revenues (from 48 per cent), the board of directors reluctantly approved the payment of a 4 per cent annual dividend in 1922, despite the fact that the rate of exchange had failed to improve at all (see Appendix).[11]

II

Brazilian Traction's management took the decision to expand operations with considerable trepidation owing to the increasing instability of the 'Old Republic.' Alexander Mackenzie favoured the Rio de Janeiro politician Nilo Peçanha to succeed President Epitácio Pessoa in 1922. Peçanha, a wily veteran of factional politics, had proven his 'soundness' on financial and other questions over a long career and especially during his brief presidency in 1909–10. The alternative was Artur da Silva Bernardes from the state of Minas Gerais, an inflationist and a strong economic nationalist antagonistic to foreign corporations. Despite the hostility of the armed forces, Bernardes was elected, but in July 1922, some Rio army officers who supported Peçanha rose in revolt. Disaffected by the election outcome, mounting social and economic problems, and a growing lack of confidence in the corrupt élite accommodation politics of the republic, these junior officers staged a brief, bungled, and in the end quixotic rebellion. When the rising collapsed, the zealots barricaded themselves in a coastal blockhouse; then, after a day or so of indecision, boldly marched out into the bewildered Carioca crowd, hoping to raise the population by their brave example, only to be cut down in a shootout on Copacabana beach.[12]

As expected, the new president, himself embattled by regional discontents and open military opposition, showed little sympathy for Brazilian Traction's problems. At Ilha dos Pombos the new dam was inching its way across the Paraíba from the state of Rio de Janeiro towards the Minas Gerais shore. Minas politicians undoubtedly interpreted the dam as the first step in a wholesale invasion by Brazilian Traction of the locally controlled electric utility industry. The state government fought to limit the power concession to a term of thirty years with the right to fix electricity rates and to acquire the plant without compensation after sixty years. The company resisted these conditions, arguing that the main dam, from the

Rio shore to an island in Rio territory, would permit the generation of 45,000 horsepower. The only structure in Minas Gerais would be a diversion dam, which would ultimately permit capacity to be expanded to 160,000 horsepower. When Bernardes was asked to intervene and override the regulations in his home state, he naturally refused. At great risk, therefore, the company continued to build its dam to the far shore without a proper agreement, relying upon the tendentious argument that as a state boundary the Paraíba River fell under federal jurisdiction anyway, so that the laws of Minas Gerais did not apply.[13]

Bernardes and his supporters also hindered the renegotiation of Brazilian Traction's telephone franchise in Rio. Since the end of the war Alexander Mackenzie had been seeking changes in the consession, originally granted in 1899 to the Brazilianische Elektricitäts Gesellschaft: 'It is of supreme importance to us ... that we should get this concession extended for a long period. It has only ten years to run, and the capital account is increasing by leaps and bounds owing to the demand for telephone service which we cannot begin to meet.' In exchange he was quite prepared to lower residential rates, which were so high that the public used telephones in business establishments instead of subscribing for private lines. Mackenzie wanted to end this and impose measured service on commercial telephones. He had actually negotiated such a deal in 1919 before the prefect of Rio got cold feet.[14]

In 1921 Brazilian Traction retained the US telephone expert W.J. Hagenah to go to Brazil and examine the Rio situation. Hagenah concluded that the system had returned an income of just 0.20 per cent per annum on the capital invested in it between 1900 and 1921. Mackenzie persuaded the prefect to reopen negotiations, and in the summer of 1922 an agreement was reached to extend the franchise from 1929 to 1950 (with non-exclusive rights to 1990). Any municipal takeover would require full compensation to be paid. Measured service would be introduced for commercial lines, and charges would vary with the exchange rate of the milréis. These two changes together were expected to double current revenues.[15]

The mood of optimism evaporated the following year, however, as the new prefect of Rio, Alaor Prata Soares, a close associate of President Bernardes, applied to the courts to nullify the deal on the grounds that the abandonment of the city's right to acquire the telephone system in 1929 at less than half its capital cost involved the unlawful disposal of public property by a predecessor. Soares also alleged that tenders ought to have been called for a new franchise, and that the high rates conceded were contrary to the public interest so that the prefect should not have agreed to them. Alexander Mackenzie was certain who was behind this campaign:

There is always fairly strong nationalist feeling – usually dormant but easy to rouse – and ... President Bernardes did everything he could during his first two years in office to excite public opinion against us. He was an extremist, and there has never been anybody quite like him in public life. He alone was responsible for bringing the action to set aside the telephone contract.[16]

Although the company's lawyers were confident that its case would ultimately be sustained, experience with the Brazilian courts guaranteed that any victory would be a long time coming. While company officials were determined upon 'sitting tight and fighting to [the] last ditch legally,' Mackenzie believed that he might do better by bringing diplomatic pressure from Britain to bear upon the Brazilian government. The British ambassador was asked to raise the matter with Bernardes, and on a visit to England in 1923 Alexander Mackenzie and Miller Lash attempted to persuade the Foreign Office to warn Bernardes formally that if he did not change his tactics he would not be permitted to borrow in London, 'as the only means of getting the Brazilian government to treat British enterprises with justice.' In the end no formal diplomatic protest was made, but the house of Rothschild, Brazil's financial agent, was induced to advise Bernardes that any tampering with the telephone contract would make it difficult to borrow in Britain.[17]

Bernardes pretended that he was less bent upon nullifying the telephone contract than the prefect, but Soares showed no sign of changing his attitude. During the next couple of years, while the prefect's lawsuit inched its way towards trial, the telephone company could do little except refuse to extend service in Rio despite requests from potential subscribers, in hopes that public pressure would force the municipality to return to the bargaining table. With Bernardes's backing, however, Soares was in no hurry to reopen talks, and late in 1925 the judge of first instance upheld the city's case in its entirety. Snarling that the judge was a 'recognized incompetent' acting on orders from the president, company officials now pinned their hopes upon the appeal court, but there, too, the municipality was sustained by a narrow margin of three to two. Miller Lash ruefully admitted that 'The courts in Brazil are a pretty uncertain proposition. Although we are advised by our lawyers down there that we have an exceedingly strong case, it is impossible to tell what the result will be.'[18]

From Bernardes's point of view, attacking 'the Light' was politically shrewd. When he took office there was a civil war in Rio Grande do Sul, and in the states of both Bahia and Rio de Janeiro there were rival governments claiming legitimacy. Bernardes was forced to enter Rio clandestinely and, during the early months of his term of office, he required the physical protection of his backers. Attacking Brazilian Traction was a relatively costless means of improving the beleaguered president's popularity. The Rio manager of the Canadian Bank of Commerce reported that, 'The feeling of hostility ... to the Light and Power Co. Ltd. is not confined to the government. It is shared by a large section of the press, as is usual in every case where extensive monopolies or privileges are enjoyed by foreigners. The company is always referred to in the hostile section of the press as the "Canadian octopus." '[19]

Brazilian Traction added to this animosity through its policy of charging excessive rates for both telephone and electrical service. Because the demand for power outstripped the supply, rates were kept high; since it possessed a solidly entrenched monopoly in Brazil's two major power markets the company felt no need to cut prices to encourage consumption. With the rates clearly specified by contract and the added complication of the variable exchange rate, selling more current at a lower profit margin would probably have been a mistaken strategy. H.H. Couzens, who joined the company from the public sector, once noted that the Light's management principles were contrary to those followed by most other utilities:

When I arrived here it seemed to me that the one thing we wanted was volume of business, so as to distribute our heavy overhead and get it down to a reasonable amount per k.w. hr. All my life I have been an advocate of 'volume' – but the more I came to analyze the situation as it exists in this country the more I became convinced, as I am now, that at any rate with conditions as they now are, no other course [than keeping rates up] is likely to be more successful. In fact, I feel confident that any other course is likely to be less successful than the one which is being pursued.[20]

In Brazil the Canadian utilities behaved like classic monopolists, demanding a higher price for a lower volume of output than would otherwise have been the case.

The continuing decline in the exchange value of the milréis under Bernardes only served to feed xenophobia. In an effort to stabilize coffee prices his government printed money to buy up surplus stocks, depreciating the currency. That, of course, suited the coffee producers of São Paulo, who received higher incomes from low-priced exports. The president, however, found it politic to blame foreign interests for the fall of the milréis to 5⅜d. (or little more than one-third of its 1920 value). 'He says,' snorted Alexander Mackenzie, 'we are one of the main factors which have produced the decline through our "colossal" remittances!'[21]

There were limits to such an inflationary policy, however popular it might have been domestically in the export-oriented regions. Unable to meet its foreign obligations Brazil was eventually compelled to permit a delegation of British financial experts to draw up a prescription for recovery at the end of 1923. Supposedly invited by Bernardes, this financial mission was in fact a condition set by London bankers before they would grant a large funding loan to pay off Brazilian debts as they fell due during the next five years, a point not lost upon nationalists who resented such foreign dictation.[22]

Alexander Mackenzie hoped that the mission might force the government to behave in a more friendly fashion towards Brazilian Traction. In a lengthy and elaborate memorandum to Edwin Montagu, leader of the mission, Mackenzie insisted upon the British character of the enterprise.[23] The idea that the company was really US-based he dismissed as a mistaken notion left over from the days of F.S. Pearson, and he tried to counter directly any claim that British firms had little hope of selling equipment to Brazilian Traction. If there were any fault it lay with British industry, he claimed. When one firm had submitted a tender for a turbine recently it was discovered that it had never built one of the size required and the order had gone elsewhere. Another British company, which was supplying a big generator, had had to have the shaft forged in Czechoslovakia. High-voltage transformers from England had not given satisfactory service, but tramway motors, controllers, and cement were purchased there. Most gas-making equipment and, until 1914, all gas coal, had been bought in Britain. That gave the mission an interest in protecting Brazilian Traction, which was seeking nothing except elementary fairness: 'we have to fight our own battles. As, however, the government is supposed to be holding out this country as a suitable place for the employment of British capital, it may be useful to know how capital already here is treated.'

What information Mackenzie was able to glean about the consultations between the mission and the government, however, suggested that the bankers had diplomatically avoided naming any specific injustices that ought to be rectified if a loan were to be granted to Brazil. In the end the changes the mission suggested in its report to Bernardes included only the usual balanced budgets and cuts in spending and borrowing and the encouragement of exports and foreign investment. The report made no recommendations regarding more favourable treatment of foreign capitalists.[24]

Fiscal orthodoxy and a drastic reduction of the money supply satisfied the foreign bankers and improved the government's fiscal position, but also greatly increased political opposition to Bernardes at home. As coffee prices began to rise and the destruction of paper currency dampened inflation, the unrest that had marked President Bernardes's term of office worsened during 1924. On the second anniversary of the abortive rising of July 1922 a group of young army officers in São Paulo seized control of the city. The *Tenentes* issued a manifesto denouncing the Bernardes government and calling for a return to the principles of the pre-1889 monarchy. São Paulo remained in rebel hands for three weeks; the state governor and thousands of other Paulistas fled until loyalist forces surrounded the city and forced the rebels to retreat southward. Not until the year's end did the federal government restore effective civil order.[25]

The revolt caught Brazilian Traction at an awkward moment: Alexander Mackenzie was on one of his periodic trips overseas, leaving Billings as the senior official in Brazil. When the fighting started Billings was in Rio awaiting the arrival of a new executive, H.H. Couzens, sometime general manager of the Toronto Hydro-Electric System, who had just been recruited from a position as general manager of the municipally owned Toronto Transportation Commission. In São Paulo a Brazilian national was in charge, and Billings hastened to make his way there, arriving about a week after the fighting had broken out. Telephone contact with Rio was soon cut off, and censorship made it difficult for the head office to find out what was going on in Brazil.[26]

The company emerged pretty much unscathed. Billings observed that the system had been damaged 'very lightly indeed considering the astonishing amount of ammunition used up.' Wires and pole lines had been shot up, but despite the periodic artillery bombardments, 'it is remarkable that damage to important parts of the apparatus and equipment are not greater. In nearly every case the shells which struck in or near our stations missed the important apparatus.'[27]

Worried as he was about the lack of news reaching Toronto, Miller Lash endeavoured to be philosophical: 'Of course, even if the damage would be very heavy in São Paulo it is difficult to see how it can do any more than temporarily interfere with our operations, and the damage would have to be very large an amount before it would cripple us financially.' As soon as the fighting was over, however, the company took care to assess losses as accurately as possible; initial estimates ran to over $1 million, but ultimately a figure of $840,000 was settled upon – money that, it was hoped, might be recovered from the authorities.[28]

The 1924 rebellion did not, however, embroil Brazilian Traction in the kind of difficulties in which the Mexican utilities had found themselves. The situation in São Paulo rapidly returned to normal, even though a corporal's guard of rebels roamed the interior for another two years hoping to rekindle a popular uprising. With the mutinous army now firmly under federal control in São Paulo, the company was able to turn its full attention to the dire power shortage that was imminent there. Billings, now vice-president in charge of engineering, had already begun to plan a big new development, which would divert the flow of several rivers over the seven-hundred-metre-high Serra do Mar escarpment. The drainage basin around São Paulo emptied inland into the Paraná River, which flowed southward to reach the ocean at Buenos Aires. By the fall of 1924 Billings had realized that reversing the flow of these rivers would take a long time to complete; in the interim the board approved a plan to build another run-of-the-river plant at Rasgão on the Tietê below the original Parnaíba development, at a cost of $2.2 million. Meanwhile, a steam plant was moved from Rio de Janeiro to São Paulo and power was purchased from two other small generating stations.[29]

Problems were compounded by an 'absolutely unprecedented' dry spell and, as winter approached in March 1925, power rationing was imposed in São Paulo. Miller Lash considered the drought 'the most serious thing that has happened to us in Brazil for a good many years, the late revolution in São Paulo notwithstanding.' Though it was an act of God, he was convinced that the utility would get the major share of the blame, however unjustly: 'at least this was the experience in Mexico in 1921 where a somewhat similar condition of affairs arose.' Even though construction at Rasgão was being rushed ahead as rapidly as possible in hopes of having power by the fall of 1925, the board decided to begin the preliminary stages of the Serra project at a cost of $8 million. For once the federal government gave its approval without delay to the massive river diversions the scheme called for.[30]

Rasgão began turning out power in September 1925, although the dam was only half finished and the concrete lining of the power canal extended only thirty centimetres or so above the waterline. Meanwhile, Billings struggled to recruit a large enough workforce to rush the first stage of his Serra do Mar project to completion early in 1926. He had difficulties securing more than a third of the 3,000 men he required; the governments of other Brazilian states resented São Paulo's rapid growth and expelled the company's recruiters or subjected them to prohibitive taxation. In the end Billings had to switch over part of the crew from Rasgão, leaving that project to be finished later. By that time the rains had come again, filling the reservoirs, and power rationing had been lifted in São Paulo.[31]

To guard against future shortages, work went ahead with the Serra scheme as quickly as possible, and the first generator at the Cubatão station began to turn in the fall of 1926. This proved fortunate, as power demand in São Paulo leapt upward in the late 1920s. Ultimately, Billings decided that his original plan, which involved channelling water from all the tributaries of the Tietê into the reservoir through tunnels, was too costly. Instead he devised a more daring plan by which the entire flow of the Tietê would pass southward through the city to the mouth of the Pinheiros River. There a dam would be constructed to reverse the flow of that stream so that water could be channelled up it to another huge dam, over which it would be pumped into the Rio Grande (now the Billings) reservoir. An additional seven and a half metres of water stored there would permit a much larger development than originally planned, below the Serra do Mar, to enable the company to meet future needs.[32]

The technical brilliance of this design was much admired, and Alexander Mackenzie heartily endorsed Billings' request for a large salary increase, observing that 'What he says as to the importance of the work done is the simple truth. No one we have ever had here before could have done it. He is *creating* a 500,000 HP water power, and the sum he proposes is a merest drop in the bucket of expenditure thereon.' In fact, the project was so large, involving the shifting of five million cubic metres of fill, that the work was only one-third complete by 1931 when it was suspended owing to the Depression. Resumed three years later but not finally completed until 1950, the Serra development placed Brazilian Traction in an unassailable position in the largest industrial power market in South America.[33]

The company was able to raise the capital required for these projects *and* pay dividends primarily because President Bernardes finally shook free of the influence of the Paulista coffee planters who had shaped the economic policy of his regime since 1922. Incineration of paper currency brought deflation, which improved the rate of exchange of the milréis in 1926 by nearly 20 per cent over 1925. Aided by this the dollar value of the company's profits climbed nearly 40 per cent and led to the decision to increase the dividend rate from 4 per cent to 5 per cent at the start of 1926.[34]

III

The retirement of the hostile President Artur Bernardes in November 1926 and the succession of Paulista Washington Luís Pereira de Sousa did not immediately improve the lot of Brazilian Traction as much as might have been expected. Having captured 98 per cent of the votes cast, Washington Luís was in a strong position; he quickly announced plans for monetary reform. With such broad support, Luís's responsibility for public finance overrode his regional loyalties.[35] As part of a plan to establish a new, stable currency backed by gold, however, the government chose to fix the exchange value of the milréis at 6d., 18 per cent less than the rate prevailing during the preceding year. Alexander Mackenzie could scarcely contain his outrage at this decision. '*Monetary Reform*. This is what it is called. It ought to be sabotage or kari-kari [sic],' he ranted. 'I am getting "fed-up" with "super-men". We lived through the term of the last one, who, notwithstanding all his ill-will, never did one-fiftieth part of the harm to us that the present man is doing – and he calls himself, and thinks he is, really friendly.'[36]

Mackenzie of course approved of stabilization, but he would have preferred a much higher exchange rate. Without the government's interference Mackenzie was convinced that the rate of exchange might have reached at least 8d. in the short term, and perhaps gone higher in future. He drew up an elaborate chart to show that Brazilian Traction had invested nearly £40 million at an average exchange rate of $13\frac{9}{64}$d. This he showed to every politician he could lay his hands on, arguing that the new rate confiscated more than half of this total investment.[37] '[W]hile I extracted sympathy,' he reported,

I got no comfort. They will all support the president. To some I could speak plainly of the humiliating position Brazil was putting itself in before the world. They don't realize *that* and *will* not unless and until European and American newspapers open up and let them know.

In an effort to bring that about, Edward Peacock talked to the editor of *The Times* of London, who ran an almost verbatim version of Mackenzie's criticisms that the company's head office also got inserted in the Toronto *Mail and Empire*.[38]

All this effort proved unavailing. 'Will the patient English ox give in?' fumed Mackenzie. 'I fear he will.' The Brazilian Congress went ahead and passed the stabilization legislation, leading him to speculate darkly about the company's future. The problem was not that utility rates were too high, he told Peacock:

Our troubles with the authorities arise from other causes, and the principal one, I regret to say, is that being a foreign company we are considered fair game. I even think that a foreign company exploiting a public utility in Brazil has had its day and is becoming an anachronism.[39]

Mackenzie's pessimistic views proved ill-founded. In fact, the company prospered greatly under Washington Luís's stable exchange rate policy. The company's Annual Report for 1926 showed that Brazilian Traction's net earnings were up more than 24 per cent over the previous year, and early in 1927 the dividend was raised from 5 per cent to 6 per cent (see Appendix). By the fall of that year share prices had hit $200.[40] While earnings in Brazilian currency increased handsomely, however, dollar profits rose only marginally, as the milréis stabilized at just under the official exchange rate of 6d. Nevertheless, early in 1928 the board raised the dividend again, to 7 per cent per annum, and granted shareholders a handsome capital gain by increasing the amount of capital stock and offering them the right to subscribe for one share at par for every five held. Two hundred and twenty-eight thousand shares were subscribed for. Later that year the company decided to convert its old $100 par value common shares into new no par value shares at the rate of four new shares for one old one; the dividend rate was fixed at forty-four cents per share for the last two quarters of the year.[41]

Early in 1929 the company raised additional capital for its expansion projects by offering shareholders the right to subscribe for one Brazilian Traction share at $40 for every seven they already held. This issue, which was completely taken up, raised $31 million. During the year net profits rose almost 13 per cent, and as the exchange rate remained stable at 6d. per milréis the company was able to increase the quarterly dividend rate to fifty cents per share. In addition, a stock dividend equal to 1 per cent of the common stock was declared in December 1929, to be issued the following spring.[42]

Brazilian Traction was able to recover its financial strength during the 1920s despite the continuing decline in the exchange value of the milréis owing to booming power markets in Rio de Janeiro and São Paulo. Profits rose enough to allow dividends to be resumed, then substantially increased, while retained earnings proved sufficient to finance most of the additional construction required to expand capacity. As it had before 1914, the company demonstrated that it could operate successfully provided the rate of exchange was relatively stable, as it was from 1923 through 1930.

During the twenties Brazilian Traction met the challenge of growth despite the government's overt hostility because, over the long run, the interests of the company and those of the government were very similar. Both had large foreign obligations that spoke to the need for a stable monetary policy. And a government heavily influenced by Paulista politicians understood the importance of hydroelectricity and communications for the industrialization of the region. Over the decade the number of passengers carried on the tramways, the sales of electricity and gas, and the number of telephones in service more than doubled.[43] More important, to a management mainly concerned with profitability rather than volume of output, the common stock had been split in a five to one ratio while the dividend was maintained at the annual rate of 7 per cent. After almost a decade of manoeuvring the Supreme Court upheld the revision of the Rio Telephone franchise in 1929 by a ten to one margin. Management chose to interpret this outcome as a message to 'all foreign interests in Brazil, as the sanctity and inviolability of public contracts has been demonstrated beyond the shadow of a doubt. It is a triumph for the honourability of the judiciary of the country.' Alexander Mackenzie, now enjoying his retirement by sightseeing in far-off Egypt, wittily and succinctly celebrated the occasion by cabling Toronto from Aswan: 'Now sing the 100th Psalm.' (*Jubilate Deo*: 'O be joyful in the Lord, all ye lands ... O go your way into his gates with thanksgiving and into his courts with praise.')[44]

By that time, however, the impact of the world depression had begun to make itself felt. The coffee economy actually collapsed before the famous stock market crash. By 1929 head office had started to wonder if the rate of exchange could be maintained much longer. H.H. Couzens studied the matter, then reported from Brazil that there was no reason to expect a decline; he noted, however: 'On the basis of Sir Alexander Mackenzie's theory regarding exchange, viz. that one should hear all opinions, sum them up and then decide to do the opposite, I should have cabled you the exact opposite of what I did. Time alone will prove which is correct.'[45]

Before many months had passed Couzens's rueful premonitions proved well founded. By the end of 1929 coffee prices had begun to slide, and the Banco do Brasil was struggling to maintain the official rate of exchange. Already foreign banks were undercutting that rate, and a free market in exchange reappeared for the first time since 1926. Attempts to halt the skid in the value of the milréis during 1930 were fairly successful, but the country's substantial gold reserves were exhausted, while the price of coffee plummeted from 22.5 cents per pound in 1929 to 8 cents. By the end of the year twenty-six million sacks of beans were in storage, twice Brazil's annual average export.

Economic and social unrest intensified with the economic crisis and a factional deadlock over the presidential succession. The revolt that had been rehearsing in the regions for most of the twenties finally succeeded in October 1930 when a coup installed as dictator Getúlio Doreles Vargas, the defeated candidate in that year's presidential election.[46] Regional interests, marginalized by the Paulista–Minas Gerais dominance of federal politics and led by Vargas from the southern state of Rio Grande do Sul, finally made common cause with dissident army officers disgusted by the corruption, log-rolling, and economic mismanagement that had discredited the former regime.[47] The 'Old Republic' from which Brazilian Traction had sometimes suffered but under which it had grown up and prospered came to an abrupt end.

Management's first concern, of course, was the physical security of its property. The rebels did seize the Ilha dos Pombos powerplant as they marched on São Paulo, but no serious damage was done, mainly because the federal army offered little resistance to the rising. H.H. Couzens reported that the employees had been loyal and diligent. 'All I had to do,' he wrote to head office, 'was to sit & smoke & follow events.'

Correctly he perceived that the new Vargas regime was not going to meddle much in the company's affairs:

Our company has a real background in Brazil extending over many years – & no authority in their right mind wants to recklessly interfere with something which, through this recent affair, was about the only one factor which went steadily about its business and kept going on peacefully – externally anyway.[48]

The company could readily endorse the Vargas program –financial stabilization, industrialization, regional development, and political stability. More to the point, it could see that here was a government likely to leave it alone and with the will to carry out its intentions. Ironically the political environment for the company improved just as the international and national economies collapsed. In the first stages of the global depression the rate of exchange of the milréis slid to less than 4d., and in September 1931 the government announced suspension of interest payments on its foreign debts. Brazilian Traction's earnings and profits declined steadily until 1933. Cash dividends were suspended at the end of 1930 in lieu of stock dividends.[49]

Differential rates of industrialization during the 1920s gradually destabilized the delicately balanced factional politics of the fragile Brazilian republic. The civil disorders associated with these changes that threatened to engulf Brazil during the 'Old Republic,' especially during Artur Bernardes's presidency, did not vex the company as much as the fall in the exchange rate and the rise in economic nationalism that characterized the regime. The uprising in São Paulo in 1924 inflicted minor damage on the system there, but otherwise failed to disrupt service. Bernardes's successor, Washington Luís, proved less antagonistic to Brazilian Traction, and as a result the company was able both to expand its facilities and to reward its shareholders handsomely. The overthrow of the republic by Vargas in 1930 brought an end to vacillating fiscal and monetary policies, political instability, and government interference with Brazilian Traction, but it also marked the end of an era of economic expansion during which the company, despite its many problems, had prospered mightily.

PART FIVE

Conclusion

13

International Capitalism

By the middle of the 1920s the Canadian utilities that operated throughout Latin America and the Caribbean had become thoroughly internationalized. Although they retained their place of incorporation in Canada (as some of them do today), that was largely an address of convenience. Planned, founded, and initially financed by Canadian entrepreneurs (though in many cases with a hearty dose of Yankee push added), all the larger companies and some of the smaller ones had found it necessary to seek funds in European capital markets even before the First World War. During the twenties their nominal 'Canadian-ness' was further reduced by corporate reorganizations. Still Canada remained the main theatre and Canadians key players in the battle for control over these far-flung enterprises.

The utilities holding company, something that had originated in the United States and in Germany, became the principal threat to control by the current managerial group after the First World War. Pioneering firms, such as General Electric's Electric Bond and Share Company (EBASCO) and Stone and Webster, inspired many emulators. The booming stock markets of the 1920's created an apparently insatiable demand for the securities of such enterprises, a demand that utilities promoters were only too eager to satisfy with sometimes dangerously shaky pyramids of insubstantial paper.

I

The origins of the holding company lay in the evolution of electrical technology. Innovative managers like Samuel Insull of Chicago recognized at an early date that economies of scale in power generation, diversity of load, and an increasing load factor all pointed in the direction of larger systems.[1] By the 1920s such systems had become regional in extent in Canada, the United States, and Germany as engineers combined different energy sources (hydraulic, coal-fired, and oil-fired plants) with even more diverse types of demand, such as agriculture, mining, and pulp and paper enterprises.[2]

S.Z. Mitchell of General Electric took the lead in expanding EBASCO. He assumed that power sales would rise 6 to 8 per cent per annum, roughly doubling each decade, making small generating stations increasingly inefficient. Enterprises serving a limited area should, therefore, be folded into holding companies, which would be in a better position to raise the large sums needed to expand capacity rapidly. Each additional $1 of sales would require $5 of new plant, and such amounts of capital could not be retained from earnings, so Mitchell believed that holding companies should aim to earn a 9 per cent annual profit. Of every $100 worth of capital raised, the company should obtain $60 by selling 6 per cent bonds or debentures (carrying annual interest of $3.60), $20 from 7 per cent preference stock (annual dividend $1.40), and $20 from common stock with earnings of $4 (or a rate of 20 per cent). These rates of return would be sufficient to attract the large amounts of new investment necessary, while the small amount of common stock made it easy (yet highly profitable) for a holding company to retain control over its subsidiaries.[3]

Such loosely structured holding companies did not provide the tight, multi-divisional organization characteristic of large-scale corporations in the United States. Nevertheless they did concentrate financial control of a large number of separate units.[4] By 1924 all the largest power producers in the United States were controlled by holding companies, which together accounted for two-thirds of generating capacity; just seven holding-company groups controlled 40 per cent of production. EBASCO alone had 13 per cent.[5]

During the First World War S.Z. Mitchell undertook discussions with the Royal Securities Corporation with a view to combining all the promotions with which Max Aitken had been involved with some other Latin American utilities. Calgary Power, Porto Rico Railways, the Camagüey Company, Santiago (de Cuba) Electric Light and Traction, West India Electric, Trinidad Electric, and Demerara Electric were all to be included, along with Panama Tramway and companies in Matanzas, Cárdenas, and

Cienfuegos in Cuba. Mitchell proposed to exchange the common stock of the subsidiaries for 6 per cent preferred stock in the holding company, thus ensuring control and limiting the cost of raising funds. He made the classic arguments regarding the advantages of a conglomerate to the shareholders of the existing utilities:

1. A great diversification of risk.
2. The management under the supervision of the Electric Bond and Share Co., which has a most enviable record as to successful management of many other companies.
3. The Electric Bond and Share Company, either independently, or together with Royal Securities Corporation, would secure any moneys which might be necessary for future extensions.
4. The shareholders, instead of having shares in a small issue with a very limited market, would have shares in a large issue backed by the great prestige of the Electric Bond and Share Company, and with a very broad market.
5. In connection with any future expenditures, each of the subsidiary companies would have the benefit of the broad experience and ripe judgment of the people connected with the Electric Bond and Share Company.

I.W. Killam, who had succeeded Aitken at the head of Royal Securities when the latter moved to England, went down to the Caribbean and carefully investigated the proposition, but nothing seems to have come of the plan.[6]

Only a few relatively small utility holding companies were actually created in Canada. In 1925 Montreal stockbroker (and former Royal Securities man) A.J. Nesbitt organized the Power Corporation of Canada and commenced an aggressive program of acquisitions, crowned with a successful bid for the British Columbia Electric Railway in 1928. In 1926 Killam did create the International Power Company, which swept up a mixed bag of foreign utilities under the control of Royal Securities, including such Aitken promotions as Demerara Electric and Porto Rico Railways, as well as Venezuela Power (serving Maracaibo and Barquisimeto), and Tocayo (Venezuela) Electric, Bolivia Power (La Paz), Ouro (Bolivia) Light and Power, San Salvador Electric and Oriente Electric Light (El Salvador), and one North American operation, Newfoundland Light and Power (St John's). (See Table 11.)[7]

A few Canadian-chartered utility companies operating at home and abroad escaped the net of the holding company.[8] Jamaica Public Service

TABLE 11
Canadian Utility Groups in Latin America, 1930

1 Brazilian Traction, Light and Power Company
Subsidiaries
Rio de Janeiro Tramway, Light and Power Company (controlling
the Brazilian Telephone Company)
São Paulo Tramway, Light and Power Company
São Paulo Electric Company
City of Santos Improvement Company
Brazilian Hydro-Electric Company

Book Value of assets: $376,608,494

2 International Power Company
Subsidiaries
–wholly owned:
Venezuela Power Company
Tocayo Electric Company
–majority control of common stock:
San Salvador Electric Light Company
Oriente Electric Light Company
Newfoundland Light and Power Company
Ouro Light and Power Company
–81% of 1st mortgage bonds:
Bolivia Power Company
–controlling interest:
Demerara Electric Company
Porto Rico Railways Company

Book value of assets: $32,817,572

3 Jamaica Public Service Limited
Subsidiaries
West India Electric Company
Jamaica Light and Power Company
Jamaica Hydro-Electric Company

Book value of assets: $833,853

4 Northern Mexico Power and Development Company
Subsidiaries
Mexican Northern Power Company
Empresas Electricas Mexicanas, Inc., controls:
Compania Electrica de Tampico
Vera Cruz Electric Light, Power and Traction Company
Puebla Tramway, Light and Power Company
Compania Electricida de Merida

Book value of assets: $17,081,462

Table 11 (*Continued*)

5 Mexico Tramways Company
  Subsidiaries
    Mexican Light and Power Company, controls:
      Mexican Electric Light Company
      Pachuca Light and Power Company
      Mexican Southern Power Company
      South West Power Company of Mexico
      Toluca Electric Light and Power

Book value of assets: $105,636,184

6 Trinidad Electric Company

Book value of assets: $3,982,360

Total of all assets: $535,959,925

SOURCE *Annual Financial Review (Canadian)* 1931

Corporation (formerly West India Electric) and Trinidad Electric remained in the hands of Montreal and Halifax interests respectively. Most of the rest, however, shared the fate of the Mexican Northern Power Company, formed in 1909 by Canadians[9] to develop the Conchos River in Chihuahua. Mexican Northern fell prey to the troubles of the Revolution, but recovered after the war; reorganized as Northern Mexican Power and Development Company in 1919, it was taken over in 1929 by another General Electric subsidiary, the American and Foreign Power Company. American and Foreign Power also controlled Puebla Tramway, Light and Power, which it folded into Northern Mexican Power along with some other small Mexican undertakings.[10]

In due course the huge US holding companies also began to eye the Canadian enterprises in Mexico and Brazil (which accounted for 90 per cent of the assets of all such undertakings) as likely opportunities for expansion. During the 1920s the Electric Bond and Share Company, the American and Foreign Power Company, and Stone and Webster in the United States bought up many well-established firms on the periphery of the Brazilian Traction and Mexican Light territories. It was only a matter of time before these companies themselves became takeover targets.

Sharing the field with an aggressive, acquisition-minded conglomerate like EBASCO created problems. In the fall of 1927 Brazilian Traction began to press ahead with plans for 'broadening out' in the state of São Paulo by buying up as many small companies as possible. Wherever the Canadians went, however, they found that EBASCO had preceded them with offers, pushing up the prices demanded. 'It is an undoubted fact,' reported H.H. Couzens, 'that their negotiations and purchases make matters much more difficult for us.' Eventually EBASCO agreed in 1927 to stay out of the eastern part of São Paulo (between the capital and the coast) provided that Brazilian Traction would leave the western section alone.[11]

The close links between EBASCO and General Electric worried management at Brazilian Traction. Miller Lash pointed out that

there is no doubt about it that any manufacturer who goes into the operating game will form an unnatural competitor, as his first idea is to get orders for his material, and usually the manufacturer is not an operator and will do all kinds of things in the course of operation or competition which will injure not only himself but the people who are already on the ground.

Growing public criticism of utility conglomerates in the United States led EBASCO to pretend it was independent of GE, but that was merely a smokescreen. GE was known to be very keen to increase its overseas markets, but it might be possible to control competition from EBASCO by threatening to switch to other suppliers. Lash noted that 'the only argument that these people understand, or pay attention to, is one that shows them that if they are not careful to play the game they will lose some money by it.'

Thus Brazilian Traction had to be ready to defend itself. Sometimes concessions were required, at other times aggressive action. On occasion a rival like EBASCO pushed too hard, as when it claimed that the understanding arrived at in 1927 had included a commitment by the Canadian company to stay out of the state of Minas Gerais altogether. Alexander Mackenzie was adamant that he had never agreed to any such thing: 'we ought not to abandon this state to them and are free to negotiate where we wish.' Brazilian Traction was particularly interested in extending its telephone network in Minas Gerais, and he recommended pursuing this aggressively: 'I think we ought not to allow Electric Bond and Share Company to take any interest in telephone properties or to surround our light and power territory; it may mean larger expansion than we want, but we can afford to make sacrifices for security.'[12]

At other times concessions could be made to reinforce the ties between EBASCO and Brazilian Traction. Near the end of 1928 the US firm suggested an interconnection of their electrical systems in the state of Rio de Janeiro, so they could draw upon each other for standby service if required. The engineering staff opposed the plan as of little value because the networks operated on different frequencies requiring the installation of frequency changers, but head office took a broader view. If this token of friendship were denied, Miller Lash pointed out, EBASCO might speed up its plans for its own hydraulic developments and become less eager to purchase current. Better to make the deal, although keeping it secret so as not to offend Brazilian sensibilities too much.[13]

H.H. Couzens frequently complained that EBASCO had a poor sense of the proper way to deal with the local authorities. He particularly resented the company's publicity, because the 'underlying idea of it all is to try to create the impression here that they are a colossal organization with great benefits to confer on Brazil, and indirectly to demonstrate that they are larger than our own company.' Articles planted in the press aimed to show

that it is part of their settled plan to take over all the public utilities obtainable and form a huge organization. It is difficult to realize how they can justify such an action, which to me is contrary to their own interests, as it is to the interests of any other foreign public utility concern in the country.

He particularly resented hints that EBASCO might acquire control of Brazilian Traction.[14]

Such boasts infuriated Couzens, since he believed that they 'foster, or even ask for, public ownership to keep control in Brazil.' His fears were reinforced when the governor of Belo Horizonte insisted that his state must share in the profits of a new telephone system, on the grounds that the Americans were seeking to monopolize control of all public utilities. Couzens thought that,

As to the question of public ownership in Brazil, I do not believe that the time has yet come when it is an immediate menace to the business of our company, but I believe that there will be increasing agitation along these lines; and one thing that is likely to be used as an argument by the advocates of public ownership is the declarations which the Electric Bond & Share Company are making from time to time.[15]

Discreetly he endeavoured to warn EBASCO's local representative of the dangerous tactics his firm was using, by pointing out that recently his company had gotten wind at the last minute of a Congressional proposal to form a commission to oversee the hydroelectric industry. Brazilian

Traction had been able to use its influence to have the plan dropped before the session ended in December 1928. Was this, he asked, the sort of thing EBASCO wished? 'I went on,' he reported to Lash, 'on the lines of a semi-drunken alternation between the jocular and the serious, and was as affable as I knew how.' Meanwhile, Lash met with officials at EBASCO's head office in New York and explained why the Canadians were so concerned, extracting a promise that the publicity campaign in Brazil would be ended.[16]

Thus the two big utilities eyed each other warily, co-operating for mutual benefit on occasion but determined that neither should gain any undue advantage over the other. Early in 1929 Brazilian Traction acquired control of the British-controlled City of Santos Improvement Company, which ran the telephone and sewer systems, at a cost of $14 million. The EBASCO people grumbled that this had inflated the price of other utilities in which they were interested.[17] That summer rumours that EBASCO intended to purchase control of the Canadian firm became so intense that a public denial was finally issued. While such talk persisted for a few more months, the stock market crash hit utility holding companies particularly hard, ending any real likelihood of such a takeover.[18]

The management of Brazilian Traction thus fended off the probes of one of the largest US utilities holding companies and established a delicate *modus vivendi* with it. This was just as well, for the main takeover threat came not from its obvious rivals in the United States, but from its erstwhile friends in Europe.

II

Utility holding companies were created partly for the technological and organizational benefits they bestowed, but it also became clear during the 1920s that those who controlled them could earn extraordinarily large profits. One American, Harrison Williams, in co-operation with the investment banking house of Goldman Sachs and Company, was able to leverage the stock of Central States Electric Corporation, valued at $6 million in 1921, into securities valued at nearly $1 billion during 1928 and 1929 by promoting a series of interlocking trusts called Goldman Sachs Trading, Shenandoah and Blue Ridge Corporations.[19]

Many other smart operators in both the United States and Europe hoped to pull off the same sort of coup. That was what brought Alfred Loewenstein back to play a major role in the affairs of the three largest

Canadian utilities in Spain, Mexico, and Brazil during the 1920s, in hopes of using them as the basis for a similar pyramid of utility holding companies whose securities he could market to small investors. Though there existed sound operational reasons for the existence of some utility holding companies, Loewenstein's interest was purely financial and promotional.

Loewenstein had already made a reputation and a certain amount of money by distributing the second mortgage bonds of the Rio de Janeiro Tramway, Light and Power Company in 1908 at a time when the company faced a crisis owing to the recession. Despite his rather limited success in making a market for Rio seconds on the continent, that deal provided him with the grounds to claim later on that he had 'saved' the company in a time of crisis. Even among the cast of rather raffish characters involved with F. S. Pearson's utility promotions before the First World War, Loewenstein stood in a class by himself.[20] Born in Belgium in 1877, the son of a German *émigré*, he had entered into partnership as a banker and broker with Edouard Stallaerts soon after his twentieth birthday. Before long he began to do business with James Dunn's newly established brokerage and banking firm in London and started pushing the securities of Pearson's companies on the Brussels bourse.

The recession of 1913, however, left him severely embarrassed financially. When the war broke out in 1914 Loewenstein fled to England before the advancing German forces. Although nominally attached to the Belgian army (from which he acquired his much prized title of captain), Loewenstein seems to have spent the war years like his friend Dunn in repairing his fortunes by peddling anything he could to the Allies. He succeeded to the extent that he was able to buy a large country estate where he could indulge his passion for thoroughbred horses.

With the return of peace Captain Loewenstein re-established his brokerage business in Belgium and bought another luxurious house, while retaining his English connections. Before long he began to frequent the southwestern French resort of Biarritz, where European royalty had gone to holiday before the war. To facilitate his travels he acquired a succession of private airplanes. His flamboyant style of life as he flew from place to place accompanied by a retinue of secretaries and valets and his personal boxing coach quickly attracted the attention of the press. Loewenstein assiduously cultivated this: unlike more substantial financial figures who preferred to deal in private he realized that publicity would exaggerate his influence and importance and intimidate his opponents. Ordinary investors might thus be induced to give him their savings and their proxies for his own purposes.

After an unsuccessful attempt to create a European cartel in the production of artificial silk (rayon), Loewenstein hit upon the idea of a utilities holding company to take over the old 'Pearson group' with which he retained his connections as a board member of the Barcelona and both Mexican companies. During 1922, using borrowed funds, he acquired 60,000 preference shares of Barcelona Traction and 18,400 shares of Mexico Tramways (which, in turn, controlled Mexican Light and Power). Thereupon he announced the creation of the Belgian-based Société Internationale d'Energie Hydro-Electrique (SIDRO) and exchanged his holdings in the two utilities for its preferred and ordinary stock on generous terms.

Loewenstein and the other insiders also took as a bonus most of the 40,000 shares of 'fondateur' stock (which carried special voting rights) and rose in price to 7,000 francs each by 1925. Other buyers scrambled to subscribe for the remainder of SIDRO's ordinary and preferred stock at 250 francs each, then watched them rise to 1,000 francs within three years.[21]

Loewenstein's successful promotion brought him into contact with another European financier, Dannie Heineman, who was also to play an immensely important role in the affairs of the utilities in Barcelona, Mexico, and Brazil during the 1920s. Heineman was a European emulator of S.Z. Mitchell, already well on the way to creating a vast utilities holding company with interests in many parts of the world. Heineman, in fact, protected the Canadian companies against Loewenstein's piratical raiding. By siding with the Toronto management at critical junctures, he left the Canadians in charge even though effective control had passed to Heineman's holding company.

Dannie Heineman was born in North Carolina in 1872, but grew up in the land of his German ancestors where his mother returned in 1880 upon his father's death. Having studied electrical engineering at Hanover University, he went to work for a Berlin affiliate of General Electric, Union-Elektricitäts Gesellschaft. After gaining experience in overseeing the conversion of horsecars to electricity in Koblenz, Liège, and Brussels, in 1905 he joined a new Belgian holding company, the Société Financière de Transports et d'Entreprises Industrielles (SOFINA). Thereafter he came to play a role like that of Mitchell in the electricity supply industry both at home in Belgium and overseas.[22]

Under Heineman's management SOFINA expanded rapidly with the backing of such powerful financial institutions as the Crédit Suisse and the Gesellschaft für Electrische Unternehmungen of Berlin (which, in turn, had

ties to the Allgemeine Elektricitäts Gesellschaft [AEG] and through it to
GE).[23] SOFINA's Belgian base was the Société d'Electricité de la Région de
Malmédy (SERMA),[24] which possessed links to the French division of the
Thomson-Houston organization through its equipment manufacturing
subsidiary, the Société d'Electricité et de Mécanique. From this root SOFINA
grew rapidly after the First World War. By the mid-1920s it controlled
utilities in France, Portugal, Spain, Italy, Algeria, Turkey, Thailand, Brazil
and Argentina, the Latin American undertakings being controlled through
a Madrid-incorporated subsidiary called Compañía Hispano-Americana
de Electricidad (CHADE).[25] Heineman, who also had a distinguished career
as a diplomat and humanitarian in helping to found the Commission for
Relief in Belgium after the war, was a businessman of wide power and
influence when he became involved with the Canadian utilities.

The success of Loewenstein's SIDRO depended from the first upon Dannie
Heineman, who agreed to have SOFINA purchase a sizeable share in SIDRO,
while CHADE acquired a further interest. As a result of continuing difficulties
with his artificial-silk venture, Loewenstein found himself in financial
straits in 1924. He was forced to sell more SIDRO stock, and effective control
of the Barcelona and Mexican utilities then passed into the hands of SOFINA.
Despite this Alfred Loewenstein continued to act as though he remained
the dominant figure. So long as Dannie Heineman gave him his head that
was true, and during the next few years he made a great deal of trouble for
the managers of these utilities and their associated companies in Toronto.
In particular, he turned his sights upon the largest and most profitable of
the group, the Brazilian Traction, Light and Power Company.

Difficulties with Loewenstein were nothing new to the Canadians.
Alexander Mackenzie had already had a couple of nasty run-ins with him.
Just after the First World War the bumptious Belgian had suddenly
attempted to force his way onto the board of the Brazilian company. He
complained that the European security holders were kept in ignorance of
the internal affairs of the company, and threatened to set up a 'bureau
d'information' to demand satisfaction from management if he were not
made a director. Mackenzie, as president of Brazilian Traction, would
have none of it.[26]

One year later Loewenstein was again complaining bitterly about
Brazilian Traction. The Rio second mortgage bonds had been issued in two
separate series denominated in pounds sterling and in francs, each paying 5
per cent interest. By the end of the war the franc had become drastically
devalued against the pound, and the board decided to reduce its interest

payments by cutting future sums paid to European bondholders to reflect that decline. As a result Belgian and French bondholders would receive the equivalent of only £ 55,000 or just half the amount that would go to British residents.[27]

Here was an issue ideally suited to Alfred Loewenstein, and one with plenty of potential for embarrassing the company severely. Loewenstein could easily represent himself as the friend of the ordinary bondholder and use this to stir up the continental press against the board. Moreover, there was considerable confusion as to whether the reduction was legal. While the coupons of Rio seconds stated that interest payments were due in pounds or francs, the prospectus had used the French word '*or*,' conveying the clear implication that the company was obligated to pay the gold value of the coupons regardless of currency fluctuations. After puzzling over the problem, various lawyers in Belgium, Britain, and Canada arrived at quite different opinions. The company's counsel concluded that nobody could predict the outcome of a lawsuit, but that prospects were not bright: 'It is idle ... to shut one's eyes to the fact that the court might easily convince itself that the prominent use of the word "or" was an invitation to the prospective purchaser to treat the bonds as payment in gold or on a gold basis.'[28]

When the board stuck to its guns, Loewenstein threatened to start a suit early in 1921. The directors wavered, for they feared the damage Brazilian Traction's reputation would suffer from the drumfire of publicity about their repudiation that was certain to be set afoot in France and Belgium. Even more influential, however, was what this news might mean in Brazil. One of the company's most important hedges against a decline in the value of the milréis had always been that gas and electricity rates in Rio de Janeiro were fixed half in paper milréis and half at the notional gold exchange rate of 27d. sterling to the milréis. Up to the war the company had often received at least part payment in bullion, and thereafter the gold portion continued to be paid in paper based on milréis pegged at 27d. sterling. Gold, after all, was gold, it argued in Brazil, not paper pound notes.[29]

Yet if Loewenstein went to court (and to the newspapers) with his charges that the board had unilaterally refused to continue to pay its own bondholders the gold value promised and had substituted instead francs at their current depressed value, the Brazilian authorities were certain to seize upon this as evidence of the company's hypocrisy. Why should Brazil not treat the company in exactly the same way it did its own investors, selecting the rate of exchange that suited its immediate interests?

Prudence suggested that Alfred Loewenstein be bought off in order to keep him quiet. In the spring of 1921 the directors therefore offered to purchase from him all 15,000 Rio seconds at an agreed price over a ten-year period. So long as he held the securities the company would honour any coupons that he presented at a rate equivalent to 9s. 11d. Other continental bondholders facing reduced payments were left to fend for themselves. Despite his image as the defender of the small investor Loewenstein eagerly jumped at the offer.[30]

By 1924 Alfred Loewenstein had lost control of his new holding company, SIDRO, to Dannie Heineman of SOFINA, but he still had his sights set on gaining more influence over the affairs of Brazilian Traction, which had by then resumed paying a dividend on its common stock and was prospering. He decided, therefore, to reopen the issue of the Rio seconds in order to keep the board on the defensive and persuaded a Belgian bondholder to demand payment in gold at Toronto. When the company refused to offer anything except francs at the current rate of exchange, a lawsuit was filed in the Canadian courts.[31]

Still Alexander Mackenzie refused to budge, so in mid-1926 Loewenstein offered to make a deal with Brazilian Traction's management to end the dispute over the Rio seconds. Claiming that he now owned almost all the 15,000 bonds in the franc series, he offered to sell them back to the company for a generous cash settlement or else to take the proceeds in common stock at par. This, he was confident, would give him the right to claim his long-denied seat on the board of directors. To Miller Lash and Alexander Mackenzie his demands seemed extortionate, and they resolved to fight.[32]

Loewenstein, therefore, launched a bid to capture control of Brazilian Traction. He organized a 'super-SIDRO' chartered in Canada, called the Hydro-Electric Securities Corporation, to which he turned over his remaining SIDRO shares as well as his holdings in the Barcelona and Rio companies. He stocked the board with an array of fairly prominent European bankers and financiers from his circle of associates as well as two or three friends from Montreal. If he could raise enough money from investors, he might be able to break free of Dannie Heineman's control.[33]

With as much money as he could borrow Loewenstein set out to acquire 125,000 shares of Brazilian Traction, which he promised to turn over to Hydro-Electric Securities. This wave of buying (along with an increase in the dividend from 4 per cent to 5 per cent in 1926) helped to push up the price of the stock from around $50 in mid-1925 to $115 by August 1926. Mackenzie was infuriated by the rapid rise which made his dealings with the Brazilians much more difficult. But efforts by the London directors, Edward Peacock and Malcolm Hubbard, and other English merchant bankers friendly to the company failed to slow down this 'wild buying,' which ultimately left the Belgian, according to his own account, with 167,500 shares of the stock.[34]

Loewenstein did his utmost to publicize his new holding company to attract investor support. In September 1926 he took off for Barcelona for a self-styled 'International Conference,' where he addressed a hundred guests on the evils of Bolshevism and high taxation as well as his plans to carry on the work begun by F.S. Pearson. Loewenstein then moved on to his favourite resort, taking his party with him: 'He ran a high-class circus in Biarritz, accompanied by a campaign in the press which took such forms that I began to doubt his sanity,' snorted Edward Peacock. This included telling reporters that he had sent his airplane to Russia for caviar and to Toulouse for chickens, ('the edible variety, not the sexual,' observed Miller Lash sourly.) More seriously, various influential people, among them Peacock himself and Sir Herbert Holt of Montreal Light, Heat and Power and the Royal Bank of Canada, were said to have given their backing to his scheme to gain control of the Canadian-chartered utilities.[35]

Thoroughly rattled by this razzle-dazzle, the Canadians decided at long last that they had better offer the Belgian a seat on the board of Brazilian Traction at the earliest possible moment so that they could keep an eye on him. They did so even though all of them shared Peacock's view that

Loewenstein would, of course, wreck the operating organization of any company in a year if he were really to get control, not because of any evil intentions – quite the contrary – but because of his activities and his character. He is a market operator and splendid at that, but no man to control companies.[36]

Before anything could actually be done, however, the European financial community reacted strongly against Loewenstein's plan to launch another holding company and place his remaining SIDRO shares in it. He was known to have made the grand gesture of offering the Belgian government a $50 million interest-free loan, at the very time when he had borrowed more than $10 million to buy utility shares. His creditors got exceedingly nervous as Brazilian Traction shares slid off to near par, as it was known that the success of Loewenstein's plans rested upon a price of $120. When he announced that 24 million francs worth of his wife's jewellery had been stolen from his villa at Biarritz, cynical reporters hinted that it was a publicity stunt and that he would probably be better off with the money than the jewels just now.[37]

Finding himself in a tight spot, Loewenstein sought a temporary truce with the Canadians. When Miller Lash visited Europe in the fall of 1926 the Belgian approached him with a request to help him restore his liquidity by paying $1.5 million, for the 15,000 Rio seconds he now claimed to own. Lash was not prepared to go that far, but strung Loewenstein along while exploring other possibilities. Naturally management desired to avoid having the public learn about their enmity towards Loewenstein, as this would adversely affect the price of the company's stock. Rather, they preferred to give Loewenstein an opportunity to liquidate his borrowings in an orderly fashion. 'It is really very difficult to see how the wild Belgian hare can extricate himself without some loss of fur, or perhaps a little hide,' wrote Lash with quiet satisfaction.[38] The board hoped the combination of loss of face and loss of funds would render him more malleable in future.

That, of course, was to misunderstand the character of Alfred Loewenstein. When he realized that the directors of Brazilian Traction had no intention of bailing him out, he immediately resorted to further threats. This time the board stood firm, stiffened by a cable from Alexander Mackenzie in Rio railing against Loewenstein's 'pure impudence.' The publicity attracted by his proposal to fold the company into a utilities combine with multinational holdings had already created enough national-ist feeling in Brazil to harm it. Not only did the directors refuse to purchase any of Loewenstein's Rio seconds, but they cancelled the 1921 agreement whereby he was entitled to receive 9s. 11d. for every interest coupon presented.[39]

Twisting and turning in search of a means to avoid liquidating his holdings at a heavy loss, Loewenstein hit upon the idea of issuing masses of new SIDRO stock, which could then be exchanged for the securities of his proposed new holding company. Unfortunately he overlooked that fact that he no longer controlled SIDRO, and that Dannie Heineman and his associates disapproved of Loewenstein's plans. Since the underlying companies were not earning enough to pay interest and dividends on another heavy load of new securities, they thought the proposal thoroughly unsound. Moreover, the issue of additional stock would once more hand control to the erratic Loewenstein. At a meeting of the SIDRO board his proposal was voted down by a large majority.[40]

True to form, Loewenstein tried to rally public opinion to compensate for his weakness, convening two public meetings in Brussels, to which he invited the owners of Barcelona bonds, Rio seconds, and Brazilian Traction shares in an effort to convince them to tender their securities to his proposed Canadian holding company. He also set about to force the holding of a special shareholders meeting of SIDRO to enlarge the board and to approve an increase in the company's capitalization, in the hope that the new directors would favour his scheme.[41]

This manoeuvring seriously alarmed the management of Brazilian Traction. Alexander Mackenzie struggled to rebut criticism of such a 'fusion' plan in Brazil at the very moment when the new president's currency stabilization proposal caused the milréis to slump dramatically, a fall blamed upon foreign-controlled enterprises. The slightest hint that profits earned in Brazil were being channelled out to subsidize weaker companies in Spain or Mexico would be fatal to any request for increased rates. He threatened to resign if Loewenstein got his way. In Toronto the head office was equally agitated by hints that Sir Herbert Holt, one of Brazilian Traction's largest shareholders, was flirting with the idea of backing Loewenstein and moving control of the entire Pearson group to Montreal. Despite efforts to warn him against Loewenstein, Sir Herbert continued to keep his own counsel, which only added to the alarm felt by the Torontonians.[42]

Miller Lash saw Loewenstein on a number of occasions in an effort to persuade him to drop his plans to include Brazilian Traction in any conglomerate, warning that such a move would be certain to bring about Mackenzie's resignation as president. Other prominent financiers weighed in on the side of management, but Loewenstein refused to be deflected. Eventually, the board concluded that it would have to make a public statement concerning his invitation to Brazilian Traction shareholders to tender their stock to his new holding company. The directors approved a circular, which argued that an association between that company and utilities operating elsewhere would be detrimental and advised rejection of any tender offer.[43] Ominously, however, Sir Herbert Holt's son, Andrew, who was a director, agreed that while the shareholders should be advised of Mackenzie's fears regarding 'fusion,' it should be recorded in the minutes that he reserved his judgment concerning any future offer of a share exchange by Loewenstein.[44]

All attention now centred upon the special shareholders' meeting of SIDRO scheduled to be held on 22 December 1926 in a theatre in Brussels. Loewenstein concentrated upon rounding up proxies supporting his proposals, while the Canadians looked on anxiously. Fortunately for them,

Dannie Heineman, who represented the interests of SOFINA on the SIDRO board, came down firmly against Loewenstein's plans. He regarded them as nothing more than a personal power grab engineered through the stock market, and refused to have anything to do with a hostile takeover of Brazilian Traction. Heineman wanted to get on with business as usual and had 'no time to waste in endless discussions of the fantastic schemes of a boxing financier.' Although Heineman was not prepared to give any further support to Loewenstein's plans, the outcome remained uncertain until the other SIDRO shareholders had declared themselves.[45]

Almost a thousand curious SIDRO stock owners crowded into the theatre for the special meeting.[46] From the outset it was clear that there were not enough proxies to permit the company's capital to be increased. All that Loewenstein could hope for was approval to add to the size of the board, which might then propose the increase of capital to the annual meeting early in the new year. Called upon to address the crowd, Loewenstein attacked the current management of SIDRO, holding himself out as the representative of the average shareholder and referring to his ambitious plans to form a larger conglomerate. He sat down to applause.

Dannie Heineman then got up and mercilessly dissected Loewenstein's scheme. He made clear that SOFINA would not submit to one-man control of SIDRO and would immediately sever its connection with the company if Loewenstein got his way. He was followed by the president of SOFINA's subsidiary, CHADE (which also held a sizeable stake in SIDRO), who noted that all the benefits from an increase in the capital would go to the insiders who held the 'fondateur' shares. By that time the meeting had turned against Loewenstein, whose efforts to reply to these charges were met with boos and hisses. Seeing that the tide had turned decisively against him, he abstained when the motion to increase the number of directors was finally put and it was lost by 218,992 to zero.[47]

In the face of this rebuff Alfred Loewenstein could do little except begin to liquidate his holdings of Brazilian Traction stock to meet the demands of his creditors. To the relief of the company's board he was able to do this without bringing about a dramatic fall in the price of the stock. The directors celebrated their victory (and helped maintain share prices) by announcing an increase in the dividend to 6 per cent per annum early in 1927.[48]

III

Having thwarted one hostile takeover the management of Brazilian

Traction kept an especially wary eye out for any repetition. It was not long in coming. In the spring of 1927 a very large number of bearer warrants began to be purchased, until ultimately there were more than 313,000 outstanding, the equivalent of nearly one-third of the company's share capital. What made the board nervous was that the names of the warrant-holders were not registered on the books, so that it was virtually impossible to ascertain who was buying. It seemed that the warrants were simply being taken up by continental buyers impressed with the company's prospects and its close links with Dannie Heineman's SOFINA. Since warrants once acquired by individuals rarely reappeared on the market, this wave of buying actually benefited the price of the company's stock by decreasing the size of the float.[49]

Rumours continued to swirl, however, especially after Loewenstein announced the organization of yet another holding company. Chartered in Quebec, the International Holding and Investment Company took over his shares in both an existing British company of the same name (in which were lodged Loewenstein's artificial-silk interests) and in its predecessor, Hydro-Electric Securities. He hoped to induce the public to subscribe for 123,000 shares in the new company at a price of $150 each, raising more than $18 million to help finance his takeover of Brazilian Traction.

Loewenstein's fortunes seemed to be undergoing a remarkable recovery. Forced to liquidate most of his holdings of Brazilian Traction stock to satisfy his creditors, he had been unceremoniously booted off the board of his own creation, SIDRO, after his defeat at the meeting in Brussels in December 1926. Yet Loewenstein was never one to lose confidence in his plans and abilities, and before long he had netted sizeable gains from his artificial-silk cartel and recruited backers for a renewed assault on the management of the Barcelona, Mexican, and Brazilian utilities. What particularly alarmed the Canadian managers was the presence on the board of International Holding of Andrew P. Holt; did this mean that his father, Sir Herbert Holt, one of the largest shareholders in Brazilian Traction, had thrown in his lot with the rapacious Belgian?[50]

In February 1928 Loewenstein fired his opening shot; he was still a board member of Barcelona Traction and of both Mexican Light and Power and Mexico Tramways, but now he demanded a place for his nominee on the executive committees of all three companies. He also asked that one of his associates again be placed on the SIDRO board, and he began accumulating Brazilian Traction stock once more with the aim of gaining a seat on that board, too.[51]

In his campaign Loewenstein adopted his customary tactics, seeking maximum publicity to help him make his case. In mid-April he convened a public meeting in Brussels to advertise the great future of his new holding company and revealed an important element of his plans. He controlled, he said, thousands of Rio second mortgage bonds, whose coupons the present management of Brazilian Traction was refusing to honour in full. He would, therefore, acquire a large enough interest in the company to force his way onto its board and secure fair treatment for these bondholders. He proposed to go in person to Toronto and put his case to the directors of Brazilian Traction, and to make his demands for representation directly to the boards of the Mexican and Barcelona utilities. Loewenstein and his associates already claimed to control 60,000 bearer warrants of Brazilian Traction out of the more than 300,000 outstanding in Brussels. If he succeeded in his mission to Canada, other Belgian investors could be expected to rally to him and support the takeover of all the Pearson companies.[52]

This time round, the directors of Brazilian Traction and the other utilities were determined to make no concessions to Loewenstein. Miller Lash was now convinced that it had been a mistake not to reject his demands immediately in 1926, and to continue to seek an accommodation for so long. Lash thought that Malcolm Hubbard and Edward Peacock, who frequently had to deal with Loewenstein in London, were inclined to get nervous and seek to make peace with him. That was foolish, for 'he is not the kind of man that any settlement can really be made with about anything.' J.W. McConnell, a Montrealer who had joined the board of Brazilian Traction in 1925, heartily supported Lash. To give way to a series of demands emanating from a public meeting in Brussels called by advertisements in the newspapers at which refreshments were probably served was the height of folly. Soon, said McConnell, 'we would find that a bunch of stock has been bought in China, and that we would be called on to put a Chinese director on the board.'[53]

Of one thing the Canadians could be certain: they had the full support of Dannie Heineman in resisting Loewenstein's demands. The Belgian had made the mistake of criticizing Heineman for trying to buy back his SIDRO securities at fire-sale prices after the 1926 débâcle, claiming that Heineman had acted to the detriment of other SIDRO shareholders. As soon as he learned of these charges the prickly Heineman made up his mind to deny Loewenstein and his associates any place on the SIDRO board. Heineman's hostility made it certain that many European investors would hesitate to follow Loewenstein when the financial might of sofina was arrayed against him. Equally important, Heineman used his considerable influence with General Electric to make certain that they would not give the Belgian any assistance.[54]

After landing in New York, Loewenstein moved on to Montreal, adding to the rumours that he had already struck a deal with the Holts.[55] He arrived in Toronto on 2 May 1928 in a blaze of newspaper publicity intensified by his airplane with its entourage of secretaries and valets. After giving a fiery interview threatening retribution if the Rio bondholders were denied justice, he met with a committee of the board of Brazilian Traction. Loewenstein abused Heineman violently, claiming that his opponents on the sidro board had tried to 'kill' him and had used dishonest means to oust him from control. He denounced Alexander Mackenzie and Miller Lash for thwarting his takeover bid in 1926. Amid all this ranting he made only one firm demand: that the interest on the Rio second mortgage bonds be paid off at full gold value. Walter Gow pointed out that there could hardly be a settlement when the courts had already heard the lawsuit brought at Loewenstein's instigation. When he demanded more seats on the boards of the Barcelona and Mexican companies, he was told that the views of sidro would govern, since it effectively controlled these utilities. That set off another tirade against Heineman, and the meeting broke up with the promise that the boards of all the companies would meet again in a fortnight's time.[56]

Loewenstein retreated to New York, where he spent his time trying to persuade both the people at General Electric and certain influential European utility men to give him their support. Rumours were also planted in the press that Sir Herbert Holt and Canadian broker Harry Gundy were prepared to back a huge holding company organized by Loewenstein with interests in a wide range of utilities and manufacturing industries. From London, however, Peacock reported that he had run into Gundy who had made it clear that he and Holt were not planning any kind of assault upon the present management of Brazilian Traction. In Toronto the Canadians awaited the arrival of Dannie Heineman, a member of the board of the Mexican Light and Power Company, who had already suggested that they should arrange transportation for Loewenstein to 'a very warm place.'[57]

Loewenstein flew back to Toronto on 13 May to attend the Mexican Light and Power board meeting. At once Heineman demanded an opportunity to rebut the Belgian's slanderous allegations. Chairman Miller Lash agreed, despite Loewenstein's protests, and after an exchange of abuse Loewenstein stormed out of the meeting. In Heineman's words, 'Nothing happened – as we all know he disappeared like a rabbit.' That afternoon Loewenstein returned for a meeting of the Brazilian Traction directors and submitted two letters, one demanding full payment on the Rio second mortgage bonds, the other complaining that Belgian shareholders were not properly informed by or represented on the board. The issue of the bonds was tabled. E.R. Wood, acting as chairman, pointed out that because most Belgians held bearer warrants their names were unknown to management and they could not be communicated with directly.[58]

Rebuffed, Loewenstein boarded his aircraft immediately and left for New York, not even staying to learn that at the annual meeting of Barcelona Traction the following day he would lose his seat on the board of directors. All that he could do was to attempt to get his version of what had occurred in the confrontation with Heineman accepted, but his letter was rejected by the board as 'entirely at variance with the facts.' On 5 June the Rio board rejected the demand for full payment on the second mortgage bonds on the grounds that the issue was still before the courts, and the Brazilian Traction board simply referred Loewenstein's request for Belgian representation to the annual meeting.[59]

Returning to Europe Alfred Loewenstein set about collecting proxies for that meeting. Management mobilized itself, too. On the continent Dannie Heineman worked to collect votes for them, even buying proxies, a common practice in Europe. By the end of the month almost all the large Montreal and Toronto holders had been solicited successfully. News had arrived that Sir Herbert Holt had no intention of opposing the present board. By 5 July Malcolm Hubbard reported that 40 per cent of the possible votes in Europe had been collected (a remarkable achievement considering that so many of them were held as bearer warrants). With two weeks still remaining before the annual meeting the board in Toronto seemed to be in a position to deal Loewenstein one final, stinging rebuff.[60]

The chance never came. On 4 July, while flying from London to Brussels, Alfred Loewenstein fell to his death from his airplane into the English Channel. The cause of his death remains a mystery. Was it accident or suicide? A recent book by William Norris sensationalizing the event suggests that he was murdered, probably by his wife (who was not on board the plane) in collusion with his pilot. Norris, however, displays such a dim grasp of Loewenstein's business affairs (he makes the preposterous assertion that Loewenstein was 'the third richest man in the world' at the time of his death) that no attention need be paid to his book. Only someone like Loewenstein would enjoy such a *mélange* of silliness and sensationalism.[61]

Looking at Loewenstein's business affairs one might say that he jumped after Dannie Heineman pushed him. Even before his untimely death his efforts to gain control of the Barcelona, Mexican, and Brazilian utilities had been decisively ended. On the news of his death the price of the shares of his holding company declined precipitously. In Malcolm Hubbard's words, 'his death removes a great deal of trouble which one knows would have arisen in future, not only to our group of companies but to others.'[62] The annual meeting of Brazilian Traction passed without incident.

A week later the second mortgage bondholders lost their suit against the Rio de Janeiro Tramway, Light and Power Company in the Supreme Court of Ontario. The issue upon which Loewenstein had originally based his challenge to management had been undercut. To avoid the expense of further appeals the board began negotiations with the remaining bondholders, and by the end of 1928 a deal had been worked out to replace the old securities with new ones having a face value of £14 5s. and bearing interest at 5 per cent per annum.[63]

By the late 1920s Dannie Heineman had secured effective control of the three largest Canadian-chartered utilities operating abroad. In the case of Brazilian Traction the number of Canadian common shareholders increased during that decade, rising from about 47 per cent in 1922 to 54 per cent in 1926.[64] Sir Herbert Holt and J.W. McConnell were among the largest shareholders, but it is clear that they were prepared to let Heineman run the show. And he soon tightened his grip upon the Mexican companies when they went in search of $5 million worth of new capital to finance the powerhouse at the dam already built on the Lerma River. Owing to the unsettled conditions in Mexico, neither Mexico Tramways, which held more than 50 per cent of the common stock in Mexican Light and Power, nor the power company's other shareholders, was likely to take up a new allotment of shares. Heineman, however, agreed to have SOFINA advance the money over three years as required, and to purchase enough stock to repay the advances. That deal would eventually give SOFINA 114,000 out of 250,000 shares of Mexican Light and Power, which, along with its holdings in Mexico Tramways, would make its control of the utility unassailable. The directors considered themselves very fortunate to have been able to make such a deal in light of the unsettled conditions within Mexico.[65]

Alfred Loewenstein's efforts to fold the major Canadian-chartered utilities operating abroad into a single great holding company failed. In one sense that hardly mattered. By the mid-1920s the utilities in Barcelona, in Mexico, and in Brazil had already become part of SOFINA, Dannie Heineman's Belgian-based conglomerate. In another sense, however, it did matter, because so long as Heineman was content to leave the management of the companies in Toronto, that preserved some vestige of 'Canadian-ness' about the companies. In reality, though, they had become part of a system of international capitalism in which investors, owners, and managers were scattered halfway around the world.

The Canadian character of these utilities had, of course, been notional almost from the outset. The place of domicile of most of the founding entrepreneurs and the laxity of company law alone made them Canadian. Within a very few years all but the smallest of the utilities had outgrown the capacity of the capital markets in Canada to provide the necessary funds for investment and expansion. Thereafter control quickly switched to Europe where the money had been raised.

14

Closing Balance

Great enterprises are not necessarily reared by great men. Vice as well as virtue must be paid its due in the act of creation. On the balance sheet of capitalism the basest motives and most despicable characters share equal billing with noble ambition and industrial statesmanship.

Brazilian Traction, Mexican Light and Power, Mexico Tramways, Porto Rico Railways, and a host of smaller enterprises of this ilk were not promoted by the coolly rational economic men who figure so prominently in the mythology of markets. Artful deception, showmanship, shrewd manipulation, and herd instinct played a part here. No accountant's mentality conceived these utility ventures in the first instance or led Canadian investors into southern latitudes. These companies owed their existence to the raw animal spirits of enterprise.

However ardent the spirits of the promoters, the managers of these enterprises discovered in the course of time that they had to be adaptable and accommodating if they were to survive. The insiders might take their profits and run if they were lucky, or more likely lose their shirts when they misjudged the market, but the utilities endured to serve the rapidly growing urban population of Latin America. Powerdams and streetcars, generating stations and telephone exchanges stayed put, and those who ran them had to come to terms with the local authorities or lose control.

The relationship between the utility men and the policitians, that forms the backdrop to the promotional activities analysed here proved more subtle and ambivalent than any simple theory of dependency or economic imperialism might imply. When in difficulties the companies could appeal for help in London or in Washington, but the assistance they received (if any) was usually of limited value. In the final analysis they had to work out some sort of deal with the local people or risk the loss of their property. Yet the politicians, in turn, were aware that if they violated the rules of the game of international capitalism too flagrantly, they would pay for it the next time they turned to London or New York for the loans they required to keep their economies afloat. Warily, the two parties circled each other, unable to break free from one another during this epoch.

I

F.S. Pearson, 'the good Doctor' to his colleagues, was the archetypal promoter. He reversed rivers in Latin America and diverted huge flows of capital from North America and Europe into his schemes. He altered the physical and the financial landscape. He was not, however, the nascent corporation man of the twentieth century. He was a wheeler-dealer, an engineer of overweening ambition, and an unscrupulous market operator. He attracted like-minded people, men like himself who sincerely wanted to be rich.

Pearson discovered a market niche – creating integrated utility monopolies in Latin America – then exploited it to the hilt. The place did not matter much. São Paulo, Mexico City, and Rio might have been anywhere in the world. He was applying known technique on the margin. He knew how to build electrical systems; he needed capital to do it, and that brought him into the company of the leading men of the Canadian financial village, colonials perched atop swelling mounds of investment funds equally ready to take a position for high stakes.

Pearson did not persuade so much as storm. He was a whirlwind of energy; indeed it might be said that he overcame the natural friction of the banker-promoter relationship with overpowering gales of energy and optimism. He did the same thing on site visits. There was never a moment of calm reflection in his presence. He was all dash, bluster, decisiveness, and, in difficult times, denunciation. He imagined himself to be surrounded by lesser men, men of narrower vision and less manly will. Obsessions are never very pretty up close. Pearson, the indomitable promoter, was obsessed with the idea of creating the largest, most comprehensive utility monopolies possible. He would brook no opposition either from competitors in the field or from his friends in the financial markets.

Pearson and men like him lived on the edge, always in danger of having their precariously balanced paper empires collapse, always stretched to the point of nervous exhaustion. In moments of high tension, the mind and body failed, and the promoter retreated under his doctor's care to his mansion at Great Barrington in the Berkshires of Massachusetts to brood upon his fate.[1] But not for long. Soon he would be borne aloft again on some gust of hope. Then the sun would be shining, the mooring lines of his yacht unloosed, bankers and hotel men on the alert as the telegraph wires hummed with orders.

Complaints of ill health brought on by stress and overwork formed a persistent theme in the correspondence among these men. James Dunn complained constantly of problems due to the pressure of business. Even the normally invincible Max Aitken retreated to the hospital in Montreal for four weeks at a key moment in the promotion of Porto Rico Railways during the autumn of 1906.[2]

Men like these, who lived by their wits, seemed very susceptible to fad diets and folk remedies. For a time James Dunn was a great devotee of 'rhythmic breathing'; and on another occasion of a diet of watermelons. His behaviour perplexed his friend Max Aitken, who observed in his memoir: 'Periodically, he fell under the influence of some practitioner or dietician who would persuade him he was eating the wrong food. At one time he would eat nothing but vegetables, and then he would exclaim that such fare was only fit for the beasts of the field. He would switch to platefuls of beef, even a diet consisting of English farmhouse cheeses, which were sent to him from every shire – until he tired of them.'[3]

At one point Dunn persuaded his friends to take up an all-banana diet that was being promoted by the society quack Dr Fenton B. Turck. Quite apart from the nutritional superiority and related psychic benefits, Turck claimed that bananas would most certainly replace grain as the staple of the western diet (banana bread, muffins, chips, sweeteners).[4] Dunn, Loewenstein, Farquhar, Pearson, and company were particularly receptive to the message since at that time they were deeply involved in financing various banana plantations, harbour improvements, and railroads that were being promoted by Minor Keith (of the United Fruit Company) throughout Central and South America.

The banana diet and other such episodes serve to remind us that in the fashion of the classic salesman, these promoters sold themselves before they sold anyone else. And in the end they were their own largest customers. No one believed in ultimate success more than they did. At the same time they alone knew how chancy were the 'sure things' they were selling to their friends.

As a result, when the market turned decisively down in 1913 it was the promoters rather than the investors who faced bankruptcy. Having leveraged their market operations as much as possible, they were especially vulnerable. Dunn and Loewenstein were technically bankrupt by 1914; when Pearson died in 1915 the liabilities of his estate greatly exceeded its assets. Dunn and Loewenstein bounced back, several times. Only sly Max Aitken managed to extricate himself with a lasting fortune early on. He gave up company promotion in 1911 to assume quite another position of power without responsibility.

These then were the animal spirits of capitalism, the promoters and market schemers. They were driven by the thrill of creation, the excitement of the game, but above all by the rewards of winning: the country estates, the gleaming Daimlers, the chorus girls from His Majesty's and the Winter Garden theatres, the dizzying possibility of knighthoods, unending champagne-soaked weekends at Coombe Hill, at Deauville, at Lowenstein's sybaritic circus at Biarritz. These men made their own morality with their momentary winnings. It is entirely fitting that they took up Noel Coward as their court entertainer; they might well have been characters in his plays. They certainly were grist for Evelyn Waugh's mordant mill.

The *louche*, even scandalous behaviour of the promoters contrasts rather oddly with the staid character of the utility companies. Security selling might require this showmanship and talent, but management called upon other skills, other kinds of men. The Pearsons, Aitkens, Dunns, and Loewensteins might be necessary to promote these companies; but it fell to the Mackenzies, Conways, and Couzenses of the world to run them: men with a gentler touch, more refined tastes, steadier minds, and a more balanced sense of corporate responsibility.

F.S. Pearson discovered early on that the good grey Canadian bankers could be swept up by his vision, if the possibilities were demonstrated, and once caught up they could be made to put up remarkable sums of money for their time and place. Having become entangled, his Canadian associates could not easily disentangle themselves even when they wanted to, without endangering the whole adventure. Raising millions meant it was even easier for Pearson to find tens of millions more with an exasperating combination of charm and threats.

Implicit in this venturing southward was a new sense of power within the Canadian financial village. Rooted in the combination of finance and technology, this new entrepreneurship harnessed a new form of energy – electricity. The power arose from a sudden maturation of financial institutions and a momentary shift from being borrower to lender. The entrepreneurial vigour of an ascendant Canada and its abundant savings could be united with superior North American technology and sent abroad to create a new empire of capital in the tropics where northern superiority could be profitably demonstrated in other ways – light, power, efficiency, order, dynamism, progress. A hint of this doctrine may be glimpsed in the boast of Montreal's *Journal of Commerce* in 1900 that 'Canadian capital and clearer northern brains are fast turning the island of Cuba into a modern hive of industry.'[5]

Canada's early foreign investors did not, however, develop a coherent ideology of mission. Before consciousness of this new role could be articulated and packaged for mass consumption, the vision was altered by rapidly changing circumstances. Soon these ventures outstripped Canadian financial abilities. When control shifted abroad, the vision became blurred, the enterprise more ambiguous – and more peripheral to Canadian experience.

Eventually Pearson's schemes outgrew the Canadians' wildest dreams both of cost and scale. At that point he moved on, to men with stronger stomachs and deeper pockets. Even before the crisis of 1907 Pearson had begun to exhaust the Canadian capital market. Already he had begun spinning a web around a new, more adventurous crowd of British and European bankers. James Dunn and Max Aitken, who moved from Canada to Great Britain at this time, personified this shift of base from the narrow streets of the financial village of Canada to the City and the suburbs of metropolitan capitalism. Their departure for London personified the growing internationalization of the capital market and, insofar as these enterprises were concerned the eclipse of the Bank of Montreal and Cox clan groups.

The transition from national to international enterprise occurred relatively peacefully. The migration of the companies and some of the promoters themselves across the Atlantic to the very centre of capitalism and empire, London, was marked by only one mock battle pitting a notional nationalism against an ascendant imperialism – the Mexican Light and Power proxy fight in 1909. Otherwise these southern ventures floated free of the country of their birth without trauma.

At one level the James Dunns, Max Aitkens, Edward Peacocks, and Alexander Mackenzies might have been thought of as living exemplars of the new imperial doctrine – except, of course, that the Canadian imperialists would have deplored their methods and occupations, however much they might have envied their success. James Dunn was not the kind of imperialist that Andrew Macphail and Stephen Leacock had in mind.[6] The 'Canadian' companies in the Caribbean, Latin America, and Spain might have been thought of as the financial incarnation of Canadian imperialism. But they were not. In this instance capitalism was not really a form of Canadian imperialism. For the men who created these utility empires other nations were merely markets, for capital or promotions. Countries were not things to be used by or to be loyal to; they were things to use – and they were interchangeable.

II

Where, in fact, was nationality in all this? To the Brazilian, Mexican, Puerto Rican, and Spanish authorities these companies, legally domiciled in Canada, were Canadian. In Barcelona, Mexico City, São Paulo, and especially Rio de Janeiro, the very word Canadian became an epithet for the exploitive, authoritarian, reactionary, dictatorial foreigner, especially during times of labour strife. The vernacular word for the streetcars in Brazil – - *bondes* – symbolized this irritating debt to Canada.

Yet in Brazil the utility managers tried to play up their British or American associations, whichever was most useful at the moment. In Mexico even the British diplomats could not tell Canadians from Americans, and when the anguished businessmen came calling on the Foreign Office, it could not tell whether they were Canadian or American either. They were certainly not British, though in time the British government chose to take them under its wing during the Mexican Revolution. In Washington, Pearson insisted that his companies were American in all but name, and certainly where it counted, in the purchase of capital equipment. And all of this overlooked the fact that a large part of the debt and a good measure of control ended up in Belgian hands. Belgium, of course, was the Canada of Europe, a country where lax security regulations, light taxes, and loose corporate law made for convenient, comfortable, and anonymous domicile.

Finance capitalism of the sort examined here knew no borders and proclaimed no permanent loyalties, perhaps because company promotion was a special sort of business, an especially ephemeral kind. Promoters came and went, wandering wherever deals could be struck; they went where the most lucrative opportunities for the application of their talents took them. Canadians migrated from the village to the City before the war. It was not a one-way ticket. After Doctor Pearson drowned and Captain

Loewenstein fell from the sky, Jimmy Dunn came home with his knighthood to build another empire in Sault Ste Marie, Ontario.[7]

This fundamental ambiguity as to the nationality of the 'Canadian' utilities in Latin America was revealed most poignantly in 1938 following the Mexican government's takeover of the oil industry. G.R.G. Conway, the managing director of Mexico Tramways and Mexican Light and Power, fearing that the government would press ahead with its nationalization program and seize his companies, contacted the British Legation in Mexico to see what protection His Majesty's government might afford. (Conway himself was a British subject who had been sent out to manage R.M. Horne-Payne's British Columbia Electric Railway and had then moved on to manage the Mexican properties after the Revolution.) The reply from his friend Owen O'Malley offered him no comfort. 'So long as things have been normal, if such a word can be applied to anything Mexican, I am sure you have been wise to get along without asking for any support from this Legation,' O'Malley wrote, 'even supposing that diplomatic support for the Light and Power Company could have produced any effect on the Mexican authorities.' The British government would act only after receiving information as to 'the real national character (in the way in which we can use those words) of the interests either Canadian or Mexican for which you are responsible.' After long experience with such matters the Foreign Office used a rough rule of thumb to determine 'the real national character of a concern.' Just because a company was registered in Canada that did not necessarily make it a Canadian company. O'Malley explained that Foreign Office officials 'reserve to themselves the right to enquire where the real beneficiary interest of a company is held and where the real control of it is exercised.'[8] The nationality of the controlling common shareholders decided the issue.

Conway plainly backed off at this point, knowing that by this test his companies were neither British nor Canadian. Later, in 1938 when the Canadian trade commissioner to Mexico finally bestirred himself to ask if he could be of any service to these Canadian companies in a time of distress, Conway brushed him off. 'While these Companies are Canadian companies,' R.T. Young reported to his superiors in Ottawa, 'Mr. Conway stated that practically all of the stock is Belgium owned and controlled, and therefore he considers that so far as his organizations are concerned, no immediate action on the part of our authorities, or even those of the United Kingdom, would serve any good purpose.'[9]

The nationality of these tropical utilities changed over time. They were

Canadian to begin with partly by accident (through F.S. Pearson's connections) and so long as the Canadian financial system could sustain them. However, as the rapid expansion of these southern utilities overtaxed the capacity of the Canadian capital market, responsibility for financing their needs and ultimately control of them shifted to Europe. This displacement was masked by the fact that they kept their Canadian address for legal convenience. Canadians retained a substantial interest only in Brazilian Traction; by 1927 54 per cent of its shares were owned by residents of Canada.

In the final analysis it was not the nationality of the companies that mattered, for they left little imprint upon the economy from which they emerged. Where were the office towers of top and middle managers, the vast engineering and research departments, the ships steaming down the St Lawrence laden with turbines, generators, telecommunications equipment, and motors? No organic connection was forged between the nominal home of the utilities and their host countries. Canada was not the primary source of equipment, management, or engineering services. As we have noted several times Pearson bought his equipment where his deal making required, with a marked preference for the United States, and his successors continued that pattern. The initial Canadianness was a function of a highly developed and concentrated capital market that could readily mobilize savings for domestic or foreign investment.

By contrast the German and US overseas utility holding companies had their origins in electrical equipment manufacturing firms who had to create markets for their products abroad. An equipment manufacturer like Siemens and Halske in association with a merchant bank, such as the Deutsche Bank, created utilities in Europe and Latin America, later grouping them into Swiss- or Belgian-based holding companies. By these means German electrical equipment companies with a small home market nevertheless produced 46 per cent of world electrotechnical exports in 1913.[10] In the United States the General Electric Company gave rise to the Electric Bond and Share company to help finance utilities buying GE equipment. At first this was primarily a domestic operation serving the huge American market. Only later, when the US electrical equipment market had become saturated, did EBASCO become a multinational enterprise. During the course of its overseas expansion it became a threat to Brazilian Traction in the 1920s.[11] US and German electrical promotions were driven by manufacturers seeking exports. The Canadian promotions, by contrast, were essentially financial creations. In mature industrial economies the manufacturers looked abroad for markets; in Canada the bankers and deal makers in search of high yields led the way.

The Canadian case offers a curious sidelight on the connection of trade and investment between peripheral economies. In 1911 the Canadian Department of Trade and Commerce did a brief study of Canadian trade with Mexico, itself a sign that this trade was of increasing importance. Between 1900 and 1911 total trade between the two countries had risen from $205,808 to $1,713,946 annually. Throughout the period, Canadian exports to Mexico exceeded imports from Mexico by a relatively constant 2.5 to 1.

A close inspection of the goods traded, however, brings into question any suggestion of a direct linkage between investment and trade. In 1911 Canada's exports to Mexico consisted overwhelmingly of two raw materials, grain (64 per cent) and coal (25 per cent). Only 11 per cent of Canadian exports were manufactured goods. In this category iron and steel, whisky, cordage, newsprint, and drugs were the principal items of trade. Mexico exported coffee, henequen and asphalt to Canada. Natural products accounted for an overwhelming 95.5 per cent of Mexican exports. Thus when Canada and Mexico did open up trading links during the high point of Canadian investment in Mexican utilities early in the twentieth century, Canadian exports to Mexico resembled Canadian exports to the rest of the world. Basically the two countries exchanged raw materials where each had an absolute advantage, wheat for coffee.[12] The same was probably true with Brazil as well.

The capital goods required to build the hydroelectric system and extend the street railways did not come from Canadian sources. The turbines, generators, wiring, meters, switching gear, transformers, motors, rolling stock, tools, and construction materials all came from elsewhere. Generators came from Germany, transformers from the United States, ironwork from Great Britain. This pattern would be repeated in Brazil and Barcelona. The systems would be assembled from parts gathered from all over the industrial world. For day-to-day items the Pearson Engineering Company in New York acted as a centralized purchasing agent; after 1915 the combined Canadian–Latin American utility enterprises operated their own purchasing and supply company in New York. When, in 1927, for example, a US pump manufacturer complained to the State Department that Mexican Light and Power was buying all British equipment, the US authorities were able to respond decisively with a long list of itemized capital expenditures showing 'that even though the company was Canadian, and being a British concern, it might be expected to buy British, in fact most of its materials had been purchased from American concerns.' On another occasion the Department of Trade and Commerce of Canada inquired of Brazilian Traction why all its purchasing was done through its New York office. The company replied that, all other things being equal, it would prefer to buy in Canada, but 'few orders can be placed advanta-geously in Canada.' Either the prices asked were too high, or steamship schedules made delivery from other sources easier. Finally the company observed that the structure of Canadian industry sometimes prevented exports. R.C. Brown called Trade and Commerce's attention 'to the difficulty we have in connection with certain large concerns, some of which have agreements which prevent them from making export sales; this applies especially to the Canadian General Electric Company, which is typical of several others.'[13]

Most of the effective demand for goods and services exerted by these companies was thus routed through New York and into the US economy despite the fact that the company in New York responsible for these purchases was misleadingly called the Canadian Engineering Agency. Great Britain, whose Foreign Office bore the brunt of the political demands of these companies, certainly did not benefit as an exporter in anything like its proportion of the amount of capital provided. One of the factors that makes this complex international flow of capital so curious is that US industry became its principal beneficiary. British, European and Canadian capital was routed through Canadian companies to buy largely American equipment for operations in Latin America.

Apart from the earnings these securities provided in excess of compara-ble Canadian opportunities, it cannot be said that these Latin American investments provided either a trade or institutional benefit to Canadian capitalism commensurate with their scale. Nor did the promotion of these companies have any lasting impact upon the institutions of Canadian capitalism. No large-scale utilities conglomerate rose built upon the capital provided by the Bank of Commerce and the Bank of Montreal, staffed by Canadians, doing business all over the world. These were essentially financial creations rather than products of managerial capitalism. The equivalent of the amount of investment required for a transcontinental railroad did not give rise to a corresponding corporate institution. Control remained outside –outside the corporation and eventually outside the country, in the hands of financiers weighing the relative advantages of investment on three continents.

These companies reflect, in their loosely integrated form, the importance of promoters rather than managers, of finance rather then production. They represented an early form of *rentier* capitalism or finance capitalism that would later become characteristic of Canadian economic development.[14] The holding company, with its small head office of investment managers, rather than the modern corporation with its growth-perpetuating strategic planning and research core, would be the peak institution of Canadian capitalism. Canadian capitalists to this day pride themselves on their lean head office staffs as a symbol of tight management; on the contrary it is a sign of their failure to create central agencies capable of generating the opportunities and technologies upon which second-generation growth depends.

From beginning to end the head office of Brazilian Traction, Mexican Light and Power, Mexico Tramways, and Barcelona Traction was little more than a room in the Blake firm's law office where the requisite legal work was carried out. A staff of two or three people handled correspondence. Purchasing was done in New York where goods were shipped to Brazil, Spain, and Mexico; local managers – especially Sir Alexander Mackenzie – enjoyed a wide degree of operating discretion, but decisions were ultimately made in London or Brussels.

On the other hand it must be said that to a certain extent these investments did create opportunities for Canadian managers and engineers. The smaller Montreal-based utilities in particular provided work for Max Aitken's creation, the Montreal Engineering Company, and other such services. Through these projects, Canadian engineers were drawn into that international pool of technical talent that roamed the world building dams, hydroelectric stations, and railroads. Foreign investment did enlarge the scope for Canadian engineers, managers, and consultants.[15]

In the final analysis what needs to be emphasized about these companies is not their nationality, but precisely their *international* character. The engineers, for example, were drawn from many countries, including Canada, but predominantly from the United States. F.S. Pearson, Hugh Cooper, R.C. Brown, and A.W.K. Billings were all Americans; Henry Holgate and F.W. Teele Canadians. Among the managers, Harro Harrsen was a US citizen; H.H. Couzens came from a British municipal corporation to the publicly owned Toronto Hydro and then the Toronto Transportation Commission, after which he moved on via his Toronto connections to Brazil. Conway, as has already been noted, was recruited in Britain to manage first a foreign-owned company in Mexico, then in Canada, and then again in Mexico. The most notable of all the managers, however, Sir Alexander Mackenzie, was a Canadian. Thus the recruitment of engineering and managerial personnel reflects the international character of these concerns. The capital and capital goods were assembled from the main centres of the industrial world; so too were the personnel. These enterprises thus linked emergent Canadian capitalism with the deeper currents of international finance flowing around the globe before the First World War.

III

Notwithstanding this ambiguity as to nationality, the Pearson group of companies relied heavily upon governments for introductions, franchises, assistance, and, occasionally, diplomatic protection. How can one characterize the relationship between the state and capital as reflected in the history of these southern ventures?

In the first instance it must be said that the state least called upon and affected by these foreign affairs was Canada, the country of origin. For most of this period Canada had no diplomatic representation in the region. Virtually the only time the Canadian government was called upon was during the controversy over the recognition of Victoriano Huerta. From time to time Sir Robert Borden was pestered by Dunn to use his influence with the British government, but that was mere surplusage. Borden had no standing in the making of British foreign policy. Canada had nothing to do either with organizing the abortive Clifton Hotel conference. Again Niagara Falls, Ontario, merely provided a convenient, neutral, non-US, non-Mexican venue. The government of Canada was not even the host, only a spectator.

Though these companies might be carrying the Canadian flag in various parts of the globe, the Canadian government maintained no formal relationship with them and vice versa. And the government of Canada did nothing to promote foreign investment. In the 1920s when the Canadian trade commissioner in Mexico was reported to be interviewing government officials seeking investment opportunities he was sharply reprimanded. 'Would urge utmost caution such matters,' Ottawa wired: 'Scarcely within your purview.'[16] Politically there was nothing to be gained from a Canadian association, except the tactical advantage of being neither British nor American during dust-ups. Standard Oil of New Jersey, for example, employed the stratagem of developing its Latin American markets using its relatively innocuous Canadian subsidiary as a stalking horse.[17]

What the promoters sought and gained from the government of Canada was benign neglect. Canadian domicile combined several extremely valuable attributes: a reputation for commercial integrity, easy incorporation provisions, and little if any effective regulation of securities markets.[18] Behind this curtain of rectitude built up over a century of commercial and public finance, private financiers pushed out the margins of the capitalist system. Because the international connections of the financial sector developed more rapidly than other sectors of the economy, the state had not caught up. And so long as the financial village traded largely within itself it was left to regulate itself. Throughout this period neither the government of Canada nor the provinces of Quebec and Ontario intruded much into the affairs of the stock exchanges. Financial gentlemen were left to regulate their own conduct. When someone broke the rules too flagrantly, the result was rejection – as in the case of Max Aitken.[19] If men failed to meet their obligations, suicide might be the only means of making amends – as was the case for James Dunn's Montreal partner in 1908. Honour and the social networks of the financial village were expected to temper financial ambition with prudence. In Canada the informal regulation of the financial village was deemed to be sufficient. As forbidding and confining as such regulations might be in certain respects, they nevertheless left a great deal of latitude for market operators.

It was also clear that, notwithstanding Pearson's nationality and best efforts, the United States remained a foreign government. The companies retained friends at court, most notably Lloyd Griscom, later ambassador to Italy. And the State Department certainly took an interest in the business activities of the Canadian companies, from time to time surveying the number of US employees and the amount trade generated. But the US government did not act overtly on behalf of these companies when requested. American policy, such as it was during the Mexican Revolution, was predicated upon concerns quite separate from – though coincident with – those of Dr Pearson and his companies. But Pearson could no more summon up recognition or intervention in Washington than he could hold that government to firm, resolute policies. A host of conflicting interests and ideals produced incoherence rather than effective protective force when it really mattered.

On the other hand the friendship of the US ambassador to these projects, especially in the case of Brazil, enhanced their prestige and lent them important competitive advantages at key moments. From the US authorities the Pearson companies received sympathy but not safety. The only state that might have intervened decisively in the Mexican Revolution effectively immobilized itself – in wartime, for its own broader strategic purposes – and Pearson could do nothing to change that.

The government upon which the Pearson companies' most persistent demands fell was that of Great Britain. This put the companies at something of a disadvantage, if the truth be known. For while Great Britain possessed enormous economic and moral influence, it lacked the means to act in a region over which another emergent power claimed hegemony. Dunn and Pearson could plead with the British government for protection during the Mexican Revolution, but even if the government were disposed to agree, it was powerless. Only the United States had both the force and the declared mandate to intervene. British influence was entirely informal, though not unimportant. But in the final analysis Great Britain could afford protection to neither persons nor property. It had influence, but not power.

Certainly the British government and its diplomats rendered these companies signal service over the years, especially Thomas Hohler, the chargé in Mexico, who did everything from negotiating strikes to advising on expropriation. At crucial points British diplomats were not merely external adjuncts but acted as operating spokesmen, with all that that implied about the importance of the linkage of state power and financial power.

At the same time it must also be observed that some representatives of the British government kept their distance from these intrusive, speculative enterprises, which did not fit the British upper-class notions of how things ought to be done. The aloofness of the governor of Jamaica, the British ambassador to Brazil at the beginning of the century, and later Sir Lionel Carden at the height of the Mexican Revolution might be cited as examples. The Foreign Office, as we have noted several times, queried the 'British-ness' and respectability of the firms until swayed by a paid lobbyist. Hohler himself had some qualms about representing 'British' companies that employed such a large number of unreliable Americans.

Thus a loose and somewhat ambiguous relationship existed between these companies when flying the British flag and the British state. As we have argued here, Pearson and his associates were most forthright and persistent in lobbying the British government over the recognition of Huerta, and they made more impact than is usually realized. That is certainly not to say, however, that Pearson and Dunn shaped British policy. The geopolitical interests of Great Britain, mainly a concern for oil supplies, shaped the views of His Majesty's government as much as concern for the capital sunk in public utilities. In the final analysis policy towards Mexico was made after taking into account the broad range of British concerns. And British policy in the region did not count for much by the twentieth century. These promoters would have each other, and us, believe that they were moving and shaking the state. However, a coincident set of interests shared by a government and some private interests is not the same thing as a determined relationship.

The Pearson group, despite its somewhat ambiguous national origins and shadowy reputation, did receive the active support and friendship of the British government during the Mexican Revolution. The group did everything in its power to cultivate that protective instinct. It did not dictate British policy, however, nor did it receive any more favourable treatment than any other British commercial interest in similar circumstances. Capital may have been stateless, but the government of Great Britain was its most consistent friend. It was not a friendship, however, from which a great deal could be expected. Though the Pearson group might beg, they did not necessarily receive. And even when they did, it was not much help.[20]

The most effective influence the Pearson companies could rely upon in their dealings with Latin American governments was the power of the market itself. Governments had to go to market for loans as well. So did their citizens. And the treatment accorded borrowers in global markets, especially the City, depended upon whether or not the country involved played by the rules of the international capitalist game. If foreign investors cried foul or were subject to 'unfair' regulation, then of course borrowers from that country could expect to pay higher interest rates, if money was to be had at all. On the other hand good relations with large foreign investors opened doors in London and New York.[21]

Thus the intimate relationship of these utilities with the world's capital market was in fact their strongest card. In the twentieth century, as interest-rate spreads and bankers' sanctions replaced gunboats and diplomatic notes, concern for 'the market' was a potent force. During the twenties Brazilian Traction appealed both to the British government and the house of Rothschild to apply pressure to the recalcitrant Brazilian authorities. The strongest power these companies possessed was, in fact, intrinsic to themselves and not extrinsic. A smoothly negotiated franchise agreement might mean a more readily negotiated refunding loan in London, or a cheaper flotation of public works debentures. These companies did their best to present themselves as the representatives of the world's capital markets, for in such a guise they could wield considerable influence.

IV

Foreign direct investment depended upon market imperfections: proprietary technological and organizational knowledge. It remains to be asked in general terms what impact this kind of foreign direct investment had upon the host countries. Did foreign investors dictate terms to weak local governments? What recourse, if any, did the host countries have? If the market was imperfect, did politics compensate?

In the first instance it must be stressed that the knowledge of hydroelectric technology and integrated utilities organization Pearson and company brought to Latin America was thoroughly up-to-date. Indeed, in many important respects Pearson charted remarkable engineering advances, extending the scope of the technology in remote, high-head situations, in long-distance transmission, and especially in the reorganization and redirection of natural hydraulic systems to produce the maximum energy output. Mexico, Brazil, and Spain received advanced technological systems at a relatively early date. The same could be said, though with reduced force, for the less adventuresome promotions of Max Aitken and the other Montrealers in the Caribbean.

It must not be forgotten that, behind all the bickering, brinkmanship, and profit taking among the promoters (matters that figure prominently in these pages), these companies were applying knowledge not easily gained and certainly not widely shared, with corresponding advantages for Latin American consumers. If the Pearson group knew how to create energy where others could not see the possibilities, it also knew how to transmit, market, and sell the product within a monopolistic, inter-corporate framework that also worked to its own best advantage. Pearson and his friends could organize utilities, create monopolies, and manage interdependent companies in such a way as to maximize the rate of return on capital invested. To the extent that this provided transportation, gas, water, electricity, and telephones sooner, more efficiently, and more cheaply than local alternatives, this too represented a net gain to the host countries. Private profit is not inconsistent with public benefit, even in a monopoly setting – though it is harder to justify.

Foreign direct investment opened up a much larger pool of capital for application to urban public services than would have been available if Brazil, Mexico, and the other countries had depended entirely upon their own resources. To that extent, therefore, efficient public services unquestionably enhanced the processes of urbanization and industrialization in the region. Cheaper, more abundant, and more regular energy, light, and communications laid down the infrastructure for manufacturing and commerce. For this net benefit a long-term price would have to be paid, but the burden of that price was a matter to be determined in continuous negotiations. It was not fixed and set for all time.

Thus foreign investment, as long as it was confined to the most technically difficult and capital-intensive opportunities, offered Latin Americans up-to-date utilities service with considerably less risk and lower transaction costs than would otherwise have been possible. The benefit would be minimized by the extent to which the host countries could deny the promoters monopoly profits, minimizing the pure rent. It is here that the broader market power of foreign capital was most effectively brought to bear. Up to 1913 the Pearson group was able to promote, finance, and operate more or less as it pleased. Local governments could stall, grumble, and interfere, but they could not fundamentally alter the situation. More damaging was the intransigence of competitors, rivals who would not submit and could not be bought, as in the case of the Guinle family of Santos.

In unusual times, when market sanctions carried less weight, host countries were able to wring the most water out of these ventures. Often this was an unintended consequence of other public policies. War and monetary deflation in Brazil combined to reduce the profitability of Brazilian Traction to more ordinary levels. In Mexico a continuous revolution, complicated by a world war, also scaled back the capitalization of these firms.

These instruments were not in the first instance conscious 'policy' vehicles directed towards the foreign investment problem; nor were they particularly discriminating tools. Their social cost is of another order of magnitude entirely. But however blunt the instrument, it was nevertheless the case that host governments did possess the power to change the terms of the international capitalist equation so as to shift things in their own favour. Public utilities, among all forms of foreign direct investment, were unusually vulnerable, embodying as they did millions of pounds of sunk, immovable capital. Integrated hydroelectric utilities were not like manufacturing firms or banks, which could pick up and move to more salubrious climes at minimal cost. The capital was committed in location-specific assets that could be abandoned only with tremendous financial sacrifice.[22] Like it or not, the company was there for the long run. Thus the very immobility of this form of investment meant that capital was more likely to seek accommodation than confrontation, to negotiate rather than fight, to seek comfort with half a loaf if the whole loaf for some reason could not be obtained.

The power relations between foreign capital and local governments were complex, by no means one way, certainly not that of superior and subordinate. If on occasion foreign investors had to bribe officials, that in itself was a recognition that someone else possessed some discretionary power, which could be purchased for the advantage of the company or, alternatively, used against it. Moreover, the power relationship between foreign capital and local governments ebbed and flowed with circumstances. Mutually dependent, nevertheless each jockeyed for advantage, trying to make the most of situations as they arose.

At first foreign capital possessed the greatest power, and friendly government could make a great deal of difference as to its profitability and growth. In Cuba, Puerto Rico, Mexico City, and São Paulo, capital flourished under the benign regime of development-minded local authorities. Where local governments animated by competing interests intruded, capital had to cope with harder bargains. Of course, information about profitability, as it became more widely available, also stiffened the resolve of local authorities in negotiations. Since differences in information lay at the basis of foreign direct investment, much depended upon the management of information: to enhance capital raising ability on the one hand without raising local resistance on the other. It was a fine line, but it could be managed.

Throughout it must be said that foreign capitalists had the distinct advantage of an extremely focused self-interest. Governments had many objectives that had to be traded off. Ruthless pursuit of a narrow self-interest through revolutions, devaluations, and hostile political regimes could nevertheless produce respectable rates of return. Again foreign capitalists had information about internal financial circumstances not available to their government antagonists, who had to guess. Foreign capitalists tended to be more successful negotiators precisely because their goals were so clear. Even with a hostile government, such as that in Brazil, or during a bloody revolution, as in Mexico, one could do more than merely survive.

Thus we do not emerge from this study convinced of the idea that foreign capitalists, operating through comprador local interests, bought their way into positions of power and dictated terms to local authorities thereafter, creating conditions of permanent dependency. The relations between foreign utilities companies and local authorities were characterized by continuous negotiations, in which alterations in the flow of information and capital, not to mention upheavals in international affairs, dramatically changed the bargaining positions of the negotiators over time. With the passage of time these companies became, in effect, local companies; their foreign association did them little good – apart from providing more direct access to international capital – and probably a good deal of harm politically. Since relations between government and utilities in all countries have been marked by intense conflict, it is difficult to separate those political difficulties connected to anti-monopoly sentiment from those connected to nationality.

Having a single interest, a massive, valuable, complex property, and many friends in the capital markets of Europe gave the companies important tactical advantages in negotiations that account for their relative success. But the wealth of detail on the preceding pages reminds us how contingent and variable that superiority might be. To focus exclusively upon the control of one agent by another or on conflicts between the foreigner and the national is to ignore other important matters, such as conflicts among the foreigners and shifting market conditions that impinged upon all parties. Professor Platt may be going too far when he argues that 'nationality is irrelevant in many or most of the cases described, since the business would have been conducted and controlled in the same way irrespective of nationality.' But he is certainly correct to point out that both parties were subject to broader market forces over which each had only very limited control.[23] Foreign direct investment depended upon international differences in technical knowledge and technique. Over time, of course, these differentials diminished as knowledge became more widely shared.

In concluding this study we must resist the temptation to make sweeping statements about the nature of entrepreneurship, international capitalism, imperialism, and dependency. These firms open only a very narrow window on the relationship of business and the state, investment and trade, finance and nationalism. And we have been looking through that window from a peripheral economy within the Atlantic system. Academic prudence requires that we not generalize beyond the evidence provided by the very special case under examination. The Canadian utilities were not a representative sample of 'capitalism' nor were they typical foreign busi- nesses – if such a thing could be said to exist. They were highly unusual in so many ways. Their dependence on international capital markets perhaps rendered them more stateless than other businesses; their sunk capital perhaps made them more susceptible to local regulation; and their monopoly character made them perhaps more profitable on the one hand but more politically vulnerable on the other.

They began as Canadian companies, though their inspiration – F.S. Pearson – and their technology were American. But they rapidly became international. The capital thus risked relied implicitly upon the political power of Europe; but in the final analysis that power could not deliver protection when it was most needed. Over the long run these companies depended most upon the vitality of local economies, the wit of their local engineers and managers, their effectiveness in local negotiations, and their ability to finance expansion out of retained earnings after 1914 and to pay a return on investment within a changing international economy.

Like the services they provided, these firms were interstitial: they fit between and connected things. They depended in part upon the much larger Atlantic state system, the economic hegemony of the European capital market, and the need for modern services that Latin Americans momentarily could not provide for themselves at this scale in their major cities. Over time each of these forces would decay, and with that the space occupied by foreign direct investment would shrink and ultimately vanish.

In time that portion of the capital that was Canadian was repatriated as the governments of Mexico and Brazil gradually nationalized their utilities in extensive, state supported, economic development programs following the Second World War.[24] Foreign private equity was exchanged for foreign public debt, a transaction that did not necessarily remove external influence over the domestic economy. But it did internalize decision making over the provision of public services. The ultimate domestication of these companies in the public sector left only their legal shells behind in Canada, kept alive for technical reasons in a few Toronto law offices. Latin American governments patriated control, but the corporate papers of the Mexican and Brazilian companies remained locked in Toronto warehouses or in the sub-basements of skyscrapers. To this day Mexican officials repair briefly to Toronto (in February) to observe the peculiar legal rites necessary to keep these corporate charters alive. This curious holdover from another time explains the somewhat puzzling fact that the government-owned Mexican Light and Power Company still turns up in the listings of Canadian corporations, recently vying with Dome Petroleum and the Canada Development Corporation as the largest money loser.[25]

As is more widely known, Brazilian Traction, renamed Brascan, sold most of its utility assets to the government of Brazil in 1978. With the proceeds Brascan turned itself into a dynamic Canadian holding company. Thereby Canadian finance capital resumed its more familiar course as it was reinvested in breweries, financial services, and natural resources. Home at last: beer, insurance, forest products and minerals – and the boys of summer.[26]

Notes

Abbreviations Used in Notes

BA Brascan Archives, Brascan Ltd, Toronto
Series:
AM Sir Alexander Mackenzie
BHE Brazilian Hydro-Electric Company
BTel Brazilian Telephone Company
BT Brazilian Traction, Light and
  Power Company
CF Current Files
DF Decimal Files
HD Historical Documents
HHC Sir H.H. Couzens
LM Loewenstein Matter
MC Miscellaneous Correspondence
OD Original Documents
Pre-1923 1923 and prior
RJTLP Rio de Janeiro Tramway, Light
  and Power Company
SPTLP São Paulo Tramway, Light and
  Power Company
Beaverbrook Lord Beaverbrook Papers
Series: A, G, H
DP Sir James Dunn Papers
HLRO House of Lords Record Office,
  London
MB Minute Book
MET Mexico Electric Tramway

Company Records (in the custody of
  Fasken and Calvin, Toronto)
MLP Mexican Light and Power
  Company Records (in the custody of
  Blake, Cassels and Graydon, Toronto)
MTC Mexico Tramway Company
  Records (see MET)
PAC Public Archives of Canada, Ottawa
Pearson LB F.S. Pearson Letterbook
PRO Public Record Office, London
Series:
CO Colonial Office
FO Foreign Office
RF Robert Fleming and Company
  Records, London
RJTLP Archives Rio de Janeiro Tramway,
  Light and Power Company Archives, Rio
  (courtesy of Duncan McDowall)
SPTLP Archives São Paulo Tramway, Light
  and Power Company Archives, São Paulo
  (courtesy of Duncan McDowall)
USNA United States National Archives,
  Washington
Series:
DF 1910–29 State Department
  Decimal Files

Preface

1 J.F. Rippy, *British Investments in Latin America* (Hamden: Archon, 1966); I. Stone, 'British Direct and Portfolio Investment in Latin America before 1914,' *Journal of Economic History* 37 (1977) 690–722, and 'British Long Term Investment in Latin America, 1865–1913,' *Business History Review* 32 (1968) 311–39; Brinley Thomas, 'The Historical Record of International Capital Movements to 1913,' in J.H. Adler, ed., *Capital Movements and Economic Development* (New York: St Martin's, 1967) 3–33, and Matthew Simon, 'The Pattern of New British Portfolio Foreign Investment, 1865–1914,' in ibid. 33–60; D.C.M. Platt, *Latin America and British Trade* (London: A. and C. Black, 1972); and M. Edelstein, *Overseas Investment in the Age of High Imperialism: The United Kingdom, 1850–1914* (New York: Columbia University Press, 1982). For current revisionist research that is likely to qualify the quantity and economic importance of this capital outflow see the essays in R.V. Turrell and J.J. Van-Helten, eds, *The City and the Empire* (London: University of London, Institute of Commonwealth Studies, 1985).
2 Charles P. Kindleberger and Peter Lindert, *International Economics* (Homewood: Richard D. Irwin, 1978) 455
3 We have been guided in matters of theory by Charles P. Kindleberger, *American Business Abroad* (New Haven: Yale University Press, 1969); Richard Caves, *Multinational Enterprise and Economic Analysis* (New York: Cambridge University Press, 1982); and N. Hood and S. Young, *The Economics of Multinational Enterprise* (New York: Longman, 1979).
4 See, for example, D.K. Fieldhouse's critique of current theories of multinational enterprise development, 'The Multinational: A Critique of a Concept,' in Alice Teichova, Maurice Lévy-Leboyer, and Helga Nussbaum, eds, *Multinational Enterprise in Historical Perspective* (New York: Cambridge University Press, 1986) 23.

Chapter 1 The Paper Givers

1 W.L. Marr and D.G. Paterson, *Canada: An Economic History* (Toronto: Macmillan, 1980) 6–9, 18–21; Simon Kuznets, *Modern Economic Growth: Rate, Structure and Spread* (New Haven: Yale University Press, 1966) 63–72.
2 *Monetary Times* 8, 22 June 1900
3 Vincent P. Carosso, *Investment Banking in America* (Cambridge: Harvard University Press, 1970)
4 Michael Bliss, *A Canadian Millionaire: The Life and Business Times of Sir Joseph Flavelle, Bart. 1858–1939* (Toronto: Macmillan, 1978)

5 Ian Drummond, 'Canadian Life Insurance Companies and the Capital Market, 1890–1914,' *Canadian Journal of Economics and Political Science* 27 (1962) 211

6 The Montreal group has not been much studied. A roster of its members has been compiled from George Harris, *The President's Book: The Story of the Sun Life Assurance Company of Canada* (Montreal: privately printed, 1928), and Merrill Denison, *Canada's First Bank: A History of the Bank of Montreal* (Toronto: McClelland and Stewart, 1967) 2 vols.

7 T.W. Acheson, 'The National Policy and the Industrialization of the Maritimes, 1880–1910,' *Acadiensis* 1 (1972) 3–28

8 *Monetary Times* 19 January 1900

9 T.W. Acheson, 'Changing Social Origins of the Canadian Industrial Elite, 1880–1910,' *Business History Review* 47 (1973) 189–217.

10 On the architecture of turn-of-the-century Canadian capitalism see William Dendy, *Lost Toronto* (Toronto: Oxford, 1978) and Leslie Maitland, *Neoclassical Architecture in Canada* (Ottawa: National Historic Parks and Sites Branch, Environment Canada, 1984). For a splendid series of examples of the descending scale of bank grandeur see the illustrations in Victor Ross and A. St L. Trigge, *The History of the Canadian Bank of Commerce* (Toronto: privately printed, 1922, 1934) 3 vols. See also Alan Gowans's agitated attack upon late-Victorian and Edwardian eclecticism in *Building Canada: An Architectural History of Canadian Life* (Toronto: University of Toronto Press, 1966) 139–44 (a 'really mature' society would not have needed such an excess of ornament and classical allusion), and Eric Arthur's more sympathetic acceptance of it in *Toronto: No Mean City* (Toronto: University of Toronto Press, 1964) 172–3, 223.

11 Edgar A. Collard, *Chalk to Computers: The Story of the Montreal Stock Exchange* (Montreal: privately printed, 1974) 19 and plates. For the inspiration see D.S. Robertson, *A Handbook of Greek and Roman Architecture* (Cambridge: Cambridge University Press, 1943) 210–1, pl. 9; and Frank Brown, *Roman Architecture* (New York: George Braziller, 1967) fig. 17. Currently this temple at Tivoli is not thought to have been a Temple of Vesta; see Frank Sear, *Roman Architecture* (London: Batsford, 1982) 20–1, pl. 10.

12 Collard, *Chalk to Computers* 15 and plates; Dendy, *Lost Toronto* 45–59; Arthur, *Toronto* 161, for descriptions and photos

13 John F. Whiteside, 'The Toronto Stock Exchange to 1900: Its Membership and Development of the Share Market,' (MA diss., Trent University, 1979) 55–6, portions of which have been printed in Whiteside, 'The Toronto Stock Exchange and the Development of the Share Market to 1885,' *Journal of Canadian Studies* 20 (1985) 64–81; *Journal of Commerce* 8 July 1898, 9 January 1903

14 *Journal of Commerce* 2 October 1896; Whiteside, 'Toronto Stock Exchange,' 169

15 These listings were not systematically recorded in the financial press, and these figures should only be taken to suggest the general outlines of the two markets.

16 Kenneth Buckley, *Capital Formation in Canada, 1896–1930* (Toronto: McClelland and Stewart, 1974) 2–17; Marr and Paterson, *Canada: An Economic History* 223–30; Phyllis Dean and W.A. Cole, *British Economic Growth, 1688–1959* (Cambridge: Cambridge University Press, 1962) 264–77; Lance E. Davis, et al., *American Economic Growth* (New York: Harper and Row, 1975) 290–310

17 Buckley, *Capital Formation* 15; Marr and Paterson, *Canada: An Economic History* 266–70. See also PAC, Finance Department Records, RG 19, E 2 B vol. 3244, file 14650, Percy A. Hurd to W.L. Griffith, 7 July 1906, for a contemporary memorandum on Colonial Loans and Investments drawn from *Burdett's Stock Exchange Official Intelligence*, comparing 1882, 1894, and 1906, and J.M. Courtney to W.L. Griffith, 3 October 1906, reconciling these estimates with those of the *Economist*.

18 *Monetary Times*, 29 Sept. 1899

19 E.P. Neufeld, *The Financial System of Canada: Its Growth and Development* (Toronto: Macmillan, 1972) 94–117

20 Neufeld, *Financial System* 242–65

21 Drummond, 'Life Insurance' 206–8, 217

22 Thomas Navin and Marian Sears, 'The Rise of a Market for Industrial Securities, 1887–1902,' *Business History Review* 29 (1955) 105–138; Whiteside, 'Toronto Stock Exchange,' 139

23 *Monetary Times* 14 August, 23 Oct. 1896

24 *Monetary Times* 'Foolish Mining Investments,' 23 Apr. 1897; 'Investment and Speculation,' 4 Aug. 1899; 'Success in Business,' 8 Dec. 1899; 'Bucket Shop Gambling,' 2 Feb. 1900; *Journal of Commerce* 'Stock Gambling,' 9 Jan., 15 May, 5 June, 31 July 1903

25 Clipping, 1902, Toronto Stock Exchange Archives; see also *Toronto Daily Star* 3 Apr. 1900 for an account of the opening of the exchange's new quarters.

26 For a more restrained account of trading on the Toronto Stock Exchange somewhat later, see E. Gordon Wills, 'The Stock Exchange and the Street,' *Canadian Banker* 58 (1951).

27 This commission was inspired by the 1905 Armstrong Committee investigation of the New York life insurance industry. See Morton Keller, *The Life Insurance Enterprise, 1885–1910* (Cambridge: Harvard University Press, 1963) 245–64. On the Canadian Royal Commission see Drummond, 'Life Insurance,' 211–16; Royal Commission on Life Insurance, *Report* (Ottawa: King's Printer, Sessional Paper No. 123a, 1907) 17.

28 *Annual Financial Review (Canadian)*, compiled by W.R. Houston, 1901 and 1902

Chapter 2 Going Abroad

1 *Monetary Times* 19 January 1900
2 See the entries for Mackenzie and Ross in Henry J. Morgan, ed., *Canadian Men and Women of the Time* (Toronto: William Briggs, 1898 and 1912); a brief biography of Porteous is contained in the finding aid to his papers in the PAC, which are the prime documentary source for the activities of his principals during the 1890s. See also T.D. Regehr, *The Canadian Northern Railway, Pioneer Road of the Northern Prairies, 1895–1918* (Toronto: Macmillan, 1976) for further insight into the personality of William Mackenzie.
3 Carl A.S. Hall, 'Electrical Utilities in Ontario under Private Ownership,' (Ph D diss., University of Toronto, 1968) 63–5; G.R. Stevens, *Canadian National Railways* vol. 2, *Towards the Inevitable, 1896–1922* (Toronto: Clarke Irwin, 1962) 23–4; C. Armstrong and H.V. Nelles, *Monopoly's Moment: The Organization and Regulation of Canadian Utilities, 1830–1930* (Philadelphia: Temple University Press, 1986) 93–137
4 PAC, C.E.L. Porteous Papers, vol. 24, Porteous to W.Y. Soper, 20 May 1895, Confidential
5 By 1893 there were 19,600 kilometres of street railways in the United States, 60 per cent using electricity, and a decade later fully 98 per cent of the 48,000 kilometres of tramway were electrified. John P. McKay, *Tramways and Trolleys: The Rise of Urban Mass Transport in Europe* (Princeton: Princeton University Press, 1976) 50–1
6 George W. Hilton, 'Transport Technology and the Urban Pattern,' *Journal of Contemporary History* 4 (1969) 126, quoted in McKay, *Tramways and Trolleys* 51
7 Canada, Department of Railways and Canals, *Railway Statistics of the Dominion of Canada* 1901 (Ottawa: King's Printer, 1902); John F. Due, *The Intercity Electric Railway Industry in Canada* (Toronto: University of Toronto Press, 1966) 37
8 J.H. Cox in the *Electrical Engineer*, quoted in McKay, *Tramways and Trolleys* 85
9 On these three cities see Charles W. Cheape, *Moving the Masses: Urban Public Transit in New York, Boston and Philadelphia, 1880–1912* (Cambridge: Harvard University Press, 1980). See also Charles H. Cooley, 'Report on the Transportation Business in the U.S. Statistics of Street Transportation,' *11th Census of the United States* vol. 50, pt 2 (1896) 681–2, quoted in T.C. Barker and Michael Robbins, *A History of London Transport* vol. 2, *The Twentieth Century to 1970* (London: George Allen and Unwin, 1974) 18.
10 McKay, *Tramways and Trolleys* 73, 95–106, and quotations from 168
11 Barker and Robbins, *History of London Transport* vol. 2, 22–6

12 PAC, Porteous Papers, vol. 2, Mackenzie to Porteous, 7 July 1895

13 Barker and Robbins, *History of London Transport* vol. 2, 26–34

14 PAC, Porteous Papers, vol. 2, Mackenzie to Porteous, 7 July 1895.

15 Asa Briggs, *History of Birmingham* vol. 2, *Borough and City, 1865–1938* (London: Oxford University Press, 1952) 94

16 PAC, Porteous Papers, vol. 3, Mackenzie to Porteous, 18 Apr. 1896

17 Ibid., vol. 17, Porteous to James Ross, 27 Apr. 1896; vol. 25, Porteous to James Ross, 5 May 1896; vol. 3, Mackenzie to Porteous, 9 May 1896

18 PAC, Bank of Montreal Papers, M-158, Directors' MB, 9 June 1896, 339

19 PAC, Porteous Papers, vol. 3, Ross to Porteous, 27 June 1896; vol. 19, Porteous to Ross, 8 July 1896

20 Ibid, vol. 3, Ross to Porteous, 27 June 1896

21 Briggs, *History of Birmingham* vol. 2, 94

22 PAC, Porteous Papers, vol. 25, Porteous to W.G. Ross, 3 Aug. 1896; Porteous to Bank of Montreal, 3 Aug. 1896

23 Ibid., vol. 4, Mackenzie to Porteous, 7 Nov. 1896

24 Report of Birmingham Subcommittee on Tramways quoted in McKay, *Tramways and Trolleys* 85–6

25 PAC, Porteous Papers, vol. 26, Porteous to Ross, 29 June 1897

26 Briggs, *History of Birmingham* vol. 2, 95–6; PAC, Porteous Papers, vol. 30, James Ross to Porteous, 13 Sept. 1900

27 Thomas P. Hughes, *Networks of Power: Electrification in Western Society, 1880–1930* (Baltimore: Johns Hopkins University Press, 1983) 227–61

28 C. Armstrong and H.V. Nelles, *The Revenge of the Methodist Bicycle Company: Sunday Streetcars and Municipal Reform in Toronto, 1888–1897* (Toronto: Peter Martin, 1977) 121–2

29 PAC, Porteous Papers, vol. 29, Porteous diary, 24 Feb. 1898; the entry for James Ross in Morgan, ed., *Canadian Men and Women* (1898); *Annual Financial Review (Canadian)* 1902, comp. W.R. Houston

30 The president was F.L. Wanklyn, who had run the street railways in Toronto and Montreal for the syndicate, with J.K.L. Ross as vice-president and James Hutchison and Abner Kingman as directors in addition to James Ross and Porteous.

31 PAC, Porteous Papers, vol. 20, Porteous to James Ross, 10 June 1898

32 Ibid., vol. 21, Porteous to James Ross, 6 Oct. 1899; vol. 8, Memorandum of Amounts of Contract for Material, etc., for Kingston, Jamaica made by C.E.L. Porteous, 20 Sept. 1900

33 *Annual Financial Review (Canadian)* 1903, 1905, 1908, 1909

34 For a list of his interests see Morgan, ed., *Canadian Men and Women* (1912).

35 C. Lintern Sibley, 'Van Horne and His Cuban Railway,' *Canadian Magazine* 41:5 (Sept. 1913) 444

36 Walter Vaughan, *The Life and Work of Sir William Van Horne* (New York: Century, 1921) 274–5 and 370–82; PAC, Gonzalo de Quesada y Arostegui Papers, Van Horne to Quesada, 21 Apr. 1909

37 Quoted in Vaughan, *Van Horne*, from which personal information has also been drawn, 381.

38 PAC, Porteous Papers, vol. 5, J.H. Hoadley to Porteous, 15 Dec. 1898

39 Charles A. Gauld, *The Last Titan: Percival Farquhar, American Entrepreneur in Latin America* (Palo Alto, Ca.: Institute of Hispanic American and Luso-Brazilian Studies, Stanford University, 1964) 11–19; *Monetary Times* 29 Dec. 1899, 19 Jan. 1900. See the ms on the life of Pearson by Stearns Morse, entitled 'The Yankee Spirit,' in BA 237–8.

40 The *New York Times*, on 30 Mar. 1900, reports the purchase of the railway; 12 May 1900 notes the formation of the syndicate; and articles on 9, 13, and 29 Nov. and 16 December comment on aspects of the tour based upon interviews with Sir William.

41 Vaughan, *Van Horne* 276–305; Gauld, *Last Titan* 26–39. Vaughan quotes Van Horne at 301.

42 The *Journal of Commerce*, 3 May 1901, 1184–6, quoted a long article from the Philadelphia *Record*

43 Vaughan, *Van Horne* 301–5, 312–18, 329–31

44 *Journal of Commerce* 17 Nov. 1899, 1309; 26 Jan. 1900, 280; on the granting of the franchise see PRO, CO 111, vol. 513, files 20424, 23260-1

45 PAC, Bank of Montreal Papers, M-158, Directors' MB, 24 Oct. 1899, 257

46 The dispute over electrolysis may be followed in PRO, CO 111, vols 519, 520, 522, 526, 527, 529.

47 *Journal of Commerce* 3 May 1901

48 Sibley, 'Van Horne and His Cuban Railway,' 451

49 PAC, Porteous Papers, vol. 21, Porteous to James Ross, 29 Aug. 1899

50 Ibid., vol. 10, E.A. Carolan to Porteous, 30 Nov., 5 Dec. 1901. Carolan was head of the Foreign Sales Department at General Electric.

51 PAC, Porteous Papers, vol. 8, J.D. Hazen to Porteous, 7 June 1900; vol. 9, Holgate to Porteous, 21 Feb. 1901

52 Ibid., vol. 13, E.H. Drury to Porteous, 28 Aug. 1905. By that time, of course, Porteous had ceased to be employed by James Ross and had fallen out with him over other business deals.

53 Ibid., vol. 22, Porteous to Dr James Johnston, 2 May 1901, Private

Chapter 3 Success in São Paulo

1 Details of Pearson's life may be found in the unpublished manuscript by Stearns Morse, 'The Yankee Spirit,' a copy of which is in BA.

2 Américo de Campos had been dispatched to Canada, apparently, as a remittance man when he met Gualco. During Gualco's visit to Brazil he met A.A. de Souza, a Campos connection, with whom he formed Gualco e de Souza Incorporadores (in which Campos also held an interest) to acquire the franchises. This account is drawn from Brascan Limited's *60 Years of Brazilian-Canadian Cooperation* (np, nd [*c.* 1960]) 2, and from BA, CF 0-7-1-41, Sir Henry Lynch to H.B. Style, 22 Sept. 1948.

3 On the development of the city and state of São Paulo see, *inter alia*, Warren Dean, *The Industrialization of São Paulo, 1880–1945* (Austin: University of Texas Press, 1969); Joseph H. Love, *São Paulo in the Brazilian Federation, 1889–1937* (Stanford, Ca.: Stanford University Press, 1980).

4 BA, SPTLP, B. 24, Report of R.C. Brown on São Paulo Railway [sic], Light and Power Company to F.S. Pearson, 1 Mar. 1899. See also Gerald Michael Greenfield, 'Lighting the City: A Case Study of Public Service Problems in São Paulo, 1885–1913,' in Dauril Alden and Warren Dean, eds, *Essays Concerning the Socioeconomic History of Brazil and Portuguese India* (Gainesville, Fla.: University Presses of Florida, 1977) 118–49.

5 BA, SPTLP, B. 24, Report by Brown to Pearson, 1 Mar. 1899

6 BA, SPTLP, MC, Memorandum 'Re Company's History, the São Paulo Gas Company by C.H.N. A[nglin],' 15 Aug. 1933; CF 0-7-141, N. Biddell to A.W.K. Billings, 13 Mar. 1934

7 BA, SPTLP, B. 69, Memorandum re 'History of São Paulo Co. Revised to July 31st, 1908 from 1906 Memorandum,' 31 July 1908; B. 24, Memorandum, unsigned, nd, received from Frederic Nicholls, July [1900?]

8 BA, CF 0-7-1-41, 'Outline History of the São Paulo Light,' by Dr Edgard de Souza, Feb. 1949

9 BA, CF 0-7-1-41, J.M. Bell to Walter Gow, 8 June 1945, enclosing extract from letter by B.F. McCurdy, 28 Mar. 1945; Gow to Bell, 22 June 1945, in which Gow observed, 'It was common knowledge here [in Toronto] in the early days that the Doctor [F.S. Pearson] had failed to interest anyone in New York in the São Paulo proposal and that in some way he heard of Sir William Mackenzie.'

10 BA, SPTLP, B. 85, Pearson to J.M. Smith, 5 May 1906

11 PAC, RG 19 E 2 B, Department of Finance Records, vol. 3181, file 11275, Sir Louis Davies to J.C. Courtenay, nd and reply, 1 Apr. 1901

12 BA, SPTLP, B. 32½, J.M. Smith to E.R. Wood, 8 June 1905, Private. Formally, 40,000 shares went to William Mackenzie, 10,000 to Cox, and 10,000 to B.F. Pearson, who reallocated them. For a list of those who received shares in this way see ibid., OD, Statement showing allotments of São Paulo stock with No. of shares issued to various subscribers, 6 Sept. 1900.

13 Morse, 'Yankee Spirit,' 243–5; BA, SPTLP, OD, 'Memorandum for Mr. [Alexander] Mackenzie, Re São Paulo Railway, Light and Power Company Limited,' May 1899

14 BA, CF 0-7-1-41, C.G.S. Shalders to A.W.K. Billings, 28 Feb. 1934; SPTLP, MC, Mackenzie to Blake, Lash, Cassels, 16 July 1899. On Prado's family see Darrell E. Levi, *The Prados of São Paulo, Brazil: An Elite Family and Social Change, 1840–1930* (Athens, Ga.: University of Georgia Press, 1987) which appeared while this book was in press.

15 BA, SPTLP, MC, A. Mackenzie to Blake, Lash, Cassels, 29 June 1899, reported that Pearson had decided not even to meet with the Viação Paulista people until the work was further under way so that the seriousness of the potential competition might lead them to reduce their demands to be bought out. The information on the rival utilities is contained in ibid., CF 0-7-1-41, 'Outline History of the São Paulo Light,' by Dr Edgard de Souza, Feb. 1949.

16 The situation in São Paulo was fully set forth in Mackenzie's three reports to his partners, the first of which is cited in n15 above, the others being dated 16 and 25 July, found in ibid., SPTLP, MC, with the quotation from the last of these. Mackenzie also reported that the Brazilian lawyers had advised against seeking legislation to confirm all the agreements, something unheard of in Brazil.

17 See BA, SPTLP, B. 24, Progress reports from the engineers dated Dec. 1899 to Feb. 1900, seven from Cooper on the powerplant (begun on 16 Sept. 1899), three from Harry Hartwell on the trolley work, and C.B. Graves to Brown, 10, 28 Feb. 1900, and the report on the transmission line from A. de Borba, 14 Feb. 1900

18 BA, SPTLP, MC, Pearson to A. Mackenzie, 19 Dec. 1899. This is also interesting as an early indication that Pearson, at any rate, recognized that in the long run the Canadian capital market could not finance such extensive schemes and that securities would ultimately have to be sold in England. The first quotation is from SPTLP Archives, São Paulo, Pearson to R.C. Brown, 19 Dec. 1899, a reference supplied by Duncan McDowall.

19 BA, SPTLP, B. 24, Mackenzie to Blake, Lash, Cassels, 24 May 1900

20 BA, SPTLP, MB, 2 Jan., 1 Feb. 1900. At the January meeting the company name was formally changed from São Paulo Railway to Tramway.

21 Ibid., B. 24, B.F. Pearson to Hanson Brothers, 14 Mar. 1900; 'List of Agreements Signed to Pool São Paulo Tramway, Light and Power Company Bonds for Sale at 95%, March 27, 1900'

Name:	Par value of bonds pooled:	Name:	Par value of bonds pooled:
W. Mackenzie	$790,000	T. Ahearn	$10,000
G.A. Cox	414,000	W.Y. Soper	10,000
B.F. Pearson	108,000	C. Porteous	10,000
W.B. Ross	130,000	D.H. Duncan	5,000
Hanson Brothers	100,000	W.P. Plummer	5,000

(Name):	(Par value of bonds pooled):	(Name):	(Par value of bonds pooled):
F. Nichols	$100,000	W.B. Torrance	$5,000
P. Burns	100,000	C.H. Kearney	5,000
D. McKeen	75,000	C.E. Hartwel	5,000
Wiley Smith	75,000	D.B. McTavish	1,000
M. Dwyer	75,000	Jno. White	15,000
Pellatt & Pellatt	25,000	J. Simmonds	15,000
H.M. Pellatt	19,000		
		Total pooled	2,097,000

Name:	Bonds not yet pooled:
J.W. Flavelle & A.E. Ames	$396,000
Provident Investment and Mortgage Co.	125,000
James Ross	100,000
W.M. Doul	80,000
T.E. Kenny	75,000
R.C. Brown	50,000
E.L. Pease & E. Heney	50,000
R.E. Harris	10,000
W.M. Botsford	5,000
Winnifred G. Burns	2,000
H. Fleming	10,000
Total not pooled	903,000
Total (both)	3,000,000

22 BA, SPTLP, B. 24, F.S. Pearson to Frederic Nicholls, 7 Apr. 1900; A. Mackenzie to Pearson, 1 May 1900. At the same time the suburban Santo Amaro steam railway was also acquired from its creditors for $28,000; see ibid., B. 31, R.C. Brown to William Mackenzie, 26 Mar. 1900.

23 BA, SPTLP, B. 24, A. Mackenzie to F.S. Pearson, 1 May 1900; Mackenzie to Blake, Lash and Cassels, 24 May, 1 June 1900; translation of article in *Correio Paulista* 8 May 1900

24 BA, SPTLP, MC, F.S. Pearson, London, to A. Mackenzie, 12 May 1900 and 19 May 1900 (from RMS *Lucania*)

25 BA, SPTLP, OD, Agreement between Banque française du Brésil (A. de Fischer) and São Paulo Tramway, Light and Power Company (W. Mackenzie), 22 June 1900; MC, Z.A. Lash to A. Mackenzie, 4 July 1900; B. 29, A. Mackenzie to F.S. Pearson, 19 July 1900

26 BA, SPTLP, B. 21½, Brown to J.M. Smith, 14 Dec. 1900

27 BA, SPTLP, B. 70, A. Mackenzie to F.S. Pearson, 26 Dec. 1900

28 BA, SPTLP, MB, 16, 17 Nov. 1900; MC, F.S. Pearson to A. Mackenzie, 31 Jan. 1901

29 Like Pearson, Leslie Perry was a graduate of Tufts and had worked for General Electric before being recruited to come to Brazil. He later joined the Pearson Engineering Company's staff. The letters that he and his wife wrote home from São Paulo were kindly made available to us by his son, Theodore H. Perry, of Neenah, Wisconsin. Quoted are Katherine R. Perry to her mother-in-law, 2 Apr. 1901, and to her mother, 12 May 1901.

30 BA, SPTLP, B. 38, F.S. Pearson to W. Mackenzie, 3 Mar. 1901

31 BA, SPTLP, OD, 'Project of a Unification Contract,' nd; MB, Front endpapers, 'Sundry Notes on the Unification Contract,' nd [17 July 1901]; MC, F.S. Pearson to A. Mackenzie, 13 July 1901; B. 29, A. Mackenzie to Z.A. Lash, 15 July 1901

32 Engineer Leslie Perry observed that the work on the powerplant and transmission line could have been completed sooner, but that supplies had been slow to arrive at the outset. Perry family papers (see n29 above), Perry to his family, 25 Nov. 1900

33 BA, SPTLP, B. 8, F.S. Pearson to Frederic Nicholls, 7 June 1901

34 Brown was not universally admired by his subordinates. According to Leslie Perry's wife, Katherine: 'One never knows when he will change his mind, and that is hard upon his men.' Perry family papers (see n29 above), Katherine Perry to her father, 13 Mar. 1901. When he left he was replaced by James Mitchell, who had been employed as General Electric's Brazilian agent.

35 For Mackenzie's views on the choice of a permanent manager see BA, SPTLP, B. 29, Mackenzie to Lash, 15 July 1901.

36 BA, SPTLP, OD, R.C. Brown to F.S. Pearson, 11 June, 8 July 1901; B. 31, D. Mulqueen to J.M. Smith, 12 Dec. 1901; B. 21, James Mitchell to SPTLP, Toronto, 16 Dec. 1901

37 BA, SPTLP, MB, 30 Apr. 1902, address of Vice-president Frederic Nicholls to shareholders meeting. SPTLP, Annual Report, 1902

38 BA, SPTLP, B. 21, James Mitchell to SPTLP, Toronto, 16 Dec. 1901. Eventually Pearson's longtime associate, Louis J. Hirt had to be sent down to put matters right in the spring of 1902. Perry family papers (see n29 above), Leslie Perry to his mother, 30 Mar. 1902

39 BA, BT, Pre-1923, 38, F.S. Pearson, Brattleboro, Mass., to J.M. Smith, 4 Aug. [1901]

40 SPTLP Archives, Pearson to Mitchell, 23 Nov. 1901; Pearson to Mitchell, 26 Sept. 1901

41 SPTLP Archives, Pearson to Mitchell, 31 Dec. 1901

42 BA, SPTLP, MC, Mitchell to SPTLP, Toronto, 14 Feb. 1902; Mitchell to A. Mackenzie, Toronto, 7 Mar. 1902; SPTLP Archives, Pearson to Mitchell, 24 June 1902. Pearson's letter follows on the heels of one in which he tells Mitchell that the company is in Brazil strictly for business and should avoid politics entirely.

43 BA, SPTLP, MB, 30 Apr., 16 July 1902; ibid., OD, Underwriting allotments for new shares, 17 July 1902, and underwriting agreement between SPTLP and A.E. Ames and Henry M. Pellatt, 17 July 1902. Stock prices may be followed in the *Annual Financial Review (Canadian)* comp. W.R. Houston.

44 SPTLP, Annual Report, 1902, Report of the President and Directors, 11 Apr. 1903; SPTLP Archives, F.S. Pearson to A. Mackenzie, São Paulo, 5 June 1903, is quoted.

45 See BA, SPTLP, B. 39, J.M. Smith to W. Mackenzie, 30 Mar. 1905.

46 BA, SPTLP, MB, 3, 29 Nov. 1904; 3,639 shares were subscribed for, the remaining 1,361 being disposed of to Dominion Securities, which earned a 1.5 per cent commission on them in addition to the 1 per cent commission it had earned as distributing agent for the entire issue.

47 BA, SPTLP, B. 41, Pearson to J.M. Smith, 29 June 1903; Pearson also forwarded the report of the British-controlled San Paulo Railway as a model, noting that it contained 'very little information.'

48 BA, SPTLP, B. 85, Report on São Paulo Tramway, Light and Power Company by F.S. Pearson, 15 Dec. 1905

49 BA, SPTLP, OD, Pearson to A. Mackenzie, 16 Apr. 1902

50 BA, SPTLP, B. 32½, E.R. Wood, London, to SPTLP, Toronto, 7 June 1905; Smith to Wood, 8 June 1905, Private; Statutory declaration by William Mackenzie and John Maitland Smith, 14 June 1905; F.A. Torrens-Johnson to the secretary, SPTLP, 25 July 1906

Chapter 4 Blame It on Rio

1 BA, SPTLP, OD, A. Mackenzie to E.R. Wood, 3 June 1902, and 'Memo as to terms upon which Alexander Mackenzie is to go to São Paulo,' nd, in Mackenzie's handwriting

2 BA, SPTLP, MC, Memorandum *re* 'Origin of the Rio Gas Company,' nd; ibid., RJTLP, A. 140, Memorandum *re* Gas Company, nd

3 BA, CF 0-7-1-41, A. Wangler to J.M. Bell, nd [Mar. 1934]. The four major companies were the Carros Urbanos, with a concession covering the central business district until 1930, the São Cristóvão line (franchised to 1950), the Villa Isabel system (franchised to 1945), and the scenic Carioca route up the mountain near the city's centre. The German-controlled Villa Isabel company also owned the Brazilianische Elektricitäts Gesellschaft, which had a thirty-year telephone franchise for the city (until 1929).

4 BA, RJTLP, A. 79, 'Memoranda Concerning the Construction Features of the Rio das Lages [sic] Dam and Power Plant,' by James D. Schuyler, 22 Nov. 1905

5 RJTLP Archives, Pearson to A. Mackenzie, 9 Apr., 5 Oct. 1903

6 RJTLP Archives, Pearson to A. Mackenzie, 9 Mar. 1904

7 BA, RJTLP, MB, 13 June, 2 Sept. 1904; RJTLP Archives, Pearson to A. Mackenzie, 4 Aug. 1904

8 See PAC, Bank of Montreal, MB, Reel M-158, 31 Mar. 1905, 22 Sept. 1905, 13 Nov. 1906; BA, SPTLP, B. 29, A. Mackenzie to J.M. Smith, 3 Dec. 1904; RJTLP, MB, 18 Nov., 10, 29 Dec. 1904.

9 BA, Brazilian Securities MB, 18 Nov. 1904; RJTLP, A. 39, 'Estimate of Cost of Construction, Earnings and Operations of Rio de Janeiro Tramway, Light and Power Co. Ltd.,' nd [1904–5]

10 We are grateful to Professor John D. Wirth of Stanford University for his helpful advice on Rio in this period. See also Jeffrey Needell, 'Making the Carioca Belle Epoch Concrete: The Urban Reforms of Rio de Janeiro under Pereira Passos,' *Journal of Urban History* 10 (1984) 383–422.

11 USNA, Minister's dispatches, Brazil, M 121, roll 73, D.E. Thomson to Secretary of State, 1 June 1905; BA, HD, A. Mackenzie to E.H. Blake, 2 May 1905; BA, RJTLP, A. 161, Memorandum *re* purchase of Carris Urbanos and São Cristóvão shares, nd [1905]; A. 166, Memorandum *re* Carioca line, nd [1905]

12 BA, RJTLP, A. 136, Pearson to Lash, 11 July 1905; Gow and Wood to Lash, 15 July 1905; RJTLP Archives, Gow to A. Mackenzie, 15 July 1905

13 BA, RJTLP, A. 151, 'To the Shareholders and Bondholders of the Gas Company of Rio ('La Société de Gaz de Rio') from E. Stallaerts and A. Loewenstein and Witteroos and Co.,' June 1905; A. 93, Walter Gow to RJTLP, Toronto, 10 Aug. 1905; A. 12, Gow to Lash, 17 Oct. 1905

14 BA, RJTLP, A. 39, Pearson to W. Mackenzie, 1 Sept. 1905; A. 44, F.A. Huntress to J.M. Smith, 3 Oct. 1905 (quoted); CF 0-7-1-41, Memorandum to the President and Board of Directors of the Rio de Janeiro Tramway, Light and Power Company, by F.S. Pearson, Vice-president, 15 Dec. 1905

15 BA, RJTLP, A. 78, Pearson to E.R. Wood, 31 Oct. 1905, Confidential
16 BA, CF 0-7-1-41, Memorandum to the President and Board of Directors of the Rio de Janeiro Tramway, Light and Power Company by F.S. Pearson, Vice-president, 15 Dec. 1905
17 BA, SPTLP, B. 40, James D. Schuyler to Pearson, 22 Nov. 1905; MB, 20 Dec. 1905; CF 0-7-1-41, Report on São Paulo Tramway, Light and Power Company, by F.S. Pearson, 1 Oct. 1906, Private and Confidential
18 BA, SPTLP, B. 27, R.J. Clark to J.M. Smith, 2 Oct. 1907
19 BA, CF 0-7-1-41, Report on São Paulo Tramway, Light and Power Company by F.S. Pearson, 1 Oct. 1906, Private and Confidential; SPTLP, B. 74, R.P. Ormsby to Z.A. Lash, 20 Nov. 1906 (quoting Pearson)
20 BA, SPTLP, B. 29, J.M. Smith to A. Mackenzie, 2 Mar. 1906; CF 0-7-1-41, Report on São Paulo Tramway, Light and Power Company by F.S. Pearson, 1 Oct. 1906, Private and Confidential; SPTLP, B. 39, J.M. Smith to E.R. Wood, 28 Nov. 1906; Smith to W. Mackenzie, 29 Nov. 1906
21 BA, RJTLP, A. 73, Wood to Pearson, 11 Dec. 1905; A. 34, J.B. Kenny to RJTLP, Toronto, 4 Dec. 1905; J.M. Smith to Kenny, 13 Dec. 1905
22 BA, CF 0-7-1-41, Report on the Rio de Janeiro Tramway, Light and Power Company by F.S. Pearson, 1 Oct. 1906, Private and Confidential
23 RJTLP Archives, Pearson to A. Mackenzie, 2 May 1906; A. Mackenzie to Dr Alcindo Guanabara, 15 May 1906
24 BA, CF 0-7-1-41, Report on the Rio de Janeiro Tramway, Light and Power Company by F.S. Pearson, 1 Oct. 1906, Private and Confidential
25 BA, RJTLP, A. 60, A. Mackenzie to J.M. Smith, 6 Nov. 1906; RJTLP Archives, A. Mackenzie to Pearson, 17 Nov. 1906 (two letters quoted)
26 BA, CF 0-7-1-41, Report on the Rio de Janeiro Tramway, Light and Power Company by F.S. Pearson, 1 Oct. 1906, Private and Confidential
27 RJTLP Archives, Pearson to A. Mackenzie, 20 Nov. 1906; A. Mackenzie to Lash, 20 Nov. 1906
28 BA, RJTLP, MB, 13 July 1906: Nicholls made it clear that as the purchase of subsidiaries and the revision of franchises was still under way 'it is not intended to print this report or to allow it to go out to the public in any way.' No balance sheet was presented.
29 BA, CF 0-7-1-41, Report on the Rio de Janeiro Tramway, Light and Power Company by F.S. Pearson, 1 Oct. 1906, Private and Confidential; RJTLP, A. 44, F.A. Huntress to J.M. Smith, 7 Nov., 5 Dec. 1906
30 BA, RJTLP, A. 60, A. Mackenzie to J.M. Smith, 6 Nov. 1906; A. 44, F.A. Huntress to Smith, 5 Dec. 1906
31 BA, CF 0-7-1-41, Report on the Rio de Janeiro Tramway, Light and Power Company by F.S. Pearson, 1 Oct. 1906, Private and Confidential; PRO, FO 368, vol. 92, no. 20902, Arthur Chapman to Sir Edward Grey, 5 June 1907, Confidential

32 PRO, FO 368, vol. 92, no. 22503, William Haggard to Grey, 13 June 1907, Confidential
33 PRO, FO 128, vol. 314, Haggard to Grey, 12 July 1907; RJTLP Archives, A. Mackenzie to F.S. Pearson, 20 Aug. 1907
34 RJTLP Archives, John B. Orr to Pearson, 11 Apr. 1904
35 BA, CF 0-7-1-41, Report on the Rio de Janeiro Tramway, Light and Power Company by F.S. Pearson, 1 Oct. 1906, Private and Confidential
36 RJTLP Archives, A. Mackenzie to Pearson, 3 Apr. 1907
37 BA, RJTLP, A. 42, A. Mackenzie to Pearson, 1 May 1907
38 BA, RJTLP, A. 60, A. Mackenzie to J.M. Smith, 4 May 1907; RJTLP Archives, A. Mackenzie to Pearson, 20 Aug., 4 Sept. 1907; Pearson to A. Mackenzie, 3 Oct. 1907; Pearson to A.B. Slater, 20 Nov. 1907
39 BA, RJTLP, A. 74, 'Estimate of the Cost of the Rio das Lages [sic] Hydraulic Development, Electrification of the Rio City Railways, and Power and Light Distribution, The Rio de Janeiro Tramway, Light and Power Company, F.S. Pearson, Dr. Sc., Consulting Engineer,' 1 May 1906; CF 0-7-1-41, Report on the Rio de Janeiro Tramway, Light and Power Company by F.S. Pearson, 1 Oct. 1906, Private and Confidential
40 BA, SPTLP, B. 37, Sperling and Company to SPTLP, 1 Feb. 1905; ibid., RJTLP, A. 53, J.H. Dunn and Co. to J.M. Smith, 9 Nov. 1905. On Horne-Payne and Mackenzie see T.D. Regehr, *The Canadian Northern Railway, Pioneer Road of the Northern Prairies, 1895–1918* (Toronto: Macmillan, 1976) 101–2.
41 BA, SPTLP, 21, British Empire Trust Company, *Record of Successful Enterprise and Profitable Investment in Canada* (nd) [July 1910]
42 BA, RJTLP, A. 68, Horne-Payne to J.M. Smith, 31 January 1906
43 BA, RJTLP, A. 80, Smith to Horne-Payne, 8 Feb. 1906
44 BA, RJTLP, A. 19, Massey Morris, Bank of Commerce, to J.M. Smith, 7 Sept. 1906; RJTLP, MB, Agendas and Papers, Memorandum from Z.A. Lash, A.W. Mackenzie, Frederic Nicholls, 20 Sept. 1906; MB, 17 Nov. 1906
45 RJTLP Archives, Pearson to A. Mackenzie, 30 Nov. 1906
46 BA, RJTLP, A. 27, Horne-Payne to Pearson, 23 Jan. 1907; PAC, DP, vol. 249, Dunn to Pearson, 15 Aug. 1906
47 PAC, DP, vol. 7, Horne-Payne to Dunn, 27 Feb. 1907, Personal; vol. 252, Dunn to Horne-Payne, 27 Feb. 1907; RJTLP Archives, Horne-Payne to W. Mackenzie, 6 Aug. 1907; BA, RJTLP, A. 130, RJTLP to J.M. Smith, London, 26 Sept. 1907, quoting Horne-Payne
48 RJTLP Archives, Pearson to A. Mackenzie, 31 July 1907
49 BA, RJTLP, A. 19, M. Morris to J.M. Smith, 22 Apr., 3, 18 May 1907
50 BA, RJTLP, A. 130½, W. Mackenzie to E.R. Wood, London, 9 July 1907; W. Mackenzie to Horne-Payne, 10 July 1907; Wood to W. Mackenzie, 10 July 1907; Horne-Payne to Mackenzie, 11 July 1907; A. 73, T.D. Semon to L.J. Hirt, 18 July 1907; Hirt to J.M. Smith, 18 July 1907

51 BA, RJTLP, A. 73, J.M. Smith to F.S. Pearson, 18 July 1907; A. 110, Memorandum *re* material delivered but not yet paid for, 26 July 1907; RJTLP Archives, Pearson to A. Mackenzie, 31 July 1907; same to same, 29 Aug. enclosing Horne-Payne to W. Mackenzie, 6 Aug. 1907; A. Mackenzie to Pearson, 2 Sept. 1907

52 RJTLP Archives, Pearson to A. Mackenzie, 29 Aug., 3 Oct. 1907

53 BA, SPTLP, B. 27, Clark to J.M. Smith, 21 Sept., 2 Oct., 5 Nov. 1907

54 BA, SPTLP, MB, 6 Apr. 1908; B. 27, Memorandum from R.J. Clark, 12 May 1908; SPTLP Archives, Pearson LB, Pearson to W.N. Walmsley, 29 Apr. 1908

55 BA, RJTLP, MB, 25 July, 2 Aug. 1907; A. 19, J.M. Smith to B.E. Walker, 31 July 1907; A. 130, R.P. Ormsby to Z.A. Lash, 24 Aug. 1907; A. 73, Pearson to Smith, 22 Aug. 1907; Smith to L.J. Hirt, 22 Aug. 1907; Hirt to Smith, 6 Sept. 1907

56 BA, RJTLP, A. 73, Pearson to Smith, 20, 21 Sept. 1907; L.J. Hirt to Smith, 26 Nov. 1907; Smith to Hirt, 27 Nov., 10 Dec. 1907, Smith to Pearson, 29 Nov. 1907; A. 130, Smith to Hirt, 27 29 Oct. 1907; Hirt to Smith, 28 Oct. 1907; A. 124, Hirt to G.G. Benfield, Nov. 1907; W.P. Plummer to Smith, 3 Dec. 1907

57 BA, RJTLP, A. 56, G.G. Benfield to Smith, 29 Oct. 1907; A. 73, Smith to Pearson, 2 Oct. 1907; MB, 14,15 Oct., 27 Nov. 1907

58 RJTLP Archives, R.J. Clark to A. Mackenzie, 1 Nov. 1907; Pearson to A. Mackenzie, 21 Nov. 1907

59 BA, RJTLP, A. 19, Smith to Pearson, 7 Dec. 1907; Smith to Walter Gow, 4 Dec. 1907: A. 44, E.D. Trowbridge to Smith, 4 Dec. 1907; RJTLP Archives, A. Mackenzie to W.H. Blake, 4 Jan. 1908

60 BA, RJTLP, A. 56, G.G. Benfield to J.M. Smith, 28 Jan. 1908; MB, 28 Mar., 15 Sept. 1908

61 BA, RJTLP, A. 36, Pearson to J.M. Smith, 28 May 1908

62 BA, RJTLP, Pearson to Fleming, 28 Apr. 1908; Fleming to Pearson, 26 May, 3 June, 30 July 1908; MB, 23 June 1908; A. 134, Deutsche Bank to Pearson, 9 Apr. 1908; Pearson to Smith, 17 June 1908

63 BA, RJTLP, A. 37, Pearson to Smith, 4 June 1908; A. 111, Smith to ? [Pearson], nd [4 June 1908]

64 BA, RJTLP, MB, 14 Apr. 1908; 15 Sept. 1908, report of the directors to the annual meeting; A. 60, A. Mackenzie to J.M. Smith, 25 May 1908; A. 73, Pearson to Smith, 7 Aug. 1908

65 BA, RJTLP, MB, 29 Apr., 3 July, 15 Sept. 1908

66 BA, RJTLP, A. 74, Pearson to E.R. Wood, 10 Mar. 1908, enclosing a memorandum dated 22 Feb. 1908

67 BA, SPTLP, Annual Report, 1908, 1909; MB, 26 Jan. 1909; Pre-1923, 77, E.R. Wood to R.M. Horne-Payne, 22 Sept. 1910

68 RJTLP Archives, A. Mackenzie to W.H. Blake, 4 Jan. 1908

69 BA, SPTLP, B. 31, A. Mackenzie to W. Mackenzie, 1 Feb. 1906;
   CF 0-7-1-31, Report on São Paulo Tramway, Light and Power Company
   by F.S. Pearson, 1 Oct. 1906, Private and Confidential; Annual Report,
   1909
70 BA, RJTLP, MB, 16 Sept. 1908, report of third annual meeting
71 BA, RJTLP, A. 74, F.S. Pearson to E.R. Wood, 6 Mar. 1908; MB, 27 Mar.
   1909, circular to shareholders; 6 Aug. 1909, report to fourth annual meeting;
   30 Dec. 1909
72 BA, RJTLP, Pre-1923, 69, Pearson to E.R. Wood, 16 Jan. 1911; MB, 3 May
   1911
73 BA, RJTLP, Pre-1923, 47, Pearson to J.M. Smith, 27 Sept. 1911;
   CF 0-7-1-41, Memorandum re 'Services of Dr. Abel Vargas,'
   Confidential, nd [Mar. 1934]; RJTLP Archives, A. Mackenzie to Pearson,
   29 Sept. 1911
74 BA, BT, Pre-1923, 88, F. A. Huntress to Sir William Mackenzie, 23 June 1915,
   gives a list of the Guinle concessions.
75 BA, BT, Pre-1923, 90, A. Mackenzie to Sir William Mackenzie, 11 May 1915
76 A, CF 0-7-1-41, Report on São Paulo Tramway, Light and Power Company by
   F.S. Pearson, 1 Oct. 1906, Private and Confidential

Chapter 5 Falling Out in Mexico

1 PRO, FO 368, vol. 32, file 27699, W.G. Muller to Sir Edward Grey, 26 July
  1906. Portions of this chapter appeared in our article, 'A Curious Capital
  Flow: Canadian Investment in Mexico, 1902–1910,' *Business History Review*
  58 (1984) 178–203.
2 In his manuscript biography of Pearson, 'The Yankee Spirit,' Stearns
  Morse gives a romantic account of Pearson's discovery of this waterfall
  250–2. Morse drew mainly upon oral tradition within the family. According
  to this account Pearson was sent to Mexico by the Bank of Montreal,
  which had been contacted previously by Vacquie. That may be, although
  we think the possibility outlined here is more likely, since Vacquie
  had no previous connections with the Bank of Montreal. Pearson's options
  are recorded in MLP, MB, 13 Oct. 1902.
3 MLP, MB, 13 Oct. 1902, for extensions to the option and the organization of
  the company in Halifax
4 Ibid., 19 Jan. 1903, for the cancellation of the first agreement and the terms of
  the new one
5 Ibid., 13 May 1903; *Canadian Engineer* (Feb. 1903) 56
6 MLP, MB, 19 Jan., 18 Mar. 1903
7 Ibid., 20 Jan. 1903
8 Ibid., 15 Mar. 1903

9 PRO, FO 50, vol. 505, Lionel Carden to the Marquis of Salisbury, 9 June 1896; vols 521 and 523 for the Anthony Gibbs and Co. protests against the Siemens and Halske invasion of its territory. On the background of Anthony Gibbs and Co. see D.C.M. Platt, ed., *Business Imperialism, 1840–1930* (Oxford: Oxford University Press, 1977) 337–70, and W.M. Mathews, *The House of Gibbs and the Peruvian Guano Monopoly* (London: Royal Historical Society, 1981).

10 MLP, MB, 13 May–20 Nov. 1903

11 John P. McKay, *Tramways and Trolleys* (Princeton: Princeton University Press, 1976) 78–9, 125–62; see also T. Hughes, *Networks of Power* (Baltimore: Johns Hopkins University Press, 1983) 175–200

12 MLP, MB, 9 Oct. 1903

13 MLP, MB, 18 Mar. 1903; Interim Report, 1906

14 Ibid., 10 Feb., 29 Nov. 1904

15 ibid., 21 Dec. 1904, 17 Apr., 5, 19, 20 June, 17 Aug. 1905

16 The parent company then leased the Mexican Electric Light property; MLP, MB, 18 Oct. 1905, 21 Aug. 1906

17 Memorandum in Regard to the Electrical Light and Power Situation in the City of Mexico, printed in lieu of an annual report in the *Annual Financial Review* (*Canadian*), comp. W.R. Houston, 1906, 172–5

18 *Annual Financial Review* 1907, 263–4; Interim Report, 1906

19 MLP, MB, 19 Dec. 1903, 4 Mar., 15 Apr., 31 Aug., 7 Apr. 1904, 7 Apr. 1905, 19 June, 17 Aug. 1905, 10 Apr. 1906; *Annual Financial Review* 1907, 263–4. Limantour and Mancera were identified as being friends of the company on the Water Commission.

20 For details of these negotiations see the MET, MB, 30 Nov. 1904; 3, 17, 24, 31 May, 7, 12, 28 June, 19 July, 30 Aug., 14, 20, 26 Sept., 9 Oct. 1905.

21 *Annual Financial Review* 1907, 265

22 MLP, MB, 24 Oct. 1904, contains an extraordinary verbatim interrogation of Hugh Cooper on the date Necaxa power would be delivered (he promised June 1905) and when the storage dams would be fully effective (he said January 1906). The death of Cooper's wife, the impossibility of meeting those deadlines, and friction with Pearson led to Cooper's release in December 1904.

23 MLP, MB, 29 Nov. 1904

24 Prospectus, Mexican Light and Power Company, 15 May 1903, printed in the *Annual Financial Review* 1903, 264–6.

25 MLP, MB, 21 June, 23 July, 18 Oct. 1905; 10 Apr., 21 Aug., 21 Nov. 1906; 28 Jan., 8 July, 30 Aug. 1907; PAC, Bank of Montreal Papers, M-158, Directors MB, 20 June 1905; 18 Aug. 1905; 13 Mar. 1906; 23 Nov. 1906; 29 Jan. 1907, for loans to the Mexican Light and Power Company and purchases of its securities

26 HLRO, Beaverbrook, A, vols 4, 7, Aitken to W.D. Ross, 18 June 1904; Ross to Aitken, 29 June 1905

27 *Annual Financial Review* 1907, 264–5; Annual Report, 1907

28 MET, MB, May 1898–Aug. 1902. Breitmeyer along with the company secretary, S.W. Jameson, took charge of day-to-day affairs; On Wernher and Beit see Geoffrey Wheatcroft, *The Randlords* (London: Weidenfeld and Nicolson, 1985).

29 P.H. Emden, *Randlords* (London: Hodder and Stoughton, 1935); Robert V. Kubicek, *Economic Imperialism in Theory and Practice* (Durham: Duke University Press, 1979), especially 53–85; Brian Roberts, *The Diamond Magnates* (London: Hamish Hamilton, 1972). MET, Annual meetings, 11 June 1902, 28 May 1903, 9 June 1904, 27 Sept. 1905

30 MET, MB, 9 May 1906; Ninth Annual General Meeting, 24 May 1906, at which a disgruntled minority shareholder, Alfred Parrish, complained bitterly of the directors' sell-out just as the company seemed on the verge of making money. He would subsequently launch a troublesome lawsuit that would be a thorn in the side of the Pearson group in London for some time thereafter.

31 PRO, FO 368, vol. 32, file 27699, W.G. Muller to Grey, 26 July 1906

32 PAC, DP, vol. 6, F.S. Pearson to James Dunn, 9 Mar. 1906, and HLRO, Beaverbrook, A, vol. 13, Aitken to C.H. Cahan, 30 Apr. 1906; MET, MB, Report of eighth Annual Meeting, 27 Sept. 1905

33 PAC, DP, vol. 249, James Dunn to Hans Schuster, 26 Mar. 1906; Dunn to Percival Farquhar, 30 Mar. 1906

34 PAC, DP, vol. 248, James Dunn to A.E. Dyment, 30 Apr. 1906. This operating company then leased the property of the Mexico Tramways Company, which was kept in existence on account of a few minority shareholders. MTC, MB, 20 Mar.–2 May 1906

35 PAC, DP, vol. 249, James Dunn to Pearson, 5 Apr. 1906; vol. 6, Sperling and Co, to Dunn, 2 Apr. 1906, Confidential; F.S. Pearson to Dunn, 18 Apr. 1906

36 Ibid., vol. 1, James Dunn to Dunfisco, London, 9, 26 May 1906; vol. 248, Dunn to William Mackenzie, 30 May 1906, Personal; vol. 5, C.L. Fischer to Dunn, 1 July 1906

37 MET, MB, 20 June 1906; PAC, DP, vol. 248, James Dunn to C.L. Fischer, 30 May 1906; Dunn to F.S. Pearson, 31 May 1906

38 MTC, MB, 8 Jan. 1908 for dividend. Unfortunately these minutes, composed in the offices of Blake, Lash and Cassels to meet the minimum requirements of Canadian company law, contain very little information about decision making or operations.

39 MLP, Annual Report, 1907; MB, 8 June 1908

40 PAC, DP, vol. 252, James Dunn to Percival Farquhar, 26 Feb. 1908

41 PRO, FO 371, vol. 480, file 20324, Reginald Tower to Sir Edward Grey, 29 May 1908, Confidential

42 PAC, DP, vol. 11, F.S. Pearson to James Dunn, 5 Aug. 1908; MLP, MB, 5 Aug. 1908; MET, MB, 7 Aug. 1908, for Pearson and Lash's authorization to negotiate, given some time after negotiations had begun

43 MLP, MB, 22, 28 Sept. 1908; PRO, FO 371, vol. 480, file 20324, Reginald Tower to Sir Edward Grey, 14 Nov. 1908, reports on Cahan's and Pearson's comings and goings.

44 PAC, DP, vol. 12, F.S. Pearson to Dunn, 25 Nov. 1908

45 HLRO, Beaverbrook, A, vol. 28, Aitken to John Scrimgeour, 19 Dec. 1908; Aitken to Dr J.E. Mortimer, 30 Dec. 1908

46 *Monetary Times* 12 Dec. 1908; 9, 16 Jan. 1909; Montreal *Star* Dec. 1908–Feb. 1909; MB, 3, 30 Dec. 1908.

47 *Monetary Times* 16 Jan. 1909; MLP, MB, 4 Jan. 1909

48 A.E. Ames and Company Archives, Company Files, Mexican Light and Power Company, Memorandum from Sir George Drummond to the Shareholders, 25 Jan. 1909.

49 Montreal *Star* 17 Feb. 1909; MB, 17 Feb. 1909

50 MLP, MB, 17 Feb. 1909. The Mexico Tramways side of this is reported only briefly at a 16 Jan. 1909 board meeting. Pearson covered the Bank of Montreal called loan with a £500,000 loan from the Bank of Scotland, MTC, MB, 25 Jan. 1909

51 *The Statist* 25 Sept. 1909; PAC, DP, vol. 19, F.S. Pearson to Dunn, 3 Aug. 1909

Chapter 6 The Money Spinner

1 These 1895 trade figures are given in the *Journal of Commerce* 5 Feb. 1897, 168–9

2 E.P. Neufeld, *The Financial System of Canada: Its Growth and Development* (Toronto: Macmillan, 1972) 125

3 PRO, CO 295, vol. 399, file 21350, Petition of William Chapman, James Hutchinson, B.F. Pearson, and C.H. Cahan, 16 Feb. 1900

4 PRO, CO 295, vol. 610, Sir Augustus Hemming to Joseph Chamberlain, 9 Oct. 1899; Crown Agents for the Colonies to Hemming, 9 Nov. 1899

5 PRO, CO 295, vol. 399, file 21350, Sir Hubert Jermingham to Chamberlain, 19 June 1900, enclosing the original petition and the report of the select committee dated 5 June 1900. The Board of Trade had to approve all electrical franchises under the Imperial Electric Lighting (Clauses) Act of 1899.

6 *Journal of Commerce* 8 Mar. 1901, 593; *Annual Financial Review (Canadian)*, comp. W.R. Houston, 1904; HLRO, Beaverbrook, G, vol. 1, Aitken to H.M. Synder, 5 July 1902

7 Lord Beaverbrook, *My Early Life* (Fredericton, N.B.: Brunswick Press, 1965); A.J.P. Taylor, *Beaverbrook* (London: Hamish Hamilton, 1972) 17, records that Aitken himself claimed to have met Stairs on a train, another story being that the young man tried to sell him a typewriter.

8 Tom Driberg, *Beaverbrook: A Study in Power and Frustration* (London: Weidenfeld and Nicolson, 1956) 43

9 HLRO, Beaverbrook, G, vol. 1, Aitken to H.M. Snyder, 5, 24 July 1902; ibid., Aitken to [?] Archbold, 16 Sept. 1902: Aitken to [?] Collas, 20 Oct. 1902

10 Royal Securities Corporation, Historical Documents, 'Memorandum of Association and Bylaws of Royal Securities Corporation Limited, Incorporated under the Nova Scotia Companies Act, April 18th, 1903,' in the possession of Merrill Lynch Canada, Inc., which kindly permitted us to examine these documents relating to one of its predecessor companies

11 HLRO, Beaverbrook, A, vol. 2, E.L. Thorne to R.E. Harris, 7 Apr. 1903; Aitken to Senator Josiah Wood, 13 July 1903

12 HLRO, Beaverbrook, A, vol. 1, A.E. Ames to Aitken, 23 May 1903; Aitken to Ames, 28 May 1903, Confidential

13 HLRO, Beaverbrook, A, vol. 2, Aitken to John Stairs, 12 June 1903 (two letters)

14 HLRO, Beaverbrook, A, vol. 2, Royal Securities to W.H. Rodgers, 11 Sept. 1903

15 Henry J. Morgan, ed., *Canadian Men and Women of the Time* (Toronto: William Briggs, 1912); Michael Bliss, *A Canadian Millionaire: The Life and Business Times of Sir Joseph Flavelle, Bart., 1858–1939* (Toronto: Macmillan, 1978) 74–5

16 HLRO, Beaverbrook, A, vol. 2, Aitken to W.D. Ross, 28 Sept. 1903

17 HLRO, Beaverbrook, A, vol. 1, Aitken to Graham Fraser, 7 Dec. 1903

18 HLRO, Beaverbrook, A, vol. 2, contains options from such prominent Maritimers as the leader of the federal Conservative party, R.L. Borden, Nova Scotia Premier George Murray, stockbrokers J.C. Mackintosh and F.B. McCurdy, and industrialist Nathaniel A. Curry, as well as the incorporators of the Royal Securities Corporation themselves; see also Aitken to Senator Josiah Wood, 13 July 1903, and Aitken to R. Wilson-Smith and Co., 19 Dec. 1903, in ibid., vol. 1.

19 HLRO, Beaverbrook, A, vol. 1, W.D. Ross to Aitken, 8 Dec. 1903; Aitken to Dr E.A. Kirkpatrick, 14 Dec. 1903

20 HLRO, Beaverbrook, A, vol. 2, Aitken to Robb, 23 Dec. 1903, and a similar letter to Vice-president William Gordon Gordon in Trinidad, dated 22 Dec. 1903, in ibid., vol. 1

21 HLRO, Beaverbrook, A, vol. 2, Aitken to D.W. Robb, 23 Dec. 1903

22 The company was guaranteed favourable publicity in Halifax by the *Herald* editor's ownership of 100 shares of stock in it. W.R. McCurdy also forwarded to Aitken clippings from the Saint John *Sun*, the Montreal *Gazette*, *Herald*, and *Star*, and the Toronto *Mail*. See HLRO, Beaverbrook, A, vol. 1, W.R. McCurdy to Aitken, 25 Dec. 1903.

23 HLRO, Beaverbrook, A, vol. 4, Aitken to Trinidad Electric, 1 Oct. 1904; W.B. Ross to Aitken, 10 Oct. 1904; Aitken to W.D. Ross, 28 October 1904; G, vol. 4, file 31, Agreement between the Trinidad Electric Company and W.M. Aitken, 5 Nov. 1904

24 HLRO, Beaverbrook, A, vol. 3, McCuaig Bros and Co. to Aitken, 13 Oct. (Personal), 8 Nov. 1904; Aitken to Clarence McCuaig, 11 Nov. 1904; McCuaig to Aitken, 17 Nov. 1904

25 HLRO, Beaverbrook, A, vol. 4, Aitken to W.D. Ross, 18 Nov. 1904 (quoted); Aitken to F.C. Clarke, 21 Nov. 1904

26 HLRO, Beaverbrook, A, vol. 18, Aitken to Cahan, 17 Apr. 1905

27 HLRO, Beaverbrook, A, vol. 3, Edward Cronyn to Aitken, 7 Oct. 1904; Aitken to Cronyn, 14, 15 Nov. 1904.

28 HLRO, Beaverbrook, A, vol. 7, Aitken to W.D. Ross, 3 Jan. 1905; Royal Securities, Historical Documents, fragment of minutes, nd [1904]

29 Royal Securities, Historical Documents, extract of MB, nd [Nov. 1905]; certificate from registrar of companies, Nova Scotia, 22 Nov. 1905. W.D. Ross was allotted 50 shares at par. Aitken owned 140 of the 1,000 shares; see HLRO, Beaverbrook, A, vol. 6, Aitken to Aitken [sic], 14 Nov. 1905 (two letters).

30 HLRO, Beaverbrook, G, vol. 18, Aitken to C.H. Cahan, 17 Apr. 1905

31 HLRO, Beaverbrook, A, vol. 5, Aitken to David Burke, 13 May, 3 June 1905; vol. 6, Aitken to Aitken [sic], 25 May 1905

32 HLRO, Beaverbrook, A, vol. 6, B.F. Pearson to Aitken, nd and 26 June 1905.

33 HLRO, Beaverbrook, A, vol. 6, [illegible] to W.W. Russell, Caracas, 13 June 1905; Aitken to G.F. Pearson, 14 Aug. 1905

34 HLRO, Beaverbrook, A, vol. 7, Aitken to W.D. Ross, 5 June 1905

35 HLRO, Beaverbrook, A, vol. 7, A.K. McLean to W.D. Ross, 30 Oct. 1905 (quoted); Aitken to F.W. Teele, 30 Oct., 11 Dec. 1905; W.B. Ross to Aitken, 5 Dec. 1905

36 HLRO, Beaverbrook, A, vol. 6, Harris to Aitken, 17 Aug. 1905; vol. 5, Aitken to James S. Harding, 17 Oct. 1905

37 Harris was annoyed because he thought that Royal Securities was beginning to encroach upon the business of Eastern Trust of which he was a director. See HLRO, Beaverbrook, A, vol. 6, Aitken to W.B. Ross, 29 Sept. 1905, Private and Confidential.

38 HLRO, Beaverbrook, A, vol. 5, Aitken to J.S. Harding, 7 Oct. 1905; Aitken to Van Horne, 16 Nov. 1905; vol. 6, Aitken to Teele, 6 Dec. 1905; vol. 10, Aitken to Teele, 6 Jan. 1906; vol. 36, Aitken to Vincent H. Meredith, 31 Mar. 1909

39 HLRO, Beaverbrook, A, vol. 10, Aitken to Teele, 5 Jan. 1906

40 HLRO, Beaverbrook, A, vol. 10, Aitken to Teele, 6 Jan. 1906

41 HLRO, Beaverbrook, A, vol. 6, Teele to Aitken, 14 Nov. 1905

42 HLRO, Beaverbrook, A, vol. 6, Aitken to Teele, 6 Dec. 1905

43 HLRO, Beaverbrook, A, vol. 5, Aitken to Van Horne, 16 Nov. 1905; vol. 6, Aitken to Teele, 6 Dec. 1905

44 HLRO, Beaverbrook, A, vol. 28, Aitken to Edward Stairs, 14 Apr. 1908

45 Teele pointed out to Aitken that when they had discussed putting it on a 3 per cent earning basis they had not taken into account the interest on the then unissued $25,000 worth of 5 per cent bonds from the original issue plus the 6 per cent on the $100,000 worth of second mortgage bonds. Together these added $7,250 per year to the company's costs. See HLRO, Beaverbrook, A, vol. 6, Teele to Aitken, 30 Dec. 1905.

46 HLRO, Beaverbrook, A, vol. 9, Van Horne to Aitken, 10 Feb. 1906; vol. 10, Teele to Aitken, 4 Apr. 1906, Personal; Teele to F.H. Oxley, 7 Nov. 1906

47 HLRO, Beaverbrook, A, vol. 10, Aitken to Teele, 19 Oct. 1906 (quoted), and vol. 17, Aitken to Teele, 31 May 1907; vol. 14, Aitken to Van Horne, 25 May 1907; PRO, CO 111, vol. 558, file 15639, Judgement of the Judicial Committee on the appeal of Demerara Electric Company v. White and others from the Supreme Court of British Guiana, 26 Apr. 1907

48 HLRO, Beaverbrook, A, vol. 14, Aitken to R.E. Harris, 11 Oct. 1907; vol. 11, H. Bradford to Aitken, 6, 19 Dec. 1907

49 PRO, CO 111, vol. 560, F.M. Hodgson to Lord Elgin, 13 Jan. 1908; HLRO, Beaverbrook, A, vol. 11, Aitken to H. Bradford, 12 Dec. 1907; vol. 36, Aitken to H. Vincent Meredith, 31 Mar. 1909

50 HLRO, Beaverbrook, A, vol. 36, Aitken to H. Vincent Meredith, 31 Mar. 1909; vol. 37, F.C. Clarke to shareholders of Demerara Electric, 15 Apr. 1909 (printed circular)

51 HLRO, Beaverbrook, A, vol. 6, Aitken to W.P. Plummer, 6 Dec. 1905; vol. 7, Aitken to W.D. Ross, 21 Nov. 1905

52 HLRO, Beaverbrook, A, vol. 6, Plummer to Aitken, 29 Dec. 1905; vol. 9, Aitken to W.B. Ross, 11 Jan. 1906

53 HLRO, Beaverbrook, A, vol. 9, Aitken to W.B. Ross, 11 Jan. 1906

54 HLRO, Beaverbrook, A, vol. 9, Aitken to P.G. Gossler, J.G. White and Co., 11 Jan. 1906

55 HLRO, Beaverbrook, A, vol. 10, Aitken to Teele, 13 Jan. 1906; vol. 8, Aitken to H.P. Bruce, 26 Jan. 1906; vol. 14, Carbo to Aitken, 31 Mar., 9 Apr. (two letters) 1906; Aitken to Carbo, 27 Apr. 1906

56 HLRO, Beaverbrook, A, vol. 8, Aitken to Cahan, 12 Jan. 1906; vol. 10, Aitken to Teele, 16 Jan. 1906; vol. 9, Aitken to Plummer, 16 Jan. 1906

57 HLRO, Beaverbrook, A, vol. 10, Teele to Aitken, 23 Mar. 1906

58 HLRO, Beaverbrook, A, vol. 6, Aitken to Teele, 6 Dec. 1905; vol. 9, Aitken and Teele to the Matanzas syndicate, Halifax, 20 Feb. 1906

59 HLRO, Beaverbrook, A, vol. 9, Aitken to C.E. Mackenzie, 15 Mar. 1906

60 HLRO, Beaverbrook, A, vol. 10, Teele to Aitken, 12 Apr. 1906; vol. 8, Aitken to A.E. Ames, 4 Oct. 1906
61 HLRO, Beaverbrook, A, vol. 9, Aitken to R.E. Harris, 25 Apr. 1906; vol. 13, Aitken to Cahan, 30 Apr. 1906
62 HLRO, Beaverbrook, A, vol. 8, Aitken to W.D. Ross, 26 Apr. 1906 (quoted); vol. 9, Aitken to R.E. Harris, 25 Apr. 1906
63 HLRO, Beaverbrook, A, vol. 8, Aitken to A.E. Ames, 4 Oct. 1906; vol. 13, Aitken to Cahan, 30 Apr. 1906
64 HLRO, Beaverbrook, A, vol. 11, Aitken to Charles Archibald, 18 June 1907; vol. 13, Aitken to W.M. Botsford, 15 June 1906
65 HLRO, Beaverbrook, A, vol. 10, Aitken to W.D. Ross, 3 May 1906; vol. 9, Van Horne to Aitken, June 15, 1906.
66 HLRO, Beaverbrook, A, vol. 10, Aitken to Teele, 12 June 1906; vol. 8, B.G. Burrill to Aitken, 17 Sept. 1906
67 HLRO, Beaverbrook, A, vol. 13, Aitken to C.H. Cahan, 30 Apr. 1906
68 HLRO, Beaverbrook, A, vol. 8, Aitken to E.G. Kenny, 11 Oct. 1906. Kenny ran Commercial Trust in Halifax, and Aitken asked him not to pass on these views to his associates, W.B. Ross and H.A. Lovett.
69 HLRO, Beaverbrook, A, vol. 1, R.A. Betancourt to Aitken, 2 Dec. 1907; Aitken to Betancourt, 5, 6 Dec. 1907; Betancourt to Aitken, 7 Dec. 1907; Aitken to Betancourt, 17 Dec. 1907. Aitken organized an 'Amusement Syndicate' to promote similar nickelodeons throughout Latin America.
70 Beaverbrook, *My Early Life* 128

Chapter 7 Making a Market

1 HLRO, Beaverbrook, A, vol. 19, H.E. Bradford to Aitken, 9 July 1908; vol. 11, same to same, 6 Dec. 1907
2 HLRO, Beaverbrook, A, vol. 9, Aitken to Harris, 1 Feb. 1906
3 HLRO, Beaverbrook, A, vol. 10, Aitken to W.D. Ross, 19 June 1906
4 See Stephen J. Randall, 'The Development of Canadian Business in Puerto Rico,' *Revista / Review Interamericana* 7 (1977) 5–20
5 HLRO, Beaverbrook, A, vol. 10, Aitken to W.D. Ross, 22 June 1906, sets out the details of the proposition and is quoted below.
6 HLRO, Beaverbrook, A, vol. 8, Aitken to Burrill, 19 Oct. 1906
7 HLRO, Beaverbrook, G, vol. 4, file 21, Underwriting agreement, Porto Rico Railways, 9 Aug. 1906; Pooling agreement re: Porto Rico Bonds, 9 Aug. 1906; Option agreement and vol. 10, Aitken to W.D. Ross, 22 June 1906 (quoted)
8 HLRO, Beaverbrook, G, vol. 4, file 21, Agreement dividing bonus stock in Porto Rico Railways, 9 Aug. 1906; A, vol. 9, Aitken to P.G. Gossler, 11 Sept. 1906

9 HLRO, Beaverbrook, A, vol. 13, Aitken to E.M. Cravath, 3 Oct. 1906; vol. 8, Aitken to R.M. Aitken (of Kitcat, Mortimer and Aitken), 12 Oct. 1906; B.G. Burrill to Mrs G.H. Aitken, 8 Sept. 1906

10 HLRO, Beaverbrook, A, vol. 9, A.D. McRae to Aitken, 11 Sept. 1906; vol. 8, Aitken to A.E. Ames, 4 Oct. 1908; vol. 10, Aitken to W.D. Ross, 24, 28 Oct. 1906; W.N. Tilley to Aitken, 12 Sept. 1906, Personal; vol. 9, Aitken to R.E. Harris, 28 Nov. 1906

11 HLRO, Beaverbrook, A, vol. 9, Aitken to W.B. Ross, 4 Oct. 1906

12 HLRO, Beaverbrook, A, vol. 9, R.E. Harris to Aitken, 16 Oct. 1906

13 HLRO, Beaverbrook, A, vol. 17, Aitken to George Stairs, 18 Mar. 1907

14 HLRO, Beaverbrook, G, vol. 4, Porto Rico Railways Subscription Agreement, 18 Mar. 1907; Appointment of J.C. Mackintosh and Company to sell Porto Rico securities, 18 Mar. 1907; Agreement between Aitken, Ames, W.D. Ross and Subscribers, 19 Apr. 1907; Appointment of A.E. Ames to sell Porto Rico securities, 19 Apr. 1907; A, vol. 15, Aitken to A.D. McRae, 2 May 1907

15 HLRO, Beaverbrook, A, vol. 15, McCurdy to Aitken, 4 Feb. 1907; vol. 12, Aitken to Burrill, 8, 14 May 1907

16 HLRO, Beaverbrook, A, vol. 17, Aitken to D.E. Thomson, 7 May 1907

17 HLRO, Beaverbrook, A, vol. 14, Harding to Aitken, 15 May, 13, 15 June 1907

18 HLRO, Beaverbrook, A, vol. 11, Aitken to Ames, 30 May 1907

19 HLRO, Beaverbrook, A, vol. 18, Aitken to J.G. White and Company, 3 Sept. 1907; vol. 16, Aitken to W.B. Ross, 3 Sept. 1907; Aitken to W.D. Ross, 4 Sept. 1907

20 HLRO, Beaverbrook, A, vol. 16, W.D. Ross to Aitken, 5 Sept. 1907

21 HLRO, Beaverbrook, A, vol. 18, Royal Securities Corporation to J.G. White and Company, 20 Sept. 1907; vol. 17, Aitken to D.E. Thomson, 4 Nov. 1907; vol. 14, C.C. Giles to M.L. Mora, 23 Nov. 1907; Giles to Aitken, 23 Nov. 1907, regarding attempts to defer the General Electric bill

22 HLRO, Beaverbrook, A, vol. 18, Aitken to J.G. White, 26 Sept. 1907; vol. 14, Aitken to Judge Henry F. Hord, 6 Nov. 1907

23 HLRO, Beaverbrook, A, vol. 18, Ramón Valdés to Aitken, 13 Oct. 1907; vol. 17, F.W. Teele to Aitken, 26 Nov. 1907, Confidential

24 HLRO, Beaverbrook, A, vol. 18, J.G. White to Aitken, 26 Dec. 1907, enclosing White to William Loeb, 26 Dec. 1907; vol. 17, Aitken to D.E. Thomson, 28 Dec. 1907, Personal

25 HLRO, Beaverbrook, A, vol. 14, Aitken to H.F. Hord, 6 Nov. 1907; vol. 17, Aitken to George Stairs, 13 Dec. 1907; vol. 27, Aitken to W.B. Ross, 27 Mar. 1908; vol. 19, A.E. Ames to Aitken, 24 Aug. 1908, Personal

26 HLRO, Beaverbrook, A, vol. 12, Aitken to Burrill, 24 Oct. 1907. For a classic account of Morgan's decisive intervention in a dramatic meeting in his magnificent library see Frederick Lewis Allen, *The Lords of Creation* (Quadrangle Books: Chicago, 1966 reprint) 112–43.

27 HLRO, Beaverbrook, A, vol. 17, Aitken to Thomson, 14 Oct. 1907; vol. 14, Aitken to Harris, 28 Oct. 1907; vol. 12, Aitken to Burrill, 16 Sept. 1907

28 HLRO, Beaverbrook, A, vol. 17, Aitken to D.E. Thomson, 4 Nov. 1907; vol. 11, Ames to Aitken, 23 Sept. 1907; Aitken to Ames, 26 Oct. 1907

29 HLRO, Beaverbrook, A, vol. 11, Ames to Aitken, 19 Oct. 1907

30 HLRO, Beaverbrook, A, vol. 16, Statement re Third Porto Rico Underwriting, 1 Nov. 1907; vol. 14, Aitken to H.F. Hord, 5 Nov. 1907

31 The activities of two of these salesmen, H.E. Bradford and W.E. Todgham, are described in Christopher Armstrong, 'Making a Market: Selling Securities in Atlantic Canada before World War I,' *Canadian Journal of Economics* 12 (1980) 438–54. The reports of the two salesmen may be found respectively in HLRO, Beaverbrook, A, vols. 11, 19, and in vol. 17.

32 For Aitken's complaints against the Camagüey underwriters, see HLRO, Beaverbrook, A, vol. 15, Aitken to T.G. McMullen, R.E. Harris, H.A. Lovett, W.B. Ross, George Stairs, and Royal Securities Corporation re F.W. Teele, 5 Nov. 1907; Aitken to McMullen, 13 Nov., 14 Dec. 1907.

33 HLRO, Beaverbrook, A, vol. 16, Aitken to W.D. Ross, 20 Dec. 1907; vol. 11, Aitken to A.E. Ames, 23 Dec. 1907; Aitken to Ames, 28 Dec. 1907; vol. 14, Aitken to Harris, 28 Dec. 1907

34 HLRO, Beaverbrook, A, vol. 16, Aitken to W.D. Ross, 26, Dec. 1907, Personal

35 HLRO, Beaverbrook, A, vol. 19, Aitken to Ames, 17 Jan. 1908; vol. 30, Ames to Aitken, 12 May 1909; Aitken to Ames, 14 May 1909

36 HLRO, Beaverbrook, A, vol. 11, A.E. Ames to Aitken, 25 Nov., 13 Dec. 1907; vol. 18, Aitken to J.G. White, 10 Dec. 1907; vol. 17, Aitken to D.E. Thomson, 4 Dec. 1907

37 HLRO, Beaverbrook, A, vol. 22, Aitken to R.E. Harris, 24 Jan. 1908

38 The party consisted of Aitken and his wife with syndicate members W.D. Ross and W.R. Johnston, stockbrokers J.S. Harding and Thornton Davidson (with his wife), investors General C.W. Drury, F.H. McGuigan, S.B. Hammond, J.E. Wood, and Charles M. Hays's daughter, along with journalist W.R. McCurdy and engineer P.S. Archibald, who were to prepare publicity on the works. See HLRO, Beaverbrook, A, vol. 26, J.M. Smith to New York and Porto Rico Steamship Company, 1 Feb. 1908.

39 HLRO, Beaverbrook, A, vol. 28, Aitken to George Stairs, 16 Mar. 1908

40 HLRO, Beaverbrook, A, vol. 28, Aitken to Stairs, 30 Mar. 1908

41 HLRO, Beaverbrook, A, vol. 28, Aitken to D.E. Thomson, 18 May 1908

42 HLRO, Beaverbrook, A, vol. 26, J.C. Mackintosh to Aitken, 18 May 1908

43 HLRO, Beaverbrook, A, vol. 19, A.E. Ames to Aitken, 21 May 1908 (quoted); vol. 30, Ames to Aitken, 20 Jan. 1909; Aitken to Ames, 21 Jan. 1909

44 HLRO, Beaverbrook, A, vol. 35, extracts of correspondence between Henry F. Hord, F.W. Teele, and Aitken, 1907–9; vol. 16, Aitken to W.B. Ross, 26 Nov. 1908

45 HLRO, Beaverbrook, A, vol. 41, Aitken to D.E. Thomson, 22 Mar. 1909; Aitken to Ramon Valdes, 10 June, 24 Nov. 1909

46 On the creation of the new company see HLRO, Beaverbrook, H, vol. 79, D.E. Thomson to F.C. Clarke, 28 Mar. 1911, and Randall, 'Development of Canadian Business in Puerto Rico,' 15–20.

47 Royal Securities, Historical Documents, Aitken to C.R. Dobbin, 10 Aug. 1903; HLRO, Beaverbrook, A, vol. 3, Edward Cronyn to Aitken, 7 Oct. 1904; Aitken to Cronyn, 14 Nov. 1904; vol. 6, Aitken to J.J.M. Pangman, 2 Mar. 1905; Aitken to H.A. Richardson, 22 May 1905; Richardson to Aitken, Cronyn, and W.D. Ross, 31 Aug. 1905; vol. 5, Burnett and Company to Aitken, 10 Apr. 1905 (telegram and letter)

48 HLRO, Beaverbrook, A, vol. 6, Aitken to R. Wilson-Smith, 28 Feb. 1905; vol. 6, Aitken to John Knight, 30 May 1905, Personal; Knight to Aitken, 8 June 1905; Aitken to himself [sic], 14 Nov. 1905 (two letters); Royal Securities, Historical Documents, R.E. Harris to Aitken, 20 Nov. 1905; Certificate from Nova Scotia Registrar of Joint Stock Companies, 22 Nov. 1905.

49 HLRO, Beaverbrook, A, vol. 9, Aitken to Killam, 30 Aug. 1906; Nesbitt to Aitken, 25 Jan., 6 Apr. 1906; Aitken to Killam, 9 Oct. 1906.

50 HLRO, Beaverbrook, A, vol. 10, Aitken to F.W. Teele, 15 Oct. 1906; vol. 8, F.C. Clarke to Aitken, 29 Oct. 1906. These services had previously been supplied by F.S. Pearson's firm in New York. Royal Securities, Historical Documents, Notes re Montreal Engineering Company Limited, nd [1963], gives 16 Sept. 1907, as the date of incorporation but vol. 11 of the Beaverbrook Papers contains a letter from R.T.D. Aitken (Max's brother) to him, January 16, 1907 on the letterhead of Montreal Engineering.

51 HLRO, Beaverbrook, A, vol. 15, Richard Wilson-Smith to Aitken, 15 Feb. 1907; Aitken to Wilson-Smith, 16 Feb. 1907

52 HLRO, Beaverbrook, A, vol. 15, Aitken to Wilson-Smith, 25 Mar. (quoted), 30 Mar. 1907; Wilson-Smith to Aitken, 27, 30 Mar. 1907; vol. 13, Aitken to Cahan, 9 May 1907

53 HLRO, Beaverbrook, A, vol. 17, Aitken to Stairs, 31 Oct. 1907

54 HLRO, Beaverbrook, A, vol. 18, Aitken to John White, 6 Nov. 1907; vol. 20, Aitken to F.K. Curtis, 31 Jan. 1908

55 HLRO, Beaverbrook, A, vol. 28, Aitken to George Stairs, 24 Jan. 1908

56 HLRO, Beaverbrook, A, vol. 20, Aitken to Cahan, 11 Feb. 1908

57 HLRO, Beaverbrook, A, vol. 28, Aitken to Stairs, 16 Mar. 1908; vol. 22, Aitken to Harris, 16 Apr. 1908

58 HLRO, Beaverbrook, A, vol. 21, Agreement between Farrell and Aitken, 1 Feb. 1908; vol. 23, Aitken to Blake Burrill, 4 Feb. 1908

59 HLRO, Beaverbrook, A, vol. 28, Aitken to Stairs, 16 Mar. 1908; vol. 22, Aitken to Harris, 16 Apr. 1908

60 HLRO, Beaverbrook, A, vol. 27, Aitken to W.B. Ross, 17 Apr. 1908; Ross to Aitken, 21 Apr. 1908

61 HLRO, Beaverbrook, A, vol. 27, Aitken to W.D. Ross, 9 May 1908, Personal

62 HLRO, Beaverbrook, A, vol. 19, Aitken to Blake Burrill, 27 May 1909; vol. 24, Aitken to R.C. Matthews, 21 Sept. 1908. See also the correspondence in ibid., G, vol. 3, file 10, and Royal Securities, MB, 22 Mar. 1911, in the possession of Merrill Lynch Canada.

63 HLRO, Beaverbrook, A, vol. 24, Aitken to R.C. Matthews, 22 Sept. 1908. In an interesting comment on the gulf between the Montreal and Toronto financial communities, Aitken observed to an English associate a few months later that, 'In Montreal we lose sight of the prominence of Mr. Wm. Mackenzie and his interests. Neither he nor the Dominion Securities are of much consequence here, and I am relieved from the nightmare of jealousy so far as that group is concerned.' See ibid., vol. 31, Aitken to I.H. Benn, 12 Jan. 1909.

64 HLRO, Beaverbrook, A, vol. 37, Aitken to Mackenzie, 25 Jan. 1909

65 HLRO, Beaverbrook, G, vol. 19, files for *My Early Life* (1958); A, vol. 40, Aitken to W.E. Stavert, 24 Nov. 1909, Personal; Royal Securities, MB, 22 Mar. 1911

66 Royal Securities, MB, 11 Nov. 1913; 6 Aug. 1914

67 HLRO, Beaverbrook, A, vol. 27, Aitken to Ross, 18 Mar. 1908

68 HLRO, Beaverbrook, A, vol. 23, Aitken to F.O. Lewis, 28 Apr. (quoted), 1 Sept. 1908; vol. 21, Aitken to Thornton Davidson, 1 Sept. 1908 (two letters)

69 HLRO, Beaverbrook, A, vol. 41, Aitken to C.A. Luhnow, 10 Nov. 1909 (quoted); vol. 30, Aitken to Charles Archer, 22 July 1909; G, vol. 19, files for *My Early Life* (1958)

70 HLRO, Beaverbrook, A, vol. 34, V.M. Drury to Brandon Gas and Power Company, 17 Aug. 1909; vol. 31, Aitken to I.H. Benn, 26 Apr. 1909; G, vol. 19, files for *My Early Life* (1958)

71 HLRO, Beaverbrook, A, vol. 9, Aitken to Harding, 21 Mar., 25 Apr. 1906; G, vol. 18, agreement between Harding and Aitken, 5 Apr. 1906

72 HLRO, Beaverbrook, A, vol. 9, Harding to Aitken, 29 Sept. 1906

73 HLRO, Beaverbrook, A, vol. 9, Harding to Aitken, 29 Dec. 1906; vol. 14, Harding to Aitken, 12 Jan., 20 Feb. 1907

74 HLRO, Beaverbrook, A, vol. 9, Aitken to W.R. McCurdy, 3 Oct. 1906; McCurdy to Aitken, 12 Oct. 1906; vol. 10, Aitken to Algernon E. Aspinall, 6 Oct. 1906

75 HLRO, Beaverbrook, A, vol. 14, Harding to Aitken, 20 Feb. 1907; vol. 12, Aitken to B.G. Burrill, 14 Feb. 1907

76 HLRO, Beaverbrook, A, vol. 14, Aitken to Harding, 13 Mar. 1907; Mackay Edgar to Aitken, 18 May 1907; vol. 16, Nesbitt to Aitken, 26 June 1907

77 HLRO, Beaverbrook, A, vol. 16, Nesbitt to Aitken, 3 June, 3, 24 July 1907; vol. 14, Mackay Edgar to Aitken, 24 July 1907.ix

78 HLRO, Beaverbrook, A, vol. 11, Ames to Aitken, 8 Oct. 1907; Aitken to Ames, 11 Oct. 1907; vol. 16, Nesbitt to Aitken, 28 Dec. 1907

79 HLRO, Beaverbrook, A, vol. 16, Nesbitt to Aitken, 5 Nov. 1907; Aitken to Nesbitt, 11 Nov. 1907

80 HLRO, Beaverbrook, A, vol. 16, Aitken to Nesbitt, 13 Nov., 12 Dec. 1907

81 HLRO, Beaverbrook, A, vol. 16, Nesbitt to Aitken, 11 Nov. 1907

82 HLRO, Beaverbrook, A, vol. 16, Aitken to Nesbitt, 3, 24 Dec. 1907

83 HLRO, Beaverbrook, A, vol. 26, Nesbitt to Aitken, 6 Jan. 1908; Aitken to Nesbitt, 15 Jan. 1908; vol. 21, G.W. Farrell to Aitken, 8 May 1908. Aitken's letter of 15 Jan. approved the contract with Dunn, but it seems never to have been signed.

84 HLRO, Beaverbrook, A, vol. 26, Nesbitt to Aitken, 15 June 1908

85 HLRO, Beaverbrook, A, vol. 19, Ames to Aitken, 10 Oct. (quoted), 11 Nov. 1908

86 HLRO, Beaverbrook, A, vol. 22, Aitken to Harris, 5 Nov. 1908

Chapter 8 Jimmy Dunn and His Circle

1 Lord Beaverbrook's *Courage: The Story of Sir James Dunn* (Fredericton, N.B.: Brunswick Press, 1961) remains the standard account. Duncan McDowall adds substantially to the biographical and business record in his book *Steel at the Sault: Francis H. Clergue, Sir James Dunn, and the Algoma Steel Corporation, 1901–1956* (Toronto: University of Toronto Press, 1984) 95–123.

2 PAC, DP, vol. 257, Dunn to B. F. Pearson, 10 Nov. 1909

3 The firm name was changed to Dunn, Fisher during the war to avoid anti-German prejudice. PAC, DP, vols 1, 2, document the arbitrage transactions in Mexican Light, Mexican Electric, and Rio Tramways stock.

4 T.D. Regehr, *The Canadian Northern Railway, Pioneer Road of the Northern Prairies, 1895–1918* (Toronto: Macmillan, 1976); Patricia Roy, 'The British Columbia Electric Railway Company, 1897–1928,' (Ph D diss., University of British Columbia, 1970); Patricia Roy, 'Direct Management from Abroad: The Formative Years of the British Columbia Electric Railway,' *Business History Review* 48 (1974) 239–59; C. Armstrong and H.V. Nelles, *Monopoly's Moment: The Organization and Regulation of Canadian Utilities, 1830–1930* (Philadelphia: Temple University Press, 1986). For lists of the securities handled by British Empire Trust see the circulars in BA, SPTLP, B. 21.

5 F. Lavington, *The English Capital Market* (London: 1921) 184. For the best description of the customs and institutions of the London capital market at this time see E.V. Morgan and W.A. Thomas, *The Stock Exchange, Its History and Functions* (London: Elek Books, 1962). See also R.V. Turrell and J.J. Van-Helten, eds, *The City and Empire* (London: University of London, Institute of Commonwealth Studies, Collected Seminar Papers No. 35, 1985) for a helpful series of interim reports on current research in the history of British overseas finance.

6 W. Turrentine Jackson, *The Enterprising Scot: Investors in the American West after 1873* (Edinburgh: Edinburgh University Press, 1968) 1–72

7 R.C. Michie, *Money, Mania and Markets: Investment, Company Formation and the Stock Exchange in Nineteenth Century Scotland* (Edinburgh: John Donald, 1981) 128, 137, 154–5, 176; H. Burton and D.C. Corner, *Investment and Unit Trusts in Britain and America* (London: Elek Books, 1968) 15–44, for the most comprehensive account. See also J.C. Gilbert, *A History of Investment Trusts in Dundee, 1873–1938* (London: P.S. King, 1939) 1–88; Hugh Bullock, *The Story of Investment Companies* (New York: Columbia University Press, 1959).

8 Gilbert, *History of Investment Trusts in Dundee* and Burton and Corner, *Investment and Unit Trusts*, provide technical details on the various forms of investment funds, their management, partial dividend, and earnings and performance records.

9 Jackson, *Enterprising Scot* 34; Bruce Lenman and Kathleen Donaldson, 'Partners' Incomes, Investment and Diversification in the Scottish Linen Area, 1850–1921,' *Business History* 13 (1971) 3

10 Burton and Corner, *Investment and Unit Trusts* 32 report that the yield on some partners' shares could be as high as 2,000 per cent in some cases.

11 John Scott and Michael Hughes in *The Anatomy of Scottish Capital* (London and Montreal: Croom Helm, 1980)

12 Located in the vault of Robert Fleming and Company, London, hereafter cited RF. The years 1909 and 1913 are incomplete. They also generously gave us a rollicking lunch in the firm's dining room that interfered somewhat with research that afternoon.

13 RF, Syndicate Book 1, 123 for a typical example

14 This compares with the 1896 portfolio of the International Investment Trust Company as reported by Burton and Corner, *Investment and Unit Trusts* 40–2: 44.8 per cent in North America (mainly railroads); 26.6 per cent South America and Mexico; 6.2 per cent other foreign, and 22.4 per cent in the UK. Railways and transportation companies accounted for 47.5 per cent of the international portfolio, utilities less than 9 per cent.

15 See above chapter 2.

16 PAC, DP, vol. 6, Sperling and Company to J.H. Dunn, 2 Apr. 1906; F.S. Pearson to Sperling and Co., Mendel and Myers, J.H. Dunn, E. MacKay Edgar, 14 Apr. 1906; vol. 249, Dunn to F.S. Pearson, 5 Apr. 1906, on the division of the Mexico Tramways underwriting

17 RF, Syndicate Books 1 and 2, box files, contain copies of the prospectus of each issue.

18 Harvard University, Baker Library Archives, H. Seligman Letterbooks, vol. 2, H. Seligman to Isaac Seligman, 1 Aug. 1910. For an account of the abortive Farquhar-Pearson attempt to weave together a new transcontinental railroad system in the United States on heavily leveraged purchases of Lehigh Valley, Wabash, Rock Island, Missouri Pacific, Denver and Rio Grande, and Western Pacific railroad securities see Charles A. Gauld, *The Last Titan: Percival Farquhar, American Entrepreneur in Latin America* (Palo Alto, Ca.: Institute for Hispanic American and Luso-Brazilian Studies, Stanford University, 1964) 198–208, and the *New York Times*, Sunday, 7 Aug. 1910.

19 Gauld, *Last Titan* 234

20 PAC, DP, vol. 252, Dunn to R.M. Horne-Payne, 19 Oct. 1907; vol. 8, Horne-Payne to Dunn, Private, 21 Oct. 1907; Agreement between F.S. Pearson, Dunn, Fischer and Company, and R.M. Horne-Payne, undated, (Nov.–Dec. 1907)

21 PAC, DP, vol. 10, N.S. Myers to Dunn, 27 May 1908

22 PAC, DP, vol. 259, Dunn to Galen L. Stone, Stone and Company, Boston, 18 July 1910

23 PAC, DP, vol. 25, Violet Asquith to Dunn, 1 June 1910; vol. 27, M. Bonham Carter to Dunn, 16 Sept. 1910

24 Beaverbrook, *Courage* 80–3; McDowall, *Steel at the Sault* 108–9; H.H. Asquith, *Letters to Venetia Stanley* (Oxford: Oxford University Press, 1982) 85, 89, 161; John Campbell, *F.E. Smith: First Earl of Birkenhead* (London: Jonathan Cape, 1983) 688–90; Noel Coward, *Present Indicative* (London: Heinemann, 1937) 214

25 PAC, DP, vol. 5, C.L. Fischer to Dunn, 30 Mar. 1906; vol. 248, Dunn to C.L. Fischer, 17 May 1906; Dunn to F.S. Pearson, Personal, 31 May 1906; vol. 6, F.S. Pearson to Dunn, 13 June 1906; vol. 5, Fischer to Dunn, 1 July 1906

26 Duncan McDowall, 'The Belgian Croesus,' unpublished paper kindly made available to us by the author, 13–14

27 Gauld, *Last Titan* 65–84

28 Ibid. 1–247; For the Dunn conduit to Paris see *inter alia* PAC, DP, vol. 5, C.L. Fischer to Dunn, 30 Sept. 1906; vol. 10, Fischer to Dunn, 11, 16, 17, 20, 26, 28, 30 June 1908; vol. 23, Fischer to Dunn, 4 Mar. 1910.

29 See for example PAC, DP, vol. 255, Dunn to Minor Keith, 2 Feb. 1909.

30 For details concerning the pool to defend Rio-Mextrams and Brazil Railway stock (called the Anuahuac·Syndicate) see the following: PAC, DP, vol. 256, Dunn to Loewenstein, 30 July 1909; vol. 19, Loewenstein to Dunn, 30 July 1909; vol. 19, Farquhar to Dunn, 3 Aug. 1909; vol. 19, Loewenstein to Dunn, 3 Aug. 1909; vol. 256, Dunn to Farquhar, 3 Aug. 1909.

31 Arnold Spitzer supplied an uncharacteristic note of levity when Spitzer wrote to James Dunn on 15 May 1913 to thank him for a book on 'Rhythmic breathing' (another of Dunn's crank enthusiasms) and to inquire whether it had finally rained in Texas, the site of two Dunn-Pearson land promotion schemes, whose promised dividends had been much delayed by drought. Spitzer was simply delighted by the reply: 'C'est avec le plus grand plaisir que j'ai reçu la communication que vous avez bien voulu me faire que la pluie était enfin tombée à San Antonio. J'espère que ça n'ira pas jusqu'à l'inondation mais que vos canaux vont pouvoir remplir leur devoir.' PAC, DP, vol. 45, Spitzer to Dunn, 23 June 1913

32 PAC, DP, vol. 258, Dunn to F.S. Pearson, 10 May 1910

33 PAC, DP, vol. 258, Dunn to Robert Fleming, 8 July 1910; Dunn to Pearson, 11 July 1910

34 See n30 above.

35 PAC, DP, vol. 262, Dunn to Pearson, 18 Mar. 1912; vol. 42, Pearson to Dunn, 14 Feb. 1913

36 PAC, DP, vol. 34, F.S. Pearson to Dunn, 3 Oct. 1911

37 RF, Syndicate Book 1, 132, 'Barcelona Traction, Light and Power Company, 5% 1st Mortgage Bonds, November, 1911'; PAC, DP, vol. 35, Louis Fleischmann (L. Messel and Co.) to Dunn, 24 Nov. 1911; vol. 262, Dunn to Thomas Aitken, Bank of Scotland, 27 Nov. 1911; vol. 262, Dunn to E.R. Wood, 18 Dec. 1911; vol. 35, E.R. Wood to Dunn, 20 Dec. 1911

38 PAC, DP, vol. 42, F.S. Pearson to Dunn, 14 Feb. 1913; RF, Syndicate Book 2, 44, 'Barcelona Traction, Light and Power Company 5% First Mortgage Bonds, March, 1913'

39 PAC, DP, vol. 263, Dunn to M.M. Warburg, 4 Oct. 1912

40 PAC, DP, vol. 43, F. Williams Taylor, Grand Hotel, Cannes, to Dunn, 26 Mar. 1913, reporting that he had sent Mr Ross on his yacht to look over the Barcelona situation

41 PAC, DP, vols. 44, 45, 46, contain a tremendous amount of correspondence among Loewenstein, Dunn, and Pearson, much of it cables dating from Dec. 1912 to the fall of 1913 dealing with these contentious matters; see also vol. 265, Dunn to Loewenstein, 15 July 1913.

42 This account is based upon the correspondence among Loewenstein, Dunn, Malcolm Hubbard, and E.R. Wood, after the fact, dealing with the problem of silencing the complainants through the French courts. See in particular PAC, DP, vol. 50, Loewenstein to Malcolm Hubbard, 1, 3, 5 Dec. 1913.

43 When the scandal blew up Rod Demmé attempted to dislodge Dunn from his associates. 'You are at present dealing almost exclusively with the Jewish element in Paris which comes through Loewenstein's connection ... I can assure you that it is essential that you do not deal exclusively with Jews in France because if ever you need some government help you won't get it that way.' PAC, DP, vol. 46, Rod A. Demmé to Dunn, Personal, 4 Aug. 1913; see also another letter of 7 Aug. 1913

44 PAC, DP, vol. 267, Dunn to Loewenstein, 8 Dec. 1912

45 PAC, DP, vol. 48, H. Wauters, Stallaerts and Loewenstein, Brussels, to Dunn, 17 Oct. 1913, including a translation of the 16 Oct. article

46 PAC, DP, vol. 49, H. Wauters to Dunn, 22 Oct. 1913; vol. 266, Dunn to Wauters, 24 Oct. 1913, sending information from the *Annual Financial Review*

47 PAC, DP, vol. 46, Pearson to Dunn, 3 Aug. 1913; vol. 265, Dunn to Loewenstein, 5 Aug. 1913; vol. 47, Loewenstein to Dunn, 6 Sept. 1913

48 PAC, DP, vol. 48, Loewenstein to Dunn, 12 Oct. 1913, and again vol. 50, Loewenstein to Dunn, Private, 5 Dec. 1913, for an itemized account of his complaints

49 PAC, DP, vol. 50, Loewenstein to Dunn, Private, 5, 12 Dec. 1913

50 PAC, DP, vol. 266, Dunn to A. Spitzer, Private, 5 Sept. 1913; Dunn to Bradley Palmer, Boston, Private, 5 Sept. 1913

51 RF, Syndicate Book 2, 64, 'Loan of £35,000 to Dunn, Fischer and Company at 8% interest,' 27 June 1913; 65, 'Loan of £200,000 to Dunn, Fischer and Company for 2 years at 8%,' 27 June 1913

52 PAC, DP, vol. 58, Dunn to to Henry Clay Frick, 27 July, 17 Aug. 1914. Some of these pawned pictures may now be seen on display in the Frick Gallery in New York.

53 PAC, DP, vol. 60, Barcelona Traction to Dunn, 30 Dec. 1914

Chapter 9 Rates of Exchange

1 BA, BT, Pre-1923, 77, Wood to R.M. Horne-Payne, 12 Sept. 1910

2 BA, DF 540.14, Pearson to W. Mackenzie, 14 Feb. 1911; SPTLP, Pre-1923, 85, Memorandum regarding São Paulo Electric Company [by F.S. Pearson], nd [June 1911]; A. Mackenzie to Pearson, 2 Aug. 1911

3 BA, SPTLP, Pre-1923, 90, Pearson to Z.A. Lash, 19 June 1911; Annual Report, 1911; MB, 10 May 1912

4 BA, SPTLP, Pre-1923, 77, J.M. Smith (dictated by E.R. Wood) to R.M. Horne-Payne, 22 Sept. 1910; Pearson to W. Mackenzie and E.R. Wood, 16 Jan. 1911; 46A, Prospectus for issue of £300,000 Perpetual Consolidated Debenture Stock in SPTLP, 10 Jan. 1911

5 BA, SPTLP, MB, 4 Mar. 1910; 8 Dec. 1911, 16 Feb. 1912

6 BA, RJTLP, MB, 9 Mar. 1909, 18 Feb. 1910; Pre-1923, 107, Walter Gow to J.M. Smith, 15 Aug. 1910

7 BA, RJTLP, MB, Circular to shareholders, 27 Mar., 9 Aug., 15 Sept., 30 Dec. 1909. As evidence of the growing dependence upon European capital, bearer warrants representing 65,000 shares were tendered from Brussels to subscribe for 1 new share for each 4 held.

8 BA, RJTLP, MB, 21 Dec. 1910; 24 Mar. 1911.

9 BA, BT, Pre-1923, 38, J.M. Smith to F.S. Pearson, 12 July 1910; RJTLP, MB, 14 Nov. 1910; 5 Jan. 1911; Pre-1923, 115, Pearson to E.R. Wood, 21 Dec. 1910; W.H. Hickman to J.M. Smith, 22 Apr. 1911

10 BA, RJTLP, MB, 24 Feb., 5 June, 17 July, 15, 25 Aug. 1911

11 BA, RJTLP, MB, 11 Nov., 8 Dec. 1911; Pre-1923, 132, W.H. Hickman to J.M. Smith, 6 Dec. 1911

12 BA, BT, MB, 2 Oct. 1912. Since the São Paulo dividend was double the 5 per cent paid by the Rio company, a special 0.83 per cent dividend was received by each São Paulo shareholder plus 2.75 BT shares for every 1 tendered. Rio shareholders got 1.6 shares for every 1 tendered, and São Paulo Electric shareholders converted on a one-for-one basis. RJTLP, Pre-1923, 139A, J.M. Smith to H.M. Hubbard, 29 Apr. 1913, shows that 98.8 per cent of Rio shares, 99.5 per cent of SP shares, and 100 per cent of SP Electric shares had been tendered.

13 BA, BT, Pre-1923, 47, J.M. Smith to BTLP shareholders, 8 May 1913; 20, G.W.G. Townley to Smith, 8 July 1913.

14 BA, BT, Pre-1923, 20, G.F. Davison to J.M. Smith, 17 June 1914; RJTLP, Pre-1923, 166, E.R. Wood to Pearson, 12 May 1914; Pearson to Wood, 13 May 1914. The paper was said to be a scandal sheet hoping to extract a payoff to keep quiet.

15 BA, RJTLP, Pre-1923, 105, A. Mackenzie to J.M. Smith, 3 Feb. 1911; Smith to Mackenzie, 18 May 1911; MB, 13 Sept. 1912

16 BA, BT, Pre-1923, 90, A. Mackenzie to Sir W. Mackenzie, 11 May 1915; F.A. Huntress to Sir W. Mackenzie, 23 June 1915

17 BA, BT, Pre-1923, 90, A. Mackenzie to Sir W. Mackenzie, 11 May 1915

18 BA, AM Confidential, vol. 1, file 261, F.A. Huntress to Pearson, 2 Dec. 1912; BT, Pre-1923, 75, Pearson to Sir W. Mackenzie, 1 Jan. 1914; 70, Pearson to W.E. Rundle, 4 May 1914

19 BA, BT, MB, 5, 6, 23 May, 30 June 1914; Pre-1923, 41, Slaughter and May to Pearson, 21 May 1914; 70, J.M. Smith to C.W. Patrick, 22 Oct. 1914; BTel, Pre-1923, 3, Pearson to Miller Lash, 26 FEb. 1915; Pearson to E.R. Wood, 29 Apr. 1915; BT, Pre-1923, 88, F.A. Huntress to Sir W. Mackenzie, 23 June 1915

20 PAC, DP, vol. 271, Dunn to Pearson, 22 Apr. 1915; vol. 62, Pearson to Dunn, 24 Apr. 1915

21 Of the many books on the *Lusitania,* one that contains some mention of F.S. Pearson (described as a 'New York financier') is Des Hickey and Gus Smith, *Seven Days to Disaster: The Sinking of the 'Lusitania'* (Collins: London, 1981) 95–6, 126, 175–6, 286.

22 BA, RJTLP, MB, 14 May 1915

23 BA, BT, Pre-1923, 41, Sir W. Mackenzie to A. Mackenzie, 13 May 1915; MB, 14 May 1915; RJTLP, MB, 14 May 1915; SPTLP, 14 May 1915

24 BA, SPTLP, B. 17, A. Mackenzie to E.R. Wood, 31 Oct. 1902; B. 29, Mackenzie to J.M. Smith, 1 Apr. 1905; B. 31, A. Mackenzie to W. Mackenzie, 1 Feb. 1906

25 BA, OD, A. Mackenzie to W.H. Blake, 2 May 1905; RJTLP, A. 74, Pearson to W. Mackenzie, 1 June 1906

26 Thomas Holloway, *The Brazilian Coffee Valorization of 1906: Regional Politics and Economic Dependence* (Madison, Wis.: Wisconsin State Historical Society, 1975) 41–3, 50–5, 89; Joseph Love, *São Paulo in the Brazilian Federation, 1889–1937* (Palo Alto, Ca.: Stanford University Press, 1980) 43–6, 191–5. See BA, SPTLP, B. 39, A. Mackenzie to W. Mackenzie, 6 Feb. 1907, for an account of the impact of coffee valorization on the companies.

27 BA, RJTLP, Pre-1923, 101, C.W. Patrick to J.M. Smith, 12 May 1914

28 BA, file 'Operation Ontario,' Memorandum on 'Operation Ontario, Interim Report no. 2, Exchange as a Factor in Brazilian Traction History and Future Policy,' by J.M. Bell, 2 Aug. 1949, Confidential; SPTLP, B. 70, D. Mulqueen to J.M. Smith, 3 Mar. 1906

29 BA, BT, Pre-1923, 38, Pearson to Sir W. Mackenzie, 7 Oct. 1914; MB, 15 Oct. 1914; 13 July 1915; Annual Report, 1914, 1915

30 BA, BT, MB, 13 July 1915; Pre-1923, 20, F. Nolan to J.M. Smith, 29 July 1915; J.C. Priestley to BT, 12 Aug. 1915

31 BA, BT, Pre-1923, 96, Huntress to R.C. Brown, 23 Oct. 1916; 90B, Mackenzie to H.M. Hubbard, 28 Oct. 1916. Mackenzie wanted Hubbard to lobby the British authorities to reverse the requisitioning.

32 BA, BT, Pre-1923, 6D, A. Mackenzie to J.M. Smith, 23 Dec. 1916

33 BA, BTel, Pre-1923, 3, 'Memorandum of Conference, Biltmore Hotel, New York, Saturday, October 21st, 1916,' quoting K.J. Dunstan; A. Mackenzie to W.E. Rundle, 20 Oct. 1916; C.M. Mauseau to National Trust, 9 Nov. 1916

34 BA, BTel, 3, W.A. Read and Company to A. Mackenzie, 17 Oct. 1916; BT, MB, 3, 13 Nov. 1916; RJTLP, MB, 13 Nov. 1916

35 BA, BT, Pre-1923, 90, J.M. Smith to A. Mackenzie, 18 Jan. 1917; 6D, Mackenzie to Smith, 12 Apr. 1917; Mackenzie to Shareholders of BT, 19 Apr. 1917

Chapter 10 In Extremis

1 University of Toronto Archives, Walker Papers, Walker to Henry J. Gardiner, 27 Feb. 1908

2 Robert Freeman Smith, *The United States and Revolutionary Nationalism in Mexico, 1916–1932* (Chicago: University of Chicago Press, 1972) x, 23–42

3 Woodrow Wilson to Sir William Tyrell, 24 Nov. 1913, quoted in Friedrich Katz, *The Secret War in Mexico: Europe, the United States and the Mexican Revolution* (Chicago: University of Chicago Press, 1981) 157. See also Peter Calvert, *The Mexican Revolution, 1910–1914* (Cambridge: Cambridge University Press, 1968) 269–71, for a more nuanced interpretation of this interview and the phrase originally quoted in Burton Hendrick's *The Life and Letters of Walter H. Page* (Garden City: Doubleday, 1923) vol. 1, 204–5.

4 Peter Calvert, *Mexico* (New York: Cambridge University Press, 1973) 41–70;
Charles C. Cumberland, *Mexico: The Struggle for Modernity* (New York:
Oxford University Press, 1968) 190–272; Roger D. Hansen, *The Politics of
Mexican Development* (Baltimore: Johns Hopkins University Press, 1971)
11–29; Raymond Vernon, *The Dilemma of Mexico's Development* (Cambridge:
Harvard University Press, 1965) 33–59. For an excellent brief account of the later
days of the Díaz regime see Alan Knight, *The Mexican Revolution* (New York:
Cambridge University Press, l986) vol. 1, 1–170.

5 Robert L. Delorme, 'The Political Basis of Economic Development: Mexico,
1884–1911' (Ph D diss., University of Minnesota, 1968) 65–124; Joseph B.
Romney, 'American Interests in Mexico: Development and Impact during
the Rule of Porfirio Diáz, 1876–1911' (Ph D diss., University of Utah, 1968)
1–8; Harry K. Wright, *Foreign Enterprise in Mexico* (Chapel Hill:
University of North Carolina Press, 1971) 51–94

6 Herbert K. May and Jose Antonio Fernandez Arena, *Impact of Foreign
Investment in Mexico* (New York and Washington: National Chamber of
Commerce and Council of the Americas, 1972) 8–12, 61–6; Vernon, *Dilemma*
51-59; Kenneth Buckley, *Capital Formation in Canada, 1896–1930* (Toronto:
McClelland and Stewart, 1974) 15; Jonathan C. Brown, 'Domestic Politics and
Foreign Investment: British Development of Mexican Petroleum, 1889–1911,'
Business History Review 61 (1987) 387–416

7 *Historia moderna de México, la vida economica* (Mexico: Editorial Hermes,
1965) vol. 8, 1089, 1156

8 Knight, *Mexican Revolution* vol. 1, 22

9 PAC, DP, vol. 256, Dunn copying Pearson's telegram to Robert Fleming, 22
May 1909; Dunn to Pearson, 10, 16, 19, 26 June, 3 Aug. 1909; Dunn to F.H.
Deacon, 20 July 1909; Dunn to Percival Farquhar, 30 July 1909; vol. 19,
Pearson to Dunn, 3 Aug. 1909; *The Statist* 3 July, 25 Sept. 1909; PRO, FO 368,
vol. 309, file 35516, 23 Sept. 1909, Sworn Statement by L. Villareal, engineer of
the Department of Development, Colonization and Industry to be forwarded
to Malcolm Hubbard

10 This promotion deserves a separate study. Late in 1908 Pearson negotiated the
purchase of several small railroads, including the now-famous tourist
attraction the Sierra Madre Pacific, and a huge expanse of virgin pine timber
land. Pearson proposed to link these regional railroads, build a huge saw-
milling complex at a town to be named after himself, and connect this regional
system to the US transcontinental railroads at El Paso through a new,
shorter, more efficient route with easier grades. Pearson hoped timber bound
for the booming US southwest would provide the freight revenue for the
Mexico North Western Railway.

In time the scheme became wildly grandiose as Pearson teamed up with
Percival Farquhar in an abortive stock market operation that attempted to

assemble a new integrated transcontinental US railroad out of the existing Lehigh Valley, Wabash, Rock Island, Denver and Rio Grande, and Western Pacific railroads. This scheme collapsed suddenly in 1910 when frightened railroad executives and the Interstate Commerce Commission realized what was happening.

The Mexico North Western, which was notionally to connect up with this system, began as a brilliant 1909 promotion in London, Brussels, and Paris – buoyed by lucrative bonuses to insiders and a 45 per cent stock bonus to large buyers such as Robert Fleming. Plagued first by construction delays and then by revolution, this company never lived up to expectations. Indeed, whatever its merits as a regional development scheme, it was a total failure financially. Details of the promotion can be followed through the Dunn Papers. The audacious raid on Wabash et al. is recounted in the *New York Times* 7 Aug. 1910, and Charles A. Gauld, *The Last Titan: Percival Farquhar, American Entrepreneur in Latin America* (Palo Alto, Ca.: Institute for Hispanic American and Luso-Brazilian Studies, Stanford University, 1964) 198–208. Our colleague at York University, Russell Chace, is examining the impact of the Mexico North Western Railway on Chihuahua. See his unpublished paper 'The Mexico North Western Railway Company, Ltd., 1908–1914.'

11 MTC, MB, 25 Jan., 15, 20, 25, 26 Feb., 5 Apr., 12 Nov. 1909, 5 Jan., 8 Mar., 22 July 1910. See also MLP, MB, 27 Mar., 2 Oct., 12 Nov. 1909, 5 Jan., 1 Mar. 1910.

12 MLP, Annual Report, 1911; PRO, FO 371, vol. 1147, file 1573, Thomas B. Hohler to Sir Edward Grey, 15 May 1911; PRO FO 368, vol. 554, file 26358, Hohler to the Foreign Office, 5, 6 July 1911. Hohler complimented Harro Harrsen, general manager of the tramway company for his reasonable manner and cool conduct during the strike, although, as we shall see, his view of Harrsen later changed. Rodney Anderson, *Outcasts in Their Own Land: Mexican Industrial Workers, 1906–1911* (DeKalb: Northern Illinois University Press, 1976) 331–8; also Knight, *Mexican Revolution* vol. 1, 424–8

13 British Science Museum Library, London, S. Pearson and Son Papers, box A4, John B. Body to Lord Cowdray, 10 Aug., 23 Nov. 1912; 3 Jan., 8 Feb. 1913. In addition to his extensive oil and railroad interests in Mexico, Lord Cowdray was the principal owner of electrical utilities in Veracruz and Tampico. See ibid., box B2. See also Desmond Young, *Member for Mexico* (London: Cassel, 1966) 42, 92, 238–9; and J.A. Spender, *Weetman Pearson: First Viscount Cowdray, 1856–1927* (London: Cassel, 1930) 180, 205–7. We are especially indebted to Professor Chace for helping us with these and many other points.

14 PRO, FO 371, vol. 1393, file 158, Francis Stronge to Sir Edward Grey, 8 Apr. 1912.

15 Thomas Hohler, *Diplomatic Petrel* (London: John Murray, 1942) 179

16 Stanley R. Ross, *Francisco I. Madero: Apostle of Mexican Democracy* (New York: Columbia University Press, 1955) 113–249; Katz, *Secret War in Mexico* 1–118; Smith, *United States and Revolutionary Nationalism in Mexico* 1–22; Peter Calvert, *Mexican Revolution* 49–130; Knight, *Mexican Revolution* vol. 1, 55–71, 247 ff

17 PAC, DP, vol. 39, H.I. Miller to E.R. Wood, 16 Oct. 1912; MTC, MB, 9 Apr. 1913; MLP, MB, 1 Nov. 1912; 9, 22 Apr. 1913; MLP, Annual Report, 1913. Riba borrowed half a million pesos for this operation. Between them the tramway and the power company paid more than $100,000 for extraordinary security precautions.

18 See for example USNA, RG 59, State Department, DF 1910–29, 812.00 / 5777, H.I. Miller, the American general manager of the Mexican North Western Railway, to T.P. Littlepage, Washington lobbyist for the company, 24 Dec. 1912. Littlepage seems to have had privileged access to the State Department.

19 PAC, DP, vol. 39, Pearson to Dunn, 29 Sept. 1912. Pearson's letter continued in a revealing fashion suggesting that, if the British government failed to act, it would be necessary to prevail upon the US government. Pearson added: 'I do not think we have any standing before the American Government, as we are a Canadian Company, and also it would antagonize the Mexican Government very much, while action from the Foreign Office in London would appear to be from security holders rather than from the Management.' See also Pearson to Dunn, 27 Oct. 1912, on the same subject.

20 PAC, DP, vol. 263, Dunn to Sir Arthur Nicholson, 1 Oct. 1912; vol. 41, Dunn to Sir William Mackenzie, 7 Jan. 1913; vol. 263, Dunn to Sir Robert Borden, 21 Jan. 1913; vol. 264, Dunn to Borden, 4 Feb. 1913

21 PRO, FO 371, vol. 1395, file 158, J.H. Dunn to Rt Hon. Arthur Nicholson, 1 Oct. 1912, and minutes; Dunn to Sir Edward Grey, 18 Dec. 1912

22 Hohler, *Diplomatic Petrel* 178

23 PAC, RG 25, vol. 1130, file 77 records the efforts of the Governor General of Canada and Ambassador Stronge on behalf of the Mexico North Western Railway throughout January 1913. See also PRO, FO 371, vol. 1671, file 87. For an excellent sketch of that extraordinary pair, Sir Francis and Lady Stronge, see Peter Calvert, *Mexican Revolution* 118–9, 153, who relies heavily upon Hohler.

24 Hohler, *Diplomatic Petrel* 184; Ross, *Francisco I. Madero* 250–340, for a gripping account of the revolt and murder; see also Katz, *Secret War in Mexico* 92–118; Michael C. Meyer, *Huerta: A Political Portrait* (Lincoln: University of Nebraska Press, 1972) 45–82; Calvert, *Mexican Revolution* 131–55; Knight, *Mexican Revolution* vol. 1, 466–90

25 PAC, DP, vol. 42, Pearson to Dunn, 11, 16 Feb. 1913; vol. 264, Dunn to Pearson, 17 Feb. 1913. At the height of the chaos Harrsen begged for protection. Dunn and Pearson sought US, British, and French help. See, for example, PRO, FO 371, vol. 1671, file 7694, Dunn Fischer and Co., to the Under Secretary of State for Foreign Affairs, 17 Feb. 1913; PAC, RG 25, vol. 1130, Stronge to Sir Edward Grey, 7 Mar. 1913 *re* Mexico North Western Railway.

26 PAC, DP, vol. 42, Harrsen to Dunn, Saturday, 19–24 [sic] Feb. 1913

27 PAC, DP, vol. 42, Harrsen to Dunn, Sunday, 19–24 Feb. 1913

28 PAC, DP, vol. 42, Pearson to Dunn, 28 Feb. 1913

29 PAC, DP, vol. 42, Pearson to Dunn, 3 Mar. 1913

30 PAC, DP, vol. 264, Dunn to Luis Riba, Personal and Confidential, 27 Feb. 1913; Pearson to Dunn, 28 Feb. 1913; vol. 42, Pearson to Dunn, 1 Mar. 1913; vol. 264, Dunn to Luis Riba, 3 Mar. 1913

31 PAC, DP, vol. 264, Dunn to Pearson, 3 Mar. (quoted), 4 Mar. 1913; Calvert, *Mexican Revolution* 163–4, reports Greenwood's visit to the Foreign office but neglects to mention his affiliation. This is unfortunate, for Calvert's basic thrust in this part of his book is to resist the argument that the British government recognized Huerta quickly under the influence of the Cowdray interests. See also Merrill Rippy, *Oil and the Mexican Revolution* (Leiden: E.J. Brill, 1972) 135–58.

32 PRO, FO 371, vol. 1671, file 6269, Report of Conversation with Hamar Greenwood, 3 Mar. 1913; PAC, DP, vol. 264, Dunn to Hamar Greenwood, 4 Mar. 1913. See Calvert, *Mexican Revolution* 163–4.

33 PAC, DP, vol. 264, Dunn to Luis Riba, 6 Mar. 1913

34 See Calvert, *Mexican Revolution*, for details, 164–6; see also Katz, *Secret War in Mexico* 156–202 for an oil-based, anti-American interpretation of British policy formation.

35 PAC, DP, vol. 264, Dunn to Riba, 7 Mar. 1913; vol. 42, Luis Riba to Dunn, 8 Mar. 1913.

36 Calvert, *Mexican Revolution* 131–66, provides the most authoritative account of the British recognition issue.

37 PAC, DP, vol. 42, Harro Harrsen to Dunn, 21 Mar. 1913. Peter Henderson notes that Harrsen (misspelled as Harrison) acted as a go-between with Orozco, but fails to note Harrsen's connections; see Peter Henderson, *Félix Díaz, the Porfirians and the Mexican Revolution* (Lincoln: University of Nebraska Press, 1981) 89.

38 PAC, DP, vol. 42, Harro Harrsen to Dunn, 21 Mar. 1913; MTC, MB, entries for spring 1913; Annual Report, 1912; MTC, MB, 17 Mar. 1913; 17 June 1913, Sixth Annual Meeting

39 PAC, DP, vol. 264, Dunn to Pearson, 3 Apr. 1914; vol. 43, Pearson to Dunn, 9 Apr. 1913; vol. 264, Dunn to Pearson, 9, 16 Apr. 1913

40 PAC, DP, vol. 44, Loewenstein to Dunn, 28 May 1913, translation

41 Smith, *The United States and Revolutionary Nationalism in Mexico* 23–42; Katz, *Secret War in Mexico* 156–202; Meyer, *Huerta* 109–126

42 PAC, DP, vol. 45, H.I. Miller to Dunn, June 1913; vol. 48, Harrsen to Dunn, 11 Oct. 1913; vol. 50, F.S. Pearson to Dunn, 30 Nov., 9 Dec. 1913; vol. 51, H.I. Miller to Pearson, 18, 23, 30, 31 Dec. 1913

43 PAC, DP, vol. 48, Pearson to Dunn, 9 Oct. 1913; Luis Riba to Mario [cable address of the firm Cancino y Riba in Mexico City], 9, 10 Oct. 1913. We are indebted to Professor Russell Chace for identification.

44 USNA, State Department, DF 1910–29, 312.41 / 81, Nelson O'Shaughnessy to Secretary of State, 8 Dec. 1913

45 PAC, DP, vol. 47, Ward E. Pearson to Dunn, 26 Aug. 1913, Private and Confidential. His contact was H.C. Lewis; see vol. 48, Ward Pearson to Dunn, 16 Oct. 1913. The lobbyist Lloyd Griscom had previously been sent to Mexico on behalf of the Pearson group during the collapse of the Madero government; see vol. 49, Ward Pearson to Dunn, 22 Nov. 1913. These US business interests seemed to be angling for an invasion that would leave Villa in charge of Chihuahua and perhaps bring the northern states into some kind of US protectorate. USNA, State Department, DF 1910–29, file 812.602 / 11, Walter Hines Page to the Secretary of State, 10 Dec. 1913

46 PRO, FO 371, vol. 1678, file 6269, Deputation headed by Hamar Greenwood to Sir Edward Grey, 18 Nov. 1913; Sir Edward Grey to Sir Cecil Spring Rice, 19 Nov. 1913; Sir Edward Grey to Sir Lionel Carden, 19 Nov. 1913. See also Calvert, *Mexican Revolution* 167–284, for an analysis of this awkward moment in Anglo-American diplomacy.

47 Loewenstein was told that the bank imposed two conditions: that tramway receipts be deposited in the Mexico City branch as soon as they were received, and that no further dividends be voted until the loan had been repaid. PAC, DP, vol. 46, Pearson to Dunn, 11 Aug. 1913; vol. 48, Dunn to Pearson, 6 Oct. 1913; Loewenstein to Dunn, 7 Oct. 1913. The loan reached £600,000 by October.

48 USNA, State Department, DF 1910–29, 312.415M57 for a file documenting the Cumbre tunnel disaster and attendant protests; PAC, DP, vol. 53, H.I. Miller to F.S. Pearson, 9 Feb. 1914, recounting the outrage; Hamar Greenwood to Dunn, 21 Mar., 16 Apr. 1914, informing him of the diplomatic response

49 PAC, DP, vol. 267, Dunn to Pearson, 7 Jan. 1914; Dunn to L. Fleischmann, 6 Jan. 1914; vol. 53, Harrsen to Pearson, 9, 10 Feb. 1914. PRO, FO 371, vol. 2032, file 213, F.S. Pearson to the Foreign Office, 2 Jan. 1914; Sir Lionel Carden to Sir Edward Grey, 10, 14 Jan. 1914. Some of these documents are copied in PAC, RG 7, G 21, 9758a, and RG 25, vol. 1132.

50 PAC, DP, vol. 53, Harro Harrsen to Pearson, 18 Feb. 1914
51 John Womack, Jr, *Zapata and the Mexican Revolution* (New York: Vintage, 1968) 191–223; Douglas R. Richmond, *Venustiano Carranza's Nationalist Struggle, 1893–1920* (Lincoln: University of Nebraska Press, 1983) 43–82
52 See Katz, *Secret War in Mexico* 253–97, for details, and Smith, *United States and Revolutionary Nationalism in Mexico* 23–42. On labour during this phase of the revolution see Marjorie Ruth Clark, *Organized Labor in Mexico* (Chapel Hill: University of North Carolina Press, 1967) 23–56, and Joe C. Ashby, *Organized Labor and the Mexican Revolution under Lazaro Cardenas* (Chapel Hill: University of North Carolina Press, 1967) 3–18.
53 Sir Thomas B. Hohler Papers (privately held), Letters, 1914, Hohler to the Foreign Office, 11 June 1914. A copy of this lengthy dispatch marked 'Very Confidential' from the Commercial Intelligence Branch, Board of Trade, dated 10 Oct. 1914, can also be found in the British Science Museum Library, London, S. Pearson and Son Papers, box A3.
54 Sir Thomas B. Hohler Papers, Letters, 1914, Hohler to Spring Rice, 8 Oct. 1914: 'Dear Springey, While the Convention was going on it was impossible to see any authority, & my file of complaints has been growing to dreadful proportions. I am in for a field day today and have a fresh big trouble on in the shape of a tramway strike which is likely to be serious.'
55 PRO, FO 371, vol. 2040, file 58596, copy of F.S. Pearson to James Dunn, 11 Oct. 1914; Hohler to the Foreign Office, 12, 14 Oct. 1914
56 PRO, FO 371, vol. 2040, file 58596, Hohler to the Foreign Office, 20, 21, 26, 28 Oct., 3, 10 Nov. 1914
57 See for details PAC, RG 7, G 21, vol. 409, J.P. Bell, Bank of Commerce, Mexico, to Hohler, 10 Nov. 1914, et seq.; see also RG 25, vol. 1149.
58 For Canadian reaction see PAC, RG 7, G 21, vol. 409, for file of cable traffic between Mexico and London on the intervention; see also PRO, FO 371, vol. 2040, file 28596, Governor General of Canada to the Colonial Secretary, 26 Oct. 1914. For US response see USNA, State Department, DF 1910–29, 812.5045 / 74-6, for telegrams from agents in Mexico; 812.78 / 4, Harro Harrsen to Senator W.J. Stone, 13 Oct. 1914; 812.78 / 6, British Embassy to Secretary of State, 14 Oct. 1914; Memorandum, 17 Oct. 1914; 812.78 / 3, Robert Lansing, Secretary of State, to Brazilian Minister, Mexico, 14 Oct. 1914.; 812.78 / 7, National Trust Company to Secretary of State, 23 Oct. 1914, Lansing to National Trust, 29 Oct. 1914; 812.78 / 9, British Embassy to Secretary of State, 20 Nov. 1914.
59 USNA, State Department, DF 1910–29, 812.78 / 13, Isidro Fabella, Mexican Ministry of Foreign Affairs to Brazilian Minister, nd
60 PRO, FO, 371, vol. 2040, file 58596, Hohler to Sir Edward Grey, 14, 20, 21, 26, 28 Oct., 10 November 1914; PAC, DP, Pearson to Dunn, 16 Oct. 1914; PAC, RG 25, vol. 1149, and RG 7, G 21, vol. 409

61 PAC, RG 7, G 21, vol. 409, C.D. Graves to Mexico Tramways, Toronto, 3 Mar. 1915; Womack, *Zapata* 224–44, for quite a different view

62 PRO, FO 371, vol. 2040, file 58596, Hohler to Sir Edward Grey, 20 Nov., 7 Dec. 1914; vol. 2395, file 27, Hohler to the Foreign Office, 4, 12, 15 Jan. 3, 18 Mar. 1915; James Dunn to M. Bonham Carter, 11 Mar. 1915; see also USNA, State Department, DF 1910–29, 812.00 / 13957, Stillman to Secretary of State, 14 Dec. 1914; PAC, DP, vol. 60, F. Cockburn, Bank of Montreal, forwarding bank's confidential reports on Mexican situation, 19 Jan. 1915; PAC, RG 7, G 21, vol. 409, F.S. Pearson to C.D. Graves, 16 Mar. 1915

63 PRO, FO 371, vol. 2402, file 48, Hohler to Sir Edward Grey, 14, 19 July 1915; vol. 2395, Hohler to Sir Edward Grey, 8 Aug. 1915

64 PRO, FO 371, vol. 2408, file 83286, Hohler to Sir Edward Grey, 7 May 1915; vol. 2401, file 48, Hohler to Foreign Office, 13 Aug. 1915

65 Richmond, *Carranza's Nationalist Struggle* 83–106, for the nationalist program. PRO, FO 371, vol. 2395, file 27, Hohler to Foreign Office, 23 Aug. 1915; vol. 2402, file 48, Hohler to Foreign Office, 28 Sept. 1915; Mexican Light and Power Company, MB, 22 Sept. 1915. Electric and street railway workers in Monterrey also struck Sir William Mackenzie's utilities in that city later in the year. In light of Hohler's memorandum on British superiority quoted above, he had the painful duty to inform the Foreign Office that much of this strike activity had been led by 'that Englishman named Butt.' See PRO, FO, 371, vol. 2404, file 48, Hohler to Foreign Office, 22, 25, 28 Dec. 1915.

66 Womack, *Zapata* 245

67 PRO, FO 371, vol. 2697, file 48, Hohler to Foreign Office, 28 Dec. 1915

68 MTC, MB, 30 Apr., 17 May 1915, for the letter and notification of Pearson's death; MLP, MB, 30 Apr., 17 May 1915, for the same. The dates and the presence only of Blake, Lash personnel at these board meetings speaks to the role of Zebulon Lash's law firm in the performance of formal corporate requirements.

69 PAC, DP, vol. 270, Dunn to Charlie Carstairs, Knoedler and Co., New York, 7 Jan. 1915

70 PRO, FO 371, vol. 2404, file 48, R. Knox Little, Receiver, Mexico Tramways and Mexican Light and Power, to Foreign Office, 30 Dec. 1915

Chapter 11 Redemption

1 Thomas Hohler, *Diplomatic Petrel* (London: John Murray, 1942) 200–1

2 Douglas Richmond, *Venustiano Carranza's Nationalist Struggle, 1893–1920* (Lincoln: University of Nebraska Press, 1983) 82–135, pp.82-135 for an examination of Carranza's economic nationalism; Robert Freeman Smith, *The United States and Revolutionary Nationalism in Mexico, 1916–1932* (Chicago: University of Chicago Press, 1972) 71–92, quotation from Alberto Pani on 77

3 PRO, FO 371, vol. 2040, file 58596, T.B. Hohler to Lord Grey, 20 Nov. 1914, enclosing Isidro Fabela to Hohler, 27 Oct. 1914

4 USNA, State Department, DF 1910–29, 812.75 / 15, Spring Rice to Bryan, 27 Dec. 1914; 812.78 / 14, Memorandum from Solicitor, State Department, 8 Jan. 1915; 812.78 / 15, Bryan to Spring Rice, 12 Jan. 1915; 812.78 / 19, Spring Rice to Bryan, 22 Feb. 1915

5 Friedrich Katz, *The Secret War in Mexico: Europe, the United States and the Mexican Revolution* (Chicago: University of Chicago Press, 1981) 292–3; Marjorie Ruth Clark, *Organized Labor in Mexico* (Chapel Hill: University of North Carolina Press, 1967) 41–2; Hohler, *Diplomatic Petrel* 220

6 PRO, FO 371, vol. 2699, file 48, Pablo González, General, Constitutionalist Army, to Graham Fulton, Acting General Manager, Mexico Tramways, 6 Jan. 1916; Fulton to Mexican Light and Power, 10 Jan. 1916; Fulton to González, 20 Jan. 1916; González to Fulton, 24 Jan. 1916; G.A. Lash to Fulton, 25 Jan. 1916; Fulton to Mexican Light and Power, 26, 27 Jan. 1916; Foreign Office to Hohler, 14 Jan. 1916; Hohler to Foreign Office, 27, 31 Jan., 15 Feb. 1916

7 PRO, FO 371, vol. 2700, file 48, Hohler to Sir Edward Grey, 22 Mar. 1916; MTC, MB, 18 Feb. 1916

8 PRO, FO 371, vol. 2701, file 48, Hohler to Foreign Office, 20 May 1916; vol. 2700, file 48, Hohler to Foreign Office, 27, 29 May 1916

9 Sir Thomas Hohler Papers (privately held), Hohler to Sir Cecil Spring Rice, 10 June, 8 Aug. 1916

10 PRO, FO 371, vol. 2703, file 48, Hohler to Foreign Office, 3, 31 July, 1, 2, 3 Aug. 1916; vol. 2704, file 48, Hohler to Foreign Office, 8 Aug. 1916

11 Clark, *Organized Labor in Mexico* 41–2

12 Richmond, *Carranza's Nationalist Struggle* 124–32; PRO, FO 371, vol. 2703, file 48, Hohler to Foreign Office, 2 Aug. 1916

13 PRO, FO 371, vol. 2704, file 48, Hohler to Foreign Office, 31 Aug. (minuted), 2 Sept. 1916

14 PRO, FO 371, vol. 2704, file 48, Hohler to Foreign Office, 17 Aug., 13, 15 Sept. 1916; USNA, State Department, DF 1910–29, 812.504 / 60-4, Parker to Secretary of State, 19 Oct., 3 Nov. 1916

15 MTC, MB, 15 Jan., 15, 21 Mar. 1917; PRO, FO 371, vol. 2697, file 138580, E.R. Peacock to Foreign Office, 19 Sept. 1917; G.R.G. Conway to R.C. Brown, Mexican Light and Power, 13 Oct. 1917; vol. 3249, file 37998, H.A.C. Cummins to Foreign Office, 14 Mar. 1918

16 Mexican economic historians might be interested in knowing the privately recorded output figures for Mexican Light and Power as a rough proxy of economic growth in activity in the capital and mining districts during the Revolution:

Year	Kilowatt hours produced	% of 1913
1910	216,207,540	65
1911	282,314,804	85
1912	316,051,724	96
1913	329,070,315	100
1914	271,328,495	82
1915	199,570,984	60
1916	234,931,529	71
1917	293,607,860	89
1918	329,424,733	100
1919	379,179,914	115
1920	427,415,480	129

SOURCE PRO, FO 371, vol. 5585, file A 4868 / 141 / 26, Cummins to Foreign Office, 13 June 1921, enclosing Conway's 'Report of the Managing Director and General Representative of the Mexican Light and Power Company Ltd., to the Attorney General of the Republic of Mexico.'

17 PRO, FO 371, vol. 3826, file 60, Cummins to Foreign Office, 20 Jan. (minuted), 22 Jan., 2 May (minuted), 7 May (minuted) 1919; USNA, State Department, DF 1910–29, 812.78 / 24, Summerlin to Secretary of State, 7 May 1919; MTC, MB, 1 May 1918; 9 Jan. 1919

18 HLRO, Beaverbrook, H, vol. 75, F.J. Cockburn, Bank of Montreal, London, to Beaverbrook, 17 Dec. 1919, Private and Confidential

19 PRO, FO 371, vol. 3826, file 60, Morgan Grenfell and Co., to Foreign Office, 1 Jan. 1919 minuted, and reply, 21 Jan. 1919

20 PAC, DP, vol. 81, E.R. Peacock to Dunn, 28 Feb. 1919, Private, enclosing copy of a letter to Sir Robert Borden, 1 Mar. 1919

21 Smith, *United States and Revolutionary Nationalism in Mexico* 133–90

22 For a vivid account of Carranza's downfall see J.W.F. Dulles, *Yesterday in Mexico: A Chronicle of the Revolution, 1919–1936* (Austin: University of Texas Press, 1961) 3–54, and Richmond, *Carranza's Nationalist Struggle* 219–40.

23 See, *inter alia*, PRO FO 371, vol. 3829, file 60, Foreign Office to Mexican Light and Power, 16 May 1919; E.R. Peacock to Foreign Office, 22 May 1919; vol. 3839, file 60, Peacock to Foreign Office, 19 June 1919; vol. 4502, file 585, Cummins to Foreign Office, 30 Apr., 4 May 1920.

24 PAC, DP, vol. 95, Newman Erb to Dunn, 28 Sept., 24 Oct. 1921; vol. 283, Dunn to E.R. Peacock, 11 Oct. 1921; vol. 96, Peacock to Dunn, 3 Nov. 1921

25 MLP, MB, 9 July 1920, and MTC, MB, 9 July 1920, contain identical records of directors' report; A.E. Ames and Company Archives, Mexican Light and Power File, Committee for the Protection of Bondholders, 11 Oct. 1920, printed circular

26 PRO, FO 371, vol. 8471, file A 6946 / 653 / 26, E.R. Peacock to Lord Askwith, 20
   Nov. 1923; vol. 9556, File A 2528 / 6 / 26, E.R. Peacock to Sir William
   Tyrrell, 22 Apr. 1924; vol. 9556, file A 6709 / 6 / 26, E.R. Peacock's address to
   the Institute of International Affairs, 'Some Aspects of the Mexican
   Problem'; vol. 10623, file 59, Memorandum from R. Vansittart, 6 Jan. 1925

27 PRO, FO 371, vol. 5585, file A 141 / 141 / 26, E.R. Peacock to Foreign Office, 4,
   7 Jan. 1921; vol. 8470, file 653P, H. Malcolm Hubbard to Foreign Office, 29
   Aug. 1923; vol. 8471, file A 6632 / 1207 / 26, E.R. Peacock to Foreign Office, 8
   Nov. 1923, itemizing the total $28,728,128 claim

28 PRO, FO 371, vol. 5585, file A 3193 / 141 / 26, Cummins to Foreign Office, 25
   Feb., 29 Apr. 1921; R.C. Brown to E.R. Peacock, 3 May 1921; Peacock to Foreign
   Office, 6 May 1921; file A 4868 / 141 / 26, Cummins to Foreign Office, 13 June 1921

29 MLP, MB, 9 Mar. 1921; A.E. Ames and Company Archives, Mexican Light and
   Power Company File, Report of the Committee for the Protection of Holders of
   Mexican Tramway, Light and Power Group to Bondholders, 30 May 1921;
   MLP, Annual Report, 1922, Report of G.R.G. Conway, 1 Nov. 1923

30 A.E. Ames and Company Archives, Mexican Light and Power Company File,
   Report of the Committee for the Protection of Holders of Mexican
   Tramway, Light and Power Group of Bondholders, 30 May 1921; see also
   MLP, MB, 26 May 1921; MTC, MB, 26 May 1921

31 MLP, MB, 18 July, 26 Sept. 1921; MTC, MB, 18 July, 11 Oct. 1921

32 MLP, MB, 17 June 1922; 31 Jan., 28 Mar., 28, 30 May, 12 July 1923

33 MLP, Annual Report, 1922, Report of G.R.G. Conway, 1 Nov. 1923

34 USNA, RG 151, Bureau of Foreign and Domestic Commerce, Memorandum
   from Ralph H. Ackerman re Mexican situation, 16 Feb. 1922, quotes Hughes.
   A translation of Article 27 is contained in the Appendix to Smith, *United States
   and Revolutionary Nationalism in Mexico* 267–70.

35 The estimated breakdown of foreign investment by countries other than the US
   and UK was as follows: France, £57,967,808; Spain, £38,645,754; Germany,
   £15,472,603; Holland, £10,417,808; Belgium, £2,131,849; Switzerland,
   £1,746,575; Italy, £986,302; Other, £3,380,137. The sectors in which US and
   British investment was concentrated were as follows:

Type of investment	United States	Britain	Total
Govt bonds	£4,520,548	£24,657,534	£29,178,082
Banks	719,178	513,699	1,232,877
Railways	27,542,466	50,428,767	77,971,233
Electricity, trams	998,630	31,613,014	32,611,644
Telephones, telegraph	143,836	—	143,836
Mining, smelting	56,712,329	13,356,164	70,068,493
Coal mining	657,534	344,178	1,001,712
Oil, refining	18,493,151	10,273,972	28,767,123

Manufacturing	2,675,342	3,328,768	6,004,110
Wholesale, retail	274,932	—	274,932
Farming, timber	21,575,342	11,301,370	32,876,712

SOURCE PRO, FO 371, vol. 9563, file A 6562 / 12 / 6, Norman King to Foreign Office, 31 Oct. 1924

36 Smith, *United States and Revolutionary Nationalism in Mexico* 128–30; in 1919 the Netherlands and Switzerland were each given one seat, and in 1921 a German firm joined. Peacock reported to the board of Mexican Light and Power on the meetings between the committee and Mexican Finance Minister de la Huerta in June, 1922; see MLP, MB, 10 July 1922

37 The Lamont–de la Huerta Agreement of 1922 and the Bucareli Conference (held at 85 Bucareli Street) are discussed in Smith, *United States and Revolutionary Nationalism in Mexico* 208–23.

38 PRO, FO 371, vol. 8470, file 653, H. Malcolm Hubbard to R.A.C. Sperling, 29 Aug. 1923

39 Smith, *United States and Revolutionary Nationalism in Mexico* 223–5; *New York Times* 13, 16 June 1924; PRO, FO 371, vol. 10623, file 57, Memorandum from R. Vansittart, 6 Jan. 1925

40 PRO, FO 371, vol. 8471, file A 9646 / 653 / 26, Peacock to Lord Askwith, 20 Nov. 1923, and minute (quoted); vol. 9556, file A 2528 / 6 / 26, Peacock to Sir William Tyrrell, 22 Apr. 1924; *New York Times* 16 June 1924

41 Smith, *United States and Revolutionary Nationalism in Mexico* 229–32

42 MLP, MB, 4 Feb. 1926; Annual Report, 1925, Report of G.R.G. Conway, 10 May 1926

43 PRO, FO 371, vol. 10623, file 57, Memorandum from R. Vansittart, 6 Jan. 1925 (quoted); minute of Vansittart, 12 Jan. 1925 (quoted). One of the go-betweens was an executive of Mexican Eagle Oil who approached Finance Minister Alberto Pani only to be told that recognition of Mexico could never be made contingent upon settlement of British claims. See ibid., Adams to Body, Whitehall Securities, 7 Jan. 1925. Like Mexican Eagle, Whitehall Securities was controlled by Lord Cowdray.

44 PRO, FO 371, file 10625, Sir Esme Howard to Foreign Office, 28 May 1925, reporting on an interview with Peacock in Washington

45 USNA, State Department, DF 1910–29, 812.504 / 612, James R. Sheffield to Secretary of State, 14 Mar. 1925, Confidential, 17 Mar. 1925 (quoted); ibid., 712.41 / 17, F.W. Gunther to Joseph C. Grew, 2 Apr. 1925; Memorandum from F.B. Kellogg, 16 Apr. 1925, Confidential

46 BA, DF 100.2, Miller Lash to A.W.K. Billings, 28 May 1925, Confidential; MLP, MB 12 May 1925 (quoted)

47 Smith, *United States and Revolutionary Nationalism in Mexico* 241–4

48 MLP, MB, 3 Sept. 1925

49 Smith, *United States and Revolutionary Nationalism in Mexico* 230–1

50 MLP, MB, 4 Feb. 1926

51 PRO, FO 371, vol. 10631, file A 6250 / 4419 / 26, Norman King to Foreign Office, 10 Dec. 1925, minuted by R. Vansittart

52 PRO, FO 371, vol. 11151, file A 5269 / 50 / 26, Esmond Ovey to Foreign Office, 15 Sept. 1926; ibid., vol. 12775, file 185, Confidential Print, Ovey to Sir Austen Chamberlain, 26 Apr. 1928, minuted by T.M. Snow, 5 June 1928

53 MLP, MB, 11 May, 16 Nov., 23 Dec. 1926; 3, 25 May, 12 Aug. 1927; A.E. Ames and Company Archives, Mexican Light and Power Company File, Report of the Board of Directors and of the Committee of Protection of Bondholders of the Mexican Light and Power Company Limited, 3 May 1927

54 MLP, MB, 23 Dec. 1926

55 James W. Wilkie, 'The Meaning of the Cristero Religious War,' in James W. Wilkie and Albert L. Michaels, eds, *Revolution in Mexico* (New York: Knopf, 1969) 159

56 Toronto *Globe* 15 Dec. 1927

57 PAC, W.L.M. King Papers, Memorandum from King, 15 Dec. 1927, C 87162

58 Toronto *Globe* 16 Dec. 1927

59 The unfolding of this dreary affair may be followed in PAC, RG 25, D 1, vol. 731, file 89, and in PRO, FO 371, vols 12779–80, file A 404-5251 / 404 / 26, which bulge with diplomatic correspondence, newspaper clippings, and other material.

60 PAC, King Papers, Secretary of State for External Affairs to [British] Secretary of State for Dominion Affairs, 25 Jan. 1928, Secret, 133538-40. The view of the British Foreign Office was that it was Fallon who was at fault. PRO, FO 371, vol. 12767, file A 31 / 31 / 26, minute on telegram dated 23 Dec. 1927

61 PAC, King Papers, Secretary of State for Dominion Affairs to Secretary of State for External Affairs, 24 Jan. 1928, Secret, 133535; 4 Feb. 1928, Secret, 133564-6

62 PAC, RG 25, D 1, vol. 731, file 89, Secretary of State for External Affairs to Secretary of State for Dominion Affairs, 16 Feb. 1928, Secret

63 PAC, King Papers, Memos and Notes, vol. 119, Memorandum from O.D. Skelton to King, 15 Dec. 1927, C 87162, and a denial from MLP and MTC in Toronto *Globe* 16 Dec. 1927

64 MLP, MB, 20 Feb. 1928; PRO, FO 371, vol. 12779, file A 404 / 404 / 26, Esmond Ovey to the Foreign Office, 17 Jan. 1928, minuted by R. Vansittart

65 PAC, King Papers, Secretary of State for Dominion Affairs to Secretary of State for External Affairs, 16 June (two letters, Secret and Personal), 28 June (Secret), 19 July 1928; Secretary of State for External Affairs to Secretary of State for Dominion Affairs, 27 June 1928, Secret and Personal, 133931-2, 133957, 134046, 133950. When the president-elect of Mexico was assassinated in July, King decided not even to send a telegram of condolence: 'Out of sight is out of mind. It might raise [the] Mexico question.' See PAC, RG 25, D 1, vol. 731, file 89, Memorandum from O.D. Skelton to King, 18 July 1928, minuted by King.

66 PAC, RG 25, vol. 1515, file 360, F.C.T. O'Hara to O.D. Skelton, 28 Dec. 1928, Confidential

67 PRO, FO 317, vol. 12775, file 185, Confidential Print, Esmond Ovey to Sir Austen Chamberlain, 26 Apr. 1928; vol. 13498, file 335, E.A. Cleugh and Miguel S. Matienzo, Joint Secretaries to the Anglo-Mexican Special Claims Commission, to Secretary of State for Foreign Affairs, 22 Aug. 1929; vol. 14243, file 916, H.M. Hubbard to V.C.W. Forbes, 31 Jan. 1930; vol. 15841, file 17, G.G. Phillips to Sir John Simon, 26 Feb. 1932

68 PRO, FO 371, vol. 15841, file 17, Courtenay Forbes to Foreign Office, 11 Feb. 1932 (minute quoted); Forbes to Sir John Simon, 12, 15 Feb. 1932; Miller Lash to Canadian and General Finance Company, 17 Feb. 1932 (minute quoted); G.G. Phillips to Simon, 26 Feb. 1932, Confidential Print

69 MLP, MB, 12 May 1927; 15 May 1928

Chapter 12 Growth in a Hostile Environment

1 BA, BT, Pre-1923, 149, E.R. Peacock to E.R. Wood, 14 Aug. 1919; BT, MB, 1, 9, 24 Oct. 1919

2 In 1921 the company secretary calculated that, as of 1914, 35 per cent of the shares were held in North America, the rest in Europe. See BA, BT, Pre-1923, 20, J.M. Smith to Greenshields and Company, 28 Oct. 1921. On the exchange see ibid., A.W. Adams to Gene Taylor, 9 Feb. 1920.

3 BA, BT, 90, Pre-1923, J. Henry Schröder and Company to Sir A. Mackenzie, 6 May 1920; H.M. Hubbard to A.W. Adams, 23 Aug. 1920 enclosing a clipping from *Canada*

4 *Annual Financial Review (Canadian)*, comp. W.R. Houston, 1921, 651; 1926, 817

5 BA, BT, Pre-1923, 39, Synopsis of proceedings at annual meeting, 28 July 1920; 90, J.M. Smith to A. Mackenzie, 10 Nov. 1920; Mackenzie to R.C. Brown, 25 Jan. 1921

6 See Joseph H. Love, *São Paulo in the Brazilian Federation, 1889–1937* (Stanford, Ca.: Stanford University Press, 1980) 37–68, 176–212; John Wirth, *Minas Gerais in the Brazilian Federation, 1889–1930* (Stanford, Ca.: Stanford University Press, 1977) 31–65, 164–84; and Joseph H. Love, *Rio Grande do Sul and Brazilian Regionalism, 1882–1930* (Stanford, Ca.: Stanford University Press, 1971) 109–35; Nathaniel Leff, *Underdevelopment and Development in Brazil*, vol. 1 (London: Allen and Unwin, 1982) 166–80

7 The correspondence regarding the loan is in BA, BT, Pre-1923, 90B and DF 011.

8 BA, BT, Pre-1923, 39, Summary of chairman's address to annual meeting, 20 July 1921; extract of stenographer's notes of annual meeting, 20 July 1921; 6A, J.M. Smith to Canadian and General Finance Company, 17 Oct. 1921. The company took care to conceal from Brazilian officials precisely what proportion of its revenues were on a gold basis; a memorandum prepared in 1925 estimated that the proportion was then about 35 per cent, although this would decrease as the milréis rose. See DF 302, Memorandum regarding effect of increased earnings on Brazilian Traction earnings, 26 Sept. 1925.

9 BA, BT, Pre-1923, 187, A. Mackenzie and E.R. Wood to Brazilian Traction, Toronto, 25 Aug. 1921

10 See Adolph J. Ackerman, *Billings and Water Power in Brazil, A Short Biography of Asa White Kenney Billings, Hydro Electric Engineer* (Madison, Wis.: the author, 1953) 11–24.

11 BA, BHE, Pre-1923, 8, E.R. Wood to Sir A. Mackenzie, 23 Mar. 1922; 3, same to same, 31 Mar. 1922; BT, MB, 8 June 1923; BT, Pre-1923, 30, Summary of proceedings at annual meeting, 3 Aug. 1922

12 For a brief account of the Copacabana rising see Neill Macaulay, *The Prestes Column Revolution in Brazil* (New York: New Viewpoints, 1974) 26–9. For Mackenzie's account see BA, BT, Pre-1923, 90C, A. Mackenzie to M. Lash, 9 July 1922.

13 BA, DF 011, A. Mackenzie to M. Lash, 9 Jan. 1924. The Minas delegation in the federal Congress was led by Ribeiro Junqueira, an important regional boss, who controlled the electrical utilities in the Leopoldina Region; see Wirth, *Minas Gerais in the Brazilian Federation* 157–8.

14 BA, BT, Pre-1923, 90, A. Mackenzie to H.M. Hubbard, 20 Feb. 1919

15 BA, BT, Pre-1923, 187, M. Lash to A. Mackenzie, 14 Oct. 1921; Hagenah to Lash, 23 Feb. 1922; 90B, Mackenzie to BT, Toronto, 2 Aug. 1922

16 BA, HHC, Confidential, vol. 4, file 5-1-7, K.H. McCrimmon to H.F. Wileman, of The *Brazilian Review* 24 Jan. 1929, Confidential, summarizes the entire course of the telephone dispute. Quoted is DF 306, A. Mackenzie to E.R. Peacock, 29 Dec. 1926, Private and Confidential.

17 BA, BT, Pre-1923, 90B, J.M. Smith to A. Mackenzie, 17 Feb. 1923 (quoted); K.H. McCrimmon to Mackenzie, 2 Mar. 1923; M. Lash to H.M. Hubbard, 9 Mar. 1923; Mackenzie to Lash, 15 Mar. 1923; BHE, Pre-1923, 8, C.A. Sylvester to Mackenzie, 7, 21 Mar. 1923; Mackenzie to Lash, 31 Aug. 1923, Confidential (quoted)

18 BA, AM, Confidential, vol. 1, file 73, K.H. McCrimmon to H.H. Couzens, 23 Dec. 1925, Confidential (quoted); DF 100.48, M. Lash to A.P. Holt, 3 Aug. 1926; DF 306, A. Mackenzie to E.R. Peacock, 29 Dec. 1926, Private and Confidential

19 BA, AM, Confidential, vol. 1, file 221 Sir John Aird to A. Mackenzie, 3 May 1923

20 BA, HHC, Confidential, vol. 2, file 1-15-0, Couzens to M. Lash, 13 Mar. 1926

21 BA, BT, Pre-1923, 90, A. Mackenzie to M. Lash, 31 Aug. 1923, Confidential; same to same, 26 Nov. 1923 (quoted)

22 BA, DF 011, H.M. Hubbard to A. Mackenzie, 29 Nov. 1923; Mackenzie to BT, Toronto, 4 Dec. 1923; Mackenzie to M. Lash, 6 Dec. 1923

23 BA, AM, Confidential, vol. 1, file 262, A. Mackenzie to Montagu, 10 Jan. 1924

24 BA, DF 306, A. Mackenzie to M. Lash, 20 Feb. 1924, Confidential; DF 011, Mackenzie to Lash, 28 Feb., 5 Mar. 1924; H.M. Hubbard to Lash, 18 July 1924, Confidential; *Report Submitted to His Excellency the President of the United States of Brazil*, by Edwin S. Montagu, PC, Sir Charles S. Addis, KCMG, Lord Lovat, KT, etc., Sir William McLintock, KBE, etc., Hartley Withers (np, 23 Feb. 1924)

25 Macaulay, *Prestes Column Revolution* 9–18; BA, DF 011.21, A. Mackenzie to M. Lash, 6 Aug. 1924. In Mackenzie's view the officers' demands were 'all moonshine – the only sincere part ... is that elements of the army are and were personally opposed to President Bernardes and evidently thought that the time had come when they could do him in.'

26 BA, DF 011.21 contains the correspondence about the revolt, which did not reach Toronto until the rebels had retreated.

27 BA, DF 011.21, Billings to M. Lash, 5 Aug. 1924 (two letters, one Confidential). Vols i and ii of this file contain photographs of the damage to the lines and of looters and barricades in the streets.

28 BA, DF 100.43, M. Lash to R.C. Brown, 26 July 1924; 011.21, Couzens to BT, Toronto, 11 Aug. 1924; Couzens to Lash, 1 Oct. 1924; BT, MB, 13 Nov. 1924; DF 011.21, K.H. McCrimmon to Lash, 15, 24 July 1937, Confidential

29 Ackerman, *Billings* 32–8; BT, MB, 9 Oct. 1924, 12 Feb. 1925

30 BA, DF 100.46, M. Lash to E.R. Wood, 18 Feb., 24 Mar. 1925 (both quoted); A.W. Adams to Wood, 13 Feb. 1925; BT, MB, 19 Mar., 11 June 1925; Ackerman, *Billings* 42–3

31 Ackerman, *Billings* 42; BA, DF 100.1, A. Mackenzie to M. Lash, 31 July 1925; DF 100.2, Billings to Lash, 9 Dec. 1925, Confidential; DF 011, H.H. Couzens to Lash, 10 Dec. 1925

32 Ackerman, *Billings* 42–6

33 BA, DF 100.2, A. Mackenzie to M. Lash, 2 Mar. 1927; Ackerman, *Billings* 54–60. Pumping began in 1944; Billings designed a reversible pump that could function as a turbine in peak periods.

34 BA, DF 100.48, M. Lash to A.P. Holt, 1 Feb. 1926; HD, 'Combined Reports on Brazilian Traction,' comp. J. Frost 26, gives various statistics for the years 1923–33.

35 Love, *São Paulo in the Brazilian Federation* 207–8

36 E. Bradford Burns, *A History of Brazil*, 2nd ed. (New York: Columbia University Press, 1980) 389–90; BA, DF 306, A. Mackenzie to M. Lash, 12 Dec. 1926; Mackenzie to E.R. Peacock, 29 Dec. 1926, Private and Confidential (both quoted)

37 BA, DF 306, 'Quadro Demonstrativo da Media das Taxas de Cambio do Capital Applicado pela Rio de Janeiro Tramway Light & Power Co. Ltd., São Paulo Tramway Light and Power Co. Ltd. e Companhias Associadas ate 31 de Decembro de 1925'

38 BA, DF 306, A. Mackenzie to M. Lash, 12 Dec. 1926 (quoted); H.M. Hubbard to Lash, 10 Dec. 1926; BT, Toronto to Hubbard, 11 Dec. 1926, Confidential

39 BA, DF 306, A. Mackenzie to M. Lash, 12 Dec. 1926; Mackenzie to Peacock, 29 Dec. 1926, Private and Confidential

40 BA, BT, MB, 13 Jan. 1927; Annual Report, 1926; DF 310.1, E.R. Wood to A. Mackenzie, 26 Sept. 1927. On 29 Sept. Mackenzie cabled in reply, 'We will now sing old [hymn number] 200.'

41 BA, BT, MB, 5, 9 Jan., 12 Apr. 1928; Annual Report, 1928

42 BA, DF 100.46, M. Lash to E.R. Wood, 8 Apr. 1929; BT, MB, 10 Jan., 11 Apr., 19 Dec. 1929; Annual Report, 1929

43 Brazilian Traction, Annual Report, 1930 25–6

44 BA, HHC, Confidential, vol. 4, file 5-1-7, K.H. McCrimmon to H.F. Wileman, 24 Jan. 1929, Confidential; DF 100.11, vol. 2, A. Mackenzie to M. Lash, 18 Jan. 1929; BT, Annual Report, 1928, report of the president, 30 Apr. 1929

45 BA, DF 306, Lash to Couzens, 22 Feb. 1929, Private and Confidential; Couzens to Lash, 23 Feb. 1929 (two letters, Confidential one quoted)

46 Burns, Brazil 395–8

47 Love, Rio Grande do Sul and Brazilian Regionalism 216–44; Jose Maria Bello, A History of Modern Brazil 1889–1964 (Stanford, Ca.: Stanford University Press, 1966) 266–78

48 BA, HD, Billings to M. Lash, 21 Oct. 1930, Strictly Confidential; Couzens to A.W. Adams, 8 Nov. 1930, Private

49 BA, DF 306, Couzens to M. Lash, 21 Mar. 1931; DF 100.1, A.W. Adams to Sir A. Mackenzie, 22 Sept. 1931; Financial Post Corporation Service, Brascan Limited (revised 14 Jan. 1981)

Chapter 13 International Capitalism

1 See Thomas P. Hughes, Networks of Power: Electrification in Western Society, 1880–1930 (Baltimore: Johns Hopkins University Press, 1983) 216–21, which in turn draws upon Samuel Insull, Central-Station Electric Service: Its Commercial Development and Economic Significance as Set Forth in the Public Addresses (1897–1914) of Samuel Insull, ed. William E. Keily (Chicago: privately printed, 1915), and Forrest McDonald, Insull (Chicago: University of Chicago Press, 1962).

2 On regional systems see Hughes, Networks of Power 366–71.

3 See Sidney A. Mitchell, S.Z. Mitchell and the Electrical Industry (New York: Farrar, Straus and Cudahy, 1960) 76–80 and Hughes, Networks of Power 385–400.

4 Alfred D. Chandler, *The Visible Hand: The Managerial Revolution in American Business* (Cambridge: Harvard University Press, 1977) 320
5 Hughes, *Networks of Power* 391–2
6 HLRO, Beaverbrook, H, vol. 77, Carl Giles to Sir W.M. Aitken, 1 Apr. 1915
7 Patricia Roy, 'The British Columbia Electric Railway Company, 1897–1928: A British Company in British Columbia' Ph D diss., University of British Columbia, 1970) 347–9; United States, Department of Commerce, Foreign Financial News, Special Circular No. 337, 18 July 1930, 'Canadian Investment in Foreign Utilities'
8 On system building in Canada see C. Armstrong and H.V. Nelles, *Monopoly's Moment: The Organization and Regulation of Canadian Utilities, 1830–1930* (Philadelphia: Temple University Press, 1986) 293–317.
9 E.B. Greenshields, Edwin Hanson, G.F. Greenwood, from Montreal; B.F. Pearson and S.M. Brookfield, Halifax; S.J. Moore, Toronto; John D. Patterson, Woodstock, Ontario
10 *Monetary Times* 12 Aug. 1927. Mexican Northern was reorganized as Northern Mexican Power and Development Company in 1919 to escape from default on its bond interest during the Revolution.
11 BA, HHC, Confidential, vol. 3, file 3-1-0, Couzens to M. Lash, 20 Sept. 1927, Confidential; Couzens to E. de Souza, 6 Oct. 1927, Confidential; Couzens to R.C. Brown, 17 Feb. 1928
12 BA, DF 013.7, A. Mackenzie to H.H. Couzens, 15 Aug. 1928, Confidential
13 BA, HHC, Confidential, vol. 1, file 1-8-7, H.H. Couzens to M. Lash, 22 Nov. 1928; Lash to Couzens, 23 Nov. 1928; Couzens to Canadian Engineering Agency, 29 Nov. 1928; Lash to Couzens, 6 Dec. 1928, Private and Confidential; Couzens to Lash, 27 Dec. 1928. Lash pointed out that EBASCO also wanted to discuss a similar interconnection with the Canadian companies in Mexico.
14 BA, DF 013.7, Couzens to M. Lash, 14 Dec. 1928 (quoted), 2 Jan. 1929, Confidential (quoted); DF 013.71, same to same, 9 Jan. 1929, Private and Confidential
15 BA, DF 013.71, Couzens to M. Lash, 6 Jan. 1929, Private and Confidential (quoted); HHC Confidential, vol. 4, file 5-4-7, Couzens to Lash, 2 Jan. 1928 [sic, 1929], Confidential
16 BA, DF 013.71, Couzens to M. Lash, 6 Jan. 1929, Private and Confidential; DF 013.7, Lash to Couzens, 29 Jan. 1929, Private and Confidential. EBASCO proved co-operative because it was seeking BT's help in shutting out some Italian interlopers representing Milan Edison, who were bidding for a franchise in the city of Campos in the state of Rio and threatening to undercut the rates charged elsewhere by the other two firms. Subsequently, Lash reported that EBASCO had adopted aggressive tactics in Mexico, with the result that the government had passed a drastic new water law to prevent its acquiring too many properties; he hoped the Brazilian authorities would not learn of this. See Lash to Couzens, October 30, 1929, Confidential.

17 BA, DF 310.15, R.O. McMurtry to D. Heineman, 8 Jan. 1929, Strictly Private and Confidential; HHC Confidential, vol. 4, file 6-1-1, M. Lash to Couzens, 5 Feb. 1929, Confidential

18 BA, DF 310.1, M. Lash to H.M. Hubbard, 15 Aug., 18 Nov. 1929, Confidential; Lash to BT, Toronto, 19 Aug. 1929

19 J.K. Galbraith, *The Great Crash*, 1929 (Boston: Houghton Mifflin, 2nd ed. 1961) 63–8

20 Most of the biographical details about Loewenstein are drawn from an unpublished biography of him by Duncan McDowall entitled 'The Belgian Croesus,' which the author has kindly allowed us to make use of, and from William Norris, *The Man Who Fell from the Sky* (Viking: New York, 1987).

21 PAC, DP, vol. 256, Dunn to R.O. Hayward, 18 Jan. 1923; vol. 295, Dunn to C. Cambie, 6 Nov. 1925

22 John Brooks, *The Games Players: Tales of Men and Money* (New York: Times Books, 1980) 149

23 According to British Electrical and Allied Manufacturers' Association, *Combines and Trusts in the Electrical Industry: The Position in Europe in 1927* (London: BEMA, 1927) 154–6, SOFINA was backed by other financial institutions including Société Centrale pour l'Industrie Electrique, Paris, Société Générale d'Entreprises, Paris, and Société Financière pour le développement de l'Industrie, Paris.

24 BEMA, *Combines and Trusts* 155–6

25 BEMA, *Combines and Trusts* 154–5

26 BA, BT, Pre-1923, 41, Loewenstein to A. Mackenzie, 26 Nov. 1918, 18 Mar. 1919; Mackenzie to Loewenstein, 30 Jan. 1919.

27 BA, BT, MB, 11 Dec. 1919. The matter was complicated further by the fact that to counteract a decline in the value of the franc bonds before the war, Loewenstein and Dunn had agreed to buy up a number of Rio seconds and resell them in Britain on condition that these franc bonds should receive a fixed interest payment of 9s. 11d. for every 12.50 franc coupon tendered in London. See RJTLP, Pre-1923, 6, F.S. Pearson to Walter Gow, 20 Feb. 1914.

28 BA, RJTLP, Pre-1923, 6, Loewenstein to BT, 26 May 1920; Walter Gow to BT, 9 June 1920 (quoted)

29 BA, BT, Pre-1923, 90, A. Mackenzie to E.R. Wood, 23 Nov. 1920

30 BA, RJTLP, Pre-1923, 6, Sir W. Mackenzie to Sir A. Mackenzie, 7 Mar. 1921

31 BA, BT, MB, 12 Jan. 1925; DF 100.46, A.W. Adams to E.R. Wood, 13 Feb. 1926

32 BA, DF 103, Loewenstein to A. Mackenzie, 3 Aug. 1926, Private and Confidential; Mackenzie to M. Lash, 6 Aug. 1926; Lash to Mackenzie, 17 Aug. 1926

33 BA, HR, LM, Prospectus for Hydro-Electric Securities Corporation, incorporated in the province of Quebec, 10 Sept. 1926

34 BA, DF 310.11, Hubbard to M. Lash, 20 Aug. 1926, Confidential; Lash to
  Hubbard, 23 Aug. 1926; Hubbard to Loewenstein, 24 Aug. 1926; Peacock to
  Loewenstein, 26 Aug. 1926, Confidential; DF 103, Peacock to Hubbard, 24
  Aug. 1926; Hubbard to Lash, 24 Aug. 1926
35 BA, DF 310.11, M. Lash to E.R. Wood, 22 Nov. 1927, enclosing text of 'Mr.
  Alfred Loewenstein's International Conference, Barcelona [September],
  1926'; Peacock to Sir Herbert Holt, 24 Sept. 1926, Confidential; Lash to A.
  Mackenzie, 20 Oct. 1926
36 BA, DF 310.11, M. Lash to A. Mackenzie, 27 Aug. 1926, Confidential;
  Mackenzie to Lash, 30 Aut. 1926, Confidential; Peacock to Sir Herbert Holt, 24
  Sept. 1926, Confidential (quoted); DF 103, Mackenzie to Lash, 9 Sept. 1926,
  Confidential
37 BA, DF 310.11, E.R. Wood to M. Lash, 11 Oct. 1926; R.H. Merry to Walter
  Gow, 14 Oct. 1926; Lash to A. Mackenzie, 20 Oct. 1926, Private and
  Confidential
38 BA, M. Lash to A. Mackenzie, 20 Oct. 1926, Private and Confidential; Lash to
  E.R. Wood, 20 Oct. 1926, Private and Confidential (quoted)
39 BA, DF, 310.11, M. Lash to BT, Toronto, 22 Oct. 1926; E.R. Wood to Lash, 23
  Oct. 1916; BT, MB, 26 Oct., 9 Nov. 1926
40 BA, DF 310.11, E.R. Peacock to Heineman, 1 Nov. 1926; Heineman to
  Peacock, 3 Nov. 1926, Personal and Confidential; M. Lash to BT, Toronto, 13
  Nov. 1926, Private
41 BA, DF 310.11, 'Exposés fait par Monsieur Alfred Loewenstein,' 6, 20 Nov.
  1926, contain the printed text of his addresses to the public meetings; H.M.
  Hubbard to M. Lash, 8 Dec. 1926, Confidential.
42 BA, DF, 310.11, A. Mackenzie to BT, 16 Nov. 1926, Confidential; E.R. Wood
  to J.W. McConnell, 17 Nov. 1926, Private and Confidential; Wood to Sir H.
  Holt, 17 Nov. 1926, Private and Confidential; Mackenzie to BT, Toronto, 28
  Nov. 1927, Confidential. By 1924 Holt had taken a large position in
  Brazilian Traction and his son, Andrew P. Holt, was appointed to the board to
  represent his interests. See DF 103, M. Lash to A. Mackenzie, 25 Aug. 1924;
  DF 100.47, Press release from McDougall and Cowans, brokers, 8 Oct. 1925.
  Young Holt had been consorting with Loewenstein for several months, having
  joined his 'circus' in September 1926. DF 310.11, Lash to Mackenzie, 20 Oct.
  1926, Private and Confidential
43 BA, DF 310.11, M. Lash to BT, Toronto, 13, 19 Nov. 1926, Private; Sir A.
  Mackenzie to BT, 20 Nov. 1926, Confidential; BT, MB, 23 Nov. 1926; Lash
  to Mackenzie, 20 Oct. 1926, Private and Confidential
44 BA, BT, MB, 23 Nov. 1926; Andrew Holt also complained bitterly when
  another member of the board leaked the news of his reservation to the press.
  See DF 310.11, E.R. Wood to A.P. Holt, 25 Nov. 1926, Personal.
45 BA, DF 310.11, H.M. Hubbard to M. Lash, 8 Dec. 1926, Confidential;
  Heineman to E.R. Peacock, 17 Dec. 1926, Personal and Confidential (quoted)

46 BT had sent an observer from London, whose report is contained in BA, DF 310.11, F.A. Schulman to H.M. Hubbard, 24 Dec. 1926, Private and Confidential, to which is attached a sixty-eight-page verbatim transcript of the proceedings.
47 BA, DF 310.11, F.A. Schulman to M. Lash, 28 Dec. 1926, Confidential
48 BA, DF, 310.11, M. Lash to E.R. Peacock, 29 Dec. 1926, Confidential; Lash to A. Mackenzie, 29 Dec. 1926, Confidential
49 On this subject see the considerable correspondence in BA, DF 310.1 in March and April 1927, and in particular, M. Lash to A. Mackenzie, 26 Apr. 1927, Confidential.
50 BA, HD, LM, Prospectus of International Holding and Investment, 22 Mar. 1928
51 BA, DF 310.11, Loewenstein to H.M. Hubbard, 17 Feb. 1928; E.R. Peacock to M. Lash, 21 Mar. 1928, Confidential; D. Heineman to Peacock, 29 Mar. 1928, Personal and Confidential.
52 BA, HD, LM, 'Report Made April 16 [1928] by Mr. Alfred Loewenstein to the Shareholders of Canadian Stocks' (printed broadsheet); DF 310.11, E.R. Peacock to M. Lash, 3 Apr. 1928, Confidential
53 BA, HD, LM, M. Lash to J.W. McConnell, 24 Apr. 1928; DF 310.11, Memorandum by Lash of telephone call to McConnell, 1 May 1928
54 BA, DF 310.11, Loewenstein to H.M. Hubbard, 17 Feb. 1928; Heineman to E.R. Peacock, 6 Apr. 1928, Personal and Confidential; Peacock to M. Lash, 19 Apr. 1928, Confidential; Hubbard to Lash, 24 Apr. 1928, Confidential
55 J.W. McConnell persistently pooh-poohed the idea that Sir Herbert Holt would support Loewenstein against the board of BT, of which his son was a member, though the elder Holt had reportedly agreed to become chairman of the board of Hydro-Electric Securities. See BA, DF 310.11, Memorandum by M. Lash of telephone call to McConnell, 1 May 1928
56 BA, DF 310.11, M. Lash to H.M. Hubbard, 2 May 1928
57 BA, DF 310.11, M. Lash to A. Mackenzie, 3 May 1928, Confidential; H.M. Hubbard to Lash, 4 May 1928, Confidential (quoted); Peacock to Lash, 11 May 1928, Confidential; HD, LM, Lash to Mackenzie, 16 May 1928, Private and Confidential
58 MLP, MB, 14 May 1928; BA, BT, MB, 14 May 1928; RJTLP, MB, 14 May 1928; DF 310.11, Heineman to M. Lash, 16 May 1928 (quoted)
59 BA, DF 310.11, M. Lash to Loewenstein, 26 May 1928; BA, RJTLP, MB, 5 June 1928; BT, MB, 5 June 1928
60 BA, HD, LM, M. Lash to H.M. Hubbard, 15 June 1928, Confidential; Hubbard to Lash, 29 June 1928, Confidential; Lash to Hubbard, 30 June 1928l; DF 310.11, Hubbard to Lash, 5 July 1928
61 Norris, *The Man Who Fell from the Sky* 3. Reviewing this egregious effort in the *New York Times Book Review*, 10 May 1987 (21), Lillian Thomas observes that Norris 'finishes by rounding up his suspects and announcing that

he doesn't know who murdered Loewenstein and that while he favors a particular suspect, his readers should feel free to draw their own conclusions. Most will conclude that Mr. Norris should solve his next mystery before he writes about it.'

62 BA, DF 310.11, Hubbard to M. Lash, 6 July 1928, Confidential
63 BA, HD, LM, Circular from Association Belge pour la défense des détenteurs de fonds publiques, 10 Dec. 1928; BT, MB, 13 Dec. 1928
64 BA, BT, Pre-1923, 199, 'Brazilian Traction Light and Power Company Limited, Statement showing the distribution of the Company's ordinary shares on the Canadian Register, held in various countries, as at April 6th, 1922'; DF 310.1, 'Brazilian Traction Light and Power Company Limited, Classification of List of Ordinary Shareholders of the Company as of record October 31st, 1927.' Before First World War one-third of Brazilian Traction's shareholders had resided in North America; see chapter 12, n2 above.
65 MLP, MB, 11 Jan., 28 May 1929

Chapter 14 Closing Balance

1 For an example of one such collapse at a critical moment in 1906, see chapter 4 above.
2 HLRO, Beaverbrook, A, vol. 10. Aitken to P.G. Gossler, 29 Sept. 1906
3 On rhythmic breathing see above chapter 8, n31; for the watermelons see Lord Beaverbrook, *Courage, The Story of Sir James Dunn* (Fredericton, N.B.: Brunswick Press, 1961) 71–2.
4 PAC, DP, vol. 266, Dunn to Turck, 3 Oct., 14 Nov. 1913; vol. 61, Panama Banana Food Company to Dunn, 24 Feb. 1915, which advertises not only banana flour, biscuits, and figs, but marmalade and Banan-Nutro, a new hot drink. Later Turck switched to a miracle serum for curing various diseases; see PAC, Sir Robert Borden Papers, OC 475, for correspondence between the two on this subject.
5 *Journal of Commerce*, undated, 1900, quoted in T. Naylor, *The History of Canadian Business* (Toronto: James Lorimer, 1975), vol. 2, 217
6 On the attitudes of the imperialists towards business see Carl Berger, *The Sense of Power: Studies in the Ideas of Canadian Imperialism, 1867–1914* (Toronto: University of Toronto Press, 1970) 193–8.
7 Duncan McDowall, *Steel at the Sault: Francis H. Clergue, Sir James Dunn and the Algoma Steel Corporation, 1901–1956* (Toronto: University of Toronto Press, 1984) chs 6–8
8 PAC, RG 20, Trade and Commerce, vol. 162, file 28916, Owen O'Malley to G.R.C. Conway, 20 Apr. 1938
9 Ibid., R.T. Young, Canadian Trade Commissioner in Mexico to the Director of the Commercial Intelligence Branch, 7 Nov. 1938, Confidential. Earlier the US State Department had come to this conclusion independently, estimating

that only about 20 per cent of the Mexico Tramways Company shares were held in Canada; see USNA, RG 59, State Department, DF 1910–29, 842.503112, Toronto Office to Ottawa Office, Bureau of Domestic and Foreign Commerce, 18 Aug. 1927.

10 Peter Hertner, 'Financial Strategies and Adaptation to Foreign Markets: The German Electro-Technical Industry and Its Multinational Activities, 1890s to 1939,' in Alice Teichova, Maurice Lévy-Leboyer, and Helga Nussbaum, eds, *Multinational Enterprise in Historical Perspective* (London: Cambridge University Press, 1986) 145–59; John P. McKay, *Tramways and Trolleys: The Rise of Urban Mass Transport in Europe* (Princeton: Princeton University Press, 1976)

11 J.W. Hammond, *Men and Volts: The Story of General Electric* (New York: J.B. Lippincott, 1941) 388, 423; Mira Wilkins, *The Maturing of Multinational Enterprise: American Business Abroad from 1914 to 1970* (Cambridge: Harvard University Press, 1974) 16, 131–4, 200–3; Sidney A. Mitchell, *S.Z. Mitchell and the Electrical Industry* (New York: Farrar, Straus and Cudahy, 1960)

12 PAC, RG 20, Trade and Commerce, vol. 61, file 19838, and vol. 189, file 27917

13 USNA, RG 151, Bureau of Foreign and Domestic Commerce, file 841, Power Plants in Mexico, Commercial Attaché in Mexico to Director of the Bureau, 19 Apr. 1927; BA, DF 015, H.R. Poussette, Director, Commercial Intelligence Service, Department of Trade and Commerce, to R.C. Brown, 16 May 1921; Brown to Poussette, 17 May, 28 June, 7 Oct. 1921, Canadian Engineering Agency, New York, to Brazilian Traction, Toronto, 15 June 1921. See on this point Glen Williams, *Not for Export* (Toronto: McClelland and Stewart, 1983).

14 For suggestive comparative studies of business structure in Europe and the United States note some interesting variations in national patterns of what might be called 'organizational style,' see H. Daems and A.D. Chandler, eds, *Managerial Hierarchies: Comparative Perspectives on the Rise of the Modern Industrial Enterprise* (Cambridge: Harvard University Press, 1980).

15 See H.V. Nelles and C. Armstrong, 'The Transfer of Electrical Technology: The Case of the Canadian Companies in the Caribbean, Mexico and Brazil, 1896–1914,' paper presented to the Society for the History of Technology, Pittsburgh, Oct. 1986.

16 PAC, RG 20, Trade and Commerce, vol. 1632, file 28916, F.C.T. O'Hara to Noel Wilde, 26 Feb. 1923. Wilde replied that the press reports were 'pure inventions.'

17 Jonathan C. Brown, 'Jersey Standard and the Politics of Latin American Oil Production, 1911–39,' in John Wirth, ed., *Latin American Oil Companies and the Politics of Energy* (Lincoln: University of Nebraska Press, 1985) 16–17

18 See for example the study of corporation law done by the British Board of Trade, *Comparative Analysis of the Company Laws of the United Kingdom, India, Australia, New Zealand and South Africa with a Memorandum Prepared for the Imperial Conference, 1907* (London 1907, rev. 1911).

19 Aitken was thought by many business leaders, including Clouston of the Bank of Montreal, to have misconducted himself over the steel and cement mergers in 1910, and he soon departed for Britain and the newspaper business.

20 See by way of comparison D.C.M. Platt, *Finance, Trade and Politics in British Foreign Policy, 1815–1914* (Oxford: Oxford University Press, 1968), which in a much broader context makes the same point about the relative autonomy of British foreign policy.

21 See chapter 12 on the role of Brazilian Traction as an intermediary for a government loan in New York.

22 See for example Linda Jones, Charles Jones, and Robert Greenhill, 'Public Utility Companies,' in D.C.M. Platt, ed., *Business Imperialism, 1840-1930* (Oxford: Oxford University Press, 1977) 77–118.

23 Platt, ed., *Business Imperialism* 6; for an overview of the literature see H.V. Nelles, 'Latin American Business History since 1965: A View from North of the Border,' *Business History Review* 59 (1985) 543–62

24 Miguel Wionczek, 'Electric Power: The Uneasy Partnership,' in Raymond Vernon, *Public Policy and Private Enterprise in Mexico* (Cambridge: Harvard University Press, 1964) 19–110; Judith Tendler, *Electric Power in Brazil: Entrepreneurship in the Public Sector* (Cambridge: Harvard University Press, 1968)

25 *Globe and Mail, Report on Business Magazine, 1000, Ranking Corporate Performance in Canada,* July 1986 and 1987. In 1986 rankings Mexican Light and Power ranked last in terms of profitability; in 1987 Dome Petroleum spared it that fate. On the other hand Mexican Light and Power is Canada's fifteenth largest employer and has the ninth fastest growing corporate revenues.

26 Brascan now controls Labatt Breweries, London Life, Hees International, and, through the brewery, the Toronto Blue Jays baseball team.

Appendix

How profitable were these southern utilities companies? How attractive were they as investments? Despite the fact that each company usually published an annual report and released regular information to the financial press, these simple questions cannot be answered with certainty. As we have demonstrated in the foregoing text, the promoters controlled information to minimize exposure to criticism and maximize private gain. Moreover, from year to year different accounting practices were followed, especially having to do with depreciation and renewals, that make precise comparisons over time extremely difficult. To give but one example: Mexico Tramways began setting aside $300,000 for depreciation beginning in 1909 when it began to make substantial profits. Secondly, it included non-operating income (essentially interest on its loans to Mexican Light and Power) only in 1912. Since this income flow almost equalled the excess revenue from tramway operations, its net rate of return on capital invested that year almost equalled its private rate of return.

Thus the publicly available information does not necessarily reflect the actual performance of the firms in a given year, nor can the data be strictly compared over time. Certainly the published figures vastly underestimate the profitability of these investments to the insiders who were part of the promotional syndicates. Rather, the published financial returns represent no more than the information that insiders were willing, or were forced, to release by exchange authorities to inform prudent outsiders weighing investment opportunities. Some data, however misleading, are better than none at all.

With these caveats in mind we offer the following extremely crude indicators of the relative performance of some of the largest firms. Data have been gathered from annual reports, W.R. Houston's *Annual Financial Review*, and in some instances from minute books and internal financial statements. The uneven nature of the data as between companies and over time prevents the calculation of finer, more rigorously analytical indices of performance. With the available material and in the interests of clarity we have calculated and listed a few simple indicators of financial performance. We have not manipulated the figures to take into account known discrepancies, or attempted to modify them to make entries consistent over time. Rather we have taken what the companies provided (as prudent outsiders would have had to), using current definitions of operating expenses, non-operating expenses, net income, book value of assets, and so forth. As a result our rough and ready methods probably overestimate net rates of return on investment in the earlier periods and underestimate them later in the twenties.

Asset values are taken from published company financial statements. Operating ratios are not part of the modern cost-accounting arsenal. We have included the figure here because these promoters were obsessed by the relationship of ordinary business expenses to total revenues, for, from a promotional point of view, the excess of revenue determined the amount of debt that could be floated. We include this calculation because of its importance to the participants and as an indication of the relationship of operating expenses to capital costs in this industry. Nowadays accountants are not much concerned about private rate of return on investment either; on the other hand economic historians are. We have calculated the private rate of return on investment in the same manner as Peter George did for the CPR, namely the excess of revenue over expenses as a percentage of assets. Such a ratio indicates the gross rate of return before capital costs, sinking fund contributions, depreciation, and dividends. Net rate of return on investment indicates residual income (after business expenses and bond interest have been met) available for distribution as dividends, sinking fund payments, renewals through reinvestment in the plant, and ongoing surplus accounts as a percentage of assets. Prices per share are recorded wherever possible as midway between the bid and asked prices at year end.

During the period of receivership, 1914–20, the Mexican companies did not publish any usable financial statements, and for that reason we have broken the Mexican statements into two series, 1903–13, and 1921–30. The Brazilian data are complicated by the fact that the São Paulo and Rio companies were not strictly similar, the latter operating a telephone utility along with gas, electric, and street railway divisions. After 1912 the consolidated company, Brazilian Traction, published certain data for its operating subsidiaries, but not enough to permit us to continue separate series for Rio and São Paulo. Thus from 1912 to 1930 the Brazilian Traction table combines data for the operating subsidiaries in both districts.

These qualifications notwithstanding, the following tables clearly reveal some of the general points raised in our text. One must bear in mind as one scans these columns of figures that very small differences in net rates of return on capital investment work out to very large differences in actual monetary returns, especially to insiders. The São Paulo property was far and away the most profitable of all the major Latin American promotions. As we have argued, the success of this initial venture sustained hopes for subsequent investments in Brazil and Mexico. The data also reveal the comparatively disappointing performance of both Rio Tramway, Light and Power and Mexican Light and Power after 1907. Rio, which cost a good deal to assemble, was never as profitable as São Paulo. Cost overruns, drought, and continuous expansion plagued the Mexican venture. On the other hand Mexico Tramways rivalled São Paulo as a money earner once it got going. Artful accounting and large loans to the power company that inflated assets and diminished rates of return disguised the true profitability of Mexico Tramways before the Revolution.

Table 3 shows the relatively strong financial performance of Brazilian Traction after 1914. Wartime insecurity and adverse exchange rates nevertheless precluded payment of dividends and thus depressed stock prices. During the twenties earning power rebounded with astonishing vigour, something that more conservative accounting procedures tactfully disguised in the 'net rate of return on investment' columns. These data also reveal how shrewdly Loewenstein timed his attack on Brazilian Traction; for there was additional value to be wrung out of the property (see the rising net rate of return on investment in the mid-twenties), as its managers revealed first by way of self-defence and then afterwards in triumph.

In Mexico the tramway and the light and power companies changed positions over time. Before the Revolution, Mexico Tramways had been the dominant partner. Indeed retained earnings and bond issues from the tramway provided the loans required to finance expansion of the power company. However, the tramway suffered much more serious damage to its property and earning potential during the Revolution. As it was labour intensive, inflation closed the gap between costs and earnings. On the other hand the light and power company emerged relatively unscathed by the 1920s with $13 million in Canadian Victory Bonds tucked away in the Bank of Commerce vaults in Toronto. The disposition of this war chest can be dimly seen in the per cent net rate of return on investment for Mexican Light and Power between 1922 and 1926, as every peso over the above operating expenses went into the hands of its eager bondholders as per the reorganization agreement. As this money passed through the hands of the tramway company, earnings from pre-revolutionary investments in the power company helped keep the tramway afloat. Thus the Mexican properties were refinanced on the strength of the power company.

The tramway, by contrast, faltered in the face of automotive competition, rising costs, and fixed fares in the twenties. Mexico Tramways in this respect shared a similar fate to that of other North American street railways, though in this instance hampered somewhat by a worn-out physical plant. In such circumstances the company had every incentive to minimize profits by charging repairs to current operating expenses. Depreciation during these years was charged to current operating expenses, thereby diminishing the private rate of return. The tramway wanted to make the situation look as grim as possible to the authorities. During some years in the 1920s the company put out statements showing that it could not even meet its current operating costs from its revenues. It nevertheless met its bond interest obligations with non-operating income earned from earlier loans to the power company. Thus the data show not only the changed financial environment, but a strategy for dealing with it.

But having said all this it must be repeated that these numbers provide only indications. It would be a mistake to rest any argument too firmly on such flawed and inconsistent data. The general downward trend in profitability may reflect the changing power relationship of sunk foreign capital within the Brazilian and Mexican economies with the passage of time. It may also simply be an artifact of much more rigorous cost allocation and a strategic conception of depreciation in the 1920s once promoters' profits were no longer the main aim.

Abbreviations Used in Appendix Tables

BVA   Book Value of Assets
ORev   Operating Revenues
ORat   Operating Ratio
ER   Excess Revenue
NI   Net Income
PRROI   Private Rate of Return on Investment
NRROI   Net Rate of Return on Investment
SP   Share Prices

TABLE 1
Financial Performance of São Paulo Tramway, Light and Power Company, 1902–11

	BVA $	ORev $	ORat %	ER $	NI $	PRROI %	NRROI %	SP $
1902	13,302,102	1,123,285	37.2	705,370	455,370	5.30	3.42	91
1903	13,729,770	1,303,175	31.0	899,427	692,977	6.55	5.05	89
1904	14,334,815	1,419,338	32.4	958,780	598,000	6.69	4.17	106
1905	14,779,884	1,908,405	33.3	1,273,833	863,951	8.62	5.85	139
1906	16,258,847	2,018,703	32.2	1,368,162	968,162	8.41	5.95	137
1907	17,229,083	2,111,523	33.9	1,395,874	730,407	8.10	4.24	112
1908	18,497,535	2,287,410	34.2	1,504,360	982,392	8.13	5.31	153
1909	19,039,847	2,439,485	34.7	1,592,859	1,008,997	8.37	5.30	148
1910	20,297,285	2,949,292	32.6	1,986,955	1,143,804	9.79	5.64	149
1911	23,302,589	3,595,277	35.5	2,320,492	1,723,469	9.96	7.40	185

TABLE 2
Financial Performance of Rio de Janeiro Tramway, Light and Power Company, 1906–12

	BVA $	ORev $	ORat %	ER $	NI $	PRROI %	NRROI %	SP $
1906	NA	5,340,779	NA	1,462,630	NA	NA	NA	NA
1907	54,608,238	6,286,200	33.6	2,127,726	NA	NA	NA	33
1908	67,316,823	7,138,246	38.3	2,730,434	870,236	4.06	1.29	78
1909	79,570,139	7,527,559	59.2	3,068,306	779,419	3.86	0.98	92
1910	87,933,363	10,960,179	50.8	5,393,092	2,296,658	6.13	2.61	102
1911	98,177,065	12,952,317	47.8	6,767,027	3,694,616	6.89	3.76	113
1912	106,130,239	NA	NA	5,283,166	2,526,220	4.98	2.38	140

TABLE 3
Financial Performance of Brazilian Traction, Light and Power Company, 1913–30

	BVA $	ORev $	ORat %	ER $	NI $	PRROI %	NRROI %	SP $
1913	118,436,180	22,724,183	45.3	12,422,822	8,112,264	10.49	6.85	91
1914	126,896,728	21,735,860	42.8	12,438,231	7,666,532	9.80	6.04	75
1915	124,588,767	18,323,523	40.3	10,934,795	5,394,802	8.78	4.33	56
1916	134,330,911	20,182,274	42.4	11,616,323	5,674,642	8.65	4.22	51
1917	138,320,501	22,902,556	45.2	12,544,336	5,266,518	9.07	3.81	40
1918	230,503,576	25,870,927	48.6	13,310,577	5,419,672	5.77	2.35	46
1919	237,978,973	30,303,827	48.1	15,741,637	7,873,967	6.61	3.31	56
1920	246,073,380	26,929,203	45.2	14,744,615	7,243,443	5.99	2.94	40
1921	249,715,723	21,036,150	42.2	12,168,673	4,537,714	4.87	1.82	28
1922	250,685,074	25,506,420	35.6	16,417,251	7,872,961	6.55	3.14	39
1923	257,386,049	24,184,761	36.6	15,332,329	7,510,459	5.96	2.92	44
1924	265,769,935	26,936,767	38.2	16,643,472	8,249,520	6.26	3.10	49
1925	275,391,263	31,243,759	44.0	17,489,445	8,848,594	6.35	3.21	67
1926	286,104,734	38,602,891	43.8	21,700,727	12,278,654	7.58	4.29	98
1927	297,838,004	38,319,989	42.4	22,054,624	12,526,241	7.40	4.21	168
1928	328,812,356	42,774,813	41.9	24,869,330	14,762,619	7.56	4.49	59
1929	368,956,552	49,351,215	43.2	28,052,961	17,605,179	7.60	4.77	57
1930	376,608,494	46,898,444	41.3	27,549,594	16,846,075	7.32	4.47	38

TABLE 4
Financial Performance of Mexican Light and Power Company, 1906–30

	BVA $	ORev $	ORat %	ER $	NI $	PRROI %	NRROI %	SP $
1906	28,661,360	1,927,097	38.3	1,187,617	350,428	4.14	1.22	56
1907	30,888,063	3,515,613	27.7	2,540,542	1,610,542	8.22	5.21	44
1908	36,454,236	3,656,495	29.6	2,575,925	1,505,925	7.07	4.13	88
1909	32,900,792	3,014,325	21.5	2,365,988	1,293,706	7.19	3.93	70
1910	44,231,926	3,495,199	28.2	2,872,540	1,605,970	6.49	3.63	86
1911	48,377,980	3,790,513	29.0	3,423,259	1,997,528	7.08	4.13	87
1912	54,719,776	4,017,269	23.1	4,074,825	2,536,815	7.45	4.64	83
1913	56,681,056	NA	NA	3,977,116	1,867,542	7.02	3.29	45
Revolution and Receivership								
1921	76,260,380	5,236,974	62.6	1,958,663	0	2.57	0.00	NA
1922	81,369,243	6,596,717	51.0	3,714,977	1	4.57	0.00	16
1923	82,518,645	7,413,971	44.0	5,108,440	522,895	6.19	0.63	20
1924	84,722,258	7,932,129	49.9	4,791,574	498,246	5.66	0.59	24
1925	87,381,211	9,284,763	51.0	5,022,218	557,120	5.75	0.64	29
1926	91,239,021	9,857,010	51.7	4,770,281	0	5.23	0.00	33
1927	93,964,835	10,213,734	50.7	4,566,838	1,264,322	4.86	1.35	50
1928	96,625,144	10,728,965	51.5	5,200,503	1,635,066	5.38	1.69	77
1929	101,014,627	11,084,771	50.6	5,477,621	1,805,713	5.42	1.79	70
1930	105,636,184	11,966,135	51.5	5,808,920	1,031,175	5.50	0.98	69

TABLE 5
Financial Performance of Mexico Tramways Company, 1907–30

	BVA $	ORev $	ORat %	ER $	NI $	PRROI %	NRROI %	SP $
1907	15,415,280	1,284,725	51.5	623,431	211,701	4.04	1.37	59
1908	17,196,805	2,653,517	50.9	1,303,262	459,648	7.58	2.67	134
1909	33,319,060	2,709,079	48.4	1,398,233	416,344	4.20	1.25	123
1910	37,204,457	2,941,267	49.1	1,498,305	644,066	4.03	1.73	117
1911	37,427,149	3,088,485	48.6	1,588,309	786,566	4.24	2.10	115
1912	42,852,402	3,411,338	47.0	1,807,888	1,462,928	4.22	3.41	112
Revolution and Receivership								
1920	52,410,142	5,503,065	85.0	826,796	NA	1.58	NA	23
1921	55,961,961	6,537,645	82.1	1,167,718	NA	2.09	NA	11
1922	57,122,684	6,133,414	88.4	1,048,958	NA	1.84	NA	18
1923	58,283,407	6,133,414	90.7	573,024	(387,844)	0.98	−0.67	33
1924	58,734,410	5,846,184	98.7	77,289	(885,708)	0.13	−1.51	26
1925	58,812,170	4,998,516	105.3	(265,127)	(1,225,325)	−0.45	−2.08	16
1926	59,105,418	4,965,640	98.9	39,252	NA	0.07	NA	15
1927	59,398,666	5,505,432	92.0	442,829	(1,120,850)	0.75	−1.89	25
1928	59,814,873	5,842,438	92.0	465,498	(1,605,902)	0.78	−2.68	41
1929	59,897,106	5,362,469	97.9	112,546	(1,560,919)	0.19	−2.61	43
1930	59,540,376	4,971,870	106.8	(336,153)	(1,674,512)	−0.56	−2.81	19

Picture Credits

Art Gallery of Ontario, Alistair Walker Collection: Edmund Walker

Bourse de Montréal: Montreal Stock Exchange

Brascan Ltd: F.S. Pearson; Lajes powerhouse; falls of the Ribeirão das Lajes; Avenida Central; Villa Isabel mule trams; electric tram on the Carioca line

Brascan Ltd, *North America in South America:* São Paulo Tramway, Light and Power dam; Brazilian labourers at Parnaíba; feeder pipe to the powerhouse at Parnaíba

Brascan Ltd, courtesy of Duncan McDowall: Serra do Mar; dignitaries at the opening of the Lajes power station; Alexander Mackenzie

Anita Brenner and G.R. Leighton, *The Wind That Swept Mexico*, courtesy of University of Texas Press: José Limantour; Porfirio Diaz; trolley cars and electric lights transform Mexico City; Pancho Villa in the presidential chair and Emiliano Zapata

Dunn family, courtesy of Rose Adeane: James Dunn

Thomas Hohler, *Diplomatic Petrel* (London: John Murray 1942): Thomas Hohler

Mexican Light and Power Company, *Annual Report:* landscape at Necaxa

Notman Photographic Archives, McCord Museum: James Ross; A.F. Gault and family; Sir William Van Horne; E.S. Clouston; Max Aitken

National Archives of Canada: St James Street, Montreal C 8842; Bank of Montreal, photo William Notman and Son C 11723; traders on the Toronto Exchange PA 135845; William Mackenzie C 23691; Zebulon A. Lash C 47346; main control dam of the Mexican Light and Power Company, Necaxa, Dunn Papers C 132634; powerhouse of the Mexican Light and Power Company, Necaxa, Dunn Papers C 132635

Toronto *Telegram*, courtesy of Commonwealth Microfilm Products: Alfred Loewenstein

Index

This book

was designed by

ANTJE LINGNER

and was printed by

University of

Toronto

Press

.

10 SHARES

NUMBER
CG76000

THE MEXICAN LIGHT AND

INCORPORATED UN

AUTHORIZED CAPITAL 853,244 PREFERRED SHARES OF THE PAR VALUE

This Certifies that _____ SPECIMEN

is the registered holder of _____

non-assessable COMMON SHARES WITHOUT NOMINAL OR PAR

and Power Company, Limited transferable one

in person or by attorney duly authorized in writ

The provisions of the Company's Supplementary

to the Preferred Shares and Common Shares respectiv

part hereof and the holder by acceptance hereof assen

by a Transfer Agent and Registrar of the Compan

In Witness Whereof the Company has caused this c

Dated

SPECIMEN

SECRETARY

THESE SHARES ARE TRANSFERABLE AT NATIONAL TRUST COMPANY, LIMITED, TORON

COUNTERSIGNED:
NATIONAL TRUST COMPANY, LIMITED, TORONTO
MONTREAL
TRANSFER AGENT AND REGISTRAR

AUTHORIZED OFFICER

BY _____ SPECIMEN

INCO

CANADIAN